PALACES OF THE

ANCIENT NEW WORLD

PALACES OF THE

ANCIENT NEW WORLD

A Symposium at Dumbarton Oaks

10th and 11th October 1998

Susan Toby Evans and Joanne Pillsbury, *Editors*

Dumbarton Oaks Research Library and Collection
Washington, D.C.

Printed in the United States of America
10 09 08   2 3 4

Reprinted as paperback, 2008. ISBN 978-0-88402-341-8

Cataloging-in-Publication Data for this volume
is on file with the Library of Congress.

ISBN 0-88402-300-1

Contents

Preface

Dumbarton Oaks has long been renowned as an institution that nurtures scholarly effort, and as a place where prestigious scholarly conferences are held. It was built, two centuries ago, to serve as a "great house" in the sense that anthropologists and art historians would use this term: a large, well-appointed building complex occupied by social elites. Thus the 1998 Dumbarton Oaks Pre-Columbian Studies Symposium on Palaces of the Ancient New World achieved a functional duality with regard to elite residences, in that it presented a wealth of information about such traditions as they existed in the archaeological cultures of the Americas, and did so within the physical setting of a beautiful and grand old house.

Therefore, there was a certain logic in holding this conference on palaces in what many scholars, worldwide, know and appreciate as their own intellectual great house. The initial idea sprang from a short talk, a *tertulia* on the palaces of Chan Chan, presented by Joanne Pillsbury at Dumbarton Oaks in fall, 1995. At that time, Susan Evans was a Fellow in residence researching Aztec palaces, and from that encounter there developed the 1998 Summer Seminar on New World Palaces, the 1998 Pre-Columbian Studies symposium, and this, the conference volume. Since then, however, there have been a number of conferences and publications on New World palaces. It is interesting, however, that so little attention has been paid to New World palaces until recently. Why might this be? I suggest that the reasons involve academic specializations combined with distinct discourses about how the past is discussed.

Although there are many exceptions to the rule, art historians have tended to focus on objects often removed from their contexts of use or not fully considered in their original settings. As for architects, the few who occasionally have taken an interest in Pre-Columbian buildings often have been inspired by design elements, the use of masses and spaces, but have not fully considered (or cared about?) the activities that once occurred in such structures. Lastly, anthropological archaeologists, especially in the hey-day of the New Archaeology, tended to be rather anti-elitist thus shying away from the homes of the upper classes. One result of this attitude is that the discourse of archaeological investigation has often not included the term "palace" nor an eagerness to employ it in referring to architecture. This is not, I submit, simply a question of academic cautiousness, but rather an active mistrust of employing the term "palace" for a Pre-Columbian case.

The best example of these kinds of terminological issues is the case of the long buildings found around the courtyards in the heart of Maya cities. These were referred to as "range structures" or similar terms for years. It has only been in recent times when the courtly life of the ancient Maya as seen in art has been confirmed through textual references, that Mayanists seem to finally have fully embraced the term "palace." A similar acceptance of the term is starting to emerge in Andean scholarship, too, although that impetus has had to overcome the commonly cited case for Andean exceptionalism.

This issue highlights the problem archaeologists face in finding a comfortable balance between utilizing English (or other European) language terms to describe phenomena in other cultures that, nonetheless, appear to share cross-cultural similarities, versus using the particular terms employed by ancient people (when available); it is the old problem of choosing between ideographic particularities and nomothetic generalizations.

Thus, some might argue that "palace," is inappropriate to use for a non-Western, ancient phenomenon because correlative social aspects may not be patterned in the same way as the Western examples. The raising of this issue is important to consider and it is noteworthy the majority of examples in this book are of elite residences known through documentary sources as well as archaeology. Perhaps a greater problem, however, is recognizing palaces or elite residences when no native or ethnohistoric texts are available to declare that palaces existed in the society in question.

As emphasized in many of the chapters in this book, palaces are very busy places sustaining a wide variety of people of different social ranks engaged in a multitude of activities among which may be craft production, military service, and, especially and quite commonly, the feeding of many people. Feasts and provisioning of courtiers, petitioners, and others, often occurs on a vast scale at palaces. Indeed, it is noteworthy that the role of food provider in the context of the palace setting is an extension or continuation of the same kind of "big man" tradition spoken of so frequently for tribal and chiefly societies. A palace might be thought to be emblematic of a state, but in many ways it is an elaboration of a chief's big house: if a "man's home is his castle," then, a chief's house is his palace. Because palaces are more than the residences of the upper class they may not be easily recognized in archaeological fieldwork. It might be easier to identify the larger house of a tribal or chiefly leader, for example, than to clearly identify the palace of a king or queen in the absence of literary sources.

These and many more issues are raised in the chapters in this book. The editors and I hope, however, that they will help to advance issues on a wide range of topics associated with palaces and offer case studies to pursue questions on the nature of elite residential architecture at other times and places in New World prehistory. I have learned much through my close association with Susan Toby Evans and Joanne Pillsbury, who did so much to make the summer seminar, the conference, and this book come about. I thank them and the authors for their hard labors and fine work. It is, therefore, a very great pleasure to introduce this volume to our reading public.

Jeffrey Quilter
Dumbarton Oaks

Palaces of the Ancient New World: An Introduction

Joanne Pillsbury

UNIVERSITY OF MARYLAND AND DUMBARTON OAKS

Susan Toby Evans

PENNSYLVANIA STATE UNIVERSITY

Palaces are generally thought of as complex residences that are used by the rulers of complex societies. In a strict sense, palaces *are* private residences, but, like their occupants, they play a public role. Palaces and other types of elite residential buildings have rarely been systematically addressed by modern scholars as a specific category of architecture in the Pre-Columbian New World. Substantial documentary and archaeological evidence exists that demonstrates the importance of palaces in the cultures of ancient Mesoamerica and the Andes. They are described in early colonial accounts, and numerous structures bearing the hallmarks of palaces have been excavated in the past one hundred years. Yet until recently, the study of this architectural form and its social roles has been relatively muted. The lack of an elementary survey of the major examples of this formal type, and their cultural contexts, has been a hindrance to scholars wishing to understand how elites in such societies operated, but it also presented an opportunity to bring together a set of studies that would provide a baseline for further research.

Inherent in the essays in this volume are questions about the social contexts of this type of architecture and what these structures reveal about the societies that made them. These palaces were seats of rulership, and we seek to understand how their architecture served to reflect and reiterate the power and legitimacy of ruling elites. The authors of these essays have investigated how palaces facilitated and supported rulers and how they functioned within the context of empires, states, and complex chiefdoms. Moreover, the essays *describe* palaces, in words and illustrations, offering the physical layouts of these buildings and evidence about how they functioned. These basic descriptions may become the most lasting contribution of this volume because they permit the reader to understand the material and documentary evidence, compare it to other case studies, and use it for further—or alternative—interpretation.

The essays in this volume concern examples ranging from the late Pre-Hispanic period in Central Mexico to the Central Andean Middle Horizon. These studies draw upon a wealth of new data available for the study of ancient American palaces, but perhaps more importantly, they bring to bear new perspectives on the subject and approach the problem of identifying and understanding ancient American palaces with new questions and new methodologies. The authors have sought to address a number of fundamental questions. For example, how do we identify a palace? In the absence of precise historical records, what is the archaeological evidence for a palace?

These questions, in turn, have led to a consideration of larger issues about the structure of power and common attributes across time and space. Is palace architecture merely domestic space writ large, or are there greater complexities, such as storage facilities and the like? Are there discernible patterns in the placement and articulation of palace buildings? What are their materials, dimensions, and amenities? What activities were conducted in palaces? Were courtyards used for the performance of ritual and presentation of tribute? What are the artifactual remains? What was the program of ornament? In what ways did it express royal or imperial rhetoric? Are connections with the divine invoked in architectural form or iconographic programs?

Patterns have begun to emerge through examination of case studies in Mesoamerica and the Andes. Although the architectural manifestations vary greatly by region, certain characteristics consistently appeared, reminding us of the central features and functions of palace architecture. For example, while in its strictest sense a palace may be a private residence, there were clearly ample spaces for public or semipublic rituals and exchanges. The courtyard as an architectural feature was prominent in nearly all of the palace examples under consideration. Restricted access was an almost universal feature of palaces, although the manner in which access was controlled varied considerably. Certain types of palaces, particularly more urban or administrative ones, often contained extensive storage facilities. As is true elsewhere in the world, however, ancient American palaces were far more than strictly bureaucratic structures. One of the other common features that came to light during the Dumbarton Oaks symposium was the importance of amenities such as gardens and displays of waterworks. Although clearly elements of pleasure and delight, such additions surely played a profound symbolic role as representative of a ruler's control over the physical environment and presumably his intimate link with divine powers.

This volume is organized roughly chronologically and by region, beginning with some of the most recent examples of palace architecture in Mesoamerica, those of the Aztec empire, and moving backward through time to Maya palaces. Following a brief discussion of the concept of the palace in the Andes, the second section of the volume follows in parallel fashion, beginning with two essays on Inca palaces, before reaching farther back to the Chimú empire and Middle Horizon polities. The final chapter, "Body, Presence, and Space in Andean and Mesoamerican Rulership," by Stephen Houston and Tom Cummins, addresses key issues in Mesoamerican and Andean governance and the implications of certain characteristics of governance for the study of palaces.

Elite residential architecture of ancient Mesoamerica is represented by essays on palaces of the Aztecs, of West Mexico, the Valley of Oaxaca, and the Maya lowlands. Aztec society was the first New World empire contacted by Europeans, and a remarkable number of sixteenth-century documents described palaces and their functions either directly or tangentially. This is in marked contrast to the number of Aztec palace remains that have survived to be investigated archaeologically. Susan Toby Evans describes Aztec palaces, and other elite residences, on the basis of a combination of documentary and material culture sources from the Central Highlands of Mexico, one of the core regions of Mesoamerican culture history.

Elsewhere in Mesoamerica, complex societies were smaller in scale, and their cultural patterns showed vigorous local development with influences from the dominating capitals of the era. West Mexico developed true palaces only in the Late Postclassic period, according to contributor Ben Nelson, and then under influence from the Central Highlands. West Mexico, however, had an indigenous centuries-old tradition of elite residential architecture, which gave rise to a distinctive palace tradition that shared the canons of the larger culture.

Ancestor veneration was an important feature of Mesoamerican life, but seldom did it reach the level of elaboration found in the Valley of Oaxaca and Mixteca regions, as Ernesto González Licón describes in his chapter. The ruling family naturally depended upon its ancestors for validation of status and treated them as vital members of the family. This extended household was translated, into architectural terms, to a multigenerational residence, where the dead lay in their chamber under those of the living.

The Maya are perhaps the best-known and most investigated of all Mesoamerican cultures. In this volume, two essays focus on the Maya in order to encompass some of the variation exhibited by their elite residential architecture. One famous Maya monument declared that there were four great capitals in the southern lowlands, and that Tikal and Copán were two of them. Peter Harrison and Wyllys Andrews describe and compare the royal palaces of these important centers. Such residences represent the pinnacle of southern lowland Classic Maya society, but other elite compounds reveal nuances of wealth and power. David Webster and Takeshi Inomata discuss two elite residential situations that reveal the complexity of Maya political life. At Copán, nonroyal elites were rich and powerful and commanded the labor and resources to build impressive compounds. At Aguateca, in contrast, the Late Classic occupation seems to have been a court-in-exile, with residences of both royal and subroyal elites who had fled from Dos Pilas.

In an admirable display of counter-hegemonic reluctance to embrace nonindigenous terminology, Andeanists have been rather resistant to the use of the term *palace*. In her opening chapter, "The Concept of the Palace in the Andes," Joanne Pillsbury examines the historical sources for the avoidance of both the topic and the terminology. Nonetheless, the Andeanists represented here consider the evidence for elite residential architecture and, indeed, palaces in the Pre-Hispanic Andean past.

The section on Andean case studies begins with the Inca, our best opportunity for combining historical and archaeological data. As there was no tradition of alphabetic writing in the Andes prior to the arrival of Europeans in the sixteenth century, the only documentary sources for the study of this region came from accounts of the colonial period. Sadly, accounts of Inca palaces are few in number and woefully brief. The single best description of an Inca palace, that of Martín de Murúa (1986/87 [1611–16]), is relatively late, coming several generations after the arrival of the first Europeans in Peru. Yet this description is important for the study of Andean palaces as it not only outlines a number of the critical features of such structures but also offers tantalizing glimpses of social elements once present in the palace.

Two essays concern Inca palace architecture. "Enclosures of Power: The Multiple Spaces of Inca Administrative Palaces," by Craig Morris, is an examination of three major state palaces: Huánuco Pampa, La Centinela, and Tambo Colorado. Morris considers the variations in architectural form between these sites and places them within the larger framework of Inca statecraft. Of particular interest is the detailed examination of the distribution of ceramics at the well-preserved site of Huánuco Pampa. Here the archaeological record fills in the historical one in a most intriguing way: Morris argues that the distribution pattern can tell us about activities that took place in the palace compound, perhaps even revealing the identities of specific social groups that inhabited distinct parts of these compounds.

"Lifestyles of the Rich and Famous: Luxury and Daily Life in the Households of Machu Picchu's Elite," by Lucy Salazar and Richard Burger, addresses a specific type of Inca elite residence: the royal estate. Great strides in the study of these estates have been made in recent years (e.g., see Niles 1999), and Salazar and Burger take a close look at one of the most famous, Machu Picchu. This site has been admired since its spectacular appearance in the scholarly and popular literature in the early twentieth century and our understanding of it has increased dramatically with the discovery of documents linking it to the *panaca* or descent group of one of the major Inca rulers, Pachacuti (Rowe 1990). Salazar and Burger's careful ongoing analysis of the archaeological collections from the site have greatly enriched knowledge of the activities and social groups inhabiting this spectacular site.

Joanne Pillsbury and Banks Leonard, in "Identifying Chimú Palaces: Elite Residential Architecture in the Late Intermediate Period," move us farther back to the Late Intermediate period with a study of the palace compounds of Chan Chan, the capital of the Chimú culture. The kingdom of Chimor, as it was called in early colonial documents, flourished for centuries on the north coast of Peru before falling to the Inca in the late fifteenth century. Pillsbury and Leonard consider the palaces of the kings of Chimor, drawing upon new historical, archaeological, and art historical evidence. The authors of this essay analyze the *ciudadelas*, monumental enclosures that served as the palaces of the lords of Chimor during their lifetime and upon death, their mausolea. Pillsbury and Leonard study possible antecedents to the *ciudadela*, and implications for changes in rulership in the Late Intermediate period.

In "Palaces and Politics in the Andean Middle Horizon," William Isbell analyzes features of Inca and other historically known palaces. Isbell has established a set of architectural features that one might expect to find in ancient Andean palace compounds. With this list in hand, Isbell sets out to identify elite residential architecture at the Middle Horizon capital of Huari, in Peru's Central Highlands, and at the Bolivian site of Tiwanaku. In this broad-reaching essay, Isbell questions long-held assumptions about the meaning and function of well-known architectural forms, and situates important new discoveries from Huari within his model of Andean kingship.

As centers of rulership, palaces were places for ceremony, bureaucracy, administration, and production. An understanding of the political organization and governance of a society is crucial for understanding palaces. In the final essay, Stephen Houston and Tom Cummins take up the issue of how rulers and palaces served as embodiments of power in these complex societies of the New World.

Acknowledgments Most of these essays were first presented at a Dumbarton Oaks symposium in Pre-Columbian Studies in October 1998. Three other papers presented at that time, by Colin McEwan, Linda Manzanilla, and Alan Kolata, were not available for publication in the present volume. Several of the participants convened a summer seminar at Dumbarton Oaks in 1998 to organize materials and discuss New World elite residential architecture in a systematic manner. This seminar was attended by George Andrews, Susan Toby Evans, Ernesto González Licón, William Isbell, Joanne Pillsbury, Jeffrey Quilter, and David Webster. Assistance on the symposium and subsequent manuscript production was provided by Lisa DeLeonardis, Jean-François Millaire, Magali Morlion, and Mary Pye, as well as Ted Putala (of Bistrot Lepic). Steve Bourget and Patricia Sarro read an early draft of the manuscript, and we are indebted to them for their helpful comments. The editors wish to thank Dumbarton Oaks for its generosity in supporting research on this topic, and to Glenn Ruby, Grace Morsberger, Christopher Dunham, David Topping, and Frances Kianka for their care in the production of this volume. A special debt of thanks is owed to Jeffrey Quilter, Loa Traxler, and Bridget Gazzo for their efforts on behalf of Pre-Columbian Studies at Dumbarton Oaks. Their efforts had a profound effect on maintaining this critical resource for scholars in our field, worldwide.

Bibliography

MURÚA, MARTÍN DE

 1986–87   *Historia general del Perú*, Manuel Ballesteros, ed. Crónicas de América 35. Historia 16
 [1611–16]   [Madrid].

NILES, SUSAN A.

 1999   *The Shape of Inca History: Narrative and Architecture in an Andean Empire*. University of
 Iowa Press, Iowa City.

ROWE, JOHN H.

 1990   Machu Picchu a la luz de documentos del siglo XVI. *Histórica* 14(1): 139–154.

Aztec Palaces and Other Elite Residential Architecture

Susan Toby Evans

PENNSYLVANIA STATE UNIVERSITY

One hallmark of complex society is the elite residence, or palace. By this standard, Aztec society of fifteenth- and sixteenth-century Central Mexico is found to be extraordinarily hierarchical and richly nuanced, with administrative palaces, pleasure palaces, and mansions, all designed to cosset their noble denizens and advertise themselves to the world as seats of authority and wealth. From detailed descriptions in documentary sources quite a lot is known about Aztec palaces and other fine houses: what went on in them, how space was used, and how Aztecs thought about palaces. In contrast, material evidence is paltry, as there are few archaeologically known examples. This essay reviews Aztec period elite residential architecture of the Basin of Mexico and adjacent regions, with an emphasis upon those palaces that served as seats of government. Synthesizing documentary and material sources reveals how the forms of these buildings reflect their function as the arena for the distinctive pattern of Aztec government-by-elite-consensus. Aztec palaces also reveal the universal human fondness for luxury and comfort.[1]

Aztec Palaces: Types and Examples

The evidence is indisputable that elite residential architecture in the Central Highlands of Mexico in the Postclassic period (i.e., A.D. 1150–1520) encompassed a wide range of forms, from rustic hunting lodges to the imperial palace of Tenochtitlan. The most common Aztec word for *palace* was *tecpan-calli*, meaning *lord/place-house*[2]

---

[1] This essay takes up in greater detail themes introduced in "Architecture and Authority in an Aztec Village: Form and Function of the *Tecpan*" (Evans 1991); more detailed interpretations of Aztec palace behavior are presented in "Aztec Noble Courts" (Evans 2001) and "Sexual Politics of the Aztec Palace" (Evans 1998a), while description and analysis of pleasure palaces and gardens can be found in "Aztec Royal Pleasure Parks" (Evans 2000).

[2] In the *Florentine Codex* (Sahagún 1963 [1569], bk. 11: 270), the Spanish gloss for *tecpan-calli* reads: "Palaces where the lords lived . . . city buildings where audiences were held and the lords and judges met to determine public lawsuits." The original text translated from Nahuatl continues: "[T]he house of the ruler, or the government house, where the ruler . . . lives, or where the rulers or the townsmen, the householders, assemble."

Tlatocacalli, on the other hand, indicates a house "where the lord usually lived"; a *tecpilcalli* was the palace of an important person; and *tlacocalli* refers to a "sumptuous [house] with many buildings" (for Spanish glosses on these terms, see p. 271).

Fig. 1 Aztec glyph for *tecpan-calli* (lord/place-house) shows the house glyph surmounted by the *copil* head-dress of office. Across its lintel is its signature disk frieze, an ancient Mesoamerican symbol for precious-ness in general and jade in particu-lar, as well as for the day as a measure of time.

(Fig. 1).[3] Early Colonial period documentary sources in the native tradition used the word *tecpan* as shorthand for many kinds of palaces of ruling lords, regardless of special functions. Where the ruler was living, that was his (or, very occasionally, her) *tecpan*. Spanish sources sometimes used the word *tecpan* but more frequently called them *casas reales*, *palacios*, or, distinguishing the pleasure palaces, *casas de recreo*. The word *tecpan* is still in use in Mexico today, used interchangeably with *casas de comunidad* or simply *comunidad*, referring to an administrative palace or community building (Ponce de Léon and Siller 1985: 25). This meaning has survived the Colonial period because the native tradition of local political administration was maintained, whereas pleasure palace and mansion sites were appropriated by Spanish lords and rebuilt to Spanish taste.

It is appropriate to use the English term *palace* in regard to the Aztec *tecpan*, and also to use associated conceptual analogs such as *pleasure palace* because the Aztecs used *tecpan* in many of the same general senses attributed to *palace*. Most commonly, the term meant the home of a hereditary lord, and it also took on associated meanings, such as seat of govern-ment, place of riches and art, and idyllic retreat amidst scenery and diversions.

Aztec palaces in general comprised three main functional types: (a) *administrative pal-aces* were local places of government and residences of local rulers; this plan was dominated by a large entry courtyard, which served as a meeting space, surrounded by suites of special

---

[3] The disk motif in association with rulership occurs as early as the Middle Formative, for example, appearing on Monument 1 (The King) at Chalcatzingo, and in Guerrero wall paintings depicting richly garbed figures who were no doubt nobles. That the meanings of jade/preciousness and the day as a unit of time would overlap is understandable, given the deep tradition of lords as monopolizing knowledge of calendrics.

purpose rooms; (b) *mansions* of wealthy nobles and commoners were luxurious residences built in conformance to sumptuary laws; (c) *pleasure palaces* and *retreats* had diverse functions expressed through forms ranging from hay-bale barracks at religious shrines to luxurious aeries carved out of cliff faces, as at Nezahualcoyotl's baths at Texcotzingo.

With its emphasis on administrative *tecpans*, this essay only briefly considers mansions and pleasure palaces, but Aztec palaces in general comprise a polythetically distributed set of features. They all share some features with each other, but there seem to have been no strict rules governing local variations on form and function. Functional types form sloppy clusters of features. For example, pleasure palaces were famed for gardens, but administrative palaces also had gardens, and garden development was as avidly pursued by Aztec nobles as it was by English lords several centuries later (Evans 2000). Administrative *tecpans* were defined by the signature large entry courtyard, but entry courtyards characterized many Postclassic period residences in the Central Highlands (and in other times and places), and presumably this feature was present in Aztec palaces of all functional types, even if hypertrophied in such imperial administrative *tecpans* as Motecuzoma II's palace in Tenochtitlan or the palaces of Texcoco.

Of the hundreds of Aztec palaces that once stood in the Basin of Mexico and adjacent regions, we have solid, substantial evidence—ethnohistorical and/or archaeological remains— from only a few dozen, most of them administrative *tecpans* (Fig. 2; Table 1). Of imperial palaces, there are extensive descriptions by people who lived in them or who knew people who lived in them, but not one of the imperial palaces has been excavated systematically, nor is this likely to occur because their remains lie deeply buried beneath modern cities. However, in the last few years several smaller *tecpans* have been archaeologically investigated. The combination of sources permits a broad reconstruction of different types of palaces.

Administrative *Tecpans*

The system of administrative *tecpans* in the Basin of Mexico, the Aztec core area, linked all communities having governmental functions, from the most powerful imperial capital, Tenochtitlan, administering a far more extensive tribute empire than that of any of Mesoamerica's antecedent or contemporaneous societies, down to large villages where tributes from adjacent smaller villages were gathered.

The Basin of Mexico encompassed ca. 7,000 sq km. In this area a large, dense population (1 million inhabitants in 1519 [Sanders 1992: 179]) lived in all habitable zones, from drained swamps to arid hills terraced with agave (maguey). The largest community, urban Tenochtitlan, had a population of ca. 100,000.[4] The basin's several thousand farming villages had populations ranging from dozens to hundreds (Sanders, Parsons, and Santley

---

[4] Motolinía (1951: 266) wrote: "In all of our Europe there are . . . few cities of parallel size and dimension that have so many surrounding and well-ordered towns . . . I doubt if there is any town so excellent and opulent as Tenochtitlan and so thickly populated."

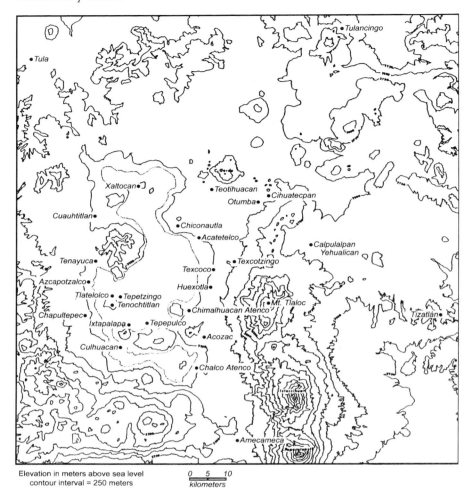

Elevation in meters above sea level
contour interval = 250 meters

0   5   10
kilometers

Fig. 2 Central Highlands, Mexico, with locations of Late Postclassic period palaces discussed in the text

1979). The Aztec political and settlement hierarchy operated dendritically from the highest authority level, that of the rulers of Tenochtitlan and Texcoco, down through the ramifying tribute system of city-states (Charlton and Nichols 1997; Hodge 1997; Smith 2000), each ruled by a *tlatoani* (pl. *tlatoque*), who was a member of one of a set of related noble dynasties. At the lowest level, low-ranking members of such dynasties served as lords of the larger villages (Evans 1993). Communities at all levels were administered from *tecpans*, which were simultaneously seats of government and the primary residences for ruling lords.

How many administrative *tecpans* were there in the Basin of Mexico at the time of European contact? Probably well over five hundred: at least two imperial *huetecpans* (Tenochtitlan and Texcoco),[5] more than fifty city-state *tecpans* (administrative residences of

[5] While Tacuba (Tlacopan) figured importantly in the Triple Alliance of the Aztecs, little is known of its *tecpans*, and the most important Tepanec *tecpan* may have been at Azcapotzalco.

Table 1 Palaces of the Late Postclassic Central Highlands of Mexico by Site Name

Site name	Name and type	Lord's title and name	Domain/ province	Date[a]	Data type	Plan
Acatetelco[b]	horticultural garden	*huetlatoani* of Texcoco	Acolhua	1400s	s. arch.? s. ethno.	abstract
Acozac	*tecpan*, city-state	*calpixqui*	Acolhua	≤ 1520	sig. arch.	partial
Acxotlan	*tecpan*	*tlatoani*	Chalco	———	frag. ethno.	none
Amecameca	*tecpan*, city-state	*tlatoani*	Chalco	≤ 1520	frag. ethno.	none
Azcapotzalco	*tecpan*, city-state	*tlatoani*; Maxtla	Tepaneca	1430s	frag. ethno.	none
Calpulalpan	horticultural garden	*huetlatoani* of Texcoco	Acolhua	1430 ≥	frag. ethno.	none
Chalco	mansion?	*tlatoani*	Chalco	———	frag. ethno.	none
Chalco Atenco	*tecpan*, city-state	*tlatoani*	Chalco	1470s	frag. ethno.	none
Chapultepec	imperial retreat	*huetlatoani* of Tenochtitlan	Mexica	1420s ≥	s. arch. sig. ethno.	none
Chiconautla	*tecpan*, city-state	*tlatoani*	Acolhua	≤ 1520	sig. arch.	partial
Chimalhuacan Atenco	*tecpan*, city-state	*tlatoani*	Acolhua	≤ 1520	sig. arch. s. ethno.	partial
Cihuatecpan	*tecpan*, village	headman	Acolhua	≤ 1520	sig. arch.	complete
Cuauhtitlan	*tecpan*, city-state	*tlatoani*	Tepanec	1300 ≥	s. ethno.	none
Cuexcomate	*tecpan*, village	headman	Huaxtepec[c]	≤ 1520	arch.	complete
Culhuacan	*tecpan*, city-state	*tlatoani*	Mexica	1550s?	ethno.	none
Huexotla	pleasure palace	*tlatoani*	Acolhua	≤ 1520	frag. ethno.	none
Ixtapalapa	*tecpan*; city-state	*tlatoani*; Cuauhtemoc	Mexica	1519	sig. ethno.	none
Otumba	mansion	noble lord; FC Ixtlilxóchitl	Acolhua	1515 ≥	frag. arch.	none
	tecpan or other elite residence	*tlatoani*?	Acolhua	≤ 1520	frag. arch. frag.ethno.	none

Site name	Name and type	Lord's title and name	Domain/ province	Date[a]	Data type	Plan
Tenayuca residences?	elite	nobles?	Tepaneca	≤ 1520	frag. arch.	none
Tenochtitlan	new imperial *huetecpan*	*huetlatoani,* Motecuzoma II	Mexica	1502–20	frag. arch frag. ethno.	abstract
	old imperial *huetecpan*	*huetlatoani,* Axayacatl, Itzcoatl, Motecuzoma I	Mexica	1430s?–1521	sig. ethno.	abstract
	pleasure garden, zoo: "Place of Whiteness"	*huetlatoani*	Mexica	≤ 1520	ethno.	none
	pleasure garden?, zoo: fierce beasts	*huetlatoani*	Mexica	≤ 1520	ethno.	none
	pleasure garden, Ahuehuetitlan	*huetlatoani* of Tenochtitlan	Mexica	≤ 1520	frag. ethno.	none
	mansion	noble lord; Cuauhtemoc	Mexica	≤ 1520	frag. ethno.	none
	administrative (residential?) palace	Cihuacoatl	Mexica	≤ 1520	frag. ethno.	none
Teotihuacan	mansion	noble lord; FC Ixtlilxóchitl	Acolhua	1515 ≥	frag. ethno.	none
Tepepulco	game reserve	*huetlatoani* of Tenochtitlan	Mexica	≤ 1520	ext. ethno. some arch.	none
Tepetzingo	game reserve	*huetlatoani* of Tenochtitlan	Acolhua	1470s–1520	ext. ethno.	none
Texcoco	*tecpan,* or mansion *Cillan* or *Zilan*	*huetlatoani* of Texcoco or other noble	Acolhua	1300s, 1400s	frag. ethno.	none
	imperial *huetecpan*	*huetlatoani;* Nezahualcoyotl	Acolhua	1430s ≥	sig. ethno.	abstract
	imperial *huetecpan*	*huetlatoani;* Nezahualpilli	Acolhua	1470s ≥	sig. ethno.	none
	Axoquentzin's mansion	noble lord; Axoquentzin	Acolhua	1470s?	frag. ethno.	none
	mansion; Tecpilpan	noble lord; FC Ixtlilxóchitl	Acolhua	1515–20	frag. ethno.	none

Site name	Name and type	Lord's title and name	Domain/ province	Date[a]	Data type	Plan
	mansion	noble lord, Iztacquautzin	Acolhua	Nezpil's reign	frag. ethno.	none
	mansion or *tecpan*	noble lord, later *huetlatoani*, Cacama	Acolhua	1515–20	frag. ethno.	none
	mansions	400+ noble lords	Acolhua	1521	frag. ethno.	none
	tecpan or *huetecpan*	*tlatoani* or *huetlatoani*, Quinatzin	Acolhua	1300s	sig. ethno.	abstract
Texcotzingo	imperial retreat	*huetlatoani* of Texcoco	Acolhua	1450s ≥	s. arch. sig. ethno.	none
Tlatelolco	*tecpan*, city-state	*tlatoani*	Mexica	≤ 1473; restored 1521	s. arch. ext. ethno.	none
Tulancingo	*tecpan*	*tlatoani*	Acolhua	≤ 1520	frag. ethno.	none
Xaltocan	*tecpan*	*tlatoani* or *calpixqui*	Acolhua	≤ 1520	frag. ethno.	none
Yautepec, Morelos	*tecpan*, city-state	*tlatoani*	Huaxtepec[c]	≤ 1520	sig. arch.	partial
Yehualican	horticultural garden	*huetlatoani* of Texcoco	Acolhua	≤ 1520	sig. arch. sig. ethno.	partial

Notes: arch. = archaeology; ethno. = ethnohistory; ext. = extensive; frag. = fragmentary; s. = some; sig. = significant.

[a] ≥ appended to a year indicates the start date for a timespan; ≤ appended to a year indicates an end date for a timespan.

[b] Also known as Atenco and El Contador Park. [c] Tributary to the Triple Alliance of Aztecs.

tlatoque, and, in a few cases, of the *calpixque* stewards, who replaced some *tlatoque*), and perhaps three to five hundred *tecpans* in small towns and villages.[6] The highest lords, the *huetlatoque* of Tenochtitlan and Texcoco, lived in the largest and most elaborate administrative *tecpans*—the *huetecpans*—*hue* in these words conveying the sense of *revered, respected, great, elder*, as in Huehueteotl, the old god of the hearth. In the main courtyards of these *huetecpans*, imperial policies were discussed and decided, and the decisions were sent on to be discussed in the courtyards of *tecpans* of city-state capitals, and from there, directives were distributed at the local level by the *tlatoani*'s vassal and junior kin, the local village headman (or occasionally headwoman), a noble who lived in a *lord-place*, a *tecpan*, and there consulted with household heads as to political policy and local civic administration (Evans 1989, 1993).

Tecpan Form and Function

The form of the *tecpan* is dominated by a large courtyard, opening onto the community plaza, which is best seen as a kind of mega-courtyard for the community. Hernán Cortés became so accustomed to this layout that he judged the limits of Mexica influence by it. Traveling south to the Gulf of Honduras after the conquest of Tenochtitlan, he arrived at Çinacantençintle (Chacujul, Guatemala, just upstream from Lake Izabal) and found:

> [A] great square where they had their temples and shrines . . . roundabout in the same manner as those of Culua [Mexica] . . . since leaving Acalan we had seen nothing of this kind . . . I collected my people together in one of those great rooms . . . the whole town . . . was very well laid out and the houses were very good and built close together. (Cortés 1986 [1519–26]: 397–398)

Moreover, modern observers have noted that this characteristic plaza-centered civic architecture sets up its own internal contrasts between the solid pyramid and open plaza (Robertson 1963: 24–25), and the whole civic layout contrasted sharply with contemporaneous European cities. Regarding Francisco Cervántes de Salazar's (1953 [1554]) description of Mexico City's *plaza mayor*, the Zócalo, George Kubler (1948) noted:

> Public plazas of this character do not occur in the medieval towns of Europe . . . the monumental concept of the plaza is anti-medieval [because European squares grew out of markets at juncture of traffic arteries, thus] the great plaza of Salamanca was an irregular, unplanned void within the urban solid. The Mexican plazas, on the other hand, are unprecedented in general European practice, but for a very few exceptions. Their form is suggested, not in coeval European towns, but in Italian theory of the fifteenth and sixteenth centuries, where the relation be-

---

[6] A city-state *tlatoani* administered an average of about forty tributary farming villages, and some of these were more nucleated nodes of local administration. In the Teotihuacan Valley a settlement pattern of one larger village with modest civic-ceremonial focus in each set of four to six farming villages was typical (Evans n.d.b).

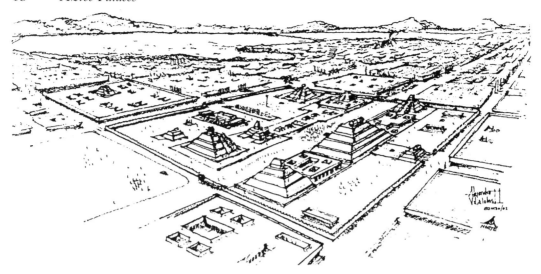

Fig. 3 Ceremonial center, Tenochtitlan-Mexico, 1519, looking toward the northwest. Motecuzoma II's palace (*bottom, center*) opening upon the plaza. To its north (*center*) is the Great Temple precinct; to its west is Axayacatl's palace. Reconstruction drawing by Alejandro Villalobos Pérez (1985: 62). Used with permission.

tween open spaces and house blocks was an object of constant study in the ideal urban layout, by . . . Alberti . . . Filarete. (98)

The community's main plaza, adjacent to the entry courtyard, sometimes functioned as a kind of palace anteroom. In Figure 3, Tenochtitlan's Templo Mayor, Axayacatl's *tecpan* where Cortés and company were lodged, Motecuzoma II's *tecpan*, and the plaza that linked them are depicted. This was a common pattern: The *tecpan* shared the civic-ceremonial focus of the community with the plaza and, where present, the ritual precinct, especially the main pyramid.

In larger towns, in addition to the palace and plaza, the civic-ceremonial focus included other elite residential and special purpose buildings, such as dance and music halls, schools and ball courts. In rural areas of the Aztec period Basin of Mexico, the pyramids and mountaintop shrines that were major ritual places were often spatially distinct from the villages. Within many rural villages, the administrative palace and plaza may have served as the main focus for ceremonial events, with rituals and festivals being carried out there as well as at isolated shrines and pyramids. It has long been observed that the plaza was the forerunner of the open-air chapel of the Colonial period (McAndrew 1965). The palace courtyard, a slightly more privileged plaza, was another locus of ritual, and thus another logical ancestor of the open-air chapel. The palace courtyards of Tizatlán, Tlax., for example, were the settings for ritually contextualized feasts in which spiritual transcendence was achieved through drunken violence (Pohl 1998).

Consider the Aztec plaza-palace courtyard relationship as part of a series of nested spatial-political relationships pertaining to the palace, an arrangement wherein the most interior palace space was the most privileged, and the most private. This was made explicit by several of the sumptuary laws promulgated by Motecuzoma Ilhuicamina:[7]

> 1. The king must never appear in public except when the occasion is extremely important and unavoidable . . . 3. Only the king and the prime minister Tlacaelel may wear sandals within the palace. No great chieftains may enter the palace shod, under pain of death . . . 11. In the royal palace there are to be diverse rooms where different classes of people are to be received, and under pain of death no one is to enter that of the great lords or to mix with those men [unless of that class himself]. Each one is to go to the chambers of his peers. (Durán 1994 [1581]: 208, 210)

These laws laid out a code of withholding royal and noble presence that was based on the spatial layout of the palace and the accessibility of the persons of the ruler and lords: the king's presence should be strictly limited, just as access to various parts of the palace was strictly limited. This provides a nice example of the body politic as political capitol, along the lines discussed by Stephen Houston and Tom Cummins (this volume).

Within the palace, the entry courtyard was the largest and most public space. Its physical and sociological centrality reflected the importance of rhetoric in achieving political and ethical consensus in Aztec society. The Aztec ruler's title, *tlatoani*, means *chief speaker*, and skill at poetry and argument was regarded as the hallmark of the truly masterful noble, one worthy of having a *tecpan*. One son of Texcocan ruler Nezahualpilli was put to death for building a palace without his father's permission and before having achieved significant mastery of either warfare or rhetoric (Alva Ixtlilxóchitl 1975–77 [1600–40]: II: 169; also I: 549). The courtyards were forums for debate and showing off. A gifted speaker could persuade others and mark himself as a coming leader in front of other nobles, who had gathered to listen, discuss, and judge.

Administrative Palaces of the Imperial Capitals: The *Huetecpans*

Almost no archaeological evidence remains of the several great *huetecpans* of the major capitals, but there is considerable written documentation of palace layout and courtly practices from chroniclers. These descriptions emphasize the large size and sumptuousness of the *huetecpans* at the time of European intrusion, as would befit the administrative residences of two of the most powerful rulers on earth.

Their empire and wealth had been gained within the century before Cortés's arrival, and so the tradition of great palaces at Aztec capitals had little time depth. Documentary sources and evidence from other *tecpans* indicate that the earliest rulers' houses were probably modest, of perishable materials, and near or perhaps at the earliest central temple (see Cuauhtitlan, pp. 35–36).

---

[7] Motecuzoma Ilhuicamina, the first Motecuzoma, ruled 1440–69. Laws similar to the ones he promulgated governed behavior in Postclassic period palaces of the Mixteca Alta (see González Licón, this volume).

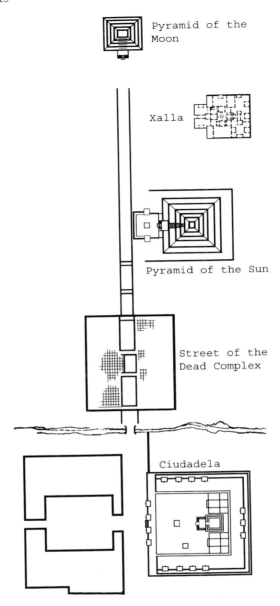

Pyramid of the Moon

Xalla

Pyramid of the Sun

Street of the Dead Complex

Ciudadela

Fig. 4 Simplified plan, Teotihuacan's monumental core along the Street of the Dead. Three complexes possibly served, in turn, as the city's administrative palaces: Xalla, the Ciudadela compounds, and the Street of the Dead complex.

The political and architectural antecedents of the Aztec palace have been addressed in detail elsewhere (Evans n.d.a; Sanders and Evans n.d.). Here, it is relevant to point out that the Aztecs used their cultural predecessors in Central Mexico to bolster their authority, associating themselves with the cultures of Teotihuacan and Tula. They used the ancient monumental heart of Teotihuacan for their own rituals, but its Terminal Formative and

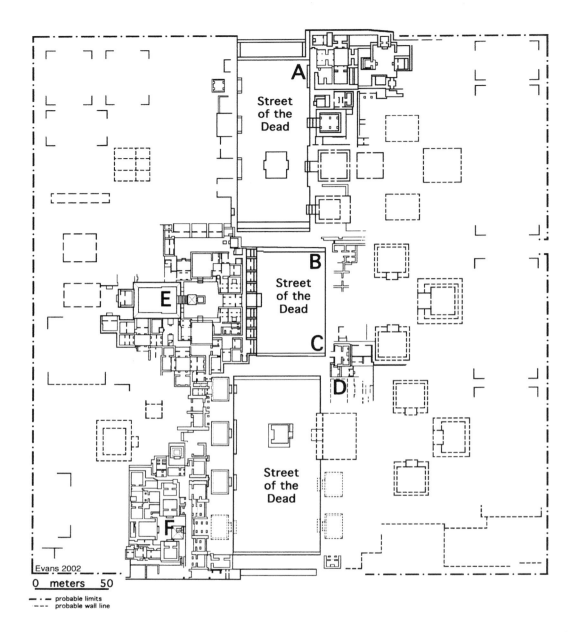

Fig. 5 Street of the Dead Complex, Teotihuacan. This vast system of formal spaces and informal "backstage" domestic rooms would have been well-suited to the administration of Teotihuacan's government and trading network. The Street of the Dead itself is embraced by the complex and may have served as its main courtyard. From Rubén Cabrera Castro (1982); Rubén Cabrera Castro, Ignacio Rodriguez G., and Noel Morelos G. (1982, 1991); René Millon, Bruce Drewitt, and George Cowgill (1973); and Noel Morelos García (1993); see also Cowgill (1983, 1997), Manzanilla and López Luján (2001), and Wallrath (1967). *Key*: A = Viking Group; B = Plaza East habitations; C = *escaleras superpuestos*; D = 1917 excavations; E = west plaza (*plaza oeste*) compound; F = *edificios superpuestos*.

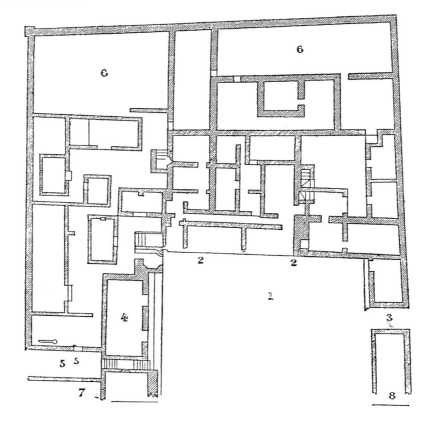

Fig. 6 Plan, Palacio Tolteca, Tula. Possibly this city's royal residential and administrative palace during its apogee in the eleventh and twelfth centuries, this palace was excavated by Désiré Charnay (1888). Unfortunately, no scale is associated with this plan, but if the size of most rooms conforms to the dimensions of other residential buildings, then the main courtyard (Charnay's 1) would have been substantial, opening onto the southern part of Tula's main plaza and surmounted by a dais room. (Charnay's 4 was the dais room, which he called the reception apartment.) From Charnay (1888: 107).

Classic period administrative palaces (Figs. 4, 5) had long lain in ruins, probably buried by the time of the Late Postclassic period. The Aztecs actively helped along Tula's process of decline, looting its sculptures and installing them in their own ceremonial precincts. Tula's royal palace may have been the Palacio Tolteca excavated by Désiré Charnay (1888) in the 1880s (Fig. 6). In contrast to Teotihuacan's Street of the Dead complex, the Palacio Tolteca had a layout similar to that of the typical Aztec palace, with a large main courtyard serving as an intermediary space between the dais room and the plaza.

Tenochtitlan and Texcoco claimed cultural descent from Tula, but neither was yet a thriving city during Tula's Early Postclassic period of hegemony. Texcoco, an older city than Tenochtitlan, had the older documented palace (see Palace of Quinatzin, Texcoco, Fig. 9, p. 25) and had far fewer rulers than did Tenochtitlan during the important period from 1430 to 1521. Numbers of rulers brings up the question of whether the Aztecs followed a tradition of building a new palace for each new ruler. The answer seems to be yes and no. In Texcoco, Nezahualcoyotl's palace was the dominant administrative palace—the *tecpan*— for about a century, beginning with its establishment in the decades after 1430. Nezahualcoyotl's successor, Nezahualpilli, built his own palace, but it seems to have served as a *tlatocacalli* and his house while he was a *tlatoani*, while the *tecpan*, the seat of government, remained at Nezahualcoyotl's palace (Umberger n.d.). Between 1430 and 1521, Tenochtitlan had many more rulers than did Texcoco, and at least several of them established *tecpans*, but there does not seem to have been a tradition of a new *tecpan* for each new ruler. For example, the *conquistadores* consistently cite two Tenochtitlan palaces that were the center of governmental activity: Motecuzoma's and Axayacatl's. They also mentioned many other rich houses, for example, that of Cuauhtemoc, who became Tenochtitlan's last ruler in 1520, but never discussed these as places of government activity. Yet some sources indicate that Cuauhtemoc's establishment was the palace of his father, Ahuitzotl (ruled 1486–1502; Umberger [n.d.] cites Alcocer 1973 [1935]). However, Ahuitzotl may have lived in this palace and governed from Axayacatl's palace, which was just to the south.

Rulers probably rebuilt and expanded existing palaces (see Axayacatl's palace, Tenochtitlan, Fig. 7, p. 22). If the first palace in early Tenochtitlan was at the temple, then, by the 1420s and 1430s, the city's ambitious dynasts would have required more substantial quarters for their administrative residences (Morales Schechinger 1993: 46). It may have been by this time that the rulers' *tecpan* was established west of the Great Temple precinct, at the location of Axayacatl's palace, which was named after the Tenochca ruler Axayacatl (ruled 1469–80), who enlarged it. It was also known as Montezuma's Old Palaces or Montezuma I's palace after the Tenochca ruler Motecuzoma Ilhuicamina (ruled 1440–69), who built or rebuilt it.

Administrative Palaces of Tenochtitlan

Axayacatl's palace, Tenochtitlan. Arriving in Tenochtitlan on November 8, 1519, Cortés (1986 [1519–26]) was greeted by Motecuzoma Xocoyotzin on the causeway leading to the central plaza.

> [H]e . . . continued up the street . . . until we reached a very large and beautiful house which had been very well prepared to accommodate us. There he . . . led me to a great room facing the courtyard through which we had entered. And he bade me sit on a very rich throne. (85)

In thus describing Axayacatl's palace, Cortés focused on the key elements of the Aztec palace: the courtyard and dais room. Motecuzoma's actions installed Cortés as lord in this palace.

Axayacatl's palace in Tenochtitlan covered a large block west of the Templo Mayor precinct.[8] It was ca. 180 x 190 m, somewhat smaller in area than that of Motecuzoma's new

---

[8]   The area is bounded by Calle de Tacuba (N), Calle Francisco Madero (S), Avenida Brasil (E), and Avenida Chile (W). Most sources agree on this location; see Ignacio Alcocer (1927); Pedro Alvarez y Gasca

palaces. Construction of the royal palace at this location may have begun in the time of Itzcoatl (ruled 1428–40). Further rebuilding took place in the early 1450s; a flood in 1449 heavily damaged the city, so that in the early 1450s, when Central Mexico was suffering from crop failures, Motecuzoma Ilhuicamina requisitioned work crews from other polities for construction at the Great Temple and at the *casas reales* (Chimalpahin 1965 [ca. early 1600s]: 99) as a means of getting work in exchange for grain distributions to the needy. In 1475, during Axayacatl's reign, an earthquake necessitated rebuilding (Lombardo de Ruiz 1973: 83), and Chalcans were required to send work crews and material for palace construction.

Sometime after 1502, Motecuzoma Xocoyotzin built his New Palaces and Axayacatl's palace was kept as lodging for important visitors and as a repository of family wealth, two features that intersected when the important visitors were Spaniards searching for gold. Andrés de Tapia (1963 [ca. 1534]: 38), one of Cortés's company, recalled that Cortés "saw a doorway that seemed recently closed off with stone and mortar. He . . . found a large number of rooms with gold in jewels and idols and featherwork."

Another eyewitness, Bernal Díaz del Castillo (1956 [1560s]), recounted the same events:

> They took us to lodge in some large houses, where there were apartments for all of us, for they had belonged to the father of the Great Montezuma, who was named Axayaca, and at that time Montezuma kept there the great oratories for his idols, and a secret chamber where he kept bars and jewels of gold, which was the treasure that he had inherited from his father Axayaca, and he never disturbed it. (194)

Although this should not be taken as evidence of ancestral cult practices on the order of those of the Inca, it does indicate how Aztec palaces functioned as dynastic monuments and shrines.

The Spaniards immediately coerced Motecuzoma into living at Axayacatl's palace with them, and the focus of Tenochtitlan's courtly life thus shifted back there. For many months, the Spaniards and the Aztec lords lived together amicably, together enjoying the pleasure-seeking and conniving life of the noble court, a life dominated by gambling, sex, feasting, hunting, and political turmoil coming to a fast boil.

The lid blew off the Azteco-Hispanic hybrid noble court with the first Spanish offensive in Tenochtitlan, the massacre of Aztec nobles dancing in the Templo Mayor precinct, next door to Axayacatl's palace. The Spaniards retreated into the palace as it was attacked by the Tenochca, as depicted in the *Lienzo de Tlaxcala* (1979 [ca. 1550]; Fig. 7), in which Axayacatl's palace is distilled into a huge courtyard surrounded by rooms, with the court-

---

(1971); Sonia Lombardo de Ruiz (1973); Marquina (1960) cited by Lombardo de Ruiz (*lám.* 27); Carlos Romero Giodano (1969); Manuel Toussaint, Federico Gomez de Orozco, and Justino Fernández (1990 [1938]). A location east of the Templo Mayor has also been suggested; see José Benítez (1929) and Roque Cevallos Novelo (1979 [1977]): 171, 176.

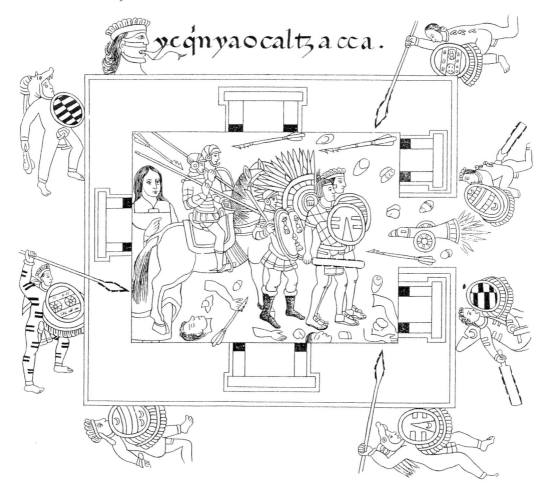

Fig. 7 The Spaniards defend themselves against Aztec attack. Plan, Axayacatl's palace, Tenochtitlan. From the *Lienzo de Tlaxcala* (1979 [ca. 1550]: ill. 14).

yard serving as an arena for political argument of the most violent sort. Here the Spaniards learned firsthand the defensive advantages of a pattern of suites of rooms around an entry courtyard: It created a blank exterior wall and also provided roofs from which to attack the attackers. The experience of defending an Aztec administrative palace lent the Spaniards insight, as they formulated their strategies of attacking Aztec palaces themselves more than a year later.

Palace of Motecuzoma II or Motecuzoma Xocoyotzin, Tenochtitlan.

The palace inside the city in which he lived was so marvelous that it seems to me impossible to describe its excellence and grandeur. Therefore, I shall not attempt to describe it at all, save to say that in Spain there is nothing to compare with it. (Cortés 1986 [1519–26]: 109)

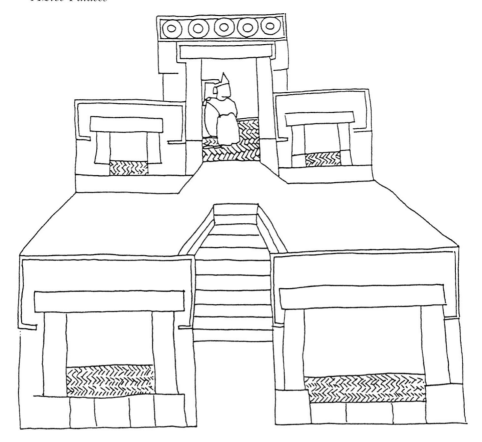

Fig. 8 Motecuzoma II's palace, Tenochtitlan. From the *Codex Mendoza* (1992).

Cortés's speechlessness on this topic is as frustrating as the only extant portrait of the palace, from the *Codex Mendoza* (1992; Fig. 8). Tapia (1963 [ca. 1534]) says a little more, describing how Cortés visited Motecuzoma to convince him to reside with the Spaniards at Axayacatl's palace:

> He went to Moctezuma's palace, where there were many things worthy of notice . . . Moctezuma met him and took him into a hall where he had his dais. About thirty of us Spaniards went in with him, while the rest stayed at the door of the building. (38)[9]

Motecuzoma's palace in Tenochtitlan covered a huge square block, ca. 200 x 200 m, somewhat larger than today's National Palace, which now overlies it, because it encom-

---

[9] The Anonymous Conqueror (1969 [1917]: 73) relates: "I entered more than four times the house of the chief Lord without any other purpose than to see things, and I walked until I was tired, and never saw the whole of it." However, this writing, while genuinely contemporary with the time of the Spanish Conquest, may have been that of an individual recounting the experiences of others.

passed land south of the Royal Canal (Guadalupe Victoria 1991).[10] Motecuzoma's palace featured a large entry courtyard, which opened onto the city plaza (see Fig. 3). In the courtyard, hundreds of courtiers spent their days, gossiping, feasting, and waiting for royal business to be conducted. Around the entry courtyard, suites of rooms surrounded gardens and smaller courtyards.

Little is known of this *tecpan* from archaeological evidence, but features of its layout can be reconstructed from descriptions and from the space it occupied.[11] From the perspective of design, Motecuzoma's palace followed earlier Aztec palaces in terms of features (though it no doubt expressed them with surpassing sumptuousness), but would have differed from many older palaces in the formality of its design, because it was built as a single unit to fill a limited urban space, rather than growing by accretion from a smaller core building into the surrounding open space (see Cuexcomate, Valley of Morelos, p. 41, and Cihuatecpan, Teotihuacan Valley, Basin of Mexico, p. 42). Motecuzoma II clearly had his palace designed for a generous block of Tenochtitlan's prime real estate, and its layout was likely to have been more engineered and more formal than the sprawling, organically grown palaces of less densely occupied cities.

Administrative Palaces of Texcoco

In Texcoco, a less nucleated city than Tenochtitlan, the imperial *tecpan* palaces ranged over larger areas. Three major palaces are well-documented, and in spite of the ambiguity noted above as to whether Nezahualpilli's establishment was a *tecpancalli* or *tlatocacalli*, it is described here, with the other two major palaces.

Palace of Quinatzin, Texcoco. Old administrative palaces stayed in use: We have seen how Axayacatl's palace became quarters for honored guests. In Texcoco, the palace of King Quinatzin was still a valuable building and grounds in the mid-sixteenth century, when its plan was drawn for a legal battle for ownership (Cline 1966, 1968).[12]

Built in the fourteenth century by Quinantzin, the [p]alace . . . was for many years the principal feature of Texcoco, housing the ruler and his court. Although over-

[10]   Estimates vary. According to Alejandro Villalobos Pérez (1985: 62), Motecuzoma's palace would have measured ca. 150 x 175 m, but the National Palace measures 180 x 200 m (Galindo y Villa 1890: 123). "The Royal Mansion, or Royal Palace, was originally the residence of Moteczoma II. The land occupied by this complex of buildings, situated in the heart of Mexico City, was granted to Hernán Cortés by the king of Spain in 1529. The heirs of the conqueror sold the property to the Spanish government in 1562, and it was there that the Viceregal Palace was constructed. Today this enormous building is the Palacio Nacional of the Federal Government of Mexico." (Horcasitas and Heyden, in Durán 1971 [1574–79]: 180, note 1)

[11]   Excavations in the interior of the present National Palace revealed some Aztec period sherds but no architectural evidence (Besso-Oberto G. 1975; Valverde L. 1982). Excavations in the *Zócalo's* southeast corner, which would have been adjacent to the southwest corner of the palace, revealed cell-like rooms, which possibly functioned as sweatbaths (*temascales*; Lombardo de Ruiz 1973: 157).

[12]   Quinatzin's dates of rule may have been 1298 to 1357, according to the Mappe Tlotzin (in Cline 1966: 82–83). Other sources use 1261 as a starting point and 1331 as his date of death.

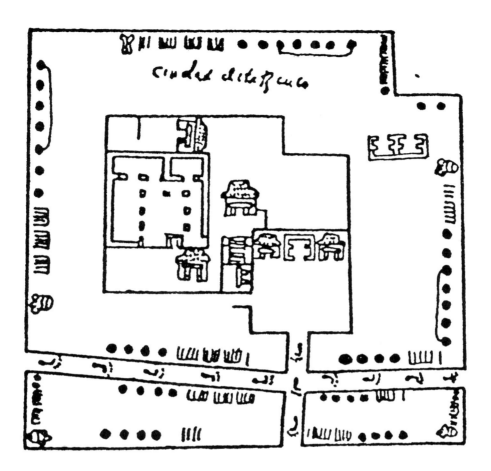

Fig. 9 Quinatzin's palace, Texcoco. From the Oztoticpac lands maps, ca. 1540 (Cline 1966: 89).

> shadowed by the buildings erected by Nezahualcoyotl and Nezahualpilli, it served
> as council hall for the lords of Texcoco up to the time of the Spanish [C]onquest.
> (Cline 1966: 92–93)

This plan (Fig. 9), from the Oztoticpac lands maps (ca. 1540), shows an entry courtyard providing the point of access between public space and the more private, presumably residential quarters beyond it. It is tempting to see Quinatzin's palace as a kind of archetype for the *tecpan* of the Early Postclassic, but this is a highly abstract plan probably reflecting changes in layout since its original building.

Between Quinatzin and his great-grandson Nezahualcoyotl, the most illustrious palace builder in Pre-Columbian Mesoamerica, Texcoco's palace history is vague. The palaces known as Cillan or Zilan (Alva Ixtlilxóchitl 1985 [1600–40]: II: 114) may have been built and occupied during this interval, or these names may have a more general meaning, referring to Quinatzin's establishment, and, at times, to Nezahualcoyotl's.

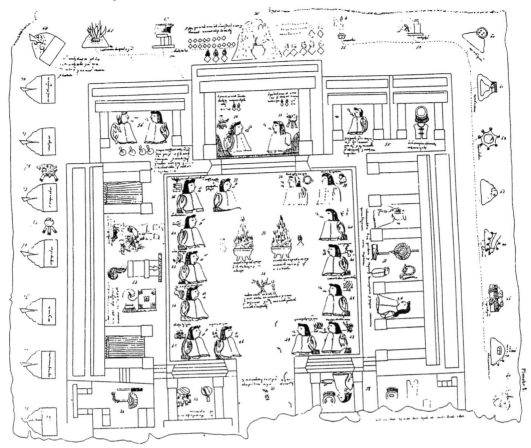

Fig. 10 Plan, Nezahualcoyotl's palace, Texcoco: "Room 1, the court, shows judges. Room 2 has Nezahualcoyotl and Nezahualpilli ... seated on their straw thrones. Rooms 3 and 4 are the armory and the keeper of the arms; rooms 20–22 the council of finance, i.e., collection of tribute; rooms 15 and 18 are the council of war; room 14 the hall of the kings of Mexico and Tlacopan; rooms 8 and 12, the hall of science and music" (Robertson [1977: 15, citing Boban 1891: I: 228–242]); a passageway (*center, lower area*) leads to the plaza and its market (Alva Ixtlilxóchitl 1985 [1600–40]: II: 94, n. 2). From the *Mapa Quinatzin* (see Robertson 1963: fig. 3). The original is in the Bibliothèque Nationale de France, Paris.

Nezahualcoyotl's palace, Texcoco. The famous *Mapa Quinatzin* plan of Nezahualcoyotl's palace (Fig. 10) has guided thinking for many years about the form and function of the Aztec palace, and the components of this plan are familiar: central courtyard, dais room, and platforms with various purposes. The plan dates from 1541 and shows Nezahualcoyotl facing his son Nezahualpilli, who was a lad of eight when his father died in 1472. In the main courtyard are the *tlatoque* of the principal city-states in the Texcocan domain at the time of European intrusion. Thus the scene depicted on the map is a historical composite, possibly showing a ritualized convocation of the *huetlatoani*, his heir, and their liege lords.

Documentary sources indicate that Nezahualcoyotl built his palace after taking the throne of Texcoco in the early 1430s and before the completion of his imperial retreat, Texcotzingo, which seems to have occurred in the 1460s. No doubt construction of his palace complex was an ongoing project, as was the development of the extensive gardens it included. The complex may have encompassed an area measuring nearly 1 sq km (i.e., 821.5 x 1,037 m), as claimed by Texcocan noble chronicler Alva Ixtlilxóchitl, but he tended to exaggerate his family's history.[13] However, in contrast to Motecuzoma's palace-on-a-city-lot, Nezahualcoyotl's establishment had room to grow, and adjacent special purpose buildings such as ball courts and schools may have been incorporated into this property. Alva Ixtlilxóchitl wrote ca. 1600 that Nezahualcoyotl's palace had two *patios principales*—one that was a *plaza y mercado* and became the central plaza of Colonial-era Texcoco and the other that was the interior patio depicted in the *Mapa Quinatzin*. It was here that fires constantly blazed in the braziers and Nezahualcoyotl's council of lords met (Alva Ixtlilxóchitl 1985 [1600–40]: II: 93), according to the *Mapa Quinatzin*.

The palace was still in use in the early 1520s, when for more than three years it was the home of Pedro de Gante, one of the earliest Christian proselytizers. Archaeological evidence is spotty. The site known as Los Melones may represent some part of Nezahualcoyotl's palace (Gillmor 1954–55), and its remains include a tower and walls finished with a coating of *tezontle* gravel (pumice) mixed with lime plaster (Noguera 1972).

Nezahualpilli's palace, Texcoco. Nezahualcoyotl's son Nezahualpilli (ruled 1472–1515) built his own separate palace in 1481, while those of Nezahualcoyotl and Quinatzin remained in use. Nezahualpilli's palaces were located in the center of Texcoco, but their exact location is, at present, not known. Alva Ixtlilxóchitl described them as smaller than Nezahualcoyotl's but more sumptuous, and having more features like gardens and baths and observatories (Alva Ixtlilxóchitl 1985 [1600–40]: II: 150). Highly regarded as a seer and wizard, Nezahualpilli saw the importance of monumental building projects as statements of public power.

Torquemada (1975–83 [1615]), writing in the early 1600s, recalled:

> I have seen all the palaces of Nezahualpilli [including touring the ruins with members of Nezahualpilli's family, who were able to describe to him the functions of certain architectural features (4: 186)] . . . They said that he was a great astrologer and valued much understanding the movements of the celestial bodies . . . and at night he would go up to the flat roofs of his palace and from there watched the stars . . . At least I know to have seen a place in his houses, on top of the flat roofs for four walls no higher or wider than a *vara*, with enough room for one man lying down and in each corner there was hole where one put a pole from which was draped a canopy. And asking '[W]hat was this for?' one of his

---

[13] Fernando de Alva Ixtlilxóchitl (1985 [1600–40]) wrote: "[D]e oriente a poniente . . . mil doscientos treinta y cuatro varas y media, y . . . de norte a sur . . . novecientas y setenta y ocho varas" (II: 93), assuming that the *vara* = 0.84 m (Heyden 1994: 593).

grandchildren (who was showing me through the house) told me that it was from the king Nezahualpilli for when at night he was with his astrologers and watched the heaven and the stars, from where I inferred to be true that which people said of him; and I think that raising the walls a *vara* off the surface and adding a ceiling of cotton or silk [awnings] . . . offered a better way of observing the sky (1: 260).

Nezahualpilli used such vantage points for humanitarian purposes as well:

[H]e had made an observatory in his palace, covered with lattices so that one could see and not be seen, and from there he used to watch the people who came to the markets and on seeing some poorly dressed woman with children he would confer with his servants to learn about her and her needs and would clothe her and her children and feed them from the granaries for a year; this was very common for him. (Torquemada 1: 261)

Torquemada further noted that the palace also provided hospital space for orphans and the ill.

Alva Ixtlilxóchitl (1975–77 [1600–40]: II: 151) wrote:

For the part that falls to the north of those houses and near the kitchens, were granaries of admirable size, in which the king had an considerable quantity of maize and other grains in order to use in famine years [such as 1505 and 1506, when Nezahualpilli opened the granaries for his subjects. Each granary] held four or five thousand *fanegas*, and all was in such good order and well-ventilated that the grain lasted many years. On the south side were the gardens and mazes, that with the height and size of the palace were guarded from cold winds from the north, and on the east side there was a pond with an aviary. (Alva Ixtlilxóchitl II: 151)

The women's quarters of Nezahualpilli's palace were the focus of several lurid stories designed to emphasize the perils of sexual encounters outside strict behavioral boundaries (Alva Ixtlilxóchitl II: 164–165; Evans 1998a: 171–172, 177–178; Evans 2001: 262–264; Zorita 1994 [1566–70]: 130–131).

Torquemada wrote:

I have seen . . . within his gardens still remain buildings of some of the palaces built for the king's women, who went to the royal palace by a road and footpath made by hand of cut stone and stucco . . . high off the ground and . . . so narrow that one had to walk single file. (4: 186)

In the early 1500s the palaces were the loci of some of the earliest omens signaling the end of the Aztec empire. Nezahualpilli found celestial portents while using his rooftop observatory, and deep inside the palace he received from a gate-crashing hare the news of "the arrival of other people who have come through our doors without resistance" (Torquemada 1: 294).

Nezahualpilli's palaces were occupied in 1521 by the Spaniards (Torquemada 2: 143). Motolinía (1951: 267) described Nezahualpilli's palace as "large enough to accommodate an army. It had many gardens and a very large pond which they used to enter in boats through a canal below the ground."

> [Quartered there, Cortés commanded his men] under pain of death, not to leave the house without [his] permission. The house was so large that had we Spaniards been twice as many we could still have put up there very comfortably . . . Toward sunset, certain Spaniards climbed onto some high roofs from where they could survey the whole city (Cortés 1986 [1519–26]: 171–172).

Later, Cortés's Tlaxcalan allies vandalized the palace, including the "large apartment that was the general archive of his papers, on which were painted many ancient things" (Pomar 1941 [1582]: 3–4).

> [Nezahualpilli's son] Ixtlilxochitl . . . went to the [c]ity of Texcoco, where he . . . found the city sacked and ruined by the Tlaxcalans. He ordered everything repaired and cleaned, especially the palaces of his father and grandfather and those of other lords (Alva Ixtlilxóchitl 1969 [1600–40]: 54).

City-State *Tecpans*

Probably because city-state capitals often retained native governors, their *tecpans* tended to continue in use into the Colonial period, and there is significant information, both archaeological and/or ethnohistorical, pertaining to the layout and rooms function of eight such *tecpans* in the Basin of Mexico and one in the adjacent Valley of Morelos.[14] They are discussed below in alphabetical order by site name.

Acozac: El Palacio. El Palacio is one of the most complete *tecpan*-palace type residences known from the Aztec period Basin of Mexico. It was occupied throughout the Postclassic period and into the Colonial era. Prior to 1418, the ruler was a *tlatoani* (*señor*; Alva Ixtlilxóchitl 1975–77 [1600–40]: I: 327), and Acozac provided service to the Texcoco royal palace (Alva Ixtlilxóchitl II: 89–90; Offner 1983). After Nezahualcoyotl regained control of Texcoco in the 1430s, Acozac's status was changed: It remained an administrative center for the Acolhua domain but was ruled by a *calpixqui*, a steward of the Texcoco *huetlatoani* (Gibson 1964: 40).[15] However, the palace remained in use and would have retained its same functions because the *calpixqui* was still a lord, although one without dynastic pretensions.

---

[14] Less is known about the form of Aztec period elite residential architecture at Culhuacan. Colonial period wills mention *tecpans* (Cline and Léon-Portilla 1984: 228, 233, 246, 248, 249). At Tenayuca, recent excavations have revealed a "palacio o conjunto residencial de alta jerarquía [palace or adjoining residence of high status]" (Limón Boyce 1997: 10–11]).

[15] Nezahualcoyotl transformed several *tlatoani* towns into *calpixque* outposts, and all were located at the boundaries of his domain. This was possibly a deliberate effort to stabilize these regions against the ever-present threat of pretensions of independence on the part of dynastic lords (Evans and Gould 1982: 295–297).

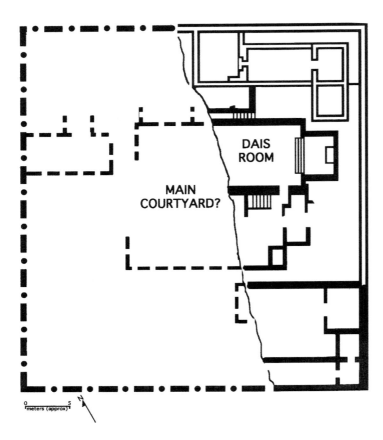

DAIS ROOM

MAIN COURTYARD?

0 meters (approx) 5

N

Fig. 11 Dais room (*upper right*) and possible main courtyard area (*center*), plan, El Palacio, Acozac. Redrawn from Richard Blanton (1972; *broken lines*), Jürgen Brüggemann (1983; *solid lines*), and Eduardo Contreras Sánchez (1976; *broken lines alternating with filled circles*).

Fig. 12 Plan, civic-ceremonial architecture, Ixtapaluca Viejo, Ix-A-26, Acozac. Note the palace's proximity to the ball court, temples, and plaza. Redrawn from Richard Blanton (1972), Jürgen Brüggemann (1983), and Eduardo Contreras Sánchez (1976).

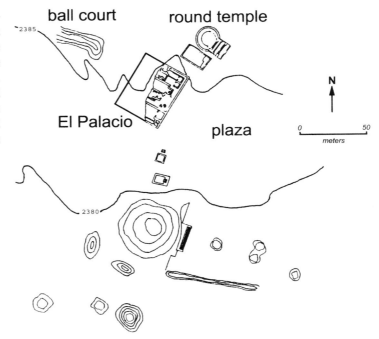

ball court

round temple

2385

El Palacio

plaza

N

0 50 meters

2380

Over half the mound encompassing the building was recently destroyed by a road cut, but fortunately, archaeological recovery operations revealed a surviving intact side (southeast wall) ca. 45 m long. The building was probably ca. 45 sq m, given Eduardo Contreras Sánchez's estimate of original extent and the square plan of known Aztec *tecpan*-palaces (Fig. 11). This would have provided ca. 2,000 sq m of interior space. The palace featured a largish courtyard presumably connected to the building entrance on the now-destroyed northwest side (Contreras Sánchez 1976). With its red-painted walls, its imposing frontage on the town's main plaza, and proximity to the ball court and large temples, El Palacio provides an excellent example of the *tecpan*'s place in the civic-ceremonial center (Fig. 12) because it is the only known archaeological evidence in the Basin of Mexico of a palace associated with a ball court, a pattern known from the ethnohistorical record and from countless archaeological examples elsewhere in Mesoamerica.

The hillside site of Acozac sloped down toward the southeast and was dominated by a view of magnificent Mt. Iztaccihuatl, which was appropriated as an important feature in orienting the civic-ceremonial buildings: The façade of the palace was framed by the mountain, a view visible down the length of the site's ball court.[16] The propinquity of palace and ball court and the orientation of the palace to the ball court and other features demonstrate broader, pan-Mesoamerican patterns and also show that there was considerable flexibility in how the component architectural parts were arrayed.

Amecameca. Entering the Basin of Mexico on their approach to Tenochtitlan, Cortés (1986 [1519–26]: 80) and company stopped at Amecameca and "were quartered in some very good houses belonging to the lord of the place." The palace continued in use after the Conquest, and is mentioned by Chimalpahin (1965 [ca. early 1600s]): 245) in the context of the Early Colonial period problem of native noble polygyny and also as the residence of Fray de Valencia in 1533 (253), suggesting that other friars followed the lead of Pedro de Gante, finding *tecpan*s an ideal place to live and preach.

Azcapotzalco. Azcapotzalco was a capital of the Tepanecs, overlords of the Mexica of Tenochtitlan and the Acolhua of Texcoco prior to the Tepanec War of the early 1430s, which resulted in the takeover of the Tepanec domain by the Mexica and Acolhua. The Tepanec had a curious division of functions with regard to their capitals, with Tlacopan/Tacuba serving as the main center (Durán 1994 [1581]: 14), whereas Azcapotzalco was the place of "the court and the kings of the Tepanecs" (61).

Archaeological explorations in the area included excavation of the Early Postclassic

---

[16] The most prominent civic-ceremonial building at Acozac (Ixtapaluca Viejo, Ix-A-26) is the Templo Mayor, which is 10 to 12 m high. The first civic-ceremonial building in this area to be systematically studied was a ball court, the first ever found in the Basin of Mexico, which was investigated by H. B. Nicholson, Frederick Hicks, and David Grove (Grove and Nicholson 1967). Richard Blanton (1972) mapped the site and drew plans of several residences, including *Tlatel* 116, which was apparently the same as El Palacio later excavated by archaeologists from the Instituto Nacional de Antropología e Historia (Contreras Sánchez 1976), and Gebäude 49, as described by Jürgen Brüggemann (1983).

Fig. 13 Azcapotzalco palace. From plancha 8, *Códice Xolotl*. Nezahualcoyotl, with coyote-head name glyph above his head (*right*), enters the palace, carrying an offering of flowers for Maxtla (*center*), who has a knotted loincloth above his head. The flowers at Maxtla's feet represent his feigned indifference to Nezahualcoyotl, whom he ignores as he sits "on a dais with the ladies and concubines of his [murdered] uncle, the King Chimalpopoca [of Tenochtitlan]." From Fernando de Alva Ixtlilxóchitl, *Historia Chichimeca* (118), quoted in the *Códice Xolotl* (1980) [1553–69]: 107; "Adjoining the palace is indicated the plaza" (107). Detail redrawn from the original.

period Coyotlatelco mound at Santiago Ahuizotla (Tozzer 1921) and other excavations by Manuel Gamio and others (described in Umberger 1996a: 260–261). The palace of Tezozomoc may have been different from that of his heir, Maxtla. Both rulers excelled at intrigue and staging dramatic political scenes. Three important elements of the Aztec palace are indicated in an illustration from the *Códice Xolotl* (1980 [1553–69]; Fig. 13): the plaza (*lower section*), the main courtyard (*upper section*), and the dais (*upper section, lower left*).

Chiconautla. Perhaps the best-known Aztec city-state palace is the Chiconautla building excavated by George Vaillant (n.d.) in the 1930s, argued to be the administrative *tecpan* of the *tlatoani* of that lakeshore town. The plan has been published extensively (Vaillant 1966), often juxtaposed with the *Mapa Quinatzin* plan, and is a familiar feature of books on the Aztecs. The plan presented here (Fig. 14) is more complex, redrawn from Vaillant's field drawings and notes, which have been recently edited and published (Vaillant and Sanders 2000: 786). However, given the courtyard-and-dais focus of the Aztec palace, it is clear that

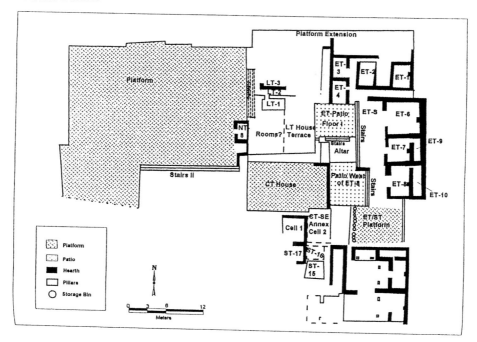

Fig. 14 Palace plan, Chiconautla. Redrawn from George Vaillant's original notes. It is far more detailed than that usually presented for this building (e.g., Vaillant 1966), but it still reveals only the building's domestic section (Vaillant and Sanders 2000: 786).

the Chiconautla plan presents only part of a compound of buildings, and its functions, beyond being residential and of the Aztec period (Elson 1999), are unclear. This section of the building, with its relatively small rooms, many featuring *tlequil*-style hearths, may have been the private quarters of a much larger *tecpan* building, which would have included a main courtyard and dais room.

Chimalhuacan Atenco. One of Texcoco's city-states (Gibson 1964: 43), Chimalhuacan Atenco had a *tecpan* that is documented by descriptive and physical evidence. It is shown at the top of the map from the 1579 *Relación geográfica* (Fig. 15) as a glyphlike, simple front-view Aztec house with a disk frieze set on a platform (Paso y Troncoso 1979 [1890]). The gloss on the platform says "El Tianguiz" (The Market). West of the platform is a much larger building, El Monasterio.

Recent excavations on the town's principal platform have uncovered the remains of an extensive Aztec period building thought to be the *tecpan* (Fig. 16). The plan of the archaeological zone shows the *tecpan* on the east. On the west is the Templo Viejo de San Andrés, the ruins of a very early Colonial period chapel, possibly overlying a Pre-Columbian ceremonial building.

The *tecpan's* southeast corner has been excavated (García, Ramírez, Gámez, and Córdoba 1998). The excavated portion of the building measures ca. 20 x 30 m, and the east side is

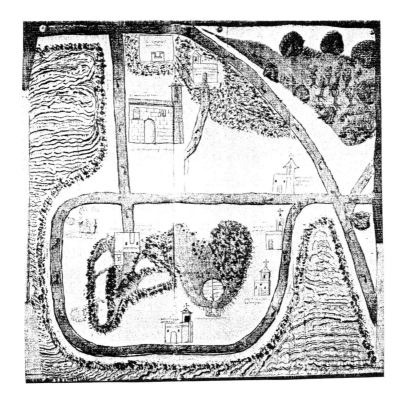

Fig. 15 Chimalhuacan Atenco. Note the *tecpan* (*top, center*), viewed upside down, and El Monasterio (*center*). From Francisco del Paso y Troncoso (1979 [1890]: VI: 69).

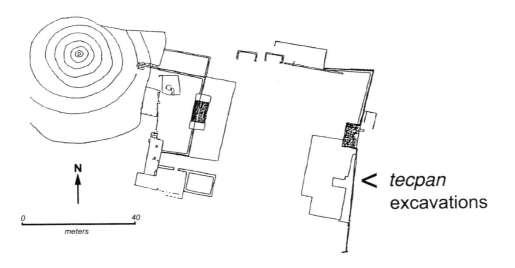

Fig. 16 Civic-ceremonial architecture, plan, Chimalhuacan Atenco. Note *tecpan* excavations on the mound's east side. Redrawn from Raúl García et al. (1998: pl. 1).

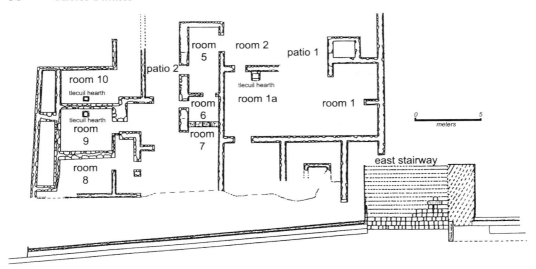

Fig. 17 Palace plan, Chimalhuacan Atenco. Excavation revealed wall bases in the building's south-east quadrant. Note *tlecuil*-hearths in rooms 1a, 9, and 10 and the east stairway (*lower right*). Redrawn from Raúl García et al. (1998: fig. 1).

dominated by a wide staircase (Fig. 17). The dimensions of the building were probably ca. 55 m north–south and perhaps 30 to 40 m east–west. There are about a dozen rooms and hallways in this section, and thus the whole building may have contained thirty to forty separate rooms. Its layout is difficult to reconstruct in terms of the typical *tecpan* rooms-around-the-courtyard pattern because the hallway that provided access from the east stair-way would have bisected such a courtyard. This brings up the problem of the orientation of this building. The *Codex Mendoza* illustration of Motecuzoma II's *tecpan* (see Fig. 8) has been used as a prototype for a hypothetical reconstruction (Fig. 18) centered on the stair-way and positing a kind of dais room west of the excavated portion of the structure.

Patio 1 was slightly sunken relative to the platform of rooms (1, 1a, 2) around it. Several suites of rooms are found beyond the patio and the platform: rooms 5, 6, 7, 8, and 9 are accessed from patio 2 and may have been habitation rooms. Cut-stone hearths (*tlecuiles*) were installed into the floors of several rooms (for contexts of *tlecuiles* at Monte Negro, see González Licón, this volume). Some of the smaller, unheated rooms may have been storage areas for household goods, tribute payments coming into the city-state or being trans-shipped to Texcoco or market goods. The right to hold a market was held by the dynasty ruling a particular town, and sellers at the market "paid the *tlatoque* for market privileges" (Gibson 1964: 356). The *tlatoani*'s role in administering the market may have been reflected architecturally in the orientation of the courtyard and dais room toward the marketplace.

Cuauhtitlan. The Annals of Cuauhtitlan (1992) document *tecpan* evolution rather than format, but the information is pertinent to other *tecpans*, such as those in Tenochtitlan. Early in the town's history, the ruler lived in a "straw-house."

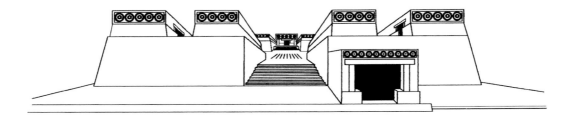

Fig. 18 Palace reconstruction, Chimalhuacan Atenco. The staircase at center is in the middle of the building's east side in the plan of the excavation. Redrawn from Raúl García et al. (1998: pl. 2).

[For example, in 1024] a Cuauhtitlan lady named Itztacxilotzin was inaugurated to govern the nation. Her mound and her straw-house were in Izquitlan Atlan . . . [Then, in 1035, a new ruler built] a new straw-house, or palace house. That is where he started it, and so that is where the rulers' residence was, etc. [In 1368, rulership was inherited by Lady Ehuat.] And she, too, lived at the temple of Mixcoatl, which had been the royal residence. (39, 72)

These passages and others indicate the custom of establishing the residence of the ruler at the town's main temple, a custom that may have been practiced when Tenochtitlan was founded.[17] However, in 1418 a ruler from Tlatelolco "came and founded a dynasty . . . came there to build his palace house" (81). The Early Colonial period *tecpan* is illustrated in the *Codex San Andrés* (Galarza 1963) as a *tecpan* glyph (i.e., house glyph with the superposed disk frieze along the top of the building).

Ixtapalapa. The city-state of Ixtapalapa was ruled by Cuitlahuac, "[l]ord of the town" and Motecuzoma II's brother (Tapia 1963 [ca. 1534]: 38). In 1519 the *tecpan*-palace was under construction and probably was one of the most luxurious in the Aztec empire, since it was being built by one of the empire's most powerful men, with access to labor and resources on a grand scale. On November 7, 1519, the night before they first arrived in Tenochtitlan, the Spaniards stayed there. Descriptions by Cortés and Díaz del Castillo are worth quoting at length, being among the most complete in the Mesoamerican ethnohistoric literature, providing key facts about quality of finishing and use of cotton cloth, as well as conveying a sense of the importance of landscape design in these palaces. Apparently, the Spaniards found extraordinary the Aztec use of the lakeshore setting in the layout of the house—how the lake as an ecological zone was appropriated into water features in landscaping and how the lake was an important transport avenue, which was integrated into the traffic flow pattern of the *tecpan* through "driveway" canals.

---

[17] *The Annals of Cuauhtitlan* (1992: 72, 74) continue: "[In 1373, a new ruler, who also] resided . . . at the temple of the devil Mixcoatl . . . [In 1379, another new ruler, whose] straw-house was in the same place where the temple of Mixcoatl was. There he lived as ruler." The ruler installed in 1390 continued this tradition.

Cortés (1986 [1519–26]) wrote:

> [In] Iztapalapan . . . the chief . . . has some new houses, which, although as yet
> unfinished, are as good as the best in Spain; that is, in respect of size and work-
> manship both in their masonry and woodwork and their floors, and furnishings
> for every sort of household task; but they have no reliefs or other rich things
> which are used in Spain but not found here. They have many upper and lower
> rooms and cool gardens, with many trees and sweet-smelling flowers; likewise
> there are pools of fresh water, very well made and with steps leading down to the
> bottom. There is a very large kitchen garden next to his house and overlooking it
> a gallery with very beautiful corridors and rooms, and, in the garden a large
> reservoir of fresh water, well built with fine stonework, around which runs a well-
> tiled pavement so wide that four people can walk there abreast. It is four hundred
> paces square, which is sixteen hundred paces around the edge. Beyond the pave-
> ment, toward the wall of the garden, there is a latticework of canes, behind which
> are all manner of shrubs and scented herbs. Within the pool there are many fish
> and birds. (82–83)

Díaz del Castillo (1956 [1560s]) was similarly impressed.

> And then when we entered the city of Iztapalapa, the appearance of the palaces in
> which they lodged us! How spacious and well built they were, of beautiful stone
> work and cedar wood, and the wood of other sweet scented trees, with great
> rooms and courts, wonderful to behold, covered with awnings of cotton cloth.
> When we had looked well at all of this, we went to the orchard and garden, which
> was such a wonderful thing to see and walk in, that I was never tired of looking at
> the diversity of the trees, and noting the scent which each one had, and the paths
> full of roses and flowers, and the many fruit trees and native roses, and the pond of
> fresh water. There was another thing to observe, that great canoes were able to
> pass into the garden from the lake through an opening that had been made so that
> there was no need for their occupants to land. And all was cemented and very
> splendid with many kinds of stone [monuments] with pictures on them, which
> gave much to think about. Then the birds of many kinds and breeds which came
> into the pond. I say again that I stood looking at it and thought that never in the
> world would there be discovered other lands such as these. (191)

The exact dimensions of Cuitlahuac's palace are not known. Its layout seems to have
centered on "great rooms" and courtyards, and it was well integrated into its lakeshore
setting, with gardens and pools overlooked by "upper . . . rooms [and] a gallery" and surrounded by pavement walkways ca. 4 m wide. Quality of finishing was high, and at least
some of the pools were apparently finished masonry (*de cal y canto*; Torquemada 1975–83
[1615]: bk. 3, chap. 21: 394), with steps leading toward the bottom. They must have been
well-sealed because they contained freshwater in an area adjacent to the saline lake. Díaz

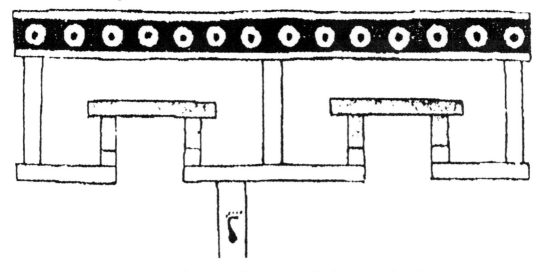

Fig. 19 *Tecpan*-palace, Ixtapalapa. From *Relación de Iztapalapa* (1580).

del Castillo's comments on the use of cotton awnings help us understand the amenities provided within the great open-courtyard spaces so important to Aztec palace life, and also give insight into noble use of cotton, a major tribute item.

The Spaniards burned Ixtapalapa in the War of Conquest, destroying Cuitlahuac's palace. Díaz del Castillo (1956 [1560s]: 191) remarks that the palace (and much else) was gone: "Of all these wonders that I then beheld to-day all is overthrown and lost, nothing left standing." After the Conquest, Cortés claimed many pieces of property, including some in Ixtapalapa, and these were listed as part of his estate in his legal papers (*Archivo General de Indias* 1940 [1570]: 57).

Sixteenth-century depictions of a *tecpan*-palace at Ixtapalapa, found in the *Mapa de México* (1986 [ca. 1550]) and the map from the *Relación de Iztapalapa* (1986 [1580]; Fig. 19), represent either a rebuilding of Cuitlahuac's palace or a separate *tecpan*. An archaeological survey of Ixtapalapa found the Aztec period remains of the town to underlie modern occupation (Blanton 1972: 152–156; Sanders, Parsons, and Santley 1979: 161, 163). The evocatively named Conjunto Palacio area identified in a survey of Aztec period *chinampas* is so called after a nearby street of the same name (Avila López 1991: 38 and fig. 8).

Tlatelolco. Tenochtitlán's sister city until 1473, Tlatelolco became its least important *barrio* after Tenochca ruler Axayacatl took advantage of Tlatelolcan royal marital discord and other circumstances to take over the city and its lucrative long-distance trade monopoly (Evans 1998a: 174–176). The temple and palace were ruined in the process.

[T]he [P]re-Hispanic palace was probably on the east side of the market, at the site of the [c]olonial *tecpan* . . . and may have originally been built early in the reign of Tlacateotl, who succeeded to the throne in 8 House, 1409. (Umberger 1996a: 256, 257; see also Barlow 1987)

Fig. 20 *Tecpan*-palace, Santiago Tlatelolco. From *Códice del tecpan* (1939 [1576–81]).

It seems to have been rebuilt by the time of the Spanish Conquest, when Cuauhtemoc was military governor of Tlatelolco before his succession to the Tenochtitlan throne and when he lived in this location (Flores Marini 1968: 53). Although the *tecpan*s of the Colonial period are beyond the scope of this essay, it is important to note that Tlatelolco's *tecpan* was rebuilt on the same location (Fig. 20) and is now part of the Three Cultures Archaeological Park in Mexico City, which is dominated by remains of the Tlatelolcan temple-pyramid. Of the Pre-Columbian *tecpan*, only its location remains.[18]

Yautepec. In the Valley of Morelos, just south of the Basin of Mexico, Yautepec was a city-state capital ruled by a *tlatoani* at the time of European contact. In the town's civic-ceremonial center, the *tlatoani*'s palace was built on a platform east of the pyramid-plaza (Fig. 21; Smith et al. 1994). The palace's platform measures ca. 95 m east-west x 75 m north-south (Vega Nova 1996: 162), surmounted by a 35 x 50 m palace mound, with deposits of successive rebuildings measuring ca. 1.5 m deep below the present height of the mound (Vega Nova 1996: 153). Excavation in the southwest corner has yielded rooms that are decidedly small and utilitarian (Fig. 22), with kitchen and other domestic detritus. In this early stage of research, generalizing about their layout of rooms is not possible, but the only known courtyard is both small and isolated. The palace mound is located just east of other civic-ceremonial buildings such as the town's pyramid, but in the palace's earliest stages of occupation, its western façade was closed to both the pyramid and the plaza. Over time, this side was opened to plaza activity, a point worth noting because it indicates flexibility in layout and orientation of various components of the civic-ceremonial center.

In the course of the excavations, seventeen burials were uncovered, mostly in flexed posture in simple graves (i.e., not in constructed tombs), with no particular pattern of

---

[18] The *Diccionario Porrúa* (1976: 2059) offers this definition: "tecpan (palacio). Edificio construido en el mismo sitio en que se halló la casa real de los señores de Tlatelolco. Tuvo varia fortuna. El nuevo edificio se terminó en 1776 y se destinó a una escuela de artes y oficios para niños pobres, en especial de raza indígena y de la parcialidad de Tlatelolco, en cuya plaza se halla, mirando al Poniente." Later versions seem to have been juvenile houses of correction.

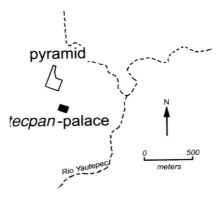

Fig. 21 *Tecpan*-palace platform mound (*blackened rectangle*) in relation to the pyramid (*above*), Yautepec,
Morelos. Redrawn from Hortensia de Vega Nova
(1996: fig. 5).

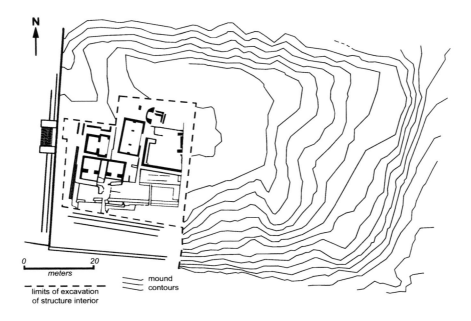

Fig. 22 *Tecpan*-palace, palace mound, plan, Yautepec. Note limits of excavation
(*broken lines*) and mound contours (*wavy lines*). Redrawn from Hortensia de
Vega Nova (1996: figs. 14–16).

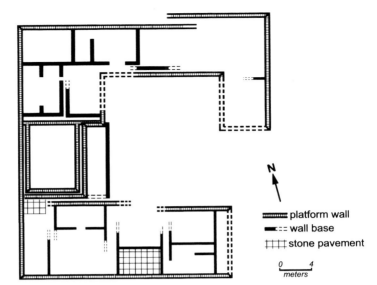

Fig. 23 *Tecpan*, patio group 6, plan, Cuexcomate, Morelos. Note wall bases (*solid and broken lines*), platform walls (*blackened rules with vertical lines*), and stone pavement (*crosshatching*). Redrawn from Michael E. Smith et al. (1989: 195, fig. 7).

platform wall
wall base
stone pavement

0   4
meters

orientation; only three had associated grave offerings. Two seem to have been sacrificial victims, both adult women, one decapitated and the other dismembered (Vega Nova 1996: 157). It was the practice in Aztec times for a deceased lord to be accompanied into the afterlife by attendants, including women (Pomar 1941 [1582]: 35–36), but the lack of context makes any interpretation completely hypothetical.

Village *Tecpans*

Surveys of the nearly continuous Aztec farming villages over the terraced piedmont of the Central Highlands have revealed that some villages had modest monumental architecture, which may have served as local foci for the tribute payments and dispute arbitration of several adjacent villages. That centralized government would ramify down to the village level during the Late Postclassic is understandable, given the high density of population and the propensity of polygynous nobles to have more offspring than could be supported in the city-state capitals. It would make perfect sense to establish local *tecpans*, staffed by members of cadet branches of city-state dynasties (Evans 1993, 1998b: 339–340).

Cuexcomate, Valley of Morelos. Excavations at the Aztec period village of Cuexcomate in the Valley of Morelos revealed a set of associated buildings on a platform encircling a patio, which has been interpreted as "the residence of a noble household" (Smith et al. 1989: 194). The complex is ca. 29 x 31 m (Fig. 23), with a central patio ca. 10 x 15 m. The *tecpan* grew over time, beginning with two separate houses, which were then leveled and a small platform built over their remains (Smith 1993: 44). This was later covered by a more extensive platform with six separate houses. The final extension of the platform created more space for the construction of larger buildings. The more dispersed building style—the *casas* approach to covering the range of necessary functions—is particularly characteristic

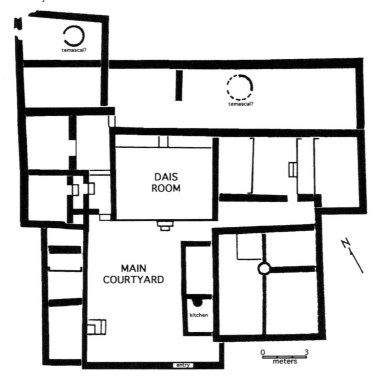

Fig. 24 Probable *tecpan*, plan, Structure 6, Cihuatecpan, Mexico. Note
the dais room (*center*) behind the main courtyard and a kitchen (*right*);
the entry is in the main courtyard's front wall (below); possible
sweatbaths (*temascales*) are to the rear (*top, left, and center*).

of buildings in warmer climates of regions like Morelos, in comparison with the colder
Basin of Mexico. The *tecpan* faces the downslope vista of the site, opening onto a plaza,
across which is a pyramid.

Cihuatecpan, Teotihuacan Valley, Basin of Mexico. The only complete physical remains in
the Basin of Mexico of a building conforming to the Aztec *tecpan* plan were found at the
village site, Cihuatecpan (Evans and Abrams 1988: 118–181).[19] Structure 6 measures 25 x
25 m (Fig. 24), the smallest of probable *tecpan*s known from archaeological evidence, small
enough to fit into a corner of the main courtyard of Motecuzoma's *tecpan* at Tenochtitlan or
Nezahualcoyotl's at Texcoco. Yet it was three times larger than the biggest of the other two

[19] The name of the site means *woman-lord-place*. In tracing the etymology of the word *tecpan* and its
associated forms, I encountered *cihuatecpan* as a town name, most notably as a *barrio* of Tenochtitlan. Hence this
term can be interpreted in various ways: as the *palace of the wife or wives of the ruler* and as the palace of
Cihuacoatl, the minister of internal affairs. A recent spate of ethnohistoric documents dealing with rulership
has provided clear instances of women ruling as *tlatoque* (see Cuauhtitlan, p. 35); were the record fine-grained
enough, it would probably reveal that the village heads were sometimes female. Thus the community name
Cihuatecpan could have been derived from a local incident of female rulership.

hundred buildings at the site, almost all of them houses of commoners, and it conforms well to the *tecpan* pattern of disproportionately large entry courtyard, dais room, and suites of rooms around the courtyard.

Aztec farmhouses commonly featured an entry courtyard flanked by residential and work rooms, and this pattern is to some degree the seminal version of the Aztec palace. Structure 6 had a more formal pattern. The entry courtyard was disproportionately large, 8.3 x 9.7 m, with a packed-earth floor and stuccoed walls decorated with a wide band of deep red paint. The dais room opposite the entryway was reached by a staircase from the courtyard. Along the back wall of the dais room, an embedded pavement of adobe bricks extended from either side of a centrally placed *tlequil*-style, cut-stone hearth. Other rooms around the central courtyard include raised platforms that may have served to accommodate special guests at meetings and feasts or to store goods for tribute.

Concerning the *Mapa Quinatzin* depiction of Nezahualcoyotl's palace, Donald Robertson (1977: 15) wrote: "The interesting thing about this reconstruction is that the building is both monumental and symmetrical and that it has a series of smaller buildings. . . in the open corners," and Cihuatecpan Structure 6 provides archaeological evidence confirming this pattern. Behind Structure 6's central courtyard were four suites of residential rooms, presumably for the lord and his several wives and their children, plus other relatives and hangers-on. Quarters for palace workers may have been separate from the palace—the shabbiest house we excavated was next to the palace, and it may have housed the *tecpan pouhque* (palace people). In the back of Structure 6 were two service yards with circular stone wall bases, possibly *temascales* (sweatbaths), judging from their shape, location, and associated artifacts, which consisted of fragments of figurines, mostly of Xochiquetzal, the goddess of healthy fertility and textile arts, reflecting two of the main concerns of Aztec women.

Structure 6's construction history was established from features of wall bonding and abutting, room levels, and ceramic typology and hydration dates from sherds and obsidian blades from floor contexts and room fill (Evans and Freter 1996). The construction chronology (Fig. 25) showed that the northeast corner of the building was built first, then the courtyard and some habitation suites, and finally the service yards and platforms. The resulting building (Fig. 26) remained in use until 1603 when the colonial government ordered its abandonment.

Mansions and Pleasure Palaces

The administrative *tecpan* announced the Aztec political process through its layout, whereas Aztec mansions and pleasure palaces, while also elite residences, expressed political organization in indirect ways. They are worth summarizing for what they reveal about the use of wealth gained from political position.

STAGE 1

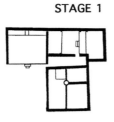

STAGE 2

STAGE 3

Fig. 25 Structure 6's three-stage construction history, Cihuatecpan, Mexico

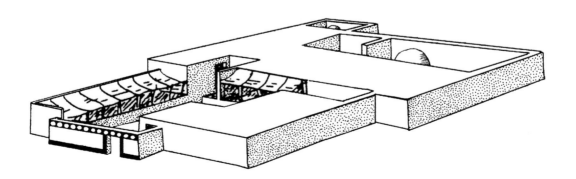

Fig. 26 Reconstruction, Cihuatecpan, Mexico

Mansions.

> [A]ll the lords who were subject to Mexico had houses in the city. These lords resided there much of the time because Moteuczom, great lord that he was, took delight in holding court. (Motolinía 1951: 272)

Mansions included the homes of nobles and nonnobles—luxurious houses of wealthy entrepreneurs like *pochteca* long-distance merchants, of nobles who gained an income from farm plots but lived in cities, of mature and accomplished offspring of powerful rulers, of diplomats, and of foreign allies maintaining residences in the imperial capitals. In Tenochtitlan there would have been dozens of these houses; the Spaniards wrote about laying siege to several neighborhoods of fine houses, especially those along canals. Most notable was Cuauhtemoc's house, inherited from Ahuizotl (Alvarez y Gasca 1971). In Tlatelolco there were also noble houses: Axayacatl had a palace built there after conquering the city in 1473, and wealthy merchants maintained large residences, although these homes may have had modest exteriors; chroniclers report that merchants were careful to conceal the extent of their wealth so as not to inspire jealousy among the nobles.

Outside Tenochtitlan-Tlatelolco, there would have been mansions in other capitals, especially Texcoco and the twelve *pochteca* merchant headquarters towns. During the Spanish Conquest, to ransom his brother, Ixtlilxóchitl sent to Texcoco "for the gold which had remained in the palaces of his father and grandfather . . . together with the gold and silver taken from the houses of four hundred other lords in the city." (Alva Ixtlilxóchitl 1969 [1600–40]: 55) This suggests that there were probably hundreds of mansions in the basin and adjacent regions, mostly in the largest cities.

No recognizable archaeological evidence of such residences remains, but they are known from descriptions of feasts and other functions that took place within them and also from citations of the architectural features that could only be used with the permission of the ruler: part of the sumptuary laws that demonstrated the conflict between the status-seeking individual's urge to display wealth and taste and the ruler's wish to limit such displays to himself and his clients.[20] These features were the architectural parlance of the palace world; to use them announced to the world the right to own a palace, a right only a king could grant.

The mansion that Nezahualpilli built for his older brother, Axoquentzin, rewarded a military victory against Chalco, and the mansion was a copy of the Chalcan king's palace (Umberger 1996b: 92–93). Nezahualpilli sent an architect, mason, and artist to study the building's plan and features. This incident shows how palaces functioned as status symbols—win a great victory, get a great palace—and also how individual innovations of design in architecture and landscaping were closely noted and became fashionable.

---

[20] Diego Durán (1994 [1581]: 209): "Only the great noblemen and valiant warriors are given license to build a house with a second story; for disobeying this law a person receives the death penalty. No one is to put peaked or flat or round additions upon his house. This privilege has been granted by the gods only to the great."

Nezahualpilli had one of his own sons executed for building a palace without his permission. Descriptions of this incident emphasize the severe justice kings had to deploy, even unto their own law-breaking offspring, but the subtext provides information as to who deserved a palace. Alva Ixtlilxóchitl 1975–77 [1600–40] describes how the son, Iztacquauhtzin, came to be executed.

> [W]ithout [Nezahualpilli's] permission he built some palaces to be his dwelling, without having achievements to merit it; because the laws stipulated that although he was a hereditary prince he could not build rich houses nor decorate them with bunches of feathers, until he had been through four battles, and had captured at least four officers, experienced military men, that had [achieved] in knowledge all the [grades] that were necessary for a wise man, philosopher, orator and poet, and at least had achieved skill in some of the mechanical arts, and being approved in one of these things, with the permission of the king could have achieved this . . . because the other way had the death penalty, so they carried out this law on Iztacquauhtzin. (II: 169; also I: 549)

Retreats, Pleasure Palaces, and Gardens

Nezahualpilli may have consoled himself by retreating to one of his numerous country palaces. Aztec nobles developed many properties for their recreational and contemplative potential, and they built pleasure palace residences at such sites, as well as creating gardens within their *tecpan* palaces. Gardens were treasured by nobles, who embowered the many courtyards of their palaces with trees, vines, and flowering plants. The right to cultivate certain plants was covered by sumptuary laws, and for a noble family to lose the privilege of developing impressive gardens was somewhat like banishment from paradise. Such matters call forth unanswered—probably unanswerable—questions of the floral gradations of noble privilege: Like symbols in a heraldic crest or ribbons on a veteran's chest perhaps the flowers in the gardens spoke a well-understood language of earned and inherited privilege.

In the Basin of Mexico, there were perhaps several dozen permanent pleasure palaces and a handful of ephemeral palaces. The development of pleasure parks in the fifteenth century by the related dynasties of Tenochtitlan and Texcoco became a fascinating contest of elite-status rivalry (Evans 2000). Beginning in 1420, four different types of pleasure parks were established and/or refined: imperial retreats, horticultural gardens, urban zoological and memorial parks, and game reserves (see Table 1). I should note that spiritual and ritual functions were ever-present at these pleasure palaces, which were often located at or near existing shrines, especially hot springs and mountaintops with commanding views.

> [T]he gardens of flowers and sweet-scented trees, and the many kinds that there were of them, and the arrangement of them and the walks, and the ponds and tanks of fresh water . . . and the baths which he had there, and the variety of small

birds . . . and the medicinal and useful herbs that were in the gardens. It was a wonder to see, and to take care of it there were many gardeners. Everything was made in masonry and well cemented, baths and walks and closets, and apartments like summer houses where they danced and sang . . . as a consequence of so many crafts being practi[c]ed among them, a large number of skilled Indians were employed. (Díaz del Castillo 1956 [1560s]: 214)

Lords also had temporary palaces, encampments at spiritual retreats and military outposts. The Spaniards describe comfortable quarters being made up for them quickly, using bales of straw or thatch. This must have been similar to the quarters constructed for kings when they traveled, for example, on the yearly pilgrimage of the lords to the shrine atop Mt. Tlaloc.

Palace as Power, Palace as Offering, Palace as Art

Having reviewed the main types of Aztec palaces and some notable examples, we can ask what do Aztec palaces signify in broader cultural terms. When we consider the Mesoamerican sequence of cultural development, the final century was unsurpassed in terms of the territory made to serve as a catchment zone for a few related royal families. The Aztecs managed to control far more land and collect much more wealth than any competing polity or predecessor. This remarkable concentration of resources gave rise to elite conspicuous consumption patterns similar to those of the Old World's flashier archaic agrarian states, Rome and Babylon, for example, wherein the rulers' facilities were a means of announcing high status and investing wealth.

Many complex societies have administrative palaces, but far fewer also have horticultural gardens and imperial retreats carved into cliffs. The range of variation in palace types and sizes, the sumptuary laws—these are all indications that concentration of wealth is extreme and that high value was placed on expressions of wealth that stressed social position and taste.

It is fortunate that so much is known about Aztec palaces. Spanish soldiers and clerics stayed in them for months before hostilities broke out, fortified themselves within the palaces during the conflict, and as soon as the Conquest was over staked claims to palatial property. Spaniards admired and later imitated palace settings and layouts, responding to two major aspects of the Aztec palace: (a) The beauty and certain comforts of these places were appreciated by Cortés and his men, and (b) The effectiveness of the central courtyard as a forum for political action and rhetorical expression impressed Catholic proselytizers, who used this design as a natural place of instruction and consensus for the young nobles they needed to convert in their spiritual conquest.

Early on, the Spaniards recognized the Aztec palace form as crucial to shaping Aztec attitudes because of the role of the courtyard. In this strongly hierarchical social structure, ideas and policies affecting multitudes were first argued before a group of powerful elites, in the courtyards of the palaces. Pedro de Gante, a strong proponent of conversion by co-opting pagan religious forms and sacred places, had spent his first three years in Mexico living in Nezahualcoyotl's palace in Texcoco. There he gained such respect for the court-yard as element of rhetorical process that he had the influential schools for elite Aztec youth built in that form. Advocating the use of native customs as a context for conver-sion, Fray de Gante saw how the *tecpan* courtyard served as an arena for discourse, par-ticularly for the sermons that Aztec elders regularly preached to those assembled.[21] Fray de Gante sensed the customary power inherent in the courtyard-and-dais architectural layout, and he copied the design for the influential native chapel and school, San José de Los Naturales, which was erected in the patio of the convent of San Francisco in Mexico City (Maza 1972: 33).[22]

Thus the *tecpan* courtyard became the prototype for the open-air chapel, a forecourt in front of churches. Services were held for Spaniards in the enclosed church, and for natives in the open-air chapel (McAndrew 1965). The position of the dais room, the tradi-tional seat of power, was spatially held by the enclosed church, where Spaniards attended services. In terms of preaching to the natives, the dais function was assumed by the preach-ing stations, the pulpits at the corners of the open courtyard. This was a spatial expression of the assumption of the power of the Aztec lords by the Spaniards, and priests in particular, with regard to direct contact with the people. The Aztec aristocracy was as a whole sector of society demoted to a position inferior to that of Spaniards (Gibson 1960).

This Spanish colonial appropriation of the functional dichotomy of Aztec palace form, with dais and courtyard representing ruler and ruled, is enormously revealing about Aztec palaces and the close relation they have demonstrated between architectural forms, func-tions, and societal and political meanings. In contrast to Spanish elite houses, and the con-ventions of Iberian noble architecture, the Aztec administrative-residential palace represented its distinctive societal meaning, its courtyard and dais room shaping social and civic identity and linking the lords and their people.

Acknowledgments The research into Aztec palaces from which this essay was derived was initiated with excavations at Cihuatecpan, near Otumba, Edo. de Mex., under the auspices of the Instituto Nacional de Antropología e Historia, México, D.F., and funded by a grant from the National Science Foundation, Washington, D.C. Further research was undertaken at Dumbarton Oaks, aptly termed by Saburo Sugiyama "the Chicomostoc of Mesoamerican research." I much appreciate the help and support of Jeffrey Quilter and Bridget Gazzo at Dumbarton Oaks in making one of the world's best research libraries of its kind also one of the world's most accessible. This volume, and the conference before it, would not have been possible without Joanne Pillsbury: enthusiastic and energetic co-organizer, incisive co-editor, and insightful scholar. It has been a privilege working with her, and I appreciate her comments on my ideas about Aztec palaces, as well as those by David Webster, William Sanders, Patricia Sarro, and other reviewers of this manuscript.

[21] See, e.g., the *huehuetlatolli* speeches recorded in Frances Karttunen and James Lockhart (1986, 1987 [1581]).

[22] The *tecpan* courtyard is the formal category missing from James Lockhart (1992: 428, table 10.1) under the table subheading "Stage 1 (1519 to ca. 1545–50)" provided for his "Arts and Architecture" data.

Bibliography

ALCOCER, IGNACIO

1927   Ubicación del palacio de Axayacatl. *Anales del Museo Nacional de Arqueología, Historia y Etnografía* 5: 91–96.

1973   *Apuntes sobre la antigua México-Tenochtitlan*. Instituto Nacional de Antropología e
[1935]   Historia, México, D.F.

ALVA IXTLILXÓCHITL, FERNANDO DE

1969   *Ally of Cortés. Account 13: Of the Coming of the Spaniards and the Beginning of Evangelical*
[1600–40] *Law*. With a foreword by D. K. Ballentine, trans. Texas Western Press, El Paso.

1975–77   *Obras históricas*, 3rd ed., 2 vols. Edmundo O'Gorman, ed. Serie de Historiadores y
[1600–40]   Cronistas de Indias 4. Universidad Autónoma de México, México, D.F.

1985   *Obras históricas*, 4th ed., 2 vols. Edmundo O'Gorman, ed. Serie de Historiadores y
[1600–40]   Cronistas de Indias 4. Universidad Autónoma de México, México, D.F.

ALVAREZ Y GASCA, PEDRO

1971   *La Plaza de Santo Domingo de México, siglo XVI*. Instituto Nacional de Antropología e
Historia, México, D.F.

ANNALS OF CUAUHTITLAN

1992   *History and Mythology of the Aztecs: The Codex Chimalpopoca. Annals of Cuauhtitlan and Legend of the Suns*. John Bierhorst, ed. and trans. University of Arizona Press, Tucson.

ANONYMOUS CONQUEROR

1969   *Narrative of Some Things of New Spain and of the Great City of Temestitan Mexico*. M. H.
[1917]   Saville, trans. and ann. Kraus Reprint, New York. [Cortés Society, New York]

ARCHIVO GENERAL DE INDIAS

1940   Archivo General de Indias 1940 [1570]. Relación de lo que valieron las rentas del
[1570]   marqués del Valle en los años de 1568 y 1569, hecha por Juan de Cigorondo, contador de dicho Estado, *Papeles de Simancas*, Estante 59, cajón 4, legajo 3, Seville, Spain. In *Epistolario de Nueva España, 1505–1818*, edited by Francisco del Paso y Troncoso, 11:5–60. Antigua Libreria Robredo, de José Porrúa e Hijos, Mexico.

AVILA LÓPEZ, RAÚL

1991   *Chinampas de Iztapalapa, D.F.* Serie Arqueología. Instituto Nacional de Antropología e Historia, México, D.F.

BARLOW, ROBERT H.

1987   *Tlatelolco: Rival de Tenochtitlan. Obras de Robert H. Barlow*, vol. 1. Jesús Monjarás-Ruiz, Elena Limón, and María de la Cruz Paillés H., eds. Instituto Nacional de Antropología e Historia, México, D.F., and Universidad de las Américas, Puebla, Pue.

BENÍTEZ, JOSÉ R.

1929   *Historia gráfica de la Nueva España*. Cámara Oficial Española de Comercio, México, D.F.

BESSO-OBERTO G., HUMBERTO

    1975   Excavaciones arqueológicas en el Palacio Nacional. *Boletín* 14 (n.s.): 3–24.

BLANTON, RICHARD E.

    1972   *Prehispanic Settlement Patterns of the Ixtapalapa Peninsula Region, Mexico.* William T. Sanders et al., eds. Occasional Papers in Anthropology 6. Pennsylvania State University, University Park.

BOBAN, EUGÈNE

    1891   *Documents pour servir à l'histoire du Méxique. Catalogue raisonné de la collection de M. E.- Eugène Goupil*, 2 vols. Leroux, Paris.

BRÜGGEMANN, JÜRGEN K.

    1983   Acozac. *Beiträge zur Allgemeinen und Vergleichenden Archäologie* Band 5: 323–334.

CABRERA CASTRO, RUBÉN (ED.)

    1982   *Teotihuacan 80–82. Primeros resultados.* Proyecto Arqueológico Teotihuacan. Instituto Nacional de Antropología e Historia, México, D.F.

CABRERA CASTRO, RUBÉN, G. IGNACIO RODRIGUEZ, AND G. NOEL MORELOS (EDS.)

    1982   *Memoria del Proyecto Arqueológico Teotihuacan 80–82*, vol. 1. Colección Científica 132. Serie Arqueológia. Instituto Nacional de Antropología e Historia, México, D.F.

    1991   *Teotihuacan 1980–1982. Nuevas interpretaciones.* Colección Científica 227. Serie Arqueológia. Instituto Nacional de Antropología e Historia, México, D.F.

CERVÁNTES DE SALAZAR, FRANCISCO

    1953   *Life in the Imperial and Loyal City of Mexico in New Spain* (Minnie Lee Barrett
    [1554]   Shepard, trans.). With an introduction and notes by Carlos Eduardo Castañeda. University of Texas Press, Austin.

CEVALLOS NOVELO, ROQUE

    1979   El Templo Mayor de México-Tenochtitlan. In *Trabajos arqueológicos en el centro de la*
    [1977]   *ciudad de México*: 169–182. E. Matos Moctezuma, ed. Instituto Nacional de Antropología e Historia, México, D.F.

CHARLTON, THOMAS H., AND DEBORAH L. NICHOLS

    1997   Diachronic Studies of City-States: Permutations on a Theme. Central Mexico from 1700 B.C. to A.D. 1600. In *The Archaeology of City-States*: 169–207. Deborah L. Nichols and Thomas H. Charlton, eds. Smithsonian Institution Press, Washington, D.C.

CHARNAY, DÉSIRÉ

    1888   *The Ancient Cities of the New World Being Voyages and Explorations in Mexico and Central America from 1857–1882.* Harper, New York.

CHIMALPAHIN CUAUHTLEHUANITZIN, DOMINGO FRANCISCO DE SAN ANTÓN MUÑÓN

    1965   *Relaciones originales de Chalco Amaquemecan.* S. Rendón, ed. Fondo de Cultural
[ca. early 1600s]   Económica, México, D.F.

CLINE, HOWARD F.

    1966   The Oztoticpac Lands Map of Texcoco, 1540. *Quarterly Journal of the Library of Congress* 23: 76–115.

    1968   The Oztoticpac Lands Map of Texcoco, 1540: Further Notes. *Thirty-Seventh International Congress of Americanists, Actas y Memorias* 3: 119–138.

CLINE, S. L., AND MIGUEL LEÓN-PORTILLA

    1984   *The Testaments of Culhuacan.* Latin American Center Publications. University of California, Los Angeles.

CODEX MENDOZA

    1992   *A Facsimile Reproduction of Codex Mendoza*, vol. 3. Frances F. Berdan and Patricia Rieff Anawalt, eds. University of California Press, Berkeley.

CÓDICE DEL TECPAN DE SANTIAGO TLATELOLCO

    1939   *Investigaciones históricas*, bk. 1, 3: 243–264.
  [1576–81]

CÓDICE XOLOTL

    1980   Charles E. Dibble, ed. Serie Amoxtli 1. Instituto de Investigaciones Históricas.
  [1553–69] Universidad Nacional Autónoma de México, México, D.F.

CONTRERAS SÁNCHEZ, EDUARDO

    1976   La zona arqueológica de Acozac, México; temporada 1973–1974. *Boletín* 16 (n.s.): 19–26.

CORTÉS, HERNÁN

    1986   *Hernán Cortés: Letters from Mexico.* Anthony Pagden, ed. and trans. Yale University
  [1519–26] Press, New Haven, Conn.

COWGILL, GEORGE L.

    1983   Rulership and the Ciudadela: Political Inferences from Teotihuacan Architecture. *Civilization in the Ancient Americas: Essays in Honor of Gordon R. Willey*: 313–343. R. Leventhal and A. Kolata, eds. University of New Mexico, Albuquerque, and Harvard University, Cambridge, Mass.

    1997   State and Society at Teotihuacan, Mexico. *Annual Review of Anthropology* 26: 129–161.

DÍAZ DEL CASTILLO, BERNAL

    1956   *The Discovery and Conquest of Mexico.* Genaro García, ed., and A. P. Maudslay, trans.
  [1560s] With an introduction by Irving A. Leonard. Farrar, Strauss, and Cudahy, New York.

DICCIONARIO PORRÚA

    1976   *Diccionario Porrúa de historia, biografía, y geografía de México*, 4th ed. Editorial Porrúa, México, D.F.

DURÁN, DIEGO

  1971   *Book of the Gods and Rites and the Ancient Calendar.* Fernando Horcasitas and Doris
  [1574–79] Heyden, eds. and trans. University of Oklahoma Press, Norman.

  1994   *The History of the Indies of New Spain.* Doris Heyden, trans. and ann. With an
  [1581]   introduction by Doris Heyden. University of Oklahoma Press, Norman.

ELSON, CHRISTINA M.

  1999   An Aztec Palace at Chiconautla, Mexico. *Latin American Antiquity* 10: 151–167.

EVANS, SUSAN TOBY

  1989   House and Household in the Aztec World: The Village of Cihuatecpan. In *Households
            and Communities*: 430–440. S. MacEachern, D. J. W. Archer, and R. D. Garvin, eds.
            Archaeological Association of the University of Calgary, Calgary, Alberta.

  1991   Architecture and Authority in an Aztec Village: Form and Function of the *Tecpan*. In
            Land and Politics in the Valley of Mexico: 63–92. H. Harvey, ed. University of New
            Mexico Press, Albuquerque.

  1993   Aztec Household Organization and Village Administration. In *Prehispanic Domestic
            Units in Western Mesoamerica*: 173–189. R. Santley and K. Hirth, eds. CRC Press,
            Boca Raton, Fla.

  1998a   Sexual Politics in the Aztec Palace: Public, Private, and Profane. *RES: Journal of
            Anthropology and Aesthetics* 33: 165–183.

  1998b   Toltec Invaders and Spanish Conquistadors: Culture Contact in the Postclassic
            Teotihuacan Valley, Mexico. In *Studies in Culture Contact*: 335–357. James G. Cusick,
            ed. Occasional Paper 25. Center for Archaeological Investigations, Southern Illinois
            University, Carbondale.

  2000   Aztec Royal Pleasure Parks: Conspicuous Consumption and Elite Status Rivalry.
            Studies in the History of Gardens and Designed Landscapes 20: 206–228.

  2001   Aztec Noble Courts: Men, Women, and Children of the Palace. In *Maya Royal
            Courts*: 237–273. Takeshi Inomata and Stephen Houston, eds. Westview, Boulder,
            Colo.

  n.d.a   Palaces and Political Power in Classic and Postclassic Central Mexico: Antecedents
            of the Aztec Tecpan. In *Ancient American Elite Residences*. Jessica Christie and Patricia
            Joan Sarro, eds. University of Texas Press, Austin (in press).

  n.d.b   A Settlement System Analysis of the Teotihuacan Region, Mexico, A.D. 1350–1520.
            Unpublished Ph.D. dissertation. Department of Anthropology, Pennsylvania State
            University, University Park, 1980.

EVANS, SUSAN T., AND ELLIOT M. ABRAMS

  1988   Archaeology at the Aztec Period Village of Cihuatecpan, Mexico: Methods and
            Results of the 1984 Field Season. In *Excavations at Cihuatecpan*: 50–234. S. T. Evans,
            ed. Publications in Anthropology 36. Vanderbilt University, Nashville, Tenn.

EVANS, SUSAN T., AND AnnCORINNE FRETER

  1996   Hydration Analysis of Obsidian from Cihuatecpan, an Aztec Period Village in
            Mexico. *Ancient Mesoamerica* 7: 267–280.

EVANS, SUSAN T., AND PETER GOULD

1982   Settlement Models in Archaeology. *Journal of Anthropological Archaeology* 1: 275–304.

FLORES MARINI, CARLOS

1968   El Tecpan de Tlatelolco. *Anales del Instituto de Investigaciones Estéticas* 37: 49–54.

GALARZA, JOAQUÍN

1963   Codex San Andrés (Juridiction de Cuautitlan): Manuscrit pictographique du Musée de l'Homme de Paris. *Journal de la Société des Américanistes* 52: 61–90.

GALINDO Y VILLA, JESÚS

1890   Epigrafía mexicana: Edificios públicos. *Anales del Museo Nacional de México* 4: 122–124.

GARCÍA, RAÚL, FELIPE RAMÍREZ, LORENA GÁMEZ, AND LUIS CÓRDOBA

1998   *Chimalhuacan: Rescate de una historia.* Municipio de Chimalhuacan, Toluca, Edo. de Mex., and Instituto Nacional de Antropología e Historia, Toluca.

GIBSON, CHARLES

1960   The Aztec Aristocracy in Colonial Mexico. *Comparative Studies in Society and History* 2: 169–196.

1964   *The Aztecs under Spanish Rule.* Stanford University Press, Stanford, Calif.

GILLMOR, FRANCES

1954–55 Estructuras en la zona de Texcoco durante el reino de Nezahualcoyotl según las fuentes históricas. *Revista Mexicana de Estudios Antropológicos* 14(1): 363–371.

GROVE, DAVID C., AND H. B. NICHOLSON

1967   Excavación de un juego de pelota en Ixtapaluca Viejo, Valle de México. *Boletín* 22: 17–19.

GUADALUPE VICTORIA, JOSÉ

1991   Noticias sobre la antigua plaza y el mercado del volador de la Ciudad de México. *Anales del Instituto de Investigaciones Estéticas* 62: 69–91.

HEYDEN, DORIS

1994   Glossary. In Diego Durán, *The History of the Indies of New Spain*: 581–593. Doris Heyden, trans. and ann. With an introduction by Doris Heyden. University of Oklahoma Press, Norman.

HODGE, MARY G.

1997   When Is a City-State? Archaeological Measures of Aztec City-States and Aztec City-State Systems. In *The Archaeology of City-States*: 209–227. Deborah L. Nichols and Thomas H. Charlton, eds. Smithsonian Institution Press, Washington, D.C.

KARTTUNEN, FRANCES, AND JAMES LOCKHART

1986   The Huehuehtlahtolli Bancroft Manscript: The Missing Pages. *Estudios de Cultural Nahuatl* 18: 171–179.

KARTTUNEN, FRANCES, AND JAMES LOCKHART (EDS.)

1987   *The Art of Nahuatl Speech: The Bancroft Dialogues.* Latin American Center Publications,
[1581]   University of California, Los Angeles.

KUBLER, GEORGE

1948   *Mexican Architecture of the Sixteenth Century,* 2 vols. Yale University Press, New Haven,
Conn.

LIENZO DE TLAXCALA

1979   *Lienzo de Tlaxcala. Publicado por Alfredo Chavero. Mexico 1892.* Editorial Cosmos,
[ca. 1550]   México, D.F.

LIMÓN BOYCE, MORRISON

1997   Tenayuca: Primer sede de los chichimecas en la Cuenca de México. *Expresión
Antropológica* 3: 7–15.

LOCKHART, JAMES

1992   *The Nahuas after the Conquest.* Stanford University Press, Stanford, Calif.

LOMBARDO DE RUIZ, SONIA

1973   *Desarrollo urbano de México-Tenochtitlan según las fuentes históricas.* Instituto Nacional de
Antropología e Historia, México, D.F.

LÓPEZ LUJÁN, LEONARDO, AND LINDA MANZANILLA

2001   Excavaciones en un palacio de Teotihuacan: Proyecto Xalla. *Arqueología Mexicana*
9(50): 14–15.

MANZANILLA, LINDA, AND LEONARDO LÓPEZ LUJÁN

2001   Exploraciones en un posible palacio de Teotihuacan: El Proyecto Xalla (2000–2001).
Tezontle, Boletín del Centro de Estudios Teotihuacanos 5: 4–6.

MAPA DE MÉXICO

1986   *Mapa de México Tenochtitlan y sus contornos hacia 1550.* Miguel León-Portilla and
[ca. 1550]   Carmen Aguilera, eds. Celanese Mexicana, México, D.F.

MAPA QUINATZIN

1959   In Donald Robinson, *Mexican Manuscript Painting of the Early Colonial Period*: 135–
[ca. 1542]   140 (pls. 13, 46, 47). Yale University Press, New Haven, Conn.

MARQUINA, IGNACIO

1960   *El Templo Mayor de México.* Instituto Nacional de Antropología e Historia, México,
D.F.

DE LA MAZA, FRANCISCO

1972   Fray Pedro de Gante y la capilla abierta de San José de Los Naturales. *Artes de México*
150: 33–38.

McANDREW, JOHN

1965   *The Open-Air Churches of Sixteenth-Century Mexico.* Harvard University Press,
        Cambridge, Mass.

MILLON, RENÉ, BRUCE DREWITT, AND GEORGE COWGILL

1973   Maps. In *Urbanization at Teotihuacan, Mexico*, vol. 1, pt. 2: *The Teotihuacan Map.* René
        Millon, ed. University of Texas Press, Austin.

MORALES SCHECHINGER, CARLOS

1993   Propiedad urbana méxica y la estructura de Tenochtitlan. *Cuadernos de Arquitectura
        Mesoamérica* 23: 37–58.

MORELOS GARCÍA, NOEL

1993   *Proceso de producción de espacios y estructuras en Teotihuacan.* Colección Científica 274.
        Serie Arqueología. Instituto Nacional de Antropología e Historia, México, D.F.

MOTOLINÍA (TORIBIO DE BENAVENTE)

1951   *Motolinía's History of the Indians of New Spain.* Frances Borgia Steck, ed. and trans.
        Academy of American Franciscan History, Washington, D.C.

NOGUERA, EDUARDO

1972   Arqueología de la región Tetzcocana. *Artes de México* 151: 75–96.

OFFNER, JEROME A.

1983   *Law and Politics in Aztec Texcoco.* Cambridge University Press, Cambridge, Eng.

DEL PASO Y TRONCOSO, FRANCISCO

1979   *Papeles de Nueva España: Segunda serie, geografia y estadística: Relaciones geográficas de la
[1890]   diocesis de México, 1579–1582.* Editorial Cosmos, México, D.F.

POHL, JOHN M. D.

1998   Themes of Drunkenness, Violence, and Factionalism in Tlaxcalan Altar Paintings.
        RES: Journal of Anthropology and Aesthetics 33: 183–207.

POMAR, JUAN BAUTISTA

1941   *Relaciones de Texcoco y de la Nueva España*: 1–64. Pomar-Zurita. Editorial Salvador
[1582]   Chavez Hayhoe, México, D.F.

PONCE DE LÉON, PABLO CHICO, AND JUAN ANTONIO SILLER

1985   La influencia náhuatl en la terminología arquitectónica. *Cuadernos de Arquitectura
        Mesoamérica* 4: 23–30.

RELACIÓN DE IZTAPALAPA

1986   In *Relaciones geográficas del siglo xvi: México*, vol. 1: 36–42. Rene Acuña, ed. Edición de
[1580]   René Acuña 7. Serie Antropológica 65. Instituto de Investigaciones Antropológicas,
        Universidad Autónoma de México, México, D.F.

ROBERTSON, DONALD

    1963   *Pre-Columbian Architecture*. Braziller, New York.

    1977   Domestic Architecture of the Aztec Period: Mapa de Quinatzin. In *Del Arte: Homenaje a Justino Fernandez. Arte prehispánico,* vol. 1: 11–18. Instituto de Investigaciones Estéticas, México, D.F.

ROMERO GIODANO, CARLOS

    1969   *Las Casas Viejas de Moctezuma: Historia de una institución*. Banco Nacional Monte de Piedad, México, D.F.

SAHAGÚN, BERNARDINO DE

    1963   In *Earthly Things. Book 11 of the Florentine Codex*. C. E. Dibble and A.J.O. Anderson,
    [1569]   trans. and ann. School of American Research, Santa Fe, N.M., and the University of Utah, Salt Lake City.

SANDERS, WILLIAM T.

    1992   Ecology and Cultural Syncretism in 16th-Century Mesoamerica. *Antiquity* 66: 172–190.

SANDERS, WILLIAM T., AND SUSAN TOBY EVANS

    n.d.   Rulership and Palaces at Teotihuacan. In *Ancient American Elite Residences*. Jessica Christie and Patricia Joan Sarro, eds. University of Texas Press, Austin (in press).

SANDERS, WILLIAM T., JEFFREY R. PARSONS, AND ROBERT SANTLEY

    1979   *The Basin of Mexico: The Cultural Ecology of a Civilization*. Academic Press, New York.

SMITH, MICHAEL E.

    1993   Arquitectura y sociedad en sitios rurales postclásicos en el oeste de Morelos: El Proyecto Morelos Postclásico. *Cuadernos de Arquitectura Mesoamericana* 24: 39–51.

    2000   Aztec City-States. *A Comparative Study of Thirty City-State Cultures*: 581–595. Mogens Herman Hansen, ed. Royal Danish Academy of Sciences and Letters, Copenhagen.

SMITH, MICHAEL E., PATRICIA AGUIRRE, CYNTHIA HEATH-SMITH, KATHRYN HIRST, SCOTT O'MACK, AND JEFFREY PRICE

    1989   Architectural Patterns at Three Aztec-Period Sites in Morelos, Mexico. *Journal of Field Archaeology* 16: 185–203.

SMITH, MICHAEL E., CYNTHIA HEATH-SMITH, RONALD KOHLER, JOAN ODESS, SHARON SPANOGLE, AND TIMOTHY SULLIVAN

    1994   The Size of the Aztec City of Yautepec: Urban Survey in Central Mexico. *Ancient Mesoamerica* 5: 1–11.

TAPIA, ANDRÉS DE

    1963   The Chronicle of Andrés de Tapia. *The Conquistadors*: 19–48. Patricia de Fuentes, ed.
    [ca. 1534] and trans. Orion, New York.

TORQUEMADA, JUAN DE

1975–83   *Monarquia indiana*, 7 vols. Miguel Leon-Portilla, ed. Instituto de Investigaciones
[1615]   Históricas, Universidad Autónoma de México, México, D.F.

TOUSSAINT, MANUEL, FEDERICO GOMEZ DE OROZCO, AND JUSTINO FERNÁNDEZ

1990   *Planos de la Ciudad de México, siglos xvi y xvii.* Universidad Autónoma de México,
[1938]   Mexico, D.F.

TOZZER, ALFRED M.

1921   Excavation of a Site at Santiago Ahuitzotla, D.F. Mexico. *Smithsonian Institution
Bureau of American Ethnology Bulletin* 74.

UMBERGER, EMILY

1996a   Appendix 3: Material Remains in the Central Provinces. *Aztec Imperial Strategies*:
247–264. F. F. Berdan et al., eds. Dumbarton Oaks, Washington D.C.

1996b   Art and Imperial Strategy in Tenochtitlan. *Aztec Imperial Strategies*: 85–106.
F. F. Berdan et al. eds. Dumbarton Oaks, Washington D.C.

n.d.   Remarks presented at a conference entitled Ancient American Palaces: Rulership
and Ornament, at the Center for Advanced Study in the Visual Arts, National
Gallery of Art, Washington, D.C., February 1997.

VAILLANT, GEORGE C.

1966   *Aztecs of Mexico* (rev. ed.). S. B. Vaillant, ed. Penguin, Baltimore.

n.d.   Report on the 1935 Excavation at Chiconautla. Manuscript on file, American
Museum of Natural History, New York.

VAILLANT, GEORGE C., AND WILLIAM T. SANDERS

2000   Excavations at Chiconautla. In *The Teotihuacan Valley Project Final Report*, vol. 5: *The
Aztec Period Occupation of the Valley*, pt. 2: *Excavations at T.A. 40 and Related Projects*:
757–787. William T. Sanders and Susan Toby Evans, eds. Occasional Papers in
Anthropology 26. Pennsylvania State University, University Park.

VALVERDE L., ADRIÁN

1982   Algunos hallazgos arqueológicos en el centro de la Ciudad de México, 1790–1980.
Anales de Antropología 19: 45–49.

VEGA NOVA, HORTENSIA DE

1996   Proyecto de Investigación Arqueológica en Yautepec, Morelos. In *Memoria, III
Congreso Interno del Centro INAH Morelos a los xx años de su fundación*: 149–168.
Instituto Nacional de Antropología e Historia, Centro Regional Morelos,
Cuernavaca, Mor.

VILLALOBOS PÉREZ, ALEJANDRO

1985   Consideraciones sobre un plano reconstructivo del recinto sagrado de México-
Tenochtitlan. *Cuadernos de Arquitectura Mesoamérica* 4: 57–63.

WALLRATH, M.

1967   The Calle de Los Muertos Complex: A Possible Macro-Complex of Structures near
        the Centre of Teotihuacan. In *Teotihuacan XI Mesa Redonda* (2 vols.), vol. 1: 11–122.
        Sociedad Mexicana de Antropología, México, D.F.

ZORITA, ALONSO DE

1994   *Life and Labor in Ancient Mexico: The Brief and Summary Relations of the Lords of New*
[1566–70]   *Spain.* With an introduction by Benjamin Keen, trans. University of Oklahoma Press,
            Norman.

Elite Residences in West Mexico

Ben A. Nelson

Arizona State University

This essay is an examination of social practices and processes associated with elite residential architecture in West Mexico. High-status buildings in this part of Mesoamerica are interesting for different reasons than those in more urbanized regions. The West Mexican examples expose important principles about the spread of sociopolitical complexity and the incorporation of multiple traditions into a civilization. At the same time, they reveal differences in elite power strategies in core versus marginal areas and within West Mexico itself. Tracing the threads of practices associated with elite residences allows us to understand how the fabric of social power was constructed in West Mexico and elsewhere.

Some observable regularities include the following: (a) palaces may exist in the absence of urban development; (b) palaces were uncommon in West Mexico and probably were an exclusively Postclassic phenomenon; (c) at least as early as the Early Classic (i.e., 100 B.C.–A.D. 400), the elite built "protopalaces," which embodied some of the symbolic principles that distinguish palaces from other residences; (d) although operating within distinct local traditions, the architects of elite residences made use of common canons to connote power; (e) the architecture of social power often encompassed not only built space but the entire landscape; (f) palaces per se tended to occur in areas of West Mexico that had contact with the Basin of Mexico and had developed economic, as well as ideational, bases of social power.

Before delineating these issues and discussing the architectural patterning, I define terms such as *palace* and *West Mexico* and also mention some theoretical points of departure. The discussion moves rather widely in time (Table 1) and space (Fig. 1).

Palaces

The definition of palaces is inextricably linked with the nature of political power, which is variably constituted according to local traditions, so that palaces and other elite-related architecture must be understood in local terms. For purposes of this essay, *palaces* are the residences of the principal power holders in stratified polities. The occupants are not merely of high status, but are first-order nobility; the existence of palaces is part of what distinguishes the residents materially from mere members of a privileged class. Political power in societies that use palaces seems to be closely linked with economic power, so that

Table 1   Periods Mentioned in Text

Period	Date
Early Classic	100 B.C.–A.D. 400
Middle Classic	400–600
Late Classic/Epiclassic	600–900
Early Postclassic	900–1150
Late Postclassic	1150–1521
Tarascan	1521–1522[a]
Huichol	1724–present

[a] The dates of Spanish observation of the Tarascans prior to their surrender to the empire.

palaces tend to be constructed with corvée labor (Sanders 1974). Palaces are durable statements of social and economic order and about the place of particular occupants in that order. Built to actively reinforce such distinctions, palaces are overtly more elaborate in materials and size than other residences, have a different internal spatial syntax than commoners' residences, and are often embellished with religious or cosmological symbols, which may hark to an idealized past or to origin accounts. Political actors may appropriate religious symbolism and attach it to personal residences as a strategy in the construction of social power.

Looking for palaces in West Mexico, or anywhere else, one is immediately faced with a question: what to look for without knowing the strategies and symbols that were used to construct power. Two different approaches are used here. First, ethnographic descriptions of rulership and, to some extent, elite architecture provide one point of departure. Second, the general principles discussed above suggest some characteristics of palaces. Thus, palaces may exhibit or embody symbolism that is ethnographically associated with rulership. In addition, they should be noticeably different in size, centrality, construction materials, and internal organization from other local residences; palaces are not just large, formal versions of ordinary residences.

West Mexico

West Mexico is a huge region, encompassing up to half of Mesoamerica, depending

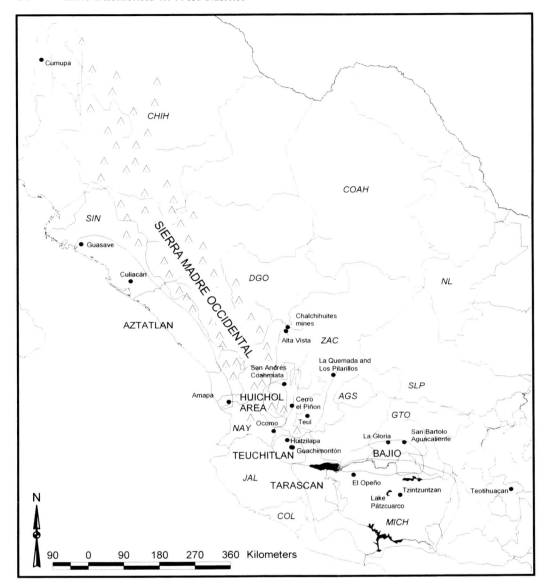

Fig. 1 West Mexico locations discussed in text. Illustration by Jean Baker.

on how the two are defined. For this essay, it roughly includes present-day Aguascalientes, Colima, Durango, Guanajuato, Michoacán, Jalisco, Nayarit, Sinaloa, and Zacatecas. Some archaeologists do not consider West Mexico to be part of Mesoamerica; others suggest that it becomes incorporated only in the Postclassic period (i.e., 900–1521). While this debate is largely definitional, embedded in it are important signals about the emergence of palaces and other elite residences. For example, there is the sensible argument that Pre-Hispanic Mesoamerica was a multiethnic civilization that affected, and was affected by, a multiplicity of traditions (Braniff 1975; Meighan 1974; Pollard 1997; Schondube B. 1987; Weigand

1985). This argument implies a need for sensitivity to variation in the grammar and syntax of architecture. At the same time, statements by Schondube B. (1980: 408), and Fernández and Deraga (1995: 197) that state-level organization was absent in West Mexico until the formation of the Tarascan entity, show that palatial architecture is unlikely to be found at many times and in many places in West Mexico. The scale and elaboration of architecture in West Mexico does not generally match that of other Mesoamerican regions.

Archaeologists lack accepted nomenclature to describe the different regions that make up West Mexico; for convenience, I distinguish core versus frontier West Mexico and sometimes coastal versus interior West Mexico. The location of the West Mexican core or cores varies through time. By *core*, I mean an area of heightened development, high-population density, and sociopolitical complexity. In the Late Formative, there is a core related to shaft tomb developments in Nayarit, Jalisco, and Colima. In the Early Classic, there is a core of circular patio-banquette complexes of Jalisco, Zacatecas, and Michoacán. The Late Classic (i.e., 600–900) or, as I prefer to call it, the Epiclassic[1] sees what may be a minor core development in the Zacatecas-Aguascalientes-Guanajuato region. In the Postclassic, there is the well-known Tarascan core and, in addition, another core associated with the Aztatlán horizon on the coast. The distinction between coastal and interior West Mexico, fairly obvious as to location, is a natural one marked by the Sierra Madre Occidental. Also of interest are the more restricted local cultural traditions defined by archaeologists.

Contrasts in Colonial Period Rulership and Associated Architecture

One key to deciphering elite architecture is to understand variations in rulership recorded by the Spanish colonists. The temptation to make facile projections onto the more remote past must be avoided, but one can legitimately derive propositions about differences in styles of rulership and the associated architecture and then see whether they seem applicable in Pre-Hispanic contexts. It is useful to array the ethnographic examples on a scale of complexity while remaining sensitive to the pitfalls of reductionism. Complexity refers here to the spatial extent of a polity and its degree of hierarchy or to the extent to which social power is concentrated in the hands of a few individuals (Nelson 1995). Among sedentary peoples whom the Spaniards mention, the Tarascans and the Huichol represent the extremes of hierarchy and scale, whereas certain peoples on the west coast represent intermediate formations.

The Tarascans were the only state-level society in contact-period West Mexico. Their capital, Tzintzuntzan, is recorded in the *Relación de Michoacán* and has been partially excavated (Cabrera Castro 1987; Rubín de la Borbolla 1941). Pollard (1982: 251) characterizes the Tarascan state as strongly centered around a single royal family, without the competing factions that characterized Central Mexican states. The palace was faced with a colonnade and situated in a prominent position overlooking Lake Pátzcuaro. A force of some three thou-

---

[1] The Epiclassic, a contested concept, seems useful in this region because much of the development of ceremonial centers appears to coincide roughly with the period between the fall of Teotihuacan and the rise of Tula.

sand state workers was responsible for the construction of royal buildings. The royal family may have had exclusive rights to the means of production in several sectors of the economy (Pollard 1982: 258), and Tzintzuntzan received tribute through a number of subordinate centers. The royal family controlled the allocation of tribute absolutely. Despite having these characteristics of sociopolitical complexity and individualizing practices of rulership, the population in the Tarascan core was distributed in a number of centers around the lake, forming a moderately dispersed settlement pattern.

The Huichol, as ethnographically known, exemplify less hierarchical principles of leadership. They regarded themselves as egalitarian (Grimes and Hinton 1969), avoiding individual aggrandizement and reaching decisions by negotiation and consensus. Tribute, material or otherwise, was paid to no local political center. Early documents also mention that the heads of main villages would convene to decide important issues (e.g., Rojas 1992: 98), suggesting that there was no overarching authority beyond what the Spaniards refer to as the *municipio*. The Huichol were politically integrated by the cargo system as well as a round of maize-oriented ritual, which regularly brought together representatives of residential groups (Fikes n.d.). Although the cargo system may have been in part a response to colonial demands for articulation with national powers (Chance 1990) and decisions about land tenure and other resources may have been concentrated in certain lineages—as among the Pueblo of the American Southwest (Brandt 1994)—it must also have been an expression of indigenous principles, as Gibson (1965) argues for other colonial forms of political organization in New Spain. The contrasts in concentration and individuation of power with those of the Tarascan polity are significant.

Phil Weigand (1998: 412–419) suggests that the Huichol of the sixteenth and seventeenth centuries were part of a hierarchically organized, regional *Nayarita* system of sociopolitical organization headed by a single "house," to which tribute and obeisance were paid. He notes that the political leaders of the Huichol and some of their neighbors were described by the Spaniards as *cacique* and *tlatoani*, and suggests that the ancient system of authority is overlain by layers of more recent, nationally oriented, political organization and is now nearly unobservable. Unfortunately, the subsurface archaeology of the Huichol in the early Colonial period is unattested, making it difficult to assess the architectural signature of the postulated regional hierarchy.

Modern Huichol patterns of architecture and settlement pattern are fascinating expressions of the current political system, in which hierarchy seems to be deliberately obscured. Their ceremonial centers, which also serve as commercial and political nodes, are removed both vertically and horizontally from the rest of the settlement pattern; they are located on mountain ridges while the majority of the population lives in the more agriculturally viable canyons (Grimes and Hinton 1969). Consistent with the Huichol world view, these locations emphasize the sacred nature of politics and position the living leaders to consult with ancestral spirits, who are thought to be the true governors of all matters (Lumholtz 1902; Negrín 1985). I have learned through my visits to one center, San Andrés Coahmiata, that many families maintain houses there, even though they do not live in the village for most of the year. The houses are for use during ceremonial times, when the village suddenly becomes densely populated with celebrants.

Huichol architecture includes no individual structures that resemble palaces; indeed, there is little obvious differentiation among dwellings, although this is a subject that merits more investigation. Most houses are of relatively humble construction; strong architectural statements would not be expected in a context where equality is emphasized, and political offices are periodically rotated among different holders. Very likely, the statement as to who holds power is made by the act of having a house in the ceremonial center or not, even though families reportedly have complete autonomy in choosing where to build. Thus the actions that associate political power with architecture appear to be (a) locating one of the family's dwellings in the center of a relatively aggregated population, as most families live in dispersed hamlets; and (b) situating that center in an elevated location, which is not particularly desirable from a subsistence perspective. The Huichol pattern provides a baseline for the subtlest expression of elitism in West Mexican architecture.

The towns encountered along the west coast by early explorers such as Nuño Beltrán de Guzmán and Francisco de Ibarra represent intermediate examples of scale and hierarchy. Not described in great detail, the towns were much larger than those of the sierra, yet the settlement pattern was also dispersed. Towns consisted of loosely clustered adobe structures, which were strung along major rivers and built on mounds to avoid flood damage. Mound height and area may have been indicators of social power. One particularly strong architecturally related political statement was recorded by Ibarra in the town of Cumupa, located in a canyon somewhat inland of the coastal plain, probably in present-day northern Sinaloa. There residents hung bones of slain enemies on the outsides of dwellings (Hammond and Rey 1928: 175). Such a symbolic statement would logically be associated with centers of power and elitism of the sort established through achievements in warfare. As shown below—in the subsection on the Malpaso-Chalchihuites, the Altos of Jalisco, and the Bajío de Guanajuato—such symbolism seems to have been quite relevant in Pre-Hispanic times.

The above ethnographic cases suggest a number of principles, in addition to the widely recognized cross-cultural ones, that might have structured the architectural expressions of power in ancient West Mexico. First, all of the ethnographic examples, even the Tarascan, exhibit some degree of dispersion at the intracommunity scale. The importance of this observation is that, in a West Mexican context, physical dispersion of a community does not rule out the concentration of political power or the use of palatial architecture. In this sense, West Mexican seats of power appear to have departed significantly from those of Central Mexico or the Maya area; it is conceivable that such divergence was deeply rooted in time. Rather than using such differences to exclude the region from Mesoamerica, we might think of the differences among the regions as alternative means of expressing dominance relationships. In other words, West Mexican palaces do not necessarily have to be part of urban settlements. Was such the case for ancient West Mexico?

Second, there is a strong correspondence in the Tarascan-Huichol contrast between the degree of social hierarchy and the configuration of central-place architecture. Both examples have dispersed settlement patterns, yet only one is overtly hierarchical; that hierarchy is clearly stated in the architecture of the central place by way of monumental scale, costly materials, internal functional differentiation, and religious associations that one might predict on a cross-cultural basis, manifested in uniquely Tarascan style. Are such distinctive, elaborate buildings found in West Mexico in Pre-Hispanic times?

Third, the Tarascan and Huichol examples indicate some of the ways in which West Mexican groups used the landscape to affirm social power. Political centers in both societies are located in elevated, sacred places. Huichol political leaders move cyclically about the landscape, not only performing rituals in the ceremonial centers, but also visiting the dispersed hamlets that make up the great bulk of the settlement pattern. The periodic gathering of the population at ceremonial centers is another form of landscape use that involves affirmation of the political order. It is not clear that the west coast groups used these strategies to mark their political arrangements. Are there relationships between landscape use and the political order in ancient West Mexican societies?

Finally, there is a hint of a pattern that seems more strongly expressed in the archaeological record, discussed below, of an association between places of political power and the display of human remains. The example in which the bones of enemies were suspended from the walls of residences, while not specifically linked to palaces or other elite buildings, seems germane to some of the archaeological data from the Classic period.

Shaft Tombs: Palaces for the Dead?

The most distinctive and elaborate structures of the West Mexican Formative are not above-ground monuments, but shaft tombs (Fig. 2). The earliest shaft tombs at El Opeño date to ca. 1500 B.C. (Oliveros and de Los Ríos Paredes 1993), but they are far more frequent ca. 1000 B.C. to A.D. 400. Most of the literature on shaft tombs is, of necessity, oriented to the art objects that have been tragically torn from their contexts by looters (Furst 1965; Meighan and Nicholson 1989); relatively little is known of the arrangements of objects within the tombs (but see Oliveros [1974]; Ramos de La Vega and López Mestas Camberos [1996]). Archaeologists have entered a number of looted tombs and described their morphology (Long and Taylor 1966).

The functions of shaft tombs are less obvious than might be thought; it is not immediately clear whether they were built to honor high-status individuals or were crypts, which many families might have. Most of the recorded tombs are not monumental in the sense of requiring the efforts of large numbers of builders, yet they obviously signaled special regard for selected individuals. Scholars have observed that many of the tombs were reopened and entered repeatedly over time; earlier-interred remains were often moved aside to accommodate later interments. These actions are inferred not only from detailed accounts of looters who have been interviewed but, in a few cases, from direct observations of bone distribution by archaeologists (Cabrero G. and López C. 1997; Corona Nuñez 1955). The placement of successive generations of people in the tombs seems inconsistent with veneration of a particular individual, and seems more appropriate if it is ancestry in general that is being venerated.

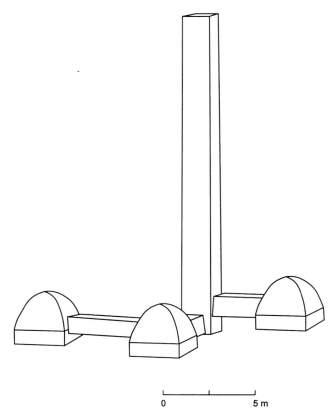

Fig. 2 Shaft tombs, El Arenal. After José
Corona Nuñez (1955: 13). Illustration
by Jean Baker.

It is the qualities of the offerings included in shaft tombs, as much as the grave
morphology, that makes it possible to think of shaft tombs as elite structures. An impressive
range of shell, greenstone, obsidian, large numbers of elaborate ceramic vessels, and other
precious objects are included in the more abundant offerings. Most notable are the famous
shaft tomb figurines. Recently, some archaeologists and art historians have advanced the
argument that shaft tombs constitute the earliest evidence of sociopolitical complexity in
West Mexico (Weigand 1996: 91). It has even been suggested, in contrast to Peter Furst's
long-held proposition that figurines portray shamans, that they instead depict rulers (Graham 1998).

If shaft tombs were a kind of palatial structure, or part of a palatial complex, they
should be infrequent within settlements, associated with the more elaborate and costly
above-ground structures, and located centrally within settlements or with respect to a group
of settlements. They might also be placed in elevated locations such as hilltops. El Opeño,
the earliest shaft tomb site, is an isolated cemetery in a moderately high spot; no associated
village or other residential architecture has been found (Noguera 1942; Oliveros 1974). The
Middle Formative example mentioned by Phil Weigand (1996: 91) consists of an isolated
burial platform that apparently served as a common mortuary facility for a dispersed and
as-yet-undocumented community.

Later, after 300 B.C., shaft tombs occurred beneath patio banquette complexes, including some of the more monumental ones (Weigand 1996). One of the few cases of shaft tombs for which we have an associated site map, however, is Huitzilapa, where a large and richly appointed shaft tomb was found beneath one of the minor patio-banquette complexes (Ramos de La Vega and López Mestas Camberos 1996: 124–125). Testing of the other complexes at the site did not reveal additional shaft tomb entrances. Shaft tombs are also found at El Piñon in association with unremarkable architecture (Cabrero G. and López C. 1997: 14). Shaft tombs have been found on the peripheries of some sites, such as El Teul (Andrew Darling, personal communication, June 1995).

Thus it is not possible to conclude that shaft tombs were consistently associated with economically powerful families or sacred places. Is the placement of the tombs below ground part of a strategy of masking power relations? Does it suggest a tradition of leadership that deliberately disassociates political and economic power (McIntosh 1999)? The contrast with what is occurring during the Late Preclassic in the Maya region is striking. There, the social and political distinctions are memorialized in flamboyant, costly, above-ground mortuary structures.

Teuchitlan

The Teuchitlan tradition is one of the most important cores of West Mexican political development. Spanning the Late Formative through Middle Classic periods (i.e., 400 B.C.–A.D. 600) and centered at a lake zone on the Nayarit-Sinaloa border, it may represent the largest concentration of human population in ancient West Mexico. Teuchitlan follows upon and incorporates the shaft tomb tradition, such that, as mentioned above, shaft tombs are found beneath some Teuchitlan patio banquette complexes. Indeed, it may be said that the Teuchitlan tradition adds residential architecture to the shaft tomb tradition.

Phil Weigand (1985, 1996) emphasizes the engineering sophistication and scale of Teuchitlan architecture; he also argues that the settlement system contains four or five tiers ranging from the largest, most complex sites to the smallest. He characterizes the Guachimontón district as "protourban" (Weigand 1985: 89); to my knowledge, he has not revised that assessment. Michael Ohnersorgen and Mark Varien (1996) write that the settlement system consists of fewer discrete levels than does Weigand, but their analysis suggests enough settlement complexity to support a prediction of sociopolitical hierarchy conceivably involving palatial architecture. Christopher Beekman (1996b) analyzes the strategic attributes of the settlement pattern and concludes that the Teuchitlan core was surrounded by a ring of defensive sites of a sort expected in association with a unitary, defensive state. Such organization might also indicate a strongly defined elite class.

It is not necessary to review the overall morphology of the patio-banquette complexes because Weigand (1996) has recently presented a detailed discussion of their distinctive forms, which are based upon a circular geometry (Fig. 3). The issue here is whether Teuchitlan sites have palaces, a question that may be premature, since the first monumental Teuchitlan patio-banquette complexes are only now being excavated. Existing data, which are admira-

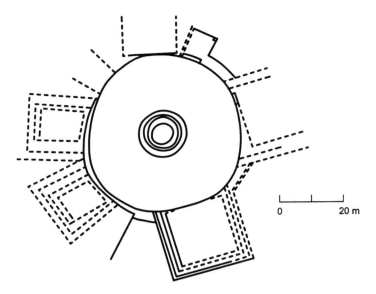

Fig. 3 Circular Teuchitlan-style patio-banquette complex, Teuchitlan site. After J. Charles Kelley (1971: 772). Illustration by Jean Baker.

bly complete given the circumstances, come from surface reconnaissance and observations of looters' pits.

On the basis of what has been published to date, I must conclude that even the largest Teuchitlan sites lack palaces. If the largest and most central structures were palatial in the sense used here, then there should be morphological differentiation among buildings; instead, the most central examples of circular architecture seem to be just larger and finer versions of the same kinds of structures occupied by ordinary residents. The larger circles tend to have more structures placed on the banquettes, fulfilling a logical possibility that is afforded by the greater amounts of available space, but no differentiation is apparent among the rooms. These structures could legitimately be called protopalatial. The repetition of like elements in the apparently contemporaneous circular complexes is suggestive of equality on some social or political dimensions and is reminiscent of the cellular or *altepetl* model of organization described by James Lockhart (1985: 9–11, 21), as opposed to more overtly hierarchical and individual-centered formations.

Weigand (1993: 100–101) mentions an intriguing group of rooms at the Caldera de Los Lobos site that is organized differently from the rest of the edifices, being rectangular rather than circular and lacking a concentric character. Although he labels it a palace, this structure does not seem to meet the criteria of centrality and elaborateness; perhaps it is part of a later occupation. Excavation data may eventually clarify its chronological position, function, and the status of its occupants.

The designers of the Guachimontón complex seem to have used the theme of associating ceremonial centers with high places; it is probably not accidental that the

Guachimontón group rings a volcano. Also, the architects clearly manipulated the attributes of size, centrality, and construction materials to make some structures more important than others. One could argue that the circular geometry precluded the construction of palaces as we conceive them—that is, large, complicated, self-contained, multiroom structures—and that the architects instead played on other attributes to accomplish their purposes. If so, excavation should eventually reveal further ornamentation or aspects of differentiation. The circular Teuchitlan complexes were replaced ca. 650 by rectangular or U-shaped ones, which, as discussed below, seem to represent a tradition that moved in from the Bajío region (Beekman 1996a: 251–256; Trombold 1990: 321); at least one of these sites, Ocomo or Oconahua, survived into the Postclassic. Weigand (1993: 147–148; 1996: 76–77, 182–183) regards the large U-shaped complex there as similar to the *tecpan* or palace form recorded of the Basin of Mexico at the time of Spanish contact. He likens it to a palace depicted in the *Mapa Quinatzin*, an interpretation that seems consistent with the surface morphology, but unfortunately, no excavations have been conducted at this site, and the rest of the surface has not been mapped.

Malpaso-Chalchihuites, the Altos of Jalisco, and the Bajío of Guanajuato

Classic and Epiclassic architecture of Guanajuato, Jalisco, Zacatecas, and Durango forms a striking contrast to that of Teuchitlan. The contrast is mainly one of rectangularity, as opposed to circularity, in the layout of the patio complexes; otherwise, the principles of arrangement and aggrandizement are quite similar. Colonnaded halls, causeways, and red-on-buff and black incised-engraved wares are other common traits of this tradition. The timing is primarily from 500 to 900, apparently beginning later than the Teuchitlan tradition, overlapping and lasting beyond it. The core of this tradition, which might be called the Bajío complex, appears to be in the Bajío region (Beekman 1996a; Braniff 1972; Cárdenas García 1996; Castañeda, Flores, and Crespo 1988; Crespo 1998; Jiménez Betts 1995; Sánchez Correa and Marmolejo Morales 1990; Trombold 1990; Weigand 1990), but the examples there, such as La Gloria and San Bartolo Aguacaliente, are not extensively excavated; more details are available for the sites in Zacatecas.

Repetitive elements, small sunken patios (Fig. 4) surrounded by rooms on an elevated banquette, are amalgamated on large, terraced hills to form visually imposing centers. Lesser sites, also consisting of rectangular patio-banquette complexes but of humbler construction, are scattered around the centers in rough clusters or aggregates. Roads interconnect settlements as well as reaching uninhabited high spots, which may be defensive lookouts or sacred places. Internal causeways connect the major components of La Quemada and also serve to mark its various entrances. The large centers, and particularly their monumental cores, are constructed of masonry, whereas lesser sites and peripheral parts of the large sites are dominated by adobe.

The large, stone-masonry colonnaded hall at La Quemada would appear to be a palace candidate (Fig. 5). In addition to being constructed of masonry rather than adobe, it sits adjacent to an oversized patio or plaza. Yet there does not appear to be a complex of

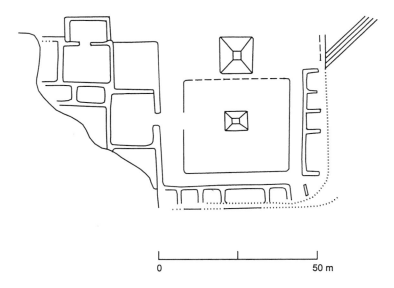

Fig. 4 Bajío-style rectangular patio–banquette complex, monumental core, La Quemada. Illustration by Jean Baker.

Fig. 5 Hall of Columns, La Quemada. Photo by Steve Northup.

other rooms associated with the Hall of Columns, as would be expected in a palace.[2] Instead, the adjacent features are the main entrance to the site, consisting of a causeway and grand staircase, and a ball court.

Unquestionably, a grammar of power was played out in these structures, yet they do not differ from the less grandiose and more peripheral patio complexes in ways that would be expected of palaces. Also, a number of other terraces at La Quemada have large structures on one side of their patios; those away from the core of the site are smaller and built of adobe. Some lesser examples have associated complexes of rooms located behind or around the large structure. Such an arrangement is found at Los Pilarillos, a site located 3.5 km to the southwest of La Quemada. The large-hall pattern is again replicated in adobe, as it is at terrace 18 of La Quemada. Terrace 18 also contains a small-scale, repeatedly plastered replica of the sites main ball court, curiously placed in the terrace's main patio.

What stands out at La Quemada is the abundance of human bone (Faulhaber 1960; Nelson, Darling, and Kice 1992; Pijoan and Mansilla 1990). La Quemada lacks obvious evidence of economic specialization or long-distance exchange; offerings are rare, and the material assemblage is impoverished in comparison with many Mesoamerican polities, even in the north. Skeletal material has been recovered from virtually every area excavated in the site, almost all disarticulated, and much of it modified in distinctive patterns. Both the Hall of Columns and the large room on terrace 18 contained such deposits.

In the case of the Hall of Columns, a large number of individuals, possibly hundreds, were apparently heaped on the floor or buried immediately beneath it; there is no published record of the stratigraphic position. In the large room on terrace 18, the bones of as many as fourteen individuals, definitely unburied, were found in positions consistent with their bodies having been suspended from rafters. A preliminary analysis suggests at least two fundamental processing patterns with variants; we (Nelson et al. 1992) argue that this dichotomy represents the differential treatment of ancestors and enemies. Biological anthropologist Debra Martin is currently working on a number of analyses to characterize the mortuary programs more thoroughly. At the time of this writing, it is believed that La Quemada is a ceremonial place partially dedicated to the preservation of human remains, both of esteemed ancestors and defeated enemies.

A stronger case can be made for the existence of a palace at Alta Vista, which also has a Hall of Columns. As at La Quemada, thousands of disarticulated human bones are found, both in temples and outdoors. Yet the architecture of Alta Vista is significantly more sophisticated, both in its intricacy and its synthesis of varied elements. The features adjacent to the hall include a pyramid and a maze of rooms known as the observatory (Aveni, Hartung, and Kelley 1982; Kelley 1976). The excavators have long maintained that Alta Vista bears a direct relationship to Teotihuacan; Charles Kelley (personal communication, February 1991) points to several specific features revealed, in recent excavations, that are reminiscent of the

---

[2] Traces of a small number of rooms are visible on what is today the front walkway of the structure; these rooms appear to have been added as an afterthought, possibly as part of a late occupation of the site.

city's palace of Quetzalpapalotl. One must agree that Alta Vista is unlike any other northern frontier center.

Several aspects of the Alta Vista economy are consistent with the accumulation of economic, as well as political, power in the ceremonial center. Unlike the Hall of Columns at La Quemada, the Alta Vista example contains subfloor offerings. Weigand describes the site as a link in a turquoise trade network linking several mineral sources in the American Southwest with numerous Mesoamerican cities; debitage as well as finished products of turquoise are found at Alta Vista. The famous Chalchihuites mines (Schiavitti 1994, n.d.; Weigand 1968), an astonishing complex of 8,000 ha of subsurface shafts and chambers, were apparently focused on the extraction of precious stones. Nicola Strazicich (n.d.) documents a higher degree of specialization in ceramic manufacturing at Alta Vista than at La Quemada. Alta Vista may be the one place on the northern frontier where the elite began to harness various bases of power—economic specialization, exchange, astronomical predictions, ancestor veneration, and warfare—to create the kind of setting in which palatial architecture was appropriate.

West Coast

This survey would be incomplete without mention of the Aztatlán tradition of the west coast, ca. 600 to 1400 (Kelley 1986; Sauer and Brand 1932). The architectural patterns of Aztatlán ceremonial centers are distinct from those of the highland lakes or interior margins of the sierra. The architects placed linear earthen mounds around plaza areas. Many of the sites, such as Culiacán (Kelly 1945) and Guasave (Ekholm 1942), have low, amorphous mounds, but those of Amapa (Meighan 1976) are large and distinct. Mound sizes vary within the center, suggesting status variation. Little direct evidence is available regarding the structures that topped these mounds, owing to soil characteristics and modern cultivation practices.

An extraordinary clay model of a building found in the Amapa excavations (Meighan 1976: 318) goes a long way toward filling out the picture of elite architecture. Clement Meighan refers to the image (Fig. 6), which is only a few centimeters high, as a *temple model*, but it could equally well be an elite residence. Festooned with heavy columns, a steeply pitched roof, and a finely crafted staircase, the building has the aesthetic qualities associated with special structures. The attributes of the staircase correlate rather precisely with those of a staircase found on one particular mound. A seeming peculiarity of the model is that the proportional sizes of mound and building are distorted, so that the mound is much smaller than expected; this difference may have been due to the artist's desire to emphasize the building; alternatively, it may be a true representation of an elaborate structure on a small mound. If so, even larger, more elaborate buildings might be expected on the largest Amapa mounds. As at most other sites discussed thus far, no definitive evidence exists for structures that could be called palaces.

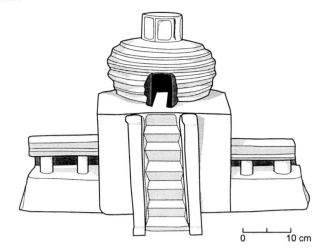

Fig. 6 Temple model, Amapa. After
Clement Meighan (1976: 318). Illustration by Jean Baker.

0   10 cm

Pre-Hispanic Tarascans

Upon the Spaniards' arrival in Central Mexico, they became aware that the Aztecs
had mortal enemies to the west. A clear line of territorial division ran through eastern
Michoacán, which was marked by garrisons on either side; penetration of the other's territory required emissaries and escorts (Pollard 1992: 5). The existence of such practices suggests that the Tarascans were politically integrated as a state; scholars have long considered
their dominion to constitute an empire. Their metallurgy and other technological and
aesthetic achievements paralleled, if not exceeded, those of Central Mexico. On the basis of
these characteristics, one might predict strongly hierarchical and individualizing rulership,
which is in fact what the documents suggested, as noted above.

How long such a political order might have existed prior to the Spaniards' arrival is
unclear. Pollard's (1996: 139) research suggests that the Tarascan state might have formed ca.
1300, when rising lake levels inundated much of the best agricultural land and stimulated
intercommunity competition for land. The necessity for being highly organized in response
to the Aztecs, on the other hand, may not have arisen until the late 1420s, when the Triple
Alliance was formed.

Tzintzuntzan, the Tarascan capital, probably holds the answers to some of these questions. When more excavation data are available, the analysis of palatial architecture should
play a great role in resolving them. The presence of both individual-centered rulership and
a palace prior to European contact are already attested archaeologically. Daniel Rubín de
La Borbolla (1944: 130–133) describes a richly appointed grave with a central individual
and sacrificed retainers, deposited in the platform fill underlying the *yácatas* of Tzintzuntzan.
The *yácatas* themselves are elaborate and distinctive enough that they might be considered
palatial. In addition, Rubén Cabrera Castro (1987: 543–547) describes a structure known as
Palace B, which consists of a complex arrangement of contiguous rooms located—depending on how they were conceived—either behind or in front of one of the *yácatas*. How far
back these burial customs and architectural patterns extend is unclear; Rubín de La Borbolla's
excavations encountered, but did not fully expose, an earlier version of the *yácatas*.

Conclusions

Palaces, if indeed they existed in West Mexico prior to the Postclassic, developed late in comparison to the Maya, Oaxacan, and Central Mexican regions. During the Early Formative, the only monumental structures are shaft tombs. It seems that no residential architecture for the living was built to complement these intriguing mortuary features until the Late Formative. Even then, and on through the Early and Middle Classic, there are no palaces in most, or perhaps all, of West Mexico. Classic period societies of West Mexico probably did not construct palaces because they did not construct power in such a way as to achieve intersections of political, economic, and ritual power among the households that competed for it (Fernández and Deraga 1995:181; Yoffee 1993:69–71). Cores of sociopolitical development, such as Teuchitlan, may have arisen without such synthesis of power bases. A possible exception, dating ca. 550 to 900 or primarily during the Epiclassic is the complex comprised of structures 2 and 3 at Alta Vista in the Chalchihuites area. This development occurs in the context of heightened economic activity, including specialized production and long-distance exchange, and a pronounced investment in observing astronomical phenomena. The proposition that the Chalchihuites rulers were *teotihuacanos* continues to be a subject of research. However, it is important to point out that most of the growth in the Bajío-Altos-Malpaso-Chalchihuites region took place in the Epiclassic, after the demise of Teotihuacan in its grandest form.

The one clear instance of palace development in West Mexico is at Late Postclassic Tzintzuntzan. This capital lies adjacent to Mesoamerican core regions, and its formation presumably was stimulated by interaction with large-scale societies there.

Among the varied array of other, more remote, and less conspicuous traditions, the archaeologist can observe strategies of architectural self-aggrandizement that are significant, even if they did not result in palaces. The elite used religious facilities as prominent fixtures in their domestic compounds. They also created spectra of spatial centrality, size, permanence, and cost across what were otherwise redundant building blocks of architectural symbolism, that is, patio-banquette complexes. Thus, elitism was marked by gradations: from adobe construction to masonry; from miniature to large ball courts; from minor temples to large ceremonial halls; and from altars to pyramids, all integral to patio-banquette complexes. Elevated locations were always chosen. A fascinating aspect of the region is the expression of similar principles in both square and circular forms, their distribution perhaps at times marking the boundaries of polities.

A widespread practice in West Mexico, particularly in its interior, was the accumulation of human bones in ceremonial centers. Both monumental public structures and elite residences were used as settings for elaborate programs of processing and displaying human remains. The fact that protopalaces, such as the Hall of Columns at La Quemada, were adorned with human remains may be one key to understanding the power-construction strategies of West Mexican elites. Contrasting combinations of customs, such as terror and physical repression along with reverential treatment of ancestral remains, seem to have characterized these populations. Above all, the social significance of architecture is best appreciated when one recognizes that Pre-Hispanic architectural patterns embraced multisite communities, such that the architecture simultaneously sacralized the landscape and ordered it politically (Tilley 1994). It is probable that no West Mexican elite residence can be fully understood without following out its causeway connections, panoptical vistas, and astronomical alignments.

Acknowledgments I am grateful to Susan Toby Evans and Joanne Pillsbury for the invitation to participate in the symposium on palaces in the New World and to Dumbarton Oaks and its staff, who made this symposium possible. George Cowgill and Phil Weigand provided useful comments on this manuscript. The fieldwork at La Quemada was conducted with the permission of the Consejo Nacional de Arqueología, Instituto Nacional de Antropología e Historia, México, D.F.; Joaquín García Bárcena, Alejandro Martínez Muriel, and José Francisco Román Gutierrez of that agency were of great assistance; Peter Jiménez Betts provided excellent technical and theoretical perspectives while overseeing the project. We especially thank Mónico García and his family for granting permission to do research on their property and for their hospitality. These excavations were supported by the following organizations: the National Science Foundation, Washington, D.C.; National Endowment for the Humanities, Washington, D.C.; Wenner-Gren Foundation for Anthropological Research, New York; Foundation for the Advancement of Mesoamerican Studies, Crystal River, Fla.; Faculty of Social Sciences, State University of New York at Buffalo; and the College of Liberal Arts and Sciences, Arizona State University, Tempe.

Bibliography

AVENI, ANTHONY F., HORST HARTUNG, AND J. CHARLES KELLEY

1982   Alta Vista (Chalchihuites), Astronomical Implications of a Mesoamerican Ceremonial Outpost at the Tropic of Cancer. *American Antiquity* 47: 326–335.

BEEKMAN, CHRISTOPHER S.

1996a   El Complejo El Grillo del centro de Jalisco: Una revisión de su cronología y significado. In *Las Cuencas del occidente de México: Epoca prehispánica* (E. Williams and P. C. Weigand, eds.): 247–291. Colegio de Michoacán with Centre d'Etudes Méxicaines et Centre-Américaines and ORSTOM, Zamora, Mich.

1996b   Political Boundaries and Political Structure: The Limits of the Teuchitlan Tradition. *Ancient Mesoamerica* 7(1): 135–147.

BRANDT, ELIZABETH

1994   Egalitarianism, Hierarchy, and Centralization in the Pueblos. In *The Ancient Southwestern Community* (W. H. Wills and R. D. Leonard, eds.): 9–23. University of New Mexico Press, Albuquerque.

BRANIFF, BEATRIZ

1972   Secuencias arqueológicas en Guanajuato y la cuenca de México: Intento de correlación. In *Memorias de la Sociedad Mexicana de Antropología, XI Mesa Redonda*: 273–323. Secretaría de Educación Pública, México, D.F.

1975   The West Mexican Tradition and the Southwestern United States. *The Kiva* 41(2): 215–222.

CABRERA CASTRO, RUBÉN

1987   Tzintzuntzan: Décima temporada de excavaciones. In *Homenaje a Román Piña Chan* (B. Dahlgren, C. Navarrete, L. Ochoa, M. Carmen Serra, and Y. Sugiura, eds.): 531–565. Serie Antropológica 79. Instituto de Investigaciones Anthropológicas, Universidad Nacional Autónoma de México, México, D.F.

CABRERO G., MARÍA TERESA, AND CARLOS LÓPEZ C.

1997   *Catálogo de piezas de las tumbas de tiro del cañón de Bolaños.* Instituto Nacional de Investigaciones Antropológicas, Universidad Nacional Autónoma de México, México, D.F.

CÁRDENAS GARCÍA, EFRAÍN

1996   La Tradición arquitectónica de los patios hundidos en la vertiente del lerma medio. In *Las Cuencas del occidente de México: Epoca prehispánica* (E. Williams and P. C. Weigand, eds.): 157–183. Colegio de Michoacán with Centre d'Etudes Méxicaines et Centre-Américaines and ORSTOM, Zamora, Mich.

CASTAÑEDA, CARLOS, LUZ MARÍA FLORES, AND ANA MARÍA CRESPO

1988   Interpretación de la historia del asentamiento en Guanajuato. In *Primera reunión sobre las sociedades prehispánicas en el centro occidente de México* (R. Brambila and A. M. Crespo, eds.): 321–356. Instituto Nacional de Antropología e Historia, México, D.F.

CHANCE, JOHN K.

1990   Changes in Twentieth-Century Mesoamerican Cargo Systems. In *Class, Politics, and Popular Religion in Mexico and Central America* (L. Stephen and J. Dow, eds.). Society for Latin American Anthropology 10. American Anthropological Association, Washington D.C.

CORONA NUÑEZ, JOSÉ

1955   Tumba de El Arenal, Etzalán, Jalisco. *Informes* 3. Institucíon de Monumentos Prehispánicos, México, D.F.

CRESPO, ANA MARÍA

1998   El Centro norte de México y sus vínculos con el occidente. In *Antropología e historia del Occidente de México: XXIV Mesa Redonda de la Sociedad Mexicana de Antropología* (R. Brambila Paz and J. L. Orozco Ampudia, eds.): 539–608. Sociedad Mexicana de Antropología y la Universidad Nacional Autónoma de México, México, D.F.

EKHOLM, GORDON F.

1942   *Excavations at Guasave, Sinaloa.* Anthropological Papers 38 (2). American Museum of Natural History, New York.

FAULHABER, JOHANNA

1960   Breve análisis osteológico de los restos humanos de La Quemada, Zacatecas. *Anales del Instituto Nacional de Antropología e Historia* 12: 131–149.

FERNÁNDEZ, RODOLFO, AND DARÍA DERAGA

1995   La Zona occidental en el Clásico. In *Historia antigua de México: El Horizonte Clásico* (L. Manzanilla and L. López Lujan, eds.), vol. 2: 197. Instituto Nacional de Antropología, México, D.F.

FIKES, JAY COURTNEY

n.d.   Huichol Indian Identity and Adaptation. Ph.D. dissertation, University of Michigan, Ann Arbor, 1985.

FURST, PETER

1965   Radiocarbon Dates from a Tomb in Mexico. *Science* 147 (3658): 612–613.

GIBSON, CHARLES

1965   *The Aztecs under Spanish Rule: A History of the Indians of the Valley of Mexico, 1519–1810.* Stanford University Press, Stanford, Calif.

GRAHAM, MARK MILLER

1998   The Iconography of Rulership in Ancient West Mexico. In *Ancient West Mexico: Art and Archaeology of the Unknown Past* (R. H. Townsend, ed.): 191–203. Thames and Hudson, New York.

GRIMES, JOSEPH E., AND THOMAS HINTON

1969   The Huichol and Cora. In *Handbook of Middle American Indians* (R. Wauchope, ed.),
        vol. 8. University of Texas Press, Austin.

HAMMOND, GEORGE P., AND AGAPITO REY (TRANS. AND EDS.)

1928   *Obregon's History of 16th-Century Explorations in Western America, Entitled Chronicle,
        Commentary, or Relation of the Ancient and Modern Discoveries in New Spain and New
        Mexico, 1584.* Wetzel, Los Angeles.

JIMÉNEZ BETTS, PETER

1995   Algunas observaciones sobre la dinámica cultural de la arqueología de Zacatecas. In
        Arqueología del norte y del occidente de México (B. Dahlgren and M. d. l. D. Soto de
        Arechavaleta, eds.): 35–66. Universidad Nacional Autónoma de México, México, D.F.

KELLEY, J. CHARLES

1971   Archaeology of the Northern Frontier: Zacatecas and Durango. In *Archaeology of
        Northern Mesoamerica: Handbook of Middle American Indians* (G. F. Ekholm and
        I. Bernal, eds.), vol. 11, pt. 2: 768–804. University of Texas Press, Austin.

1976   Alta Vista: Outpost of Mesoamerican Empire on the Tropic of Cancer. In *Las
        Fronteras de Mesoamerica: XIV Mesa Redonda*: 21–40. Sociedad Mexicana de
        Antropología, México, D.F.

1986   The Mobile Merchants of Molino. In *Ripples in the Chichimec Sea: New Considerations
        of Mesoamerican-Southwestern Interactions* (F. J. Mathien and R. H. McGuire, eds.): 81–
        104. Southern Illinois University Press, Carbondale.

KELLY, ISABEL

1945   *Excavations at Culiacán, Sinaloa.* Iberoamericana 25. University of California Press,
        Berkeley.

LOCKHART, JAMES

1985   Some Nahua Concepts in Postconquest Guise. *History of European Ideas* 6: 465–482.

LONG, STANLEY V., AND ROBERT E. TAYLOR

1966   Chronology of a West Mexican Shaft Tomb. *Nature* 212 (5062): 651–652.

LUMHOLTZ, CARL

1902   *Unknown Mexico: A Record of Five Years' Exploration among the Tribes of the Western Sierra
        Madre, in the Tierra Caliente of Tepic and Jalisco, and among the Tarascos of Michoacán.*
        Macmillan, London.

McINTOSH, SUSAN KEECH

1999   Pathways to Political Complexity in Africa. In *Beyond Chiefdoms: Pathways to
        Complexity in Africa* (S. K. McIntosh, ed.): 1–30. Cambridge University Press,
        Cambridge.

MEIGHAN, CLEMENT W.

1974   Prehistory of West Mexico. *Science* 184: 1254–1261.

MEIGHAN, CLEMENT W. (ED.)

1976   *The Archaeology of Amapa, Nayarit*, vol. 2. Institute of Archaeology, University of California, Los Angeles.

MEIGHAN, CLEMENT, AND H. B. NICHOLSON

1989   The Ceramic Mortuary Offerings of Prehistoric West Mexico: An Archaeological Perspective. In *Sculpture of Ancient West Mexico: Nayarit, Jalisco, Colima* (M. Kan, C. Meighan, and H. B. Nicholson, eds.): 29–67. Los Angeles County (Calif.) Museum of Art and the University of New Mexico Press, Albuquerque.

NEGRÍN, JUAN

1985   *Acercamiento histórico y subjetivo al Huichol*. Universidad de Guadalajara, Guadalajara, Jal.

NELSON, BEN A.

1995   Complexity, Hierarchy, and Scale: A Controlled Comparison between Chaco Canyon, New Mexico, and La Quemada, Zacatecas. *American Antiquity* 60 (4): 597–618.

NELSON, BEN A., J. ANDREW DARLING, AND DAVID A. KICE

1992   Mortuary Patterns and the Social Order at La Quemada, Zacatecas. *Latin American Antiquity* 3(4): 298–315.

NOGUERA, EDUARDO

1942   Exploraciones en El Opeño, Michoacán. In *27 Congreso Internacional de Americanistas*, vol. 1. México, D.F.

OHNERSORGEN, MICHAEL A., AND MARK D. VARIEN

1996   Formal Architecture and Settlement Organization in Ancient West Mexico. *Ancient Mesoamerica* 7 (1): 103–120.

OLIVEROS, JOSÉ ARTURO

1974   Nuevas exploraciones en El Opeño, Michoacán. In *The Archaeology of West Mexico* (B. Bell, ed.): 182–201. Sociedad de Estudios Avanzados del Occidente de México, Ajijic, Jal.

OLIVEROS, JOSÉ ARTURO, AND MAGDALENA DE LOS RÍOS PAREDES

1993   La Cronología de El Opeño, Michoacán: Nuevos fechamientos por radio-carbono. *Arqueología* 9/10: 45–48.

PIJOAN, CARMEN MA., AND JOSEFINA MANSILLA

1990   Evidencias rituales en restos humanos del norte de Mesoamérica. In *Mesoamérica y norte de México siglos IX–XII*, vol. 2 (F. Sodi Miranda, ed.): 467–478. Instituto Nacional de Antropología e Historia, México, D.F.

POLLARD, HELEN PERLSTEIN

1982   Ecological Variation and Economic Exchange in the Tarascan State. *American Ethnologist* 9 (2): 250–268.

1992   Tarascan External Relationships. A paper presented at a conference entitled Tarascan External Relationships, Center for Indigenous Studies in the Americas, Phoenix, Ariz.

1996   La Transformación de elites regionales en Michoacán central. In *Las Cuencas del occidente de México: Epoca prehispánica* (E. Williams and P. C. Weigand, eds.): 131–156. Colegio de Michoacán with Centre d'Etudes Mexicaines et Centre-Americaines and ORSTOM, Zamora, Mich.

1997   Recent Research in West Mexican Archaeology. *Journal of Archaeological Research* 5 (4): 345–384.

RAMOS DE LA VEGA, JORGE, AND LORENZA LÓPEZ MESTAS CAMBEROS

1996   Datos preliminares sobre el descubrimiento de una tumba de tiro en el sitio de Huitzilapa, Jalisco. *Ancient Mesoamerica* 7 (1): 121–134.

ROJAS, BEATRIZ

1992   *Los Huicholes: Documentos históricos.* Centro de Investigaciones y Estudios Superiores en Antropología Social con el Instituto Nacional Indigenista, México, D.F.

RUBÍN DE LA BORBOLLA, DANIEL F.

1941   Exploraciones arqueológicas en Michoacán: Tzintzuntzan, Temporada III. *Revista Mexicana de Estudios Antropológicos* 5 (1): 5–20.

1944   Orfebrería Tarasca. *Cuadernos Americanos* 3: 127–138.

SÁNCHEZ CORREA, SERGIO A., AND EMMA G. MARMOLEJO MORALES

1990   Algunas apreciaciones sobre el Clásico en el Bajío Central, Guanajuato. In *La Epoca Clásica: Nuevos hallazgos, nuevas ideas* (A. Cardos de Méndez, ed.): 267–278. Instituto Nacional de Antropología e Historia y el Museo Nacional de Antropología, México, D.F.

SANDERS, WILLIAM T.

1974   Chiefdom to State: Political Evolution at Kaminaljuyú, Guatemala. In *Reconstructing Complex Societies: An Archaeological Colloquium* (C. B. Moore, ed.): 97–116. *Bulletin of the American Schools of Oriental Research* 20 (suppl.).

SAUER, CARL O., AND DONALD D. BRAND

1932   *Aztatlán: Prehistoric Mexican Frontier on the Pacific Coast.* Iberoamericana 1. University of California Press, Berkeley.

SCHIAVITTI, VINCENT W.

1994   La Minería prehispánica de Chalchihuites. *Arqueología Mexicana* 1 (6): 48–51.

n.d.   Organization of the Prehispanic Suchil Mining District of Chalchihuites, Mexico, A.D. 400–950. Ph.D. dissertation, Department of Anthropology, State University of New York at Buffalo, 1995.

SCHONDUBE, OTTO B.

1980   La Nueva tradición. In *Historia de Jalisco: Desde los tiempos prehistóricos hasta fines del siglo XVII* (J. M. Muria and F. A. Solórzano, eds.), vol. 1: 214–258. Gobierno de Jalisco, Guadalajara, Jal.

1987   El Occidente de México: Algunas de sus características y problemas. In *Homenaje a Román Piña Chan* (B. Dahlgren, C. Navarrete, L. Ochoa, M. C. Serra, and Y. Sugiura, eds.): 403–410. Serie Antropológica 79. Instituto de Investigaciones Antropológicas, Universidad Nacional Autónoma de México, México, D.F.

STRAZICICH, NICOLA

n.d.   Pre-Hispanic Pottery Production in the Chalchihuites and La Quemada Regions of Zacatecas, Mexico. Ph.D. dissertation, Department of Anthropology, State University of New York at Buffalo, 1995.

TILLEY, CHRISTOPHER

1994   *A Phenomenology of Landscape*. Berg, Oxford.

TROMBOLD, CHARLES D.

1990   A Reconsideration of the Chronology for the La Quemada Portion of the Northern Mesoamerican Frontier. *American Antiquity* 55 (2): 308–323.

WEIGAND, PHIL C.

1968   The Mines and Mining Techniques of the Chalchihuites Culture. *American Antiquity* 33: 45–61.

1985   Evidence for Complex Societies during the Western Mesoamerican Classic Period. In *The Archaeology of West and Northwest Mesoamerica* (M. S. Foster and P. C. Weigand, eds.): 47–92. Westview, Boulder, Colo.

1990   Discontinuity: The Collapse of the Teuchitlan Tradition and the Early Postclassic Cultures of Western Mesoamerica. In *Mesoamérica y norte de México siglos IX–XI*, vol. 1 (F. Sodi Miranda, ed.): 215–222. Instituto Nacional de Antropología e Historia, México, D.F.

1993   *Evolución de una civilización prehispánica*. Colegio de Michoacán, Zamora, Mich.

1996   The Architecture of the Teuchitlan Tradition of the Occidente of Mesoamerica. *Ancient Mesoamerica* 7 (1): 90–101.

1998   Las sociedades Huicholas antes de la llegada de los españoles. In *Memoria 4 (agrupa los boletines correspondientes a 1996)* (M. d. P. c. Sánchez Alfaro, ed.): 409–432. Benemérita Sociedad de Geografiá y Estadística del Estado de Jalisco, Guadalajara, Jal.

WEIGAND, PHIL C., AND ACELIA G. DE WEIGAND

1996   *Tenamaxtli y Guaxicar: Las raíces profundas de la rebelión de Nueva Galicia*. Colegio de Michoacán, Zamora, Mich.

YOFFEE, NORMAN

1993   Too Many Chiefs? (or, Safe Texts for the 90s). In *Archaeological Theory: Who Sets the Agenda?* (N. Yoffee and A. Sherratt, eds.): 60–74. Cambridge University Press, Cambridge.

Royal Palaces and Painted Tombs:
State and Society in the Valley of Oaxaca

Ernesto González Licón

Escuela Nacional de Antropología e Historia, Mexico

Residential architecture has frequently been used as one variable to evaluate wealth differentials within a society, other important variables being the associated artifactual and ecofactual assemblages and differences in mortuary treatment among people of the same age and sex. Residential architecture reflects how social groups express residence patterns, kinship, and status. For example, spatial location with respect to a central plaza and between one residence and another is used. Elite residences, as a specific manifestation of economic power, reflect an unequal relationship among people.

How did these features develop in the Valley of Oaxaca, and how different were they from those of the neighboring Mixtec region? What were the variables involved in the transformation from the modest elite residences in San José Mogote during the Formative period to the great North Platform in Monte Albán in the Classic period, followed by the magnificent residential complexes at Mitla and Yagul in the Postclassic? Did these differences in size, construction quality, and associated materials reflect changes in social complexity? Were these changes related to political structure and economic strategies? How can we isolate the residence of the ruler—the palace—as an indicator of these political changes and social stratification? These topics are the subject of this essay.

Like language, architecture is not static: both are subject to evolutionary change and cultural adaptation (Unwin 1997). In this essay I assess the correlation between political complexity and elite residences in the Valley of Oaxaca. I analyze, from an historical perspective, changes in elite residences from the Formative to the Postclassic in the Valley of Oaxaca. Elite residences, as a material manifestation of the ruling class, are treated here as a single variable within a larger social context.

Monumental architecture, frequently associated with the burial of a society's elite members, has been used as an indicator of social stratification and political integration. In state-level societies, social stratification is institutionalized. In a state, the ruler controls both the means of production and production itself. The ruler uses part of that wealth for his own benefit and by building a house of more impressive size, design, construction materials, and decoration than his inferiors' houses.

The place where people live provides for the fundamental needs of life: shelter, sustenance, rest, spirituality (Unwin 1997). In the archaeological record, high-status individuals

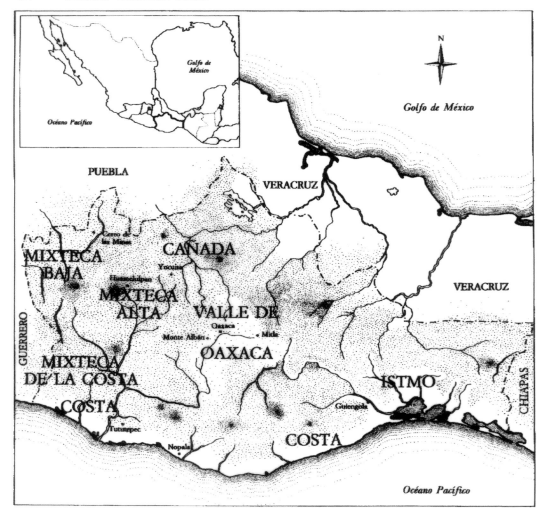

Fig. 1 Oaxaca region (González Licón 1990: 14)

will be measured in terms of personal wealth, through their association with certain kinds of luxury items, more elaborate residential architecture, and more complex funerary treatments (Chase and Chase 1992: 4). Ideological reinforcement is conferred by the place where the ruler lives. This residence is also a material expression of wealth and power for competing leaders. Elite control over specialized craft production and exchange of goods, including but not limited to, staple goods, is a means for the elite to gain power, prestige, and wealth. Leaders acquire benefits for themselves and their followers as well. In state-level societies, elite residences represent one of the most impressive material means by which the elite express and justify their position in power. With a twofold functionality, the king's residence is not only the place where the ruler and his family lived, it is also where important administrative and civic activities took place. In this sense, the ruler's residence is a reflection of his power. A politically strong government allows its ruler to build a large

Fig. 2 Valley of Oaxaca (Kirkby 1973)

palace where he can live, attend to political matters, and entertain on a grand scale. The success of a ruler is manifested in the place where he lives.

In the Valley of Oaxaca, from the earliest and humblest households to the latest and largest elite residences, the Zapotec buried their dead beneath their house floors (Figs. 1, 2). The practice was linked to the idea of an afterlife; this ancestor cult played a key social role and produced an important architectonic addition: the tomb. The strong ideological connection between the living and their ancestors is reflected in their houses where they invested considerable effort in the construction and decoration of the family tomb, which was placed beneath the main room and used by successive generations. In so doing, the Zapotecs maintained not only a symbolic and ritual connection with their ancestors, but also a physical interaction between the house of the living and the house of the dead.

In some of the best-known examples in the Valley of Oaxaca, the tomb was built so as to re-create an actual home. In this way, the inhabitants incorporated into tomb construction several common elements from their living quarters. Stairs from the house's central patio to a small vestibule in front of the tomb connected the world with the underworld. Façade decoration, antechamber, carved lintels, stone doors, and mural painting were other features shared by both tombs and houses. The traditional focus on tombs relates strongly to

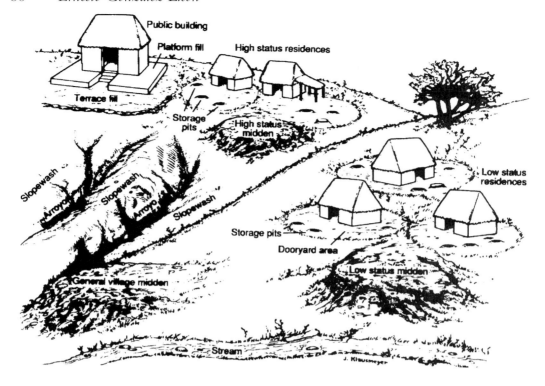

Fig. 3 High- and low-status residences, Formative village (Flannery and Marcus 1994: 26)

political, ideological, and genealogical legitimation. Offerings in tombs also relate to wealth, as does residential architecture, but there is a rich vein of complementary information about the economic and political aspects of the elite class in the analysis of formal and functional aspects of the residences and tombs in the Valley of Oaxaca.

Elite Residences in the Valley of Oaxaca

In the Valley of Oaxaca, residential architecture has been a key indicator of social inequality (Fig. 3). Wealth differences among households have been detected in San José Mogote as early as the San José phase of the Early Formative (1150–850 B.C.). The presence of jade and greenstone ornaments in some burials suggests the first differential access to these goods. However, there was no clear-cut social stratification, but rather a continuum of inequality. According to Kent Flannery and Joyce Marcus (1994: 329): "Differences among households are differences of degree rather than differences of kind." High-status houses were not only better made, but their associated households also had better access to deer meat, mica, and marine shell (Fig. 4a). Low-status houses were relatively small (3 x 5 m) one-room, wattle-and-daub structures without whitewash, which had slightly rounded corners (Fig. 4b; Marcus and Flannery 1996: 103). Ceramic similarities between San José Mogote and other larger villages in distant regions (Tlapacoya and Tlatilco in the Basin of

Fig. 4 (a) High-status residences: houses 16 and 17, San José Mogote; (b) Low-status residence: house 13, San José Mogote (Flannery and Marcus 1994: 331, 336).

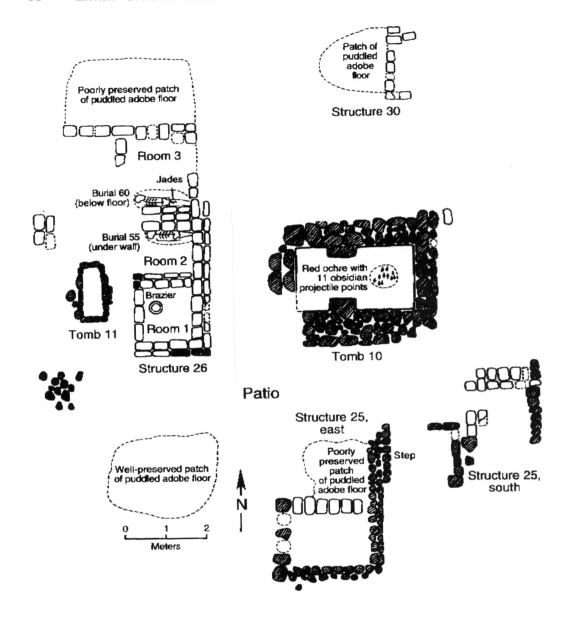

Fig. 5 Mound I: Structures 25, 26, and 30, San José Mogote (Marcus and Flannery 1996: 132)

Mexico; San Lorenzo in the gulf lowlands) indicate the development and interaction of emerging elites and greater social inequalities at those sites (Flannery and Marcus 1994: 381).

By the Middle Formative (Guadalupe phase: 850–600 B.C.; Rosario phase: 600–500 B.C.), the Etla Valley continued as a focus of settlement and was home to almost half of the valley's population; San José Mogote continued as the biggest site, with around seven hun-

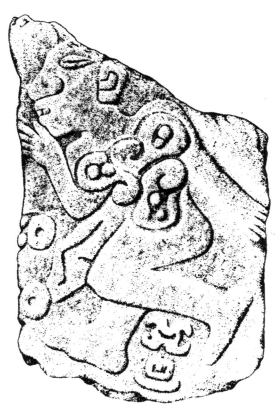

Fig. 6 Danzante, Monument 3, San José Mogote (Marcus and Flannery 1996: 129).

dred inhabitants. In San José Mogote, the change from an egalitarian to hierarchical system is evident (Blanton et al. 1981). The largest Rosario house found is located on Mound I (i.e., Structures 25, 26, 30), which is 15 m high and built over a burned temple (Fig. 5). The residence had adobe rooms around a patio. Beneath its patio floor a tomb was found. It was also the only building that had elaborate architecture and a carved monument that can be interpreted as one chief defeating another (Fig. 6). The Middle Formative site was more complex, with a *barrio* subdivision and areas of high and low status. At this site were located many more exotic materials, such as magnetite, shell, and obsidian, than in any other contemporaneous site in the Valley of Oaxaca. By the end of this phase, a hierarchical three-level system had already developed, with San José Mogote at the top, because its population was ten times larger than the second-rank sites.

With the foundation of Monte Albán (Early I phase: 500–350 B.C.) as the Zapotec state capital on top of a mountain 400 m above the valley floor, at the conjunction of three small valleys, important changes took place in the internal population dynamics of the Valley of Oaxaca, creating a qualitative change in the region's internal organization, political control, and social stratification (Fig. 7). A four-tier hierarchy was formed, and up to 155 settlements were located around the new city. Monte Albán, with almost half the total valley population, exerted great demographic and political centralization. An interregional

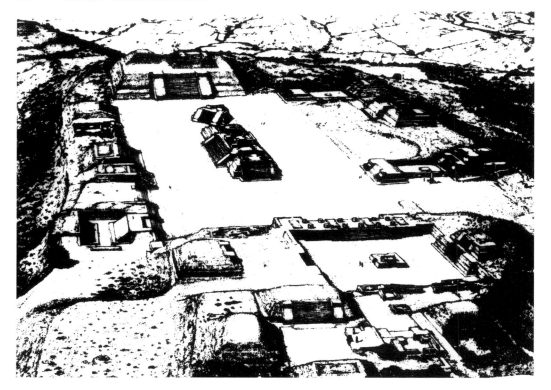

Fig. 7   Aerial view, Monte Albán (Gendrop 1976)

exchange and market system was also developed (Blanton 1978; Blanton et al. 1982; Feinman 1991; Kowalewski et al. 1989). After the foundation of Monte Albán, the populace lived on artificially leveled terraces on the hill, apparently organized into three *barrios*, which, according to Richard Blanton (1978), may indicate activities other than agriculture.

Monte Albán was a primate center, more than twice as large as the next largest center. It maintained its leadership from the Middle Formative (MA Early I: 500–350 B.C.) to the Late Classic (MA IIIb: 450–700). By the Late Formative (phase II 100/150 B.C.–A.D. 200), the Zapotec state extended its influence beyond the Valley of Oaxaca. Structure J was built (Fig. 8a) and contains up to forty stone reliefs with military themes, probably representing the sites defeated by the Zapotecs outside the valley (Fig. 8b; Marcus 1983: 106–108). The elite residences at this time were built on stone foundations, and their adobe walls were plastered with stucco. The evidence from the tombs discovered by Alfonso Caso and his associates indicates an increment in social stratification.

Depending on their location within the city, residences would have had different patio areas. Close to the central plaza, residences tended to have larger patios, with secondary patios and multiple rooms (Fig. 9). Residences located far from administrative *barrio* centers had only a single relatively small patio. On the north platform, at the northeast corner, is an elite residence with a central patio of 64 sq m. Four main rooms face the central patio, and the west room is on a higher level. Secondary patios were built at the

Fig. 8 (a) Building J, Monte Albán (González Licón 1990: 86); (b) architecture and carved motifs, Building J (González Licón 1990: 83, after Marquina 1990)

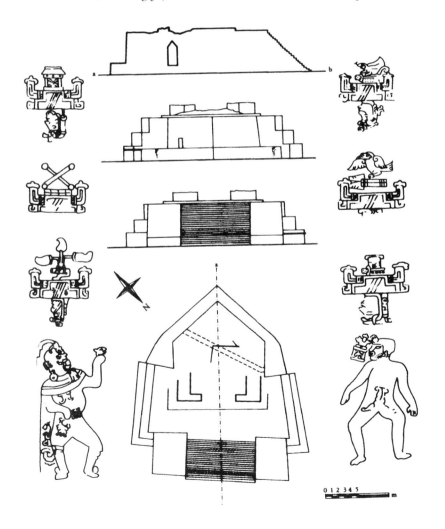

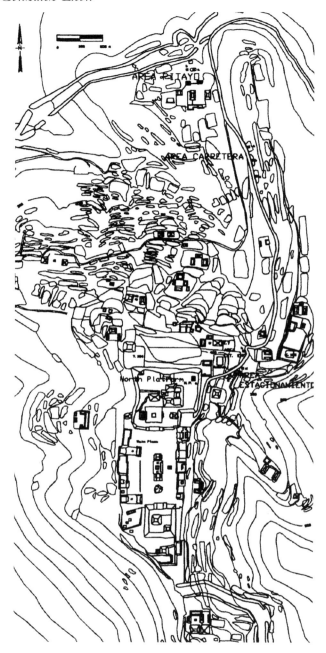

Fig. 9 Topographic map, Monte Albán (after Blanton 1978)

corners to allow access to other rooms (Fig. 10). The total house area is 750 sq m. Excavated in 1990 (González Licón n.d.), the house was dated to periods II and IIIa (Late Formative, Early Classic). Excavation revealed a high proportion of imported items, such as Teotihuacan ceramics, jade beads, and marine shells. Several floors had mica inlays. Outside the house, on the east side, all the surface was plastered up to the edge of the structure. The house drainage

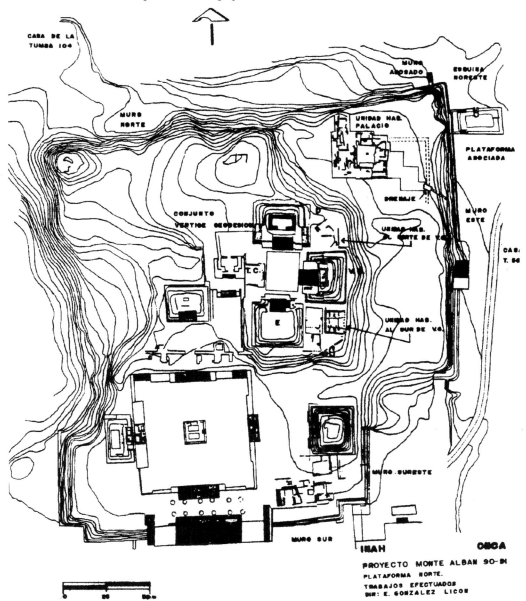

Fig. 10 North Platform, Monte Albán

system was connected to a larger one, which collected all the rainwater in that section of the North Platform. Below the central altar, a young male was buried in a seated position.

In the Mixteca Alta region, Monte Negro was also built on a hilltop during the Late Cruz or Early Ramos phase (500 B.C.–A.D. 250) in the Mixteca period (Late Monte Albán I: 300–200 B.C.; Monte Albán II: 200 B.C.–A.D. 200) in the Valley of Oaxaca. Monte Negro was contemporaneous with Yucuita, which is only 30 km to the north, and with Monte Albán in the Valley of Oaxaca at no more than 80 km to the east. There are elite residences at Monte Negro, but none can be pinpointed as the residence of Monte Negro's ruler. However, the two elite residences excavated are connected to major ceremonial structures. Temple X is the biggest structure at the site, located on the east side of the main plaza, where the inhabitants held their ceremonies. Behind Temple X, a private roofed corridor extends to the biggest house. By this means, rulers could carry out public and private activities related to their high status. This pattern is consistent with later descriptions of elite rulers, whose activities included domestic, ceremonial, and administrative duties performed in a place secluded from the population.

Each of the two elite houses in Monte Negro is located in the east-west group near administrative or ceremonial structures. Both houses have central patios surrounded by three or four rooms (the patio north of Temple T-N and the patio east of Temple X, respectively, in Acosta's terminology [1959]). A stone column was placed in each patio corner to hold a roof that extends from the frontal wall of each room. The walls were made of adobe or wattle-and-daub on stone foundations two rows high. To increase interior space, builders placed two more stone columns in each room to support the roof. Roofs were probably thatched, inclined inward through the patio to collect rainwater, since there are no signs of springs on the hilltop. The central patios are paved with small flat stones. The patios also had an impluvium system, a stone with small holes in it, that collected the rainwater and was connected to a drain. Drains were made with long flat carved stones. Four clay pipes were excavated, one of them connected to a drain, which may have been used in some cases. The existence of *tlecuil*-style hearths in the room's floors is another feature common to both temples and elite residences. *Tlecuiles* were cut-stone hearths sometimes used for ritual purposes, but, at least in Monte Negro, they were used mainly to heat the rooms. (Similar features in Aztec palaces at Chimalhuacan Atenco and Cihuatecpan, see Evans [this volume].) There is no ball court at the site. From the architectural and funerary remains, it is clear that social differences existed at Monte Negro (Acosta 1959).

In Monte Albán by the Early Classic (phase IIIa: A.D. 200–500), the North Platform was completed. It is generally assumed that the ruling elite controlled considerable economic wealth, political power, and social prestige. Even though many elite residences have been partially explored, in particular their tombs, none of these has been identified as the residence of Monte Albán's king. Juan de Córdova's sixteenth-century Zapotec vocabulary (1942 [1578]), noted that the royal ruler and his wife were addressed as *coqui* and *xonaxi*, respectively, and the name of their royal residence was known as *yoho quehui*. The residence called *the palace*, at the east side of the main plaza, and those residences associated with tombs 103, 104, and 105 (Fig. 11) are some of the most important because of their size, location, quality of construction, wall decoration, and the goods discovered inside them.

The structure located almost at the southeast corner of the Main Plaza, named the Palace (Figs. 12, 13), is the only building in that civic-ceremonial center that can be designated as a royal residence. It was built on an extended platform facing west. Reaching the house requires climbing a wide and well-made stone staircase. The only access is created by monumental stone jambs and a lintel (similar to the house of tomb 105). A narrow corridor with a left turn leads to a secondary patio and then to the main patio. Its several rooms

Fig. 11 Interior, Tomb 104, Monte Albán (González Licón 1990: 109)

are on different levels, as was common in elite houses. The thick walls and patios were made of stone and plastered. No tomb has been found here, but the same can be said of the North Platform.

Where did the rulers of Monte Albán live, and where were they buried? Archaeological data about habitational structures from period San José to period IIIb in the Valley of Oaxaca reveal a wide range of residence types (six categories in Monte Albán alone, according to Blanton [1978]). The elite residences are larger, better made, and more elaborately decorated. Nevertheless, they all have the same general plan: a central patio with four main rooms and two or four secondary patios. Their main function was residential. The enclosure of the elite residences indicates a strong intention of high-class inhabitants to isolate themselves from the rest of the population. All data indicate that the ruler lived in the North Platform, which is the largest structure at the site. From the foundation of Monte Albán until the end of the Late Classic, several houses were built in this impressive building. The residence of the ruler might be located on the north side of the sunken patio. There are several rooms that could have been used for habitation. Another possibility, at least for the Late Formative and Early Classic, is that the ruler lived in the residence located at the northeast corner of the same North Platform. The small house located south of the Mound G North Platform could have been used by the *bigaña* (Great Priest) as in Lambityeco.

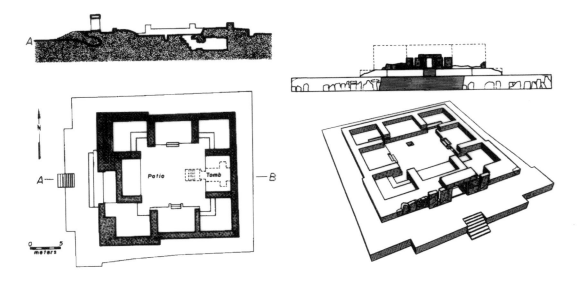

Fig. 12 Palace, Tomb 105 (Marcus and Flannery 1996: 112)

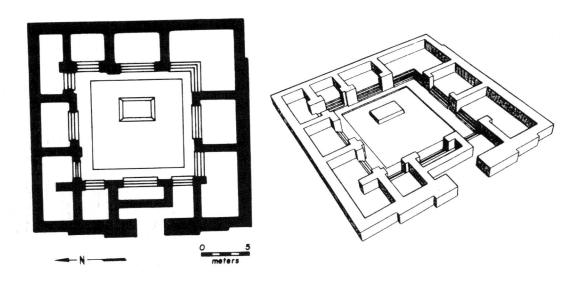

Fig. 13 Palace, Building S, Monte Albán (a) Marcus and Flannery 1983: 134, (b) Marcus and Flannery 1996: 209

Besides the city core, which concentrates the major temples and administrative buildings, Monte Albán was organized in *barrios* (Blanton 1978), but unfortunately none has been extensively excavated. Atzompa, El Gallo, Monte Albán Chico, and other complexes are examples of groups of elite residences with temples around a plaza. We can infer that the wealthy and influential lived there, but there have been as yet no detailed archaeological excavations.

After Monte Albán's decline, by the end of the Late Classic and Early Postclassic (A.D. 600–750), Lambityeco reached its peak as a small village of a larger site called *Yegüih* (*small hill* in Zapotec), with 230 mounds over an area of 75 ha located in the Tlacolula Valley. Lambityeco's inhabitants worked in salt production, boiling water from the Salado River, which runs close to the site, in big ceramic containers known as *apaxtles*. Apparently Lambityeco represents a moment of political instability between Monte Albán's decline and Yagul's florescence. Mound 195 is the tallest structure at the site, with a 6-m high pyramidal structure. Behind this building evidence was found of six high-status residences with three associated tombs. On the basis of radiocarbon tests, it has been learned that each house was occupied sequentially by five generations, each lasting from twenty-three to twenty-nine years, for a total occupation of 115 years.

The main house, called the *coqui* or *coquitao* (great lord house), was built with adobe walls plastered with stucco. The house has several rooms around two patios in a 370 sq m area. The rooms of the north patio were residential, and the larger and more elaborate rooms of the south patio were public. This patio, on its east side, has a two-level altar in typical Teotihuacan style decorated with stucco figures, representing the Lambityeco rulers and their wives. On the upper level, almost totally destroyed, appear Lord 8 Death and Lady 5 Reed, who are buried in tomb 6 in front of the altar. On the lower level to the left can be recognized Lord 4 Face and Lady 10 Monkey. To the right are representations of Lady 3 Turquoise and Lord 8 Awl. They were, respectively, the great-grandparents and grandparents of the couple represented on the upper level. Each of the male figures from the lower level holds a femur bone in his hand, representing his hereditary right to rule, which was conferred by his ancestors. In front of this altar is tomb 6, where the *coquitaos* (great lords) and their wives were buried. The tomb's façade (Fig. 14) is decorated with the typical Zapotec *tablero*, on which are represented the faces of Lord 1 Earthquake and Lady 10 Reed, parents of Lord 8 Death (Lind and Urcid 1983). Inside the tomb the remains of six individuals and 186 objects were discovered.

Just 15 m south of Mound 195 was another high-status residence of almost 400 sq m. The rooms were built around two patios oriented east-west. Between the two patios, an elevated room was built with access from the east. The two steps that connected the patio with this central room were delimited by the Zapotec *tableros*, decorated with upside-down *T*'s, and, in the front, by a monumental representation of the thunder or lightning god Cociyo. In his right hand, the god is holding a jar from which water flows and in his left are several lightning bolts, from which he takes his name. On the basis of these associated artifacts, this was the house of the *bigaña* who controlled all aspects of religion. It is probable that the *bigaña* was related to the *coqui* (ruler). He has been described as "second son of the lord." (Lind and Urcid 1983).

Fig. 14 Images of Lord 1 Earthquake and Lady 10 Reed, Tomb 6, Lambityeco (González Licón 1990)

By the Postclassic, after the collapse of Monte Albán, the Valley of Oaxaca was characterized by the lack of a regional central authority. Jalieza in the Zimatlan Valley became the largest site of period IV (A.D. 750–1000), but it never assumed Monte Albán's role. Cuilapan and Zaachila were competing centers by the Late Postclassic. In the Tlacolula Valley, Yagul and Mitla took control of exchange routes and markets. Ruling elites from other sites were freer to manage their own business. Important changes in government and political organization took place. The large urban centers such as Monte Albán or Teotihuacan had declined, opening the possibility to other smaller polities to have more authority. Several cities, strategically located and sometimes fortified, arose and competed with others to control the region.

In the Valley of Tlacolula, Mitla and Yagul are good examples of this. In Yagul the civic center is located on a volcanic tuff and distributed over several terraces. It includes structures identified as administrative public buildings around big open patios, the largest ball court in the valley, a fortress to prevent attacks from the north side, and a huge elite residence (Fig. 15). This residence is at the northwest part of the ceremonial area on an upper terrace. Construction materials were basalt slabs and river cobbles. The residence has three complexes of two patios surrounded by rooms. Apparently, the main entrance was from the

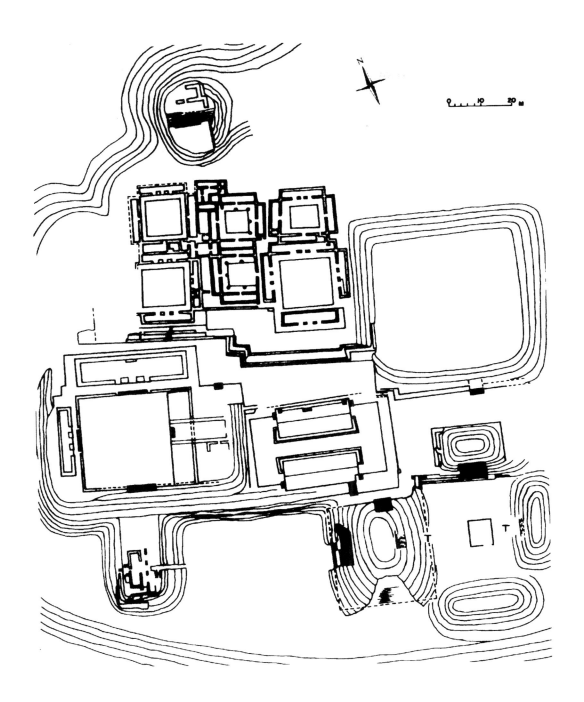

Fig. 15 General plan, Yagul (González Licón 1990: 98 after Paddock 1966)

north, although some rooms face outward, emphasizing their administrative or public functions. Minor rooms are behind or adjacent to the major ones. The poor-quality walls were
made with unaltered stone and clay, then covered with layers of mud and stucco. The patio
floors were also plastered with stucco and sometimes painted red. There are no indications
of stone lintels. Many rooms have a small *tlecuil*-style hearth at the entrance. The patio floors
were empty, with no shrine or altars. Some rooms were sealed when the palace was still in
use. The roofs were probably flat, with beams and earth on top, and plastered. Patios B and
E are the smallest and are also the only ones without a colonnaded entrance to the main
rooms. They are the only ones with a roofed corridor supported by columns and an
impluvium to channel rainwater to the drainage system (Bernal and Gamio 1974: 87). The
patios on the north side have limited access; the patios to the south had one side open and
were therefore more accessible. It is assumed that the rooms on the north patios were for
habitation and the ones on the south were for administrative matters. Patios F and D have
rooms that face outward, indicating an administrative function, but others (e.g., A, B, C, E)
are closed, with their only access from the north. The ceramics and burials found there
indicate domestic activities. There is no evidence of selection by sex or age, as in the case of
sacrifice or religious activities.

    Not far from there to the east is Mitla. (*Mictlan* is Nahuatl for *Lyobaa* in Zapotec; it
means Place of the Dead.) There are in Mitla five groups of major structures and an
undetermined number of minor constructions, such as small houses and tombs where most
of the population lived and was buried (Fig. 16). The sixteenth-century *Relaciones geográficas*
(Acuña 1984 [1580]), from the villages of Atlatlauca and Tecuicuilco, state:

> [H]ouses of the common people are very small, with one or two ground-level
> rooms where two or three Indians used to live with their wives and children.
> Houses of principals and chiefs are larger because they have more rooms and
> larger patios. Some of them have two and three patios and other rooms around
> them, with no doors, were used as antechambers . . . all materials needed to build
> the houses such as wood, limestone and thatch for the roofs are nearby. (1: 58; 2:
> 101)

In Mitla, two of the major groups, Group of the Adobe and Group of the South, are
pyramidal structures around a central plaza, probably for administrative and ceremonial
purposes. The other three similar complexes are integrated by three patios surrounded by
wide rooms and are known as the Group of the Church, the Group of the Columns, and
the Arroyo Group. They probably functioned as a combination of elite residential and
administrative structures. In the three group complexes, the north patio is smaller overall
and has smaller rooms that were probably reserved for residential activities. The central and
south patios are larger and probably were used for administrative activities. It is worth
noting the similarity between the Yagul's patios C and F and Mitla's Church Group and
Columns Group. Each patio consists of an open space limited by a banquette and corridor,
with four major rooms, with the exception of patio D, which has only three rooms (Fig. 17).

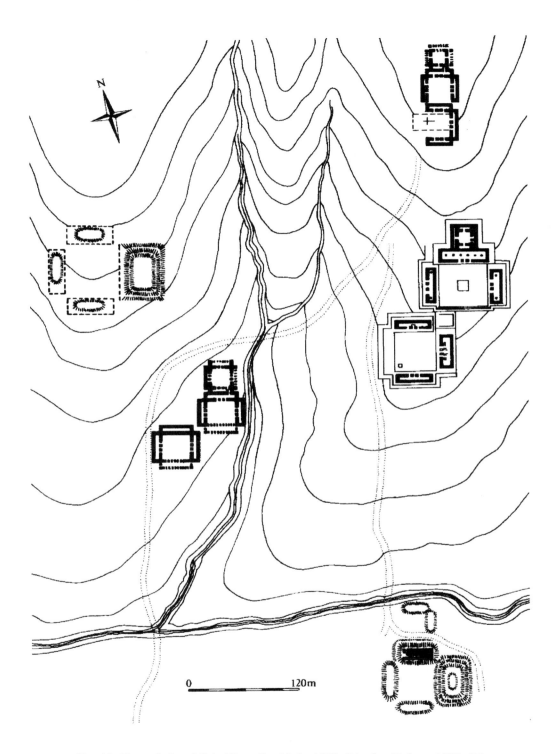

Fig. 16 General plan, Mitla (González Licón 1990: 94, after Holmes 1895–97)

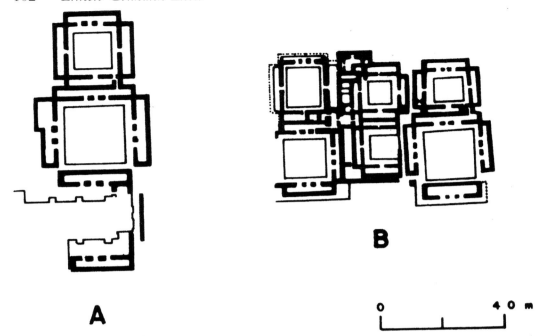

Fig. 17 Palaces, Mitla and Yagul (González Licón 1990: 95)

These three groups of buildings in Mitla have their external walls decorated with the characteristic Zapotec design of *tablero escapulario*—a stone mosaic of small, well-carved stones forming different designs of *xicalcoliuquis* or *grecas* at the interior of the *tableros*. The Group of Columns consists of three patios. Two of them—the north and central—are connected. The patios are surrounded by separate buildings with three entrances and wide rooms, although the south side was left open. There is an altar in the center of the central and larger patio.

The most important building is at the north end over a platform with a stairway. The entrance to the building is through a doorway that has three sections. It opens onto a gallery 38 m long x 7 m wide (Fig. 18). This chamber has at the center of its axis a row of six columns for supporting the flat roof, which is constructed of wood beams and stuccoed on top. At the inner wall, a narrow passage with a low roof leads to the north patio; a long, narrow room is on each side. The patio and rooms are decorated with a *greca* motif. The walls were built with a core of stone and mud and then inlaid with small cut stones to form a mosaic design. Each stone was carefully cut so as to adapt it perfectly, one to another, forming many different figures. The façade and the walls that surround the patio consist, from the bottom upward, of a *talud* surmounted by a substructure, a panel or *tablero*, and a frieze. The panels and the upper sections are decorated with *grecas*.

The Groups of the Church and Columns are similar in general plan to patios C through F in Yagul. A big patio with large rooms was designated for administrative matters, and there are other patios and rooms, much more enclosed, where it is assumed the ruler lived. According to Francisco de Burgoa (1989 [1674]), such a ruler was the *bigaña*.

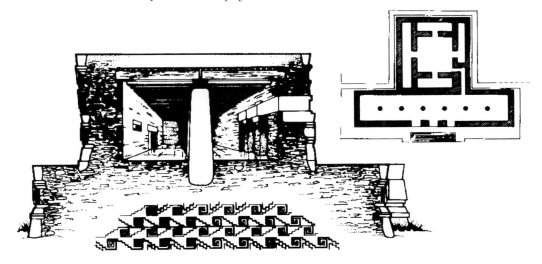

Fig. 18 Building of the Columns, Mitla (González Licón 1990: 95, after Marquina 1990, Holmes 1898–97)

[O]ne of the patios was the Great Priest palace, were he attended and lived because the place had room for everything . . . this priest was of such great authority, that even during a visit of the king, nobody dared to cross the central patio [in front of him]. To enter at any of the other three large rooms, everybody else have to use the back doors through which even the visiting chiefs had to enter. The second large room were for the priests and ministers, the third for the king when visiting, and the fourth for other chiefs and captains. And the space being so limited to such different and several families, they accepted as respect to the place, with no differences or partialities, with no other jurisdiction than that from the Great Priest, which to his sovereignty all attended. (124–125)

The south patio had a similar plan but with two tombs, one below the north building and the other beneath the east building. The building to the east is a long gallery that probably had an axial row of columns and was provided with a doorway in which stones of great size, admirably cut, served as lintels and jambs. To the center and underneath, there is a cruciform tomb internally decorated with the same *greca* mosaics as in the tableros. The only difference is that the *greca* was carved onto big stones instead of being comprised of small pieces of cut stone. The tomb below the north building has the same cruciform plan and *greca* decoration, but part of the stone roof is supported by a monolithic column, known popularly as the Column of Life. In Yagul and Mitla the residences where the ruling elites lived were also their administrative headquarters, as described in Relaciones geograficas. The differences in terms of population between Yagul and Mitla, on the one hand, and Monte Albán, on the other, are considerable. The power and authority correlation among settlements in the valley changes from the Classic to the Postclassic period. These changes were manifested in the type of government and the kind of residences that elites had in each period.

In the Nochixtlan Valley (as probably elsewhere in the Mixtec region) by the Late Classic, settlements were hierarchically organized, and their inhabitants maintained a highly stratified social system. There was no single ruler of the Mixteca, rather "the area was broken up and dominated by a group of lords claiming common descent from a few mythical ancestors" (Pohl n.d.: 33). Ronald Spores (1984) noticed that

> [E]lite residents of first-order administrative centers lived in larger, better-built houses, used more refined pottery, participated more fully in ritual and sacrificial activity, and had stronger ties to areas outside the region than did residents of second-order administrative centers. (45)

Buildings are represented extensively in Mixtec codices. Palaces and temples were the places where noble people lived and ruled. There are many kinds of houses in these hieroglyphic manuscripts. The common, lower-class house, called *xacalli* by the Aztecs, was a single structure, represented with wattle-and-daub or adobe walls and a thatched roof. These houses might have had either rounded or squared plans (Caso 1977: 32, ill. VIIIa, g). Representations of elite residential structures in Mixtec codices indicate that these were much more elaborate. Built on low platforms with their walls integrated by different segments, some examples were decorated in the Teotihuacan *talud* and *tablero* style. However, the *tableros* feature the characteristic *grecas* or *xicalcoliuquis* (Caso 1977: 32, ill. VIIIc, f). The roofs were generally flat (*terrado*), sometimes crowned with battlements (*almenas*), but thatched roofs were not unusual. The main doorway was painted red and closed with a curtain. Only half of the house was depicted when presented in a lateral view (Caso 1977: 32, ill. VIIIb).

At sites like Chachoapan, Yucuita, Nochixtlan, and Yanhuitlan, among others in the Nochixtlan Valley, elite houses were located at the settlement core, close to the main temples. The palace (*tayu* in Mixtec) had a main courtyard or patio surrounded by rooms and secondary patios, which were located at their corners. These had even more rooms adjoining them. The main patio was where semipublic or ceremonial activities usually took place. Secondary patios and their rooms were reserved exclusively as living quarters. The *tayu* was built with stone and adobe walls, with floors and walls plastered, slab-made drain systems, and external stone slab veneer. Circumscribing these elite structures were dozens of smaller single- or double-roomed structures for lower-ranking families. This combination of elite and common residences is a Postclassic characteristic of the region (Spores 1984: 49–53, 55).

The Relación of Atlatlauca and Malinaltepeque (Acuña 1984 [1580]) describes how the ruler exercised power and government from his residence, thereby illustrating the function of these multiroomed and multipatioed structures:

> The chief always had in his house one or two close relatives, the elderly, who used to live in another patio, separate from the patio where the chief lives. And all the people's complaints and requests, and embassies coming from elsewhere were attended by these old men, and after they discussed the matter with the chief they declared to the people the chief's will. (51)

The palace was the place to discuss governance issues, tax payments, land disputes among neighbors, and other ceremonial and economic matters. The ruler lived almost in total seclusion and most administrative matters were tended to by those elders who assisted him. When someone was allowed to see the ruler, he appeared in front of him barefoot to show submission and humility. (See Evans this volume for information on the sumptuary laws of Motecuzoma Ilhuicamina.) The palace represented the seat of political power. The decisions made in the palace as central office generally affected most of the population.

By the Late Postclassic, Mixtec lords settled down near Monte Albán in a village named Saayucu, the largest Mixtec community in the Valley of Oaxaca. After the Spanish Conquest, the Mixtecs from Saayucu were removed by the Dominicans, who built a convent there, in 1555. The Plaque of Yuchacaa in the Cuilapan convent gives two Mixtec dates: Year 10 Reed, Day 11 Serpent on the left and Year 10 Flint, Day 11 Death on the right (Paddock 1983: xiv). The Mixtec name of Yuchacaa, a later settlement of Saayucu means exactly the same in both Zapotec (Quicopecua) and Nahuatl (Cuilapan). Yuchacaa, under the name of Cuilapan, said by the Spanish to have been the largest community, was the administrative center for scattered groups of Mixtec-speaking communities (Paddock 1983: 53). Modern Cuilapan is located between Saayucu to the north and Quicopecua to the south (Paddock 1983: 48).

In the same Zaachila-Zimatlan arm of the valley, 10 km south of Cuilapan, is located Zaachila. This literally means *place of the real zapotes*, but it is equivalent to *place of the real Zapotecs* (Paddock 1983: 8). In 1962, the elite residential area was excavated (Caso 1966: 313–335; Gallegos 1962), in particular one elite residence with a central patio surrounded by rooms. The objects were of a style and time period similar to those found by Alfonso Caso at Monte Albán's tomb 7, the Late Postclassic (Late V) period. The house seems to have had just two occupation periods, and it was rebuilt only once, without much change from its original layout or size (Paddock 1983: 32). The patio floor in the first stage of construction covered both tombs' roofs, indicating that they were part of the original construction (Gallegos 1978: 56, 70; Paddock 1983: 36). This was part of a Zapotec tradition, according to which tombs were completed first. Multifunctional rooms were built in this residence: An altar is in the north room and a sanctuary in the west room. The east room seems to have been habitational, but the south room was so eroded that it may have been left open (Flannery 1983: 290). On the basis of ethnohistoric evidence, occupation at Zaachila during the Late Classic was important because it was the seat of Zapotec political power from which *cociyoesa* ruled. (For further discussion, see Paddock 1983.) The house, including these two tombs with their rich offering, yielded important information about the Zapotecs and Mixtecs in the Late Postclassic in the Valley of Oaxaca (see Caso 1960; 1965a, b; 1969 and Paddock 1983). For example, the relationships between the Zapotec ruler and Mixtec leaders in the valley were problematic.

Social inequality in the Valley of Oaxaca had a long trajectory. The emerging elites in San José Mogote were controlling long-distance exchange and acquired more exotic objects than their social inferiors, but the elite houses were not much different from those of the general populace. Social inequality was more evident in terms of wealth than in spatial location or house size. By the Classic period, Monte Albán was a primate center with four levels of government. Political structure and government were stable. Ideological, religious, social, and economic aspects differentiated the ruling elite. Social differences were institutionalized and much more evident. Elite residences were larger, better made, and located closer to the main plaza or at the core of a civic-ceremonial *barrio*. Spacious and well-decorated tombs were built below the main room of houses for use by family heads. High-status nobles, probably related to the king, lived in these houses.

The residence of Monte Albán's ruler on the North Platform also represents a ritual or ceremonial place. It was clearly delineated from its surroundings by its platform elevation situated in a prominent location, which served to keep the populace mindful of activities there. The North Platform was built not only to delimit the sacred space of the Main Plaza in the north, but also to distinguish this structure from the others and to prevent unauthorized entry. It was the materialization of a regional government, the place where the ruler conducted the most important religious celebrations, meetings, and festivities, and made administrative decisions. The distribution of the royal residence and the temple complexes built on the North Platform probably indicates how the ruler's activities were related to the sacred world. The most important religious and civic celebrations likely took place here. The monumental columned hall at the south end of the sunken patio represented the threshold from the Main Plaza to the royal palace. Only certain people could enter by this gate.

After the decline of Monte Albán in the Postclassic, political instability produced changes and alliances between elites with no regard for their ethnic affiliation, in contrast to the long periods of stability that characterized the Classic in the Valley of Oaxaca. By the Postclassic, military conflicts were constant, even within the same ruling family. Fragile military alliances and royal weddings among the ruling elites produced brief periods of peace. By the end of the Postclassic, political frontiers were less delimited. Zapotecs, Mixtecs, Cuicatecs, and Aztecs fought to take control of trade routes and territories. With Monte Albán disappearing, political control across the entire valley was fragmented. In the Valley of Tlacolula, Mitla was the most important city, but first Lambityeco and later Yagul were competing cities as well. Both Yagul and Mitla had fortified areas for military defense. In the Zimatlan Valley, Zaachila was the seat of political power, but Jalieza and Cuilapan were also important. Elite residences during the Postclassic were not as massive as the North Platform in Monte Albán, but they were clearly separate from the temples. Ruling elite residences in Yagul, Mitla, and Zaachila have massive stone walls, which delimit the houses. With several patios, as in Yagul and Mitla, they have clearly differentiated residential and administrative areas. Building the ruler's residence required a substantial investment of energy. Interior and exterior walls were decorated, with the Group of the Columns in Mitla as the best example.

The construction of a royal tomb was also important. Mitla and Zaachila have tombs that are rich not only in construction design and decoration, but also, as in Zaachila, in content. The tomb was regarded as the residence of the dead. For the Zapotecs, life after death and the cult of the ancestors were important because the hereditary system was based on genealogy and ancestral lines. The best example of this ancestor cult and the amount of energy invested in tomb construction is at Huijazoó. By the time of Monte Albán's decline, this site, located on the west side of the Valley of Etla, had been built over a hill in a defensive location, and it had a strategic position for trade in the Valley of Oaxaca and Mixtec region. The Huijazoó ruling elite built a tomb that reproduced a real house in toto. Its façade is fully decorated. Inside the tomb there is a central patio surrounded by four rooms. Each room entrance has carved lintels, and all the walls are stucco plastered and painted (González Licón 1990, 2001; Miller 1995). The main chamber of the tomb, representing the main room of an elite house, was above ground, with lintels and an elaborate façade. The founding families of the Huijazoó dynasty are represented here.

In conclusion, elite residential architecture in the Valley of Oaxaca reflects changes in political structure and social organization. From the almost undifferentiated residences in San José Mogote during the Formative, to the impressive residence of Monte Albán's ruler in the Classic period, to the highly decorated and wealthy residences of the rulers in the city-states of the Postclassic, these great differences reflected the evolutionary changes in political complexity of the inhabitants of the Valley of Oaxaca. The gap between elites and commoners was greater in the Classic period, and it continued into the Postclassic.

Acknowledgments I thank Susan Toby Evans for her friendship, confidence, and help throughout the editing process. I appreciate the invitation that she and Joanne Pillsbury extended to me to participate in the Dumbarton Oaks symposium Palaces of the Ancient New World. I also thank them for a wonderful research season as a fellow at Dumbarton Oaks during the summer of 1998. I thank Joyce Marcus for her insightful comments on this manuscript and for her friendship, and Mercedes de la Garza for her support and optimistic perspective. I take full responsibility for the content of this essay.

Bibliography

ACOSTA, JORGE R.

1959   *Exploraciones en Monte Negro, Tilantongo, Oaxaca.* Departmento de Monumentos Prehispánicos, Instituto Nacional de Antropología e Historia, México, D.F.

ACUÑA, RENÉ (ED.)

1984   *Relaciones geográficas del siglo XVI: Antequera,* 2 vols. Universidad Nacional Autónoma
[1580]   de México, México, D.F.

BERNAL, IGNACIO, AND LORENZO GAMIO

1974   *Yagul, el palacio de los seis patios.* Instituto de Investigaciones Antropológicas, Universidad Nacional Autónoma de México, México, D.F.

BLANTON, RICHARD E.

1978   *Monte Albán: Settlement Patterns at the Ancient Zapotec Capital.* Academic Press, New York.

BLANTON, RICHARD E., STEPHEN A. KOWALEWSKI, GARY M. FEINMAN, AND JILL APPEL

1981   *Ancient Mesoamerica: A Comparison of Change in Three Regions.* Cambridge University Press, Cambridge.

1982   *Monte Albán's Hinterland: Prehispanic Settlement Patterns of the Central and Southern Parts of the Valley of Oaxaca, Mexico,* pt. 1. Memoirs of the Museum of Anthropology 15. University of Michigan, Ann Arbor.

BURGOA, FRANCISCO DE

1989   *Geográfica descripción,* 2 vols. Biblioteca Porrúa 97. Editorial Porrúa, México, D.F.
[1674]

CASO, ALFONSO

1960   The Historical Value of the Mixtec Codices. *Boletín de Estudios Oaxaqueños* 16. Oaxaca, Oax.

1965a   Mixtec Writing and Calendar. In Gordon R. Willey, ed., *Handbook of Middle American Indians,* 3: 948–961. University of Texas Press, Austin.

1965b   Zapotec Writing and Calendar. In Gordon R. Willey, ed., *Handbook of Middle American Indians,* 3: 931–947. University of Texas Press, Austin.

1966   The Lords of Yanhuitlán. In *Ancient Oaxaca: Discoveries in Mexican Archaeology and History* (John Paddock, ed.): 313–335. Stanford University Press, Stanford, Calif.

1969   *El Tesoro de Monte Albán.* Memorias del Instituto Nacional de Antropología e Historia 3. Instituto Nacional de Antropología e Historia, México, D.F.

1977   *Reyes y reinos de la mixteca.* Fondo de Cultura Económica. México, D.F.

CHASE, ARLEN F., AND DIANE Z. CHASE

1992   Mesoamerican Elites: Assumptions, Definitions, and Models. In *Mesoamerican Elites: An Archaeological Assessment* (D. Z. Chase and A. F. Chase, eds.): 3–17. University of Oklahoma Press, Norman.

DE CÓRDOVA, JUAN

1942   *Vocabulario castellano-zapoteco.* Instituto Nacional de Antropología e Historia, México,
[1578]   D.F.

FEINMAN, GARY M.

1991   Demography, Surplus, and Inequality: Early Political Formations in Highland Mesoamerica. In *Chiefdoms: Power, Economy and Ideology* (T. K. Earle, ed.): 229–262. Cambridge University Press, Cambridge.

FLANNERY, KENT V.

1983   The Legacy of the Early Urban Period: An Ethnohistoric Approach to Monte Albán's Temples, Residences and Royal Tombs. In *The Cloud People: Divergent Evolution of the Zapotec and Mixtec Civilizations* (Kent V. Flannery and Joyce Marcus, eds.): 132–136. Academic, New York.

FLANNERY, KENT V., AND JOYCE MARCUS

1976   Evolution of the Public Building in Formative Oaxaca. In *Cultural Change and Continuity: Essays in Honor of James B. Griffin* (C. Cleland, ed.): 205–221. Academic Press, New York.

1994   *Early Formative Pottery in the Valley of Oaxaca.* Memoirs of the Museum of Anthropology 27. University of Michigan, Ann Arbor.

FLANNERY, KENT V., AND JOYCE MARCUS (EDS.)

1983   *The Cloud People: Divergent Evolution of the Zapotec and Mixtec Civilizations.* Academic Press, New York.

GALLEGOS, ROBERTO

1962   Exploraciones en Zaachila, Oaxaca. *Boletin del Instituto Nacional de Antropología e Historia* 8: 6–8.

1978   *El Señor 9 Flor en Zaachila.* Universidad Nacional Autónoma de México, México, D.F.

GENDROP, PAUL

1976   *Arte prehispánico en Mesoamérica.* Editorial Trillas, México. (First edition 1970).

GONZÁLEZ LICÓN, ERNESTO

1990   *Los Zapotecas y mixtecos: Tres mil años de civilización precolombina.* Jaca Book and Consejo Nacional para la Cultura y las Artes, México, D.F.

n.d.   Funerary Practices and Social Organization at Monte Albán, Oaxaca, México: A Paleodemographic Approach from the Late Formative to the Early Classic. A paper presented at the 62nd Annual Meeting of the Society for American Archaeology, Nashville, Tenn., April 1997.

2001   *Vanished Mesoamerican Civilizations: The History and Cultures of the Zapotecs and Mixtecs.* Sharpe Reference, Armonk, N.Y.

HOLMES, WILLIAM H.

1895–97   *Archaeological Studies among the Ancient Cities of Mexico.* Part II. Monumentos of Chiapas, Oaxaca and the Valley of México. Field Museum of Natural History, Pub. 8.16, Anthropological Series I, Chicago, Ill.

KIRKBY, ANNE V. T.

1973   *The Use of Land and Water Resources in the Past and Present Valley of Oaxaca.* Memoirs of the Museum of Anthropology, 5. University of Michigan, Ann Arbor.

KOWALEWSKI, STEPHEN A., GARY M. FEINMAN, LAURA FINSTEN, RICHARD BLANTON, AND LINDA NICHOLAS (EDS.)

1989   *Monte Alban's Hinterland: Prehispanic Settlement Patterns in Tlacolula, Etla, and Ocotlan, the Valley of Oaxaca, Mexico,* pt. 2. Memoirs of the Museum of Anthropology 23. University of Michigan, Ann Arbor.

LIND, MICHAEL, AND JAVIER URCID

1983   The Lords of Lambityeco and Their Nearest Neighbors. *Notas Mesoamericanas* 9: 78–111. University of the Americas, Cholula, Pue.

MARCUS, JOYCE

1983   The Conquest Slabs of Building J, Monte Albán. In *The Cloud People: Divergent Evolution of the Zapotec and Mixtec Civilizations* (Kent V. Flannery and Joyce Marcus, eds.): 106–108. Academic Press, New York.

MARCUS, JOYCE, AND KENT V. FLANNERY

1996   *Zapotec Civilization: How Urban Society Evolved in Mexico's Oaxaca Valley.* Thames and Hudson, London and New York.

MARQUINA, IGNACIO

1990   *Arquitectura perhispánica.* Memorias N. 1, INAH. México.

MILLER, ARTHUR G.

1995   *The Painted Tombs of Oaxaca, Mexico.* Cambridge University Press, Cambridge.

PADDOCK, JOHN

1966   *Ancient Oaxaca: Discoveries in Mexican Archaeology and History.* Stanford University Press, Stanford, Calif.

1983   *Lord 5 Flower's Family: Rulers of Zaachila and Cuilapan.* Publications in Anthropology 29. Vanderbilt University, Nashville, Tenn.

POHL, JOHN M. D.

n.d.   The Earth Lords: Politics and Symbolism of Mixtec Codices. Ph.D. dissertation, Department of Anthropology, University of California, Los Angeles, 1984.

SPORES, RONALD

1984   *The Mixtecs in Ancient and Colonial Times.* University of Oklahoma Press, Norman.

Unwin, Simon

    1997   *Analysing Architecture.* Routledge, London.

Palaces of Tikal and Copán

Peter D. Harrison

University Museum of Pennsylvania, University of Pennsylvania

E. Wyllys Andrews

Middle American Research Institute, Tulane University

In this essay, structure groups that have been called *palaces* at the sites of Tikal and Copán are compared with the purpose of noting similarities and differences. It has been noted elsewhere that the use of the term *palace* in Maya archaeology comes bearing "heavy baggage" of assumed meaning, mostly of European origin. The term stands in architectural contrast to the alternate form of *temple*, but is still only vaguely defined with reference to form and even more vaguely understood in terms of function. Recent forays into comparison of Maya sociopolitical organization with the openly European concept of the *royal court* have proved both fruitful and positive. The many functions of a royal court both in Western and non-Western societies compare favorably with the evidence for similar functions and trappings of a royal court in Classic Maya culture (Inomata and Houston 2001).

Part of the reason for our insistence that the term *palace* is inadequate for architectural explanation lies in the breadth of variety found in Maya cities both within the same city and across the landscape on differing scales. While observing the differences between Tikal and Copán we also seek anchor points of similarity either in form or function. In the first part of this essay, we describe the variety of palace-type structures in the Central Acropolis of Tikal. The second part deals with a similar examination of a specific group at Copán.

Central Acropolis at Tikal

Tikal sits on a drainage divide in the central Petén of Guatemala, on what was likely an ancient trade route between the Caribbean and the Usumacinta drainages. It is one of the largest Classic period cities constructed by the Maya, dating from the Middle Preclassic through Terminal Classic (i.e., 800 B.C.–A.D. 950), with a peak of massive monumental construction occurring in the last half of the eighth century (Fig. 1). The main ceremonial center was established in the Preclassic period in what is now called the Great Plaza. The North Acropolis, north terrace, and plaza itself are considered ceremonial precincts, but the Central Acropolis on the opposing south side of the Great Plaza bears hallmarks of residence. This complex of forty-six structures is arranged in six courtyards, which grew over

Fig. 1 Aerial view, Tikal: the Central Acropolis (*left*) and the great plaza (*right*). By Nicholas Hellmuth.

eight centuries to its present form (Fig. 2). The variety in form of structure exemplifies the diversity mentioned above, ranging from single-room buildings to three-storied structures with multiple rooms on each story. Earlier, Peter Harrison (n.d.) analyzed the variety of form in the Central Acropolis and thus defined a group of attributes that fit the function of residence to varying degrees. These attributes include the presence of multiple rooms arranged in a tandem/transverse combination, together with evidence of alteration over time, and the presence of masonry benches in a wide variety of forms with accompanying varieties of function. Long sleeping benches are a marker of permanent residence (Fig. 3). In support of the interpretation of a bed function for these benches, there are also secondary wall holes, evidence of privacy curtains and/or draped wallcoverings. Buildings used for residence frequently have added architectural elements such as low walls, used to control traffic and access. In addition, the presence of burials and caches are associated with permanent residence.

The Central Acropolis is defined as a *complex of palaces* with the implication of long-term, multi-unit phases of construction. The association of such complexes (as at the Central Acropolis) with a place of seating of the royal court has been discussed extensively (Harrison 2001b, 2003) The Central Acropolis at Tikal has been compared with Versailles, the great palace of Louis XIV of France (Harrison 2003). This comparison was based upon

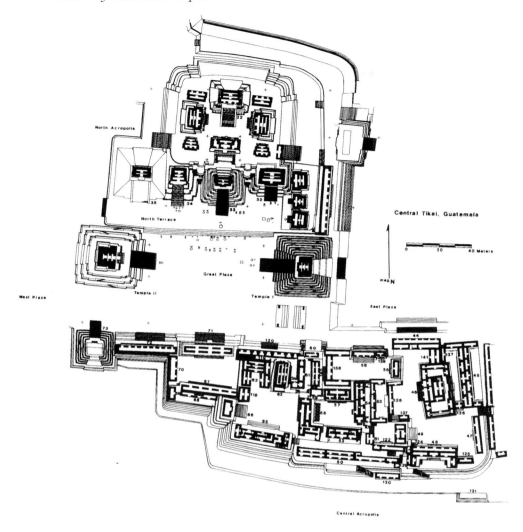

Fig. 2 Core, Central Tikal. Structure 5D-46 lies at the east end of the Central Acropolis to the south.

parallel functions and the presence of a royal court at Tikal, not singularity of construction. Versailles was built, for the most part, as a massive single-unit of effort, but the Central Acropolis was not. Rather, it grew over eight centuries to achieve its present state of complexity.

Although there is evidence buried below the Central Acropolis of structures deemed residential in function, the earliest structures do not reflect the level of wealth and opulence associated with royal courts and statehood. The seeds of the evolutionary process may be present on the surface of the bedrock of the Central Acropolis (Fig. 4), but the fluorescence of massive building in stone did not appear until the beginnings of the Early Classic period (i.e., ca. 250). Although this essay deals with the Central Acropolis at Tikal, it does not

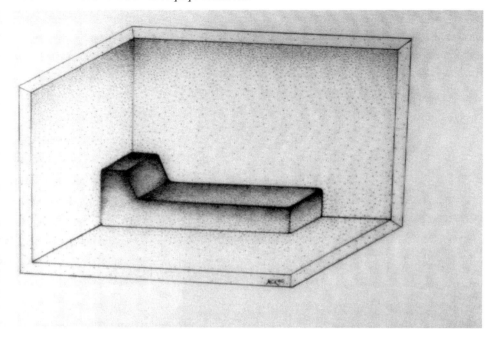

Fig. 3 Sleeping bench, reconstruction. These were commonplace in Central Acropolis structures, especially Structure 5D-63. Drawing by Amalia Kenward.

preclude that other locations of royal court functions occurred elsewhere in the city. By now, it seems clear that such functions took place at several locations around the city, possibly sequentially, but equally likely, simultaneously, as the population and complexity of Tikal increased over eight centuries (Harrison 1999).

The architecture of elite residences (and royal courts) is not expected to look exactly alike in every lowland city. Rather, comparison between and among cities is expected to be a fruitful means of seeking those attributes that express a city's individuality; those that exhibit a common form *may* share a common function. This is a subject of study that is ripe for exploration.

Preclassic: 350 B.C.–A.D. 150

For the first half-millennium of housing in the Central Acropolis much is not known for lack of excavation, but extrapolation can help fill in these gaps. In the Central Acropolis, there is solid evidence for residential function by Cauac times (i.e., A.D. 1–150) at least, and probably earlier. While the North Acropolis (see Fig. 2) was developing as a ritual and mortuary base (Coe 1990), the land on the south side of the plaza was also receiving attention from the inhabitants of this Tikal hilltop.

Because of established excavation strategies deliberately designed to counterbalance the intense depth probe of the North Acropolis, made by William Coe, the Central Acropolis excavations were oriented toward broad, extensive surface clearing rather than depth probing.

Fortunately, the latter was not ignored. Bedrock was probed in a number of locales over the surface of the Central Acropolis. Four are detailed below.

Under the Early Classic Structure 5D-71-1st, a tunnel connecting the great plaza floor sequence to the bedrock beneath Courtyard 1 was excavated. This structure is one of several "pass-through" buildings at Tikal. Such structures serve as a restricted passage from one open public space to another more private space. Incidences of such structures at Tikal offer transit always from one absolute level to another, not just from a public to a private space.

Structure 5D-71-1st dates to the later portion of the Early Classic period, likely constructed during the reign of Stormy Sky (Siyah Chan K'awil; ruled 411–458). The tunnel beneath the building revealed the presence of a Late Preclassic (i.e., Cauac) building with the same orientation (north-south) as the structure above, built on bedrock slightly above the plaza level. Although the bedrock had been modified, both for the great plaza itself and for the development of the Central Acropolis, at this particular location the bedrock rises slightly to the south of the great plaza.

Every probe that extended down to the natural rock level within the confines of the Central Acropolis's final boundaries encountered Cauac, or earlier, remains of architecture built directly upon the modified rock surface (Harrison 2000). Scant but definite Preclassic remains were uncovered in the bedrock probe in Courtyard 3 and in the tunnel that connected to this pit under Structure 5D-50, the lowest level of the five-story palace. Similarly, a horizontal probe below 5D-65, entering the eroded south face of the Acropolis from the ravine bottom, also encountered Preclassic architecture on the bedrock. In this location the bedrock beneath the Acropolis rises north-south to at least the elevation of the great plaza. As noted here and elsewhere (Harrison 2000), the bedrock beneath the Central Acropolis was modified somewhat, but its natural elevation was utilized by the earliest builders to achieve elevation of presumed dwellings above the great plaza level.

On the other hand, portions of the ravine that lie south of the Acropolis were excavated for quarrying. The extent of this type of exploitation of the ravine was never fully examined. However, two investigations have yielded a reasonable picture of its history. The western portion of the ravine was modified little or not at all, while the east end, south of Courtyard 6, was quarried extensively and paved first with rough-cut stone and then with a thick layer of black montmorillonitic clay presumably imported from Bajo de Santa Fe, which forms the eastern boundary of Tikal. This lining effectively created a watertight basin that served as a reservoir. The earliest ceramic remains recovered from this investigation were Early Classic, indicating that quarry and water-holding activities dated to this period. The water basin was rather small compared with the possible potential of the ravine. Its effectiveness depended upon the construction of the dam-*cum*-causeway, which joins the east plaza to the south side of the ravine. This artificial construction served not only to contain the water at the east end of the ravine but also to allow access to its south side.

It is known that during Early Classic times there was a construction focus on the south side of the ravine opposite the Central Acropolis (personal communications, Oswaldo Gomez July 2000; T. P. Culbert July, 1967). Gomez believes that the whole of Temple V is

Fig. 4 Palace platform, excavated and dated as Cauac period Preclassic. Immediately south of Structure 5D-46, an Early Classic residential palace, this platform was discovered only a few centimeters below Courtyard 5D-6's Late Classic floor at the east end of the Central Acropolis.

dated to late Early Classic, and there is no doubt from the stratigraphic evidence that the basal site of Temple V was occupied by architecture at this time. However, Harrison does not accept such an early date for Temple V, on grounds too complex to address here.

Returning to the roster of evidence for Preclassic architecture, a very shallow probe in Courtyard 6 demonstrated that at this location bedrock is close to the present surface and was barely modified other than leveling. This excavation revealed a Cauac structure immediately south of the Late Classic south patio of 5D-46. All that remains is a masonry platform similar to those excavated by Norman Hammond (1991) at Cuello, with large post-holes demonstrating that the structure was of perishable material (Fig. 4). There was also a dedicatory cache pit at the main entrance highly analogous to the dedicatory cache in the western stair of 5D-46. The east end of the Acropolis, specifically in the location of what is now designated Courtyard 6, was likely a residential zone from its earliest development, built almost directly on the bedrock, and that in this area there was little *vertical* growth during the next several centuries. The suggestion is that royal residence originated in the east end of the Acropolis and continued there, unbroken until the collapse. Residential function expanded into other portions of the Acropolis during the Early Classic period.

Early Classic: 250–550

Only one fully excavated structure fulfilled all of the component variables that defined

Fig. 5 Structure 5D-46, after excavation and partial reconstruction. Its central core is the Early Classic house of Jaguar Claw the Great (Chak Toh Ich'aak), which was built in the mid-fourth century. An inscribed cache vessel (see Fig. 6) was recovered beneath the west stair.

permanent residence: Structure 5D-46 (Fig. 5). In 1978, Linda Schele translated the text on the lid of a polished black carved cache vessel that had been uncovered beneath the west stair of this palace. The text reads: "Jaguar Claw the Great, ruler of Tikal, his house" (Fig. 6). Thus an interpretation originally deduced from archaeological data (Harrison n.d.) was later confirmed by textual translation (Schele and Freidel 1990). Structure 5D-46 contained *all* of the residential markers, having undergone an extraordinary amount of change, renovation, and addition over a remarkable five centuries that the building—constructed by the most important political figure in Tikal's Early Classic history, Chac Toh Ich'aak (Jaguar Claw the Great)—survived. It is likely that the initial building was constructed early in the reign of this important ruler of Tikal, ca. 330 and 350. Later, at an unknown date in the Early Classic, a second story was added to the primary first floor with access via a rare, interior *caracol* stair. In its original form, the building faced equally east-west. Both façades underwent extensive changes in their accessibility after A.D. 700. The west side remained open to an enclosed "porch," though it was sealed from the rest of the building, while the east side, through a series of progressive constructions, came to be totally enclosed, providing a degree of residential privacy similar to that of a fortress. Interior doorways connecting to the previously open west galleries were sealed, so that the palace came to have two separate parts: the eastern residential complex and a much smaller, west-facing ceremonial

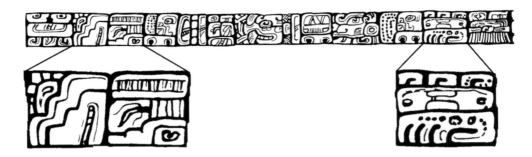

Fig. 6 Inscription, lid of the cache vessel from Structure 5D-46, whose extracted glyphs read: *na* (house), *otot* (home), Chac Toh Ich'aak (Jaguar Claw the Great). Tikal 66-5-50 was the original negative for this depiction, which was modified after a drawing by William Coe (Harrison 1999, 2000).

precinct. West-facing doors at Tikal generally are associated with a religious purpose, such as a household shrine; east-facing doors signify more daily activities including residence. The documentation of this is too lengthy to include here, although much of it was presented in an earlier work (Harrison n.d.).

Late Classic: 550–950

The influence of Teotihuacan upon the art and architecture of Tikal has been discussed extensively and used as an argument that the highland site even dominated Tikal by conquest for a time (Coggins n.d.; Stuart n.d.). The foreign influence in the Central Acropolis is limited and oddly occurs after A.D. 700, long after the highland city had collapsed. The one building (5D-57) bearing Teotihuacan-style art was partially buried, specifically its exterior art. We do not know when or how long this art survived on public view, but we do know that it was buried and covered from public view by the *tikaleños* themselves. There is no evidence to presume a long period of public exposure for this art. Rather, the good preservation of the carved stone and stucco surfaces suggests a relatively short exposure to open-air viewing, an assumption that cannot be proven. The burial of the exterior art did not, however, affect the use of the building, which continued to be open. Only partial, and mostly exterior, excavation has been realized on this palace, but it is known that the floorplan admits it into the realm of likelihood as a permanent residence. Since almost all other attributes are unknown because of lack of interior excavation, we have to rely upon the exterior decoration and the information therein contained, in glyphic text, to interpret the function of the building. The decorative panel from the upper zone of the east end was preserved because of its subsequent burial (Fig. 7), as well as a rare "orthostat" on the lower zone of the west end (Fig. 8), which was preserved for the same reason. Both depict the twenty-sixth ruler of Tikal, Hasaw Chan K'awil, in full battle armor. The east end artwork shows Hasaw with a captive from the archenemy city of Calakmul. Accompaning text identifies both the captor and the captive. That this building was commissioned by Hasaw

Fig. 7 Decorative panel, east end of the upper zone, Structure 5D-57. Hasaw Chan K'awil, Ruler 26 of Tikal, appears in full battle array with a prisoner from Calakmul. On the basis of calculations from archaeological and epigraphic materials, this building dates to A.D. 700.

Fig. 8 Carved "orthostat," west end of lower zone, Structure 5D-57. Hasaw Chan K'awil appears alone in Teotihuacan–style battle garb. Carving faces west. Drawing by Margaret Rossiter; © Peter D. Harrison.

Fig. 9 U-shaped building in Courtyard 5D-2, Structure 5D-63, Central Acropolis. Its multiple beds/ benches suggest that it served as a ceremonial guesthouse.

A.D. 700 is indisputable, but whether it was his domicile remains a theory. A throne structure was later built on the west side of the palace, a single-room building with a throne centered on the east wall, with other benches perhaps for visitors, centered on the north and west walls. This is an unusual arrangement, which did not allow observers from the outside to view the ruler on his throne. Nevertheless, it clearly was a throne room structure associated with a probable permanent residence (Harrison 2001a).

Another palace structure with interesting attributes of residence is 5D-63 (Fig. 9). There is little chance that this was a permanent residence, but almost certainly it served as a guesthouse of some kind. The building is shaped in the form of a squared *U* or in the shape of a yoke associated with the ball game. The structure contains eleven long sleeping benches, a highly disproportionate number for a typical house. While each bench *could* sleep two, there is no information on the protocol of housing guests, much less a visiting ball team, nor do we even know the size of such a team, if this was indeed the function of this unusual building. The suggestion that it was associated with such a type of guest is prompted not just by its shape but by its proximity to a ball court in the plaza below, as well as its location in an obviously prestigious and sanctified compound adjacent to the ceremonial center of the city (see Fig. 2; Hall 1975: 810; Harrison 1999: fig. 115).

A few attributes shared by the palaces at the Central Acropolis are important. All were vaulted with masonry roofs. Vertical differentiation was apparently important, since the six courtyards were all at different levels and connected by complex stair systems reminiscent

Fig. 10 Painted vessel, rollout photo. An interior palace scene, with the ceremonial reception illuminated by torchlight, depicts at least one function of a throne room. Courtesy of Justin Kerr (file K1728).

of the palace complex of Knossos in Crete. All of the vertical differentiation was achieved by artificial construction. The courtyard closest to bedrock is number 6 (see Fig. 2), the site of Jaguar Claw the Great's house. Many of the later structures were multistoried, but these multilevels were never constructed at the same time. All second and third stories were built at later dates than the first story. They often involved burial of decorative panels and brought about emphatic changes in the flow of traffic. The move was always in the direction of increased restriction of access and more regulated privacy as the city moved toward its ultimate collapse.

Another source of interpretation of the functions of such a palace complex is found in iconography, especially the painted decorative vessels of the Late Classic period. The archives made available by Justin Kerr (1989–2000) offer numerous examples of a variety of the functions of a royal court: the priest-lord receiving visitors both as captives and as lords or diplomats. Such scenes include the reception of tribute, a probable divination taking place at night by artificial light (Fig. 10), and a military event involving prisoners. All of these scenes apparently took place in palaces, including the use of throne benches upon which the receiving lord was seated. Such benches are found in many multiroomed palaces in the Central Acropolis, not just in separate throne buildings. Thus we can assume with confidence that the more complex buildings served multiple functions.

The emphasis in the scenes found on the painted vessels is different from that on public sculptures. The latter depicted the lord of the city as a warrior and conqueror (Fig. 8), often marking his important conquests. By contrast, the vessel scenes are much softer, most often depicting the lord as a scribe and diplomat. Apparently, their intended audiences were different. The lord as scribe was for private consumption, and the lord as warrior was for the public.

Fig. 11 Structure 5D-52, pre-excavation (i.e., 1959). This multistoried building may have served as a ceremonial temporary residence, probably as a men's retreat house.

At the Central Acropolis, the role of reception throne rooms underwent a marked change during the Late Classic period. Throne or reception rooms occur throughout the Acropolis within buildings of many functions, including those of royal residence (e.g., 5D-46) and included rooms in otherwise multifunctional buildings. During the Late Classic a new version of this function appears: the throne/reception building as a single-roomed structure built for the sole purpose of reception with the throne as its major feature. (Harrison 2001a). There are multiple examples of this type of structure around the Acropolis, and all are late in the stratigraphic sequence. This shift suggests that the functions of such rooms (e.g., judicial, tributary, diplomatic, ceremonial) came to be separated from the other more domestic functions of the palace as civilization moved in an upward spiral, separating home from government. Among the late throne structures are 5D-123, 5D-59, 5D-118, and the west addition of 5D-61. The separation of this function from the larger adjacent buildings was likely part of the generally late increase in security at the Acropolis.

Interpretation of hieroglyphic texts and iconography (cf. Coe and Kerr 1998) has opened the doors of perception more widely than years of digging could accomplish. However, archaeological evidence is required to corroborate these more esoteric interpretations. That they appear to complement each other is fortunate indeed for our understanding of the role of palaces in the Maya Classic.

But what of the other forty-two buildings, all called palaces, in the Central Acropolis? In the original analysis, a number of buildings were associated with residence of a different nature because many contained few of the physical attributes denoting residence. In some cases, specialized *temporary* residences, such as proposed for 5D-63 above, can be associated with differing functions, some religious, others secular. This provides a reasonable explanation for these structures. Types of temporary residence include training schools and retreat houses, an example of the latter being Structure 5D-52 (Fig. 11). It is difficult in ancient Maya culture to separate the religious from the secular, particularly when working with incomplete information derived from architectural attributes. The constant is that Maya *palace* architecture was nearly infinitely variable and supported a broad series of interconnected functions, summarized under the term *royal court*. Permanent residence was only one of these functions, and at the Central Acropolis of Tikal, it was a relatively rare function in a forty-six palace complex.

Group 10L-2 at Copán

Copán sits at the southeast corner of the Maya realm, planted in the foothills of the highlands, but sharing the Classic tradition of the lowlands. The valley was prized from earliest times. Burials of high-ranking individuals date to the end of the Early Preclassic, a Late Preclassic Copán valley boulder sculpture may show an early ruler, and inscriptions tell of kings in the Early Classic period. The beginning of a dynasty of sixteen rulers is recorded ca. 400. From the start these rulers wrapped themselves in the architectural styles, exotic furnishings, decorative imagery, literacy, and ideology of the Maya lowlands (Fash 2001; Fash, Williamson, Larios, and Palka 1992; Sharer, Miller, and Traxler 1992; Sharer, Fash, Sedat, Traxler, and Williamson 1999; Sharer, Traxler, et al. 1999). Architectural elements, funerary vessels, grave construction, and other elements in Early Classic Copán culture also showed strong ties to Teotihuacan (Sharer 2003), much as do high-status remains at Kaminaljuyú, Tikal, and other Early Classic lowland Maya sites.

The first regal structures of Yax K'uk' Mo and his successor rose from the floodplain of the Copán River early in the fifth century. The state buildings erected in the following 400 years rose steadily higher, one level atop another, to form the Copán Acropolis. (For the list of Copán kings, see Fash 2001: 79–81). Whether the concentration of royal architecture resulted from decisions to avoid occupying more agricultural land, from a desire to maintain continuity of use over sacred temples and tombs, or to create an imposing structural mass with least effort, the most important structures of the Copán kingdom were built atop one massive platform. The Acropolis, together with the huge plaza extending north from it and the buildings and monuments surrounding it constitute the Main Group. William Sanders and David Webster (1988: 530) call it *the royal compound* (Fig. 12).

During the first century or more of the dynasty, the *domestic* buildings of this royal compound were on the north side of the Acropolis. By 550, Robert Sharer (Sharer et al. 1992: 154; 1999: 248) believes, this courtyard group was abandoned, covered by fill of the next stage of the Acropolis, and the royal residential compound moved away. By 600 or earlier, members of the nobility were being buried in tombs just south of the Acropolis, in Group 10L-2, with rich furnishings appropriate to the royal family. The six known elite burials of this time in Group 10L-2 include the famous Copán Tomb 1 and Copán Tomb 2

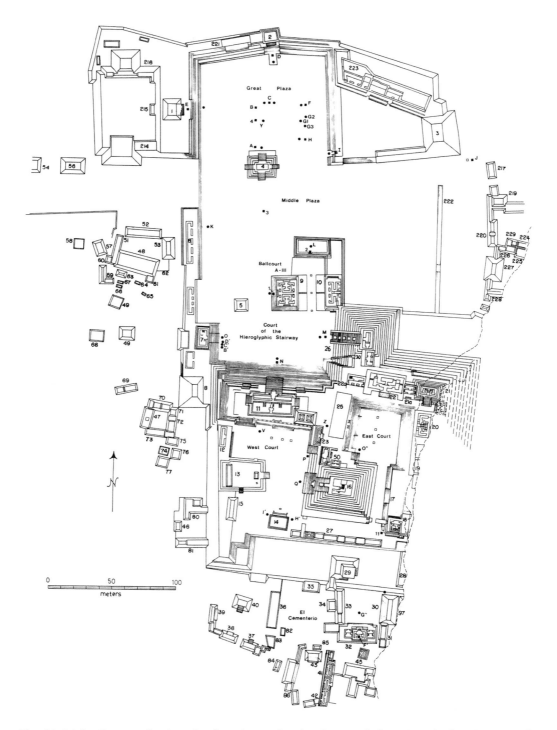

Fig. 12 Main Group of ruins, Copán: Acropolis, the Court of the Hieroglyphic Stairway, the Middle Plaza, the Great Plaza, Group 10L-2 (S), and surrounding buildings. Changes to Group 10L-2 that resulted from excavations between 1990 and 1994 are not depicted. After Fash 2001: 20, fig. 8. Courtesy of William Fash.

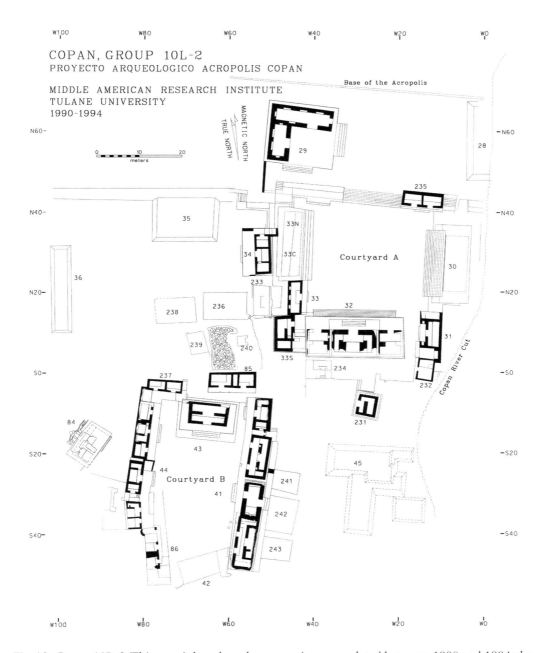

COPAN, GROUP 10L-2
PROYECTO ARQUEOLOGICO ACROPOLIS COPAN

MIDDLE AMERICAN RESEARCH INSTITUTE
TULANE UNIVERSITY
1990-1994

Base of the Acropolis

MAGNETIC NORTH
TRUE NORTH

Courtyard A

Courtyard B

Copan River Cut

Fig. 13 Group 10L-2. This map is based on the excavations completed between 1990 and 1994; the still-unexcavated Courtyard C is just off the map (W). Structure 10L-45, south of Courtyard A, has not been investigated since the late nineteenth century. The arrangement of the remaining court-yards suggests that at least one courtyard to the southeast of Courtyard A was washed away by the Copán River before 1935.

in Structures 10L-36 and 10L-38 (Fig. 13; Longyear 1952: 40–42). About fifty years later buildings were laid out around new courtyards (i.e., A, B; see Fig. 13) that were identified by inscriptions and iconography with the lineage of the founder of the Copán dynasty (Andrews and Fash 1992). Until the collapse of the central political authority at Copán ca. 820, this was the residence of at least part of Copán royalty (see Fig. 13). Yax Pasah, the sixteenth and final ruler in the dynasty, resided in the largest building on Courtyard A.

The buildings raised on the Acropolis help us to see and understand the Late Classic domestic compound within the larger context of how Copán's rulers and nobility used architecture to project their power and legitimize their rule. Most are far larger than the structures in the residential compound. The Temple of the Hieroglyphic Stairway, built by Ruler 13 (18 Rabbit) and his successor, presents the dynastic history of the site, portraying previous rulers as warriors and emphasizing war and sacrifice (Fash 1992; Fash et al. 1992). The sculpture of a smaller building attached to it emphasized death and dismemberment. Temple 22, 18 Rabbit's other major structure, is thought to have represented a sacred stone mountain with a cave where the ancestors lived. It has imagery on the interior building that placed the ruler at the center of the cosmos when he performed rituals (B. Fash 1992: 92–93; Fash 2001: 122–125; Freidel, Schele, and Parker 1993: 147–152; Trik 1939). Barbara and William Fash (1994) present evidence that Structures 10L-20 and 10L-21, once on the east side of the east courtyard but lost to the Copán River early in the twentieth century, were a prison and execution site.

Yax Pasah's two great buildings, Temples 11 and 16, have been compared in their form and iconography with 18 Rabbit's chief constructions (Fash 2001: 168–169; Schele and Freidel 1990: 322–328): the north side of Temple 11 as a huge cosmic frame and Temple 16 as a monument to the dynasty, whose members are depicted on Altar Q in front of it, with an even greater emphasis in Yax Pasah's temples on symbols of war and conquest. The south side of Temple 11 and the west courtyard, Mary Ellen Miller (1988) has argued, together create an "underwater" world, linking the living to the ancestral past. Structure 10L-22A (Fig. 14), with its adjacent dance platform, was a council house for the entire polity, depicting eight or nine permanent representatives from named places within the Copán polity (Fash, Fash, et al. 1992). The latest major building, 10L-18, was completed by Yax Pasah in 800 to contain his elaborate tomb (Becker and Cheek 1983; Fash 2001: 171). Although small compared with some of his earlier monuments, it was the most impressive tomb commissioned at Copán.

These Acropolis buildings, like the ball court and the open plazas with their huge inscribed portraits, were the public constructions of Copán rulers. They tied the living ruler and his privileged family to the supernatural world and to deified ancestral rulers of the Copán dynasty. They celebrated and justified the Classic Maya religious, social, and political order, thereby contributing to the well-being of the realm. The buildings of the king's residence, in contrast, were not public but rather a mixture of family and lineage houses and open spaces. They, too, combined ritual and administrative functions. Here were the dwellings of the ruler and *his* relatives.

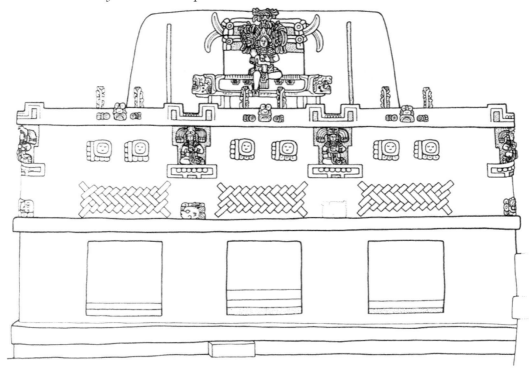

Fig. 14 Council (mat) house, reconstruction, Structure 10L-22A. Lords of the Copán kingdom, each seated above a glyph indicating a place name, ring the upper façade. A fish (*kanal*) glyph flanks the central door, facing south toward 10L-32-2nd, which is thought to have borne similar fish. From architectural data provided by Carlos Rudy Larios. Drawing and sculptural reconstruction by Barbara Fash (see Fash 1998: 251, fig. 12). Used with permission.

Group 10L-2 today consists of about twenty-five excavated buildings around Court-yards A and B (Andrews and Fash 1992; Bill n.d.; Doonan n.d.). Courtyard C just to the west and a large, complex structure south of Courtyard A have not been excavated. Because the Copán River washed away remains of Group 10L-2 east of Courtyard A before 1935, it is not known if the royal compound contained one or more additional courtyards to the east.

Yax Pasah, the last ruler in the Copán dynasty, built his house, Structure 10L-32, at the south end of Courtyard A (Fig. 15). It consists of a 2-m-high platform with a wide stair supporting three contiguous vaulted buildings. The middle edifice, resting on an upper platform accessed by five steps of massive cut stones, was dominated by a bench with side screens centered inside the wide door. On the bench in this throne room were two carved monuments. Altar F' refers to: (a) Yax Pasah "coming out in holiness" in 764, shortly after his accession; (b) a clay statue called "a gift of Chak," that he molded in 775; and (c) the "death" of this supernatural patron statue in 788 (Schele 1988, 1993, 1995; MacLeod 1989). The flanking lower buildings are a matched pair, with narrower doorways leading to a front room and wider openings leading to raised rear chambers, probably for storage or other domestic activities. The upper façade, front and back, bore full-round figures of a young

Fig. 15 House of Yax Pasah, sixteenth and final ruler of the Copán dynasty, Structure 10L-32, Group 10L-2. A broad six-step stair provides access to the first stage of the platform, which supports a second tier fronted by five steps of massive blocks. The topmost room has a broad central bench with side screens flanked by lateral chambers. Yax Pasah's bench had two carved altars. On the platform's lower stage are two identical buildings containing back rooms with raised floors. The Structure 10L-32-2nd tomb, which probably contained Yax Pasah's predecessor as lineage head, lies below the central steps in front of the 10L-32-1st doorway. Photo by William Fash, after consolidation, June 1991. Used with permission.

lord, probably Yax Pasah at the time of his accession (Fig. 16). He wore a water-lily head-dress, perhaps linking him to Chak, and was seated over a water-lily monster mask.

Inside 10L-32 are two earlier buildings, which may have been the houses of previous lineage heads. The preceding structure contained a tomb under the stair that was looted after the end of the Classic period, probably by Early Postclassic Ejar immigrants, who settled a few hundred meters to the south of Group 10L-2 (Fash 2001). The occupant was likely Yax Pasah's father, whose identity is unknown. The tomb probably did not contain the remain of Smoke Shell, the fifteenth ruler, for there is no indication that he was Yax Pasah's father. One of Yax Pasah's monuments identifies his mother as a woman from Palenque (Marcus 1992: 256–257; Schele and Grube 1987). Not one mentions his father, who was likely a noble unnamed in the Copán inscriptions. The tomb in Structure 10L-32-2nd, moreover, is less sumptuous than crypts of known Copán royalty.

Yax Pasah placed a cache under the center of his throne, a large, intact, carved fish (Fig. 17). It is similar to fragments found elsewhere in the upper fill of 10L-32, suggesting that the façade of the building that Yax Pasah replaced with his own bore numerous such fish. The meaning of the fish is indicated on the façade of Structure 10L-22A, the council house, which is thought to date to the years of the fourteenth ruler, Smoke Monkey

Fig. 16 Man wearing a water-lily headdress, reconstruction, upper façade, Structure 10L-32. These figures from the building's front and back may have been seated on a water-lily monster mask and were possibly representative of Yax Pasah, ca. 763, the year of his accession. Photo by Barbara Fash. Used with permission.

Fig. 17 Carved fish (CPN 2317) from the fill of Yax Pasah's bench, central room, Structure 10L-32-1st. Fragments of other fish and water-lily motifs, including two others from the bench, were found in the upper fill of Yax Pasah's house. They were probably from Structure 10L-32-2nd's façade (50 cm long x 28 cm high with a 48-cm-long armature).

(738–749; Fash, Fash, et al. 1992). One of the two place glyphs flanking its central doorway, facing south toward Yax Pasah's house, is a fish. Yax Pasah's *barrio*, and his family, were therefore represented on the Copán ruling council before the dedication of 10L-22A in 746, probably as far back as Ruler 12, Smoke Imix, who reigned from 628 to 695. Courtyards A and B of Group 10L-2 and the earliest set of buildings around them were laid out early in the years of Smoke Imix's rule or a few years earlier (Bill n.d.).

Yax Pasah's other structure on Courtyard A is Structure 10L-30, a 4-m-high platform, with a full-width stair similar to that of 10L-32 and with identical masonry. It supported no building and was probably used for dances and ceremonies, but with a smaller audience than might have been present on the Acropolis.

The other structures around Courtyard A predate Yax Pasah. Structures 10L-31 and 10L-33, both possibly residential, are among the earliest. Structure 10L-33, at the northwest corner of Yax Pasah's house, is a vaulted room with a C-shaped bench, a characteristic of domestic rooms, and three wall niches. The upper façade bore goggle-eye glyphs and variants of the "founder's" glyph, with which the resident family publicly claimed descent from Yax K'uk' Mo,' the founder of the Copán dynasty (Fash 1992: 101; Schele 1986, 1992). This building was contemporary with the earliest structure inside Yax Pasah's house (10L-32-3rd). An L-shaped addition of four vaulted rooms to the south of 10L-33 adjoined the earliest version of Yax Pasah's house. The new façades carried Mexican year signs, also associated with the ruling dynasty at Copán. An addition to the north side of 10L-33 created a long, high platform, probably for ritual displays and dances, that faces Yax Pasah's later ceremonial platform across the courtyard.

Structure 10L-31, just east of Yax Pasah's house, had a raised entry with small flat-roofed shrines at each side; a single vaulted room with a bench covers more than half of its floor space. The south exterior wall of 10L-31 bore a carved fish similar to those from 10L-32-2nd encountered in the fill of Yax Pasah's house. The sequence of floors in this part of Courtyard A indicates that 10L-31 was contemporary with 10L-32-3rd, the earliest building under Yax Pasah's house.

Just above Courtyard A is Structure 10L-29, a two-room, L-shaped, vaulted building that appears to have been a lineage shrine of the noble family that lived in Group 10L-2. Nikolai Grube, Linda Schele, and David Freidel call this a *waybil*, or a sleeping or dreaming place of the ancestors (Grube and Schele 1990; Houston and Stuart 1989; Schele 1993: 188–190, 441). Instead of benches, the two rooms contain eight or nine large wall niches, one of which is Ik-shaped (an inverted T), as in Copán tombs. One niche contained an intact pair of *Spondylus* shells when the vault collapsed. Burn marks on the floors inside show that offerings were repeatedly made in the corners and in the middle of the doorways.

Rectangular panels with a serpent head protruding from each corner were repeated ten times around the upper façade of 10L-29 (Fig. 18). At Palenque and Yaxchilán similar panels are called *ancestor cartouches* because they contain figures of royal ancestors. In the Terminal Classic at Chichén Itzá these serpent panels took the form of sun disks (Miller 1977; Robertson 1985: 25–31: figs. 112–138; Schele and Freidel 1990: 372, 393, 503).

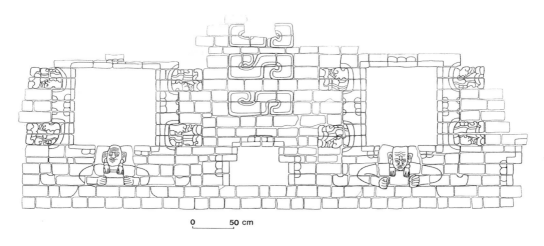

a

Fig. 18 Ancestral shrine for nobles in the lineage, reconstruction, upper west façade, Structure 10L-29, Group 10L-2: (a) a stone-by-stone reconstruction, showing only the sculptured stones with reasonably certain positions, and (b) a hypothetical configuration, where dotted motifs indicate alternative arrangements of the geometric stones that had fallen from the sunken panels. This building has been called a *waybil*, that is, a sleeping or dreaming place of the ancestors (Grube and Schele 1990; Schele 1993: 188–190, 441). The figures under its serpent panels may represent the lineage's patron deities. From an analysis by Carlos Rudy Larios. Drawings by Barbara Fash and Jodi Johnson. Used with permission.

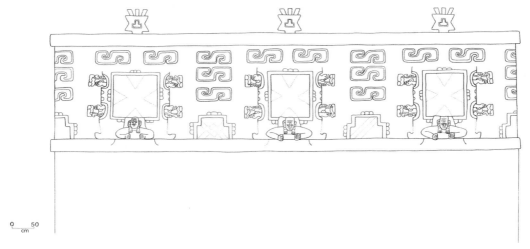

b

Fig. 19 Two-room shrine, north end of Courtyard B, Structure 10L-43, Group 10L-2. The two Late Classic buildings that formed the courtyard's original north end were designated for domestic use. 10L-43, later erected in front of them, had no sculpture, niches, or benches. A cave formation was cached inside under the floor, and a deer without a skull was buried behind the base of the rear wall. Like Structure 10L-29, the larger shrine above Courtyard A, it was neither renovated nor enlarged.

Barbara Fash (personal communication 1991) thinks the 10L-29 panels contained geometric designs, possibly kin signs. At the bottom of each panel were larger-than-life male deity heads with monkey features: wrinkled foreheads, prognathous lower faces, and large ears adorned with pendants. They resemble somewhat the monkey-men gods kneeling on the reviewing stand of 10L-11 in the west courtyard (Proskouriakoff 1946: 47–49) and the monkey-faced patron deity of noble scribes and artists described by Michael Coe (1977). These figures may have been patrons of the lineage that built this shrine. The noble family from Group 9N-8 in Las Sepulturas seems to have claimed such a relationship with a similar-appearing patron of scribes, whose image was found buried in Structure 9N-82 (Fash 1989: 67–71, fig. 45).

Courtyard A, then, was the residence of the ruler and previous heads of the lineage. The buildings surrounding it are shrines, dance and ceremonial platforms, and possible residences of important family members, all bearing sculptural motifs that reinforced the owners' status by displaying their royal ancestry and the supernatural underpinning of their earthly prominence. Courtyard B, in contrast, was surrounded by numerous residences as well as one important lineage building and shrine. All rooms on the north, west, and south sides of Courtyard B, to judge from their size and their benches, were domestic. A later shrine on a platform (10L-43), without benches, niches, or sculpture, is centered at the north end of the courtyard (Fig. 19).

Fig. 20 (On following pages) Structure 10L-41, Courtyard B, Group 10L-2 (N–S): (a) 10L-41A; (b) 10L-41B; (c) 10L-41C; and (d) 10L-41D. These separate but adjoining buildings atop a single plat-form have different interior arrangements, suggestive of different uses. This complex may have served as a lineage house for private rituals and larger ceremonies (10L-41B and C), audiences and administration (10L-41D), or warriors or priests in training; the building to the north, the latest (10L-41A), was possibly a residence for Yax Pasah.

Structure 10L-41 on the east is a line of four vaulted buildings on a 1-m-high plat-form (Andrews et al. 2003). Each building has an interior form different from the others, implying different uses (Fig. 20a–d). The central unit, 10L-41C, was for activities involving several individuals. It has doorways and stairs front and back, a niche and a wide plinth at one end, and no bench. 10L-41B, adjoining it on the north, contains a high, full-length bench against the back wall that occupied more than half of the room. The bench face contained four niches, and two large piers on the front of the bench support a double vault. The staggering of the two external doorways and the piers made the bench invisible from the outside. The south building, 10L-41D, has a bench with side and partial front walls, flanked by side chambers with niches. It is similar to Yax Pasah's throne room in 10L-32 but rendered more private by the staggering of external doorways and the front bench walls. Structure 10L-41A, at the north end, is a later three-room domestic structure that was built about the same time as Yax Pasah's house, possibly for a relative. Like many constructions on Courtyards A and B, 10L-41 was enlarged twice. Each time the individual buildings were rebuilt with a similar form, implying the persistence of distinct functions.

This complex structure has no exact parallels in the Maya area. Vaguely similar multiroom range structures at Copán and elsewhere have been suggested to be men's, youths, or priests' houses, and lineage administrative complexes. As an example, Structure 10L-223, off the northeast corner of the great plaza at Copán, is a long, four-room range structure. Charles Cheek and Mary Spink (1986) suggest that the rooms included a priestly residence, a dormitory for students or for men before ceremonies, a sweatbath, and another room for ritual purification or something similar. In 10L-41, the latest vaulted building (i.e., 10L-41A) was a noble residence, one (i.e., 10L-41D) was perhaps both a residence and a locus of ritual and administrative activities; the other two were for ritual and possibly administrative uses. Among the sculptured motifs on its façade were Tlaloc goggle eyes and Venus glyphs, hinting at Tlaloc-Venus warfare and use by warriors.

The Quiché "big houses" at Utatlán, with their many entrances and columns, may be comparable. Robert Carmack (1981: 287–290) believes these were "primarily administra-tive centers for the major lineages," suggesting that the colonnaded halls at Mayapán served the same purpose (1981: 385). Structure 10L-41 at Copán, situated near the center of Group 10L-2, was likely a multifunction ritual and administrative building used primarily by Yax Pasah's lineage, rather than by the entire Copán polity.

Courtyards A and B show a range in room size and quality, especially in domestic rooms. Rooms on Courtyard A are the largest, suggesting higher status for those who lived nearest the ruler. The smallest and most crudely constructed are on the southwest edge of

a

b

c

d

Courtyard B (Fig. 21). Scattered around the group are other small buildings and platforms without superstructures on them that show modest construction expense or were damaged and reused by individuals of lower status. These, in contrast to the simple dwellings on the southwest side of Courtyard B, which were part of the original courtyard layout, may have been the houses of retainers or clients, rather than low-ranking members of the noble lineage.

Archaeological and iconographic evidence points to Yax Pasah's residential compound as the home of at least one royal lineage throughout the Late Classic at Copán. Remains in this group contrast sharply with the royal monuments and architecture on the Acropolis. The buildings, stelae, and altars above were meant to impress inhabitants of and visitors to the Copán realm. The platforms, buildings, courtyards, and inscribed monuments below in the royal residence are smaller and more confined. They were, if not private, at least intended for a limited group affiliated with Yax Pasah's *barrio*. More than half of the buildings investigated were living quarters. The rest appear to have been for lineage ritual, display, audiences, and administration rather than legitimation of the dynasty and commemoration of events in the rulers' lives.

It is the special-purpose buildings, such as the lineage shrine and the four-building domestic, administrative, and ritual complex on the east side of Courtyard B, that set this group apart from other high-status residential complexes at Copán. Some of the courtyard groups in the Las Sepulturas zone, a few hundred meters northeast of the Acropolis, were at least as extensive, with a few buildings as large as those in this royal compound (Webster 1989; Webster, Fash, Widmer, and Zeleznik 1998; Webster and Inomata this volume). But they do not have the range of structures dedicated to lineage ritual, ceremonial display, and administration evident in Group 10L-2.

The history of the Late Classic royal residential compound at Copán—the palace—is relevant to the political organization and the nature of rulership and the state at that site, and at other Classic Maya sites. William Sanders (1989: 102) has set forth a comprehensive hierarchical model of Copán sociopolitical organization that postulates four general levels of Copán society: (a) extended family households incorporated into (b) lineages of varying sizes that, in turn, were part of (c) maximal lineages headed by a noble class. At the top was a (d) royal lineage from which was drawn the king. The archaeology and inscriptions of Group 10L-2 at Copán, however, suggest that there was no single royal lineage and that rulership rotated among more than one noble group. Yax Pasah, the sixteenth and final ruler in the Copán dynasty and the head of the (maximal?) lineage in Group 10L-2, apparently was not the son of the fifteenth ruler, Smoke Shell. Yax Pasah built his own house over the dwelling and the tomb of the previous lineage head, who must have been his father, and this individual was not Smoke Shell. Although it is not known where Smoke Shell was buried, the tomb in 10L-32-2nd is too small to have been the final resting place of a Copán king. Years of excavation in this area have not uncovered any of Smoke Shell's inscribed monuments; all of the personal monuments belong to Yax Pasah. If Smoke Shell had been Yax Pasah's father and had lived here, it is inconceivable that all of his monuments would have disappeared. These circumstances lead to the conclusion that after the death of Smoke Shell, rulership rotated to the lineage that resided in Group 10L-2.

a

Fig. 21 Structures 10L-44C (a) and 10L-86 (b), Courtyard B, Group 10L-2. These two buildings, across the paved courtyard's south end, face Structure 10L-41. Unlike the elaborate vaulted and sculptured buildings around Courtyard A and much of Courtyard B, these buildings, of poor-quality masonry, had perishable walls and pole-and-thatch roofs. Like most other courtyard structures, they were enlarged from time to time. In their final construction stage, they provided housing for lower-status individuals.

b

Several early buildings in Group 10L-2 proclaim that their owners were descendants of Yax K'uk' Mo', the founder of the dynasty, implying that the nobles who lived around Courtyard A had the right to rule, regardless of whether they had maintained power. The early buildings that stated this claim were almost certainly commissioned during the reign of Smoke Imix (ruled 628–695), the twelfth ruler. No strong evidence indicates that Smoke Imix or the three following rulers came from or lived in Group 10L-2, and so it appears that a lineage descended from Yax K'uk' Mo' that resided in the shadow of the Acropolis was out of power for most of the Late Classic, until the accession of Yax Pasah.

The model of political integration implied by this alternation of rulership requires a small number of powerful, competing lineages, rather than one royal lineage. The changes in ruling families, political upheavals, and conflict documented at other sites argue that this model better serves the Maya context.

René Viel (1999), in a study of Late Classic Copán iconography and elite political organization, has argued that the iconography of Altar Q, in front of Temple 16, and of the Temple 11 bench indicate the existence of at least two functional groups, probably corporate descent groups, which he calls *priests* and *warriors*. Each ruler at Copán had a coruler from the other group, so that power was balanced, although the preponderance of authority (i.e., ruler) belonged to one descent group during most of the Early Classic, and to the other during most of the Late Classic until Yax Pasah ascended to the throne in 763.

Although Viel states that this is a working model and although there is no independent evidence that his interpretation of the iconography is correct, his scheme fits our reconstruction of the political history of Group 10L-2. The founder, Yax K'uk' Mo', belonged to—and perhaps established—Viel's first descent group, and the builders of Group 10L-2 claimed descent from him. This group lost power during the reigns of Rulers 12, 13, and 15 until Yax Pasah, of Yax K'uk' Mo's lineage, but regained it for the final half-century before the collapse of central political authority and the subsequent abandonment of the site.

Viel thinks that Ruler 14, Smoke Monkey (ruled 738–749) was a member of Yax K'uk' Mo's group. If so, he may have come from Group 10L-2. Despite a lack of epigraphic and archaeological evidence that he was from this group, Smoke Monkey likely commissioned Structure 10L-22A, the council house, which shows the same fish–place glyph over its central doorway that is thought to have been a conspicuous and important element in the roughly contemporary façade of Structure 10L-32-2nd, the house of Yax Pasah's predecessor as lineage head. The emphasis on this toponym in these buildings may indicate a special tie between Ruler 14 and the home of Yax K'uk' Mo's descent group.

Conclusions

How well does the concept of *palace* work at Tikal and Copán? If the term is useful at these Classic Maya sites, how does a palace at one resemble a palace at the other? Obvious differences exist between the two. Tikal was a much larger city than Copán and had greater time depth. This was reflected in the greater complexity of the Central Acropolis compared with Group 10L-2 at Copán. This complexity was expressed in the vertical variability at Tikal: buildings with multiple stories and courtyards of more than one level. The growth of the Central Acropolis appears generally not to have begun with courtyards. Rather these courtyards developed through time in conjunction with several massive construction projects, such as in Courtyards 2 and 3. Both courtyards were created at different times as part of enormous additions to earlier buildings.

At Copán, there is a coherence to those parts of Group 10L-2 that have been excavated. Individual buildings do not stand alone but rather are part of a functioning whole. If we use the term *palace* for the ruler's residence at Copán, we must recognize that the spatial organization of the Maya palace was different from that of a European Palace. Instead of thinking of one large, often enclosed architectural complex, we should understand the Maya palace at Copán to include the *entire* residential compound, with several courtyards, dozens of houses reflecting widely different levels of wealth and status; special purpose constructions, such as dance and ceremonial platforms, elaborate shrines to lineage ancestors, and simple shrines; multifunction buildings, including one complex of four contiguous buildings on a single platform (i.e., 10L-41A-D) that served domestic (perhaps temporarily), administrative, and ritual purposes for the ruler's lineage; and perhaps hundreds of occupants. At the center of the Copán palace was Structure 10L-32, Yax Pasah's house, with his throne room and attached domestic or storage spaces.

There are a number of interesting contrasts between Copán and Tikal. More than the verticality of the Tikal complex separates the two. Rather the difference is between a *palace compound*, as described in Group 10L-2 at Copán, contrasted with a *complex of palaces*, as described for the Central Acropolis. The basic difference lies in the way that a set of multiple functions is associated with architecture at the two sites. In Copán, the set of functions is spread over a series of separate buildings: a palace compound. At the Central Acropolis, the same set of functions centers on a single building that was part of a complex of multifunctional buildings. Although not all buildings exhibit the palace function set, those that include the function of royal residence did contain the entire set. It is too soon to generalize that this was always so at Tikal. In fact, it is strongly suspected that further analysis will prove a temporal change in the distribution of the multiple functions of a royal household, possibly the distribution exhibited in Group 10L-2 at Copán. Single structures in the Central Acropolis parallel the European model—though not perfectly—but much more closely than at Copán. The late appearance of throne room structures as separate entities at Tikal is an example of change toward the Copán model. Whether this contrast in architectonic distribution of functional sets as related to royal residence and the royal court has a regional basis or is the result of other factors is a matter for speculation, which deserves further attention.

Acknowledgments The University of Pennsylvania Museum sponsored work in the Central Acropolis as part of the greater Tikal Project from 1962 through 1967. Project directors during this period included Robert E. Dyson Jr. and William R. Coe III. The Central Acropolis excavations were directed by Peter D. Harrison, who wishes to thank Miguel

Orrego C., Ismael Tercero, Merle Greene Robertson, Wilbur Pearson, among others, and nearly one hundred Guatemalan excavators for their contributions in the field. Illustrations in more recent times have been contributed by Margaret Rossiter, Willam R. Coe III, and Amalia Kenward. Their work is included in this paper.

The field research by Tulane University at Copán reported here took place from 1990 to 1994 as a part of the Copán Acropolis Archaeological Project directed by William L. Fash, with the permission of and supervision by the Honduran Institute of Anthropology and History (IHAH). The Copán research was supported by grants from the National Geographic Society, the U.S. Agency for International Development through the IHAH, and the Middle American Research Institute at Tulane, and by fellowships from the National Science Foundation and the Fulbright Foundation. Andrews is grateful to Bill Fash, Barb Fash, Bob Sharer, Ricardo Agurcia, Rudy Larios, David Sedat, the late Linda Schele, Joyce Marcus, Oscar Cruz, Fernando López, Kathe Lawton, David Stuart, Jim Aimers, Moncho Guerra, many graduate students from Tulane and other institutions, and all the excavators, illustrators, and technicians from IHAH and Copán Ruinas for help and friendship through the years.

The authors wish to thank both Dumbarton Oaks for the use of its magnificent facilities and the organizers of the symposium, Susan Toby Evans and Joanne Pillsbury for allowing us to present our data and insights to our colleagues.

Bibliography

Andrews, E. Wyllys, and Barbara W. Fash

1992   Continuity and Change in a Royal Maya Residential Complex at Copan. *Ancient Mesoamerica* 3: 63–88.

Andrews, E. Wyllys, Jodi L. Johnson, William F. Doonan, Gloria E. Everson, Kathryn E. Sampeck, and Harold E. Starratt

2003   A Multipurpose Structure in the Late Classic Palace at Copan. In *Maya Palaces and Elite Residences: An Interdisciplinary Approach* (Jessica Joyce Christie, ed.): 67–97. University of Texas Press, Austin.

Becker, Marshall J., and Charles D. Cheek

1983   La Estructura 10L-18. In *Introducción a la arqueología de Copán, Honduras*, vol. 2 (Claude F. Baudez, ed.): 381–500. Proyecto Arqueológico Copán. Secretaría de Estado, Despacho de Cultura y Turismo, Tegucigalpa.

Bill, Cassandra R.

n.d.   Patterns of Variation and Change in Dynastic-Period Ceramics at Copán, Honduras. Ph.D. dissertation, Department of Anthropology, Tulane University, New Orleans, La., 1997.

Carmack, Robert M.

1981   *The Quiché Mayas of Utatlán: The Evolution of a Highland Guatemala Kingdom.* University of Oklahoma Press, Norman.

Cheek, Charles D., and Mary L. Spink

1986   Excavaciones en el Grupo 3, Estructura 223 (Operación VII). In *Excavaciones en el área urbana de Copán*, tomo 1 (William T. Sanders, ed.): 27–154. Proyecto Arqueológico Copán (segunda fase). Secretaría de Cultura y Turismo, Instituto Hondureño de Antropología e Historia, Tegucigalpa.

Coe, Michael D.

1977   Supernatural Patrons of Maya Scribes and Artists. In *Social Process in Maya Prehistory: Studies in Honour of Sir Eric Thompson* (Norman Hammond, ed.): 327–347. Academic Press, London and New York.

Coe, Michael D., and Justin Kerr

1998   *The Art of the Maya Scribe.* Abrams, New York.

Coe, William R.

1990   *Tikal Report 14: Excavations in the Great Plaza, North Terrace and North Acropolis of Tikal*, 6 vols. University of Pennsylvania Museum, Philadelphia.

COGGINS, CLEMENCY CHASE

    n.d.   Painting and Drawing Styles at Tikal: An Historical and Iconographic
               Reconstruction. Ph.D. dissertation, Dept. of Fine Arts, Harvard University,
               Cambridge, Mass., 1975.

DOONAN, WILLIAM F.

    n.d.   The Artifacts of Group 10L-2, Copán, Honduras: Variation in Material Culture and
               Behavior in a Royal Residential Compound. Ph.D. dissertation, Department of
               Anthropology, Tulane University, New Orleans, La., 1996.

FASH, BARBARA W.

    1992   Late Classic Architectural Sculpture Themes in Copán. *Ancient Mesoamerica* 3: 89–
               104.

FASH, BARBARA W., AND WILLIAM L. FASH

    1994   Copán Temple 20 and the House of Bats. In *Seventh Palenque Round Table 1989*
               (Merle Greene Robertson and Virginia M. Fields, eds.): 61–67. Pre-Columbian Art
               Research Institute, San Francisco.

FASH, BARBARA W., WILLIAM L. FASH, SHEREE LANE, CARLOS RUDY LARIOS, LINDA SCHELE, JEFFREY
STOMPER, AND DAVID STUART

    1992   Investigations of a Classic Maya Council House at Copán, Honduras. *Journal of Field*
               Archaeology 19: 419–442.

FASH, WILLIAM L.

    1989   The Sculptural Façade of Structure 9N-82: Content, Form, and Significance. In *The*
               House of the Bacabs, Copán, Honduras (David Webster, ed.): 41–72. Studies in Pre-
               Columbian Art & Archaeology no. 29, Dumbarton Oaks, Washington, D.C.

    1998   Dynastic Architectural Programs: Intention and Design in Classic Maya Buildings at
               Copán and Other Sites. In *Function and Meaning in Classic Maya Architecture* (Stephen
               D. Houston, ed.): 223–270. Dumbarton Oaks, Washington, D.C.

    2001   *Scribes, Warriors and Kings: The City of Copán and the Ancient Maya* (rev. ed.). Thames
               and Hudson, New York.

FASH, WILLIAM L., RICHARD V. WILLIAMSON, CARLOS RUDY LARIOS, AND JOEL PALKA

    1992   The Hieroglyphic Stairway and Its Ancestors. *Ancient Mesoamerica* 3: 105–115.

FREIDEL, DAVID A., LINDA SCHELE, AND JOY PARKER

    1993   *Maya Cosmos: Three Thousand Years on the Shaman's Path*. Morrow, New York.

GRUBE, NIKOLAI, AND LINDA SCHELE

    1990   Royal Gifts to Subordinate Lords. *Copán Note* 87. Copán Mosaics Project, Austin,
               Texas, and the Instituto Hondureño de Antropología e Historia, Tegucigalpa.

HALL, ALICE J.

    1975   A Traveller's Tale of Ancient Tikal. *National Geographic* 148(6): 799–811.

HAMMOND, NORMAN (ED.)

1991   *Cuello, an Early Maya Community in Belize.* Cambridge University Press, Cambridge.

HARRISON, PETER D.

1999   *The Lords of Tikal, Rulers of an Ancient Maya City.* Thames and Hudson, London.

2000   Poder centralizado en Tikal: El crecimiento de la Acrópolis Central. In *XIV Simposio de Investigaciones Arqueológicas en Guatemala* (J. P. Laporte, J. S. de Suasnavar, and B. Arroyo, eds.): 233–245. Ministerio de Cultura y Deportes, Instituto de Antropología e Historia, and Asociación Tikal, Guatemala City, Guatemala.

2001a   Thrones and Throne Structures in the Central Acropolis of Tikal as an Expression of the Royal Court. In *Royal Courts of the Ancient Maya*, vol. 2 (T. Inomata and S. Houston, eds.): 74–101. Westview, Boulder, Colo.

2001b   The Central Acropolis of Tikal. In *Tikal: Dynasties, Foreigners and Affairs of State* (J. A. Sabloff, ed.): 171–206. School of American Research, Santa Fe, N.M.

2003   Palaces of the Royal Court of Tikal. In *Maya Palaces and Elite Residences* (Jessica Joyce Christie, ed.): 98–119. University of Texas Press, Austin.

n.d.   The Central Acropolis, Tikal, Guatemala: A Preliminary Study of the Functions of its Structural Components during the Late Classic Period. Ph.D dissertation, Department of Anthropology, University of Pennsylvania, Philadelphia, 1970.

HOUSTON, STEPHEN D., AND DAVID STUART

1989   *The* Way *Glyph: Evidence for "Co-Essences" Among the Classic Maya.* Research Reports on Ancient Maya Writing 30. Center for Maya Research, Washington, D.C.

INOMATA, TAKESHI, AND STEPHEN D. HOUSTON (EDS.)

2001   *Royal Courts of the Ancient Maya*, 2 vols. Westview, Boulder, Colo.

KERR, JUSTIN

1989–2000   *The Maya Vase Book*, 6 vols. Kerr Associates, New York.

LONGYEAR, JOHN M., III

1952   *Copán Ceramics: A Study of Southeastern Maya Pottery.* Publication 597. Carnegie Institution of Washington, Washington, D.C.

MacLEOD, BARBARA

1989   The Text of Altar F': Further Considerations. *Copán Note* 52. Copán Mosaics Project, Austin, Texas, and the Instituto Hondureño de Antropología e Historia, Tegucigalpa.

MARCUS, JOYCE

1992   *Mesoamerican Writing Systems: Propaganda, Myth, and History in Four Ancient Civilizations.* Princeton University Press, Princeton, N.J.

MILLER, ARTHUR G.

1977   "Captains of the Itza": Unpublished Mural Evidence from Chichén Itzá. In *Social Process in Maya Prehistory: Studies in Honour of Sir Eric Thompson* (Norman Hammond, ed.): 197–225. Academic Press, London.

MILLER, MARY ELLEN

1988   The Meaning and Function of the Main Acropolis, Copan. In *The Southeast Classic Maya Zone* (Elizabeth Hill Boone and Gordon R. Willey, eds.): 149–194. Dumbarton Oaks, Washington, D.C.

PROSKOURIAKOFF, TATIANA

1946   *An Album of Maya Architecture*. Publication 558. Carnegie Institution of Washington, Washington, D.C.

ROBERTSON, MERLE GREENE

1985   *The Sculpture of Palenque*, vol. 3: *The Late Buildings of the Palace*. Princeton University Press, Princeton, N.J.

SANDERS, WILLIAM T.

1989   Household, Lineage, and State at Eighth-Century Copan, Honduras. In *The House of the Bacabs, Copan, Honduras* (David L. Webster, ed.): 89–105. Studies in Pre-Columbian Art and Archaeology 29. Dumbarton Oaks, Washington, D.C.

SANDERS, WILLIAM T., AND DAVID L. WEBSTER

1988   The Mesoamerican Urban Tradition. *American Anthropologist* 90: 521–546.

SCHELE, LINDA

1986   The Founders of Lineages at Copán and Other Maya Sites. *Copán Note* 8. Copán Mosaics Project, Austin, Texas, and the Instituto Hondureño de Antropología e Historia, Tegucigalpa.

1988   Altar F and the Structure 32. *Copán Note* 46. Copán Mosaics Project, Austin, Texas, and the Instituto Hondureño de Antropología e Historia, Tegucigalpa.

1992   The Founders of Lineages at Copán and Other Maya Sites. *Ancient Mesoamerica* 3: 135–144.

1993   A Reexamination of U-Yak'-Chak. *Copán Note* 111. Copán Acropolis Archaeological Project, Austin, Texas, and the Instituto Hondureño de Antropología e Historia, Tegucigalpa.

1995   The Texts of Group 10L-2: A New Interpretation. *Copán Note* 118. Copán Acropolis Archaeological Project, Austin, Texas, and the Instituto Hondureño de Antropología e Historia, Tegucigalpa.

SCHELE, LINDA, AND DAVID A. FREIDEL

1990   *A Forest of Kings: The Untold Story of the Ancient Maya*. Morrow, New York.

SCHELE, LINDA, AND NIKOLAI GRUBE

1987   The Brother of Yax-Pac. *Copán Note* 20. Copán Mosaics Project, Austin, Texas, and the Instituto Hondureño de Antropología e Historia, Tegucigalpa.

SHARER, ROBERT J.

2003   Founding Events and Teotihuacan Connections at Copán, Honduras. In *Teotihuacan and the Maya: Reinterpreting Early Classic Interaction*, (Geoffrey E. Braswell, ed.): 143–165. University of Texas Press, Austin.

SHARER, ROBERT J., WILLIAM L. FASH, DAVID W. SEDAT, LOA P. TRAXLER, AND RICHARD WILLIAMSON

1999   Continuities and Contrasts in Early Classic Architecture of Central Copan. In *Mesoamerican Architecture as a Cultural Symbol* (Jeff Karl Kowalski, ed.): 220–249. Oxford University Press, New York and Oxford.

SHARER, ROBERT J., JULIA C. MILLER, AND LOA P. TRAXLER

1992   Evolution of Classic Period Architecture in the Eastern Acropolis, Copan. *Ancient Mesoamerica* 3: 145–159.

SHARER, ROBERT J., LOA P. TRAXLER, DAVID W. SEDAT, ELLEN E. BELL, MARCELLO A. CANUTO, AND CHRISTOPHER POWELL

1999   Early Classic Architecture beneath the Copan Acropolis: A Research Update. *Ancient Mesoamerica* 10: 3–23.

STUART, DAVID

n.d.   K'inich Yax K'uk' Mo' and the Early History of Copán. A paper presented at a symposium entitled "Understanding Early Classic Copán," at the 65th Annual Meeting of the Society for American Archaeology, Philadelphia, April 2000.

TRIK, AUBREY S.

1939   Temple XXII at Copán. *Contributions to American Anthropology and History* 509: 87–103. Carnegie Institution of Washington, Washington, D.C.

VIEL, RENÉ H.

1999   The Pectorals of Altar Q and Structure 11: An Interpretation of the Political Organization at Copán, Honduras. *Latin American Antiquity* 10: 377–399.

WEBSTER, DAVID L.

1989   The House of the Bacabs: Its Social Context. In *The House of the Bacabs, Copan, Honduras* (David L. Webster, ed.): 5–40. Studies in Pre-Columbian Art and Archaeology 29. Dumbarton Oaks, Washington, D.C.

WEBSTER, DAVID L., BARBARA W. FASH, RANDOLPH WIDMER, AND SCOTT ZELEZNIK

1998   The Skyband Group: Investigation of a Classic Maya Elite Residential Complex at Copan, Honduras. *Ancient Mesoamerica* 25: 319–343.

Identifying Subroyal Elite Palaces at Copán and Aguateca

David Webster

PENNSYLVANIA STATE UNIVERSITY

Takeshi Inomata

UNIVERSITY OF ARIZONA

Dumbarton Oaks was a singularly appropriate place to hold a comparative confer-ence on New World palaces. The surroundings are a reminder that the rich, the powerful, and the influential are different from the rest of us, not least in the palatial scale and varied facilities of their residences. Nor is this an ethnocentric observa-tion: In every well-documented complex society, the privileged distinguish themselves, conduct their affairs effectively, and make their lives agreeable by enhancing their domestic arrangements.

Our concern in this paper is Maya palaces, and particularly those of the lowland Classic Maya between ca. 600 and 900 A.D. More specifically, we address how such settle-ment features can be identified archaeologically and analyzed by comparing excavated palace precincts at Copán, Honduras, and Aguateca, Guatemala (Fig. 1).

Maya Palaces: Issues and Definitions

What does the term *palace* mean? We prefer a broad and simple definition: *Palaces are the residences of individuals of wealth or high social rank, along with their families and retinues, and they include facilities appropriate to the ritual, political, recreational, and economic functions of elite households and individuals as foci of social power.* We do not restrict the concept of palace to royal establishments but apply the term also to those of lesser elites. Nor do we assume that everyone who was important lived in palatial residences or that those who did were of high status. Moreover, palaces often include facilities that do not fulfill residential functions in the strict sense of the word.

Palaces are not only interesting in their own right, but as barometers of social differ-entiation, inequality, and political evolution as Lewis Henry Morgan realized at the very dawn of American anthropology. Morgan (1876) wrote a famous essay, since nicknamed

Fig. 1 Map of the Maya Lowlands, showing locations of Copán and Aguateca

"Montezuma's Dinner," that was essentially an early exercise in what we would today call deconstructionism. He argued, among other things, that when Hernán Cortés and his soldiers first entered the Mexica capital of Tenochtitlan in 1519 they were trapped by their European preconceptions into identifying as great royal palaces what were merely multiroomed apartment houses. According to Morgan, no New World people ever achieved a level of organization more complex than that of egalitarian tribal confederations. If there were no kings, or princes, or nobles, neither could there be palaces, so the Spainards were just plain deluded.

Our own summer seminar and the papers in this symposium volume show how wrong-headed Morgan was in his conceptions of native New World societies, while reminding us that his central evolutionary logic was not entirely off the mark. Where palaces are present, they can tell us something about how elite individuals or groups were organized, how they behaved, how they thought about the world, how they related to the larger society, and sometimes about specific historical events. Flannery (1998) recently included palaces as important elements in his review of the archaeological "footprints" of early state institutions.

The concept of *palace* has a long and convoluted history in Maya archaeology. Sixteenth-century Spaniards encountered impressive household facilities in both highland and lowland Maya communities. In one of the earliest commentaries, Cortés, noted that in Yucatan:

> There are houses belonging to certain men of rank which are very cool and have many rooms, for we have seen as many as five courtyards in a single house, and the rooms around them [are] very well laid out, each man having a private room. Inside there are also wells and water tanks and rooms for slaves and servants of which they have many. Each of these chieftains has in front of the entrance to his house a very large courtyard, and some two or three or four [of the houses] raised up very high with steps up to them and all very well built" (Cortés 1986: 30, 35).

Houses of such lords were usually divided into front and back sets of rooms. Front rooms were elegantly decorated and were the more "public" spaces of the house, where apparently disputes were settled and business of various kinds was transacted (Landa 1941: 87). Shrines were also maintained in elite houses, and remains of illustrious ancestors were kept for ritual purposes. When lords left their houses, they were often accompanied by sizable retinues, suggesting that considerable numbers of lesser relatives, officials, dependents, or retainers also lived with them, or at least spent much time at the elite residential precincts. Palaces were built using the labor of commoners and tended to cluster in the centers of larger settlement systems.

As Kowalski (1987) points out, Spanish observers early on began to use the word *palacio* to describe such settlement features, no doubt because functionally equivalent household facilities, albeit differently organized, characterized the contemporary European societies they knew. Two important dimensions of these early Spanish descriptions stand out: (a) as Cortés's comment makes clear, the inhabitants or situational attendants of elaborate house complexes were numerous and included individuals of different social ranks and (b) possession of impressive household facilities was not just the prerogative of rulers, but generally of people of rank and wealth. Interestingly, the first explorers of Yucatan left no descriptions of particularly large and elaborate royal palaces. It was just these kinds of places they later encountered in Central Mexico and described in the grandiose terms that so exercised Morgan. The less differentiated palaces of sixteenth-century Yucatan are probably, in Flannery's terms, a good measure of the comparative complexity, wealth, and political centralization of the Postclassic Maya and Aztecs.

But is it justified to project sixteenth-century Maya patterns back into the Classic period? The ways archaeologists have wrestled with this question reflect larger implicit or explicit conceptions of the nature of ancient Maya society and settlement. On the first night of their visit to Palenque in 1840, John Lloyd Stephens wrote that he and his party slept in the palace of a long-dead king (Stephens 1949 [1841]: 242). Early Mayanists like Stephens not only adopted the *palacio* usage from the Spanish, but also clearly thought that the Classic Maya must have resembled other ancient civilizations in fundamental ways. Their use of the palace concept is partly rooted in this comparative assumption. During the exploratory period of Maya archaeology, the label *palace* (or sometimes simply *house*) became attached to large masonry structures that were set on low platforms and that usually consisted of linear, multichambered arrangements of rooms, often with regular, modular floorplans and sometimes with more than one story.

As the theocratic model of Classic society gained acceptance in the 1920s, this comparative perspective was largely abandoned. Archaeologists continued to use the label *palace* as a purely descriptive term—that is, a default category for structures whose uses were unclear. There were no lords and kings, so there were no *palaces* in even the most general Western sense of the word.

Since 1960, many lines of evidence have undermined this theocratic perspective. The Classic Maya have been transformed from an essentially prehistoric culture to one that can be comprehended on the basis of its own texts, and inscriptions are heavily bolstered by ever more sophisticated archaeological and iconographic research. Texts provide us with the names of rulers, their families, and their attendant courtiers, and Maya art is replete with what we now know to be palace images. If by palaces we mean the residences of wealthy, powerful people of rank, then the Maya had palaces, just as such people did in all other preindustrial complex societies.

Subroyal Palaces

Royal palaces that can be plausibly connected with specific Maya kings or dynasties have long been known for Palenque, Tikal, Uxmal, and other Lowland Maya centers. Although we briefly describe one probable royal palace under excavation at Aguateca, our main theme is subroyal elite households below the level of rulers' palaces.

By *subroyal* we are not implying that these elites lacked connections by descent, marriage, or other affiliations with rulers, but simply that they situationally or permanently were excluded from the highest political office, and so required household facilities apart from royal ones. Residences of the nobles who formed the connective political tissues of Classic Maya polities promise to provide essential data on the internal workings of Classic political systems. Unfortunately and surprisingly, comparatively little extensive excavation, as opposed to mapping or test trenching, has traditionally been focused on remains of such households.

Gair Tourtellot (1993: 230, 232) points out that Mayanists still find it difficult to answer the questions "Where do elite people reside and how many were there? [After surveying currently available settlement data evidence, he concluded that we] have severe problems when we want to identify the elite on the ground." The most important of the problems he identifies are (a) recognizing elite residences using surface architectural traces; (b) associating textual information with elite residences; (c) relating known or suspected elite residences at particular centers to a larger universe of well-documented, contemporaneous settlement; (d) assessing the functional and demographic implications of specialized structures/rooms within elite residential compounds; and (e) explaining the variable configurations and locations of elite residences at major centers.

Only systematic, extensive, horizontal exposures of multistructure elite residences carried out within the context of mature, regional-scale settlement projects can effectively address these problems. Two such sets of excavations from Copán and Aguateca are compared and contrasted below. Each demonstrates conclusively the presence of palaces, and each has its own strengths and weaknesses, illustrating how archaeologists can resolve the issues raised by Tourtellot.

Copán

Copán, located in a beautiful river valley in western Honduras, is one of the most celebrated Classic Maya centers, and the capital of a major polity between ca. 426 and 820. Beginning in 1975, archaeologists from numerous institutions have investigated not only the Copán Main Group (Fig. 2)—the seat of the royal dynasty—but also lesser elite establishments (Ashmore 1991; Willey et al. 1994). Household archaeology was an especially important component of the Pennsylvania State University projects between 1980 and 1997, and many excavations focused on Classic period subroyal palaces, most notably Groups 9N-9 and 8N-11. (For background, see Melissa Diamanti [n.d.]; Andrea Gerstle [n.d.]; Julia Hendon [n.d.]; Hasso Hohmann [1995]; William Sanders [1986–90]; Richard Leventhal [n.d.]; James Sheehy [1991]; David Webster [1989a, b, 1999, 2002]; David Webster and Elliot Abrams [1983]; David Webster, Barbara Fash, Randolph Widmer, and Scott Zeleznik [1998]; David Webster, AnnCorinne Freter, and Nancy Gonlin [2000]; and Gordon Willey and Richard Leventhal [1979]).

Surrounding the Copán Main Group is a zone of dense settlement dominated by mound groups with particularly large, well-built, and ornate structures (Fig. 3). Under the old theocratic model, these would have been called *minor ceremonial centers*, and as recently as 1977 some archaeologists asserted that there were no palaces at Copán.

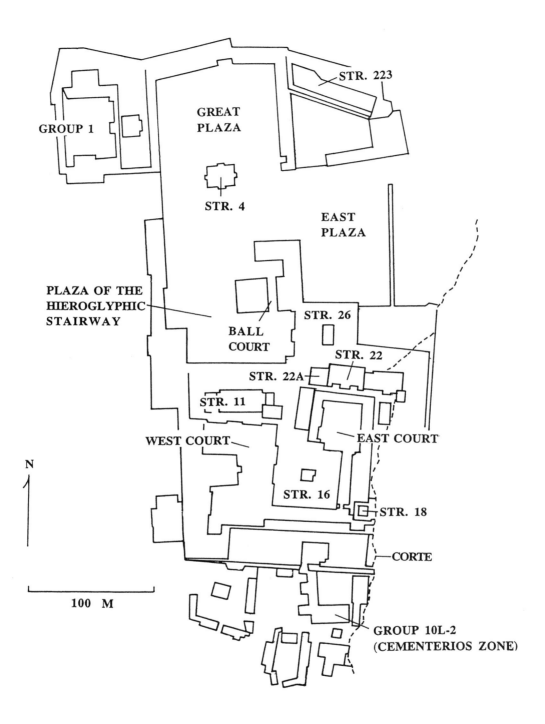

Fig. 2 Copán Main Group

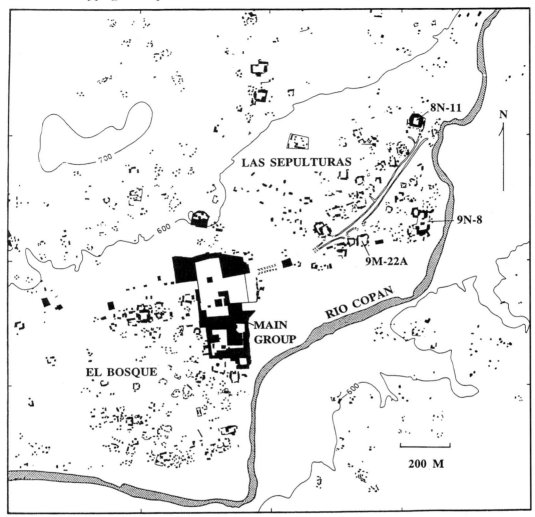

Fig. 3 The Copán urban core

We now know, to the contrary, that the Copán urban zone is distinguished by an un–usual concentration of residential groups that housed wealthy and powerful subroyal nobles.

One key to our understanding of the functions of urban core elite groups was the ability to carry out extensive lateral excavations which not only exposed scores of buildings, but also the patios and other ambient spaces around them. Such excavations are essential because they provide comprehensive evidence for the internal arrangements and character of buildings and room complexes, and also very complete data on how spaces of all kinds were used for various activities.

On the most general level we found that the several excavated groups yielded huge amounts of domestic debris, much of it from structure fill, but also from activity areas and middens. Pottery, chipped stone tools of chert and obsidian, grinding stones, and other

Fig. 4 Sculptured façade, Structure 66S, Group 8N–11, Copán. Drawing by Barbara Fash.

kinds of artifacts from these large sites essentially duplicate domestic assemblages associated with more humble rural residences (Hendon n.d.; Gonlin n.d.; Webster, Gonlin, and Sheets 1997). Moreover, in good Maya fashion the inhabitants of these ancient palaces buried many of their dead, including men, women, and children, in and around their dwellings. In short, there is no longer any doubt that these large complexes had overwhelmingly domestic functions, and so accord with one part of our palace definition.

Several lines of evidence indicate that the people who lived in these groups were rich and powerful. Many of their buildings were beautifully made of fine cut stone and had elaborately vaulted roofs. Interiors and exteriors were covered with smooth plaster, much of it painted. Some buildings had absorbed on the order of 10,000 man–days of labor (Abrams 1994), far in excess of what the immediate inhabitants could easily provide, showing that the resident families were able to draft workers from far larger social groups.

Additional indications of the high social rank of the inhabitants of these groups were the impressive programs of sculpture that graced many façades and interiors (Fig. 4). Façade sculpture on the principal buildings was often of a quality similar to that found in the Copán Main Group and royal compound. Carved benches or thrones identical to those shown in Classic Maya art were found in some buildings. One such bench uncovered in 1990 depicts a skyband, an extremely exalted symbol associated with Mesoamerican kings and other elites since Olmec times (Fig. 5).

Fig. 5 Skyband Bench, Structure 66C, Group 8N-11, Copán. Drawing by Barbara Fash.

We also learned that palatial groups at Copán are themselves variable, ranging from comparatively small, compact sets of buildings arranged around one or several patios to sprawling complexes consisting of many patios and scores of buildings. One reason for such variation is that the nobles who lived in these Copán palaces were themselves ranked according to their power, wealth, and authority. In addition, some palaces were founded much earlier than others, and over time they developed into complexes of buildings and patios that covered as much as a hectare of land (9N-8, for example, was founded earlier and grew to be much larger and more elaborate than 8N-11). Although the urban core clearly housed Maya noble families for many centuries, most of the impressive masonry buildings now visible on the surface were built between 650 and 800 when the Copán dynasty and polity were most powerful.

We still have a poor grasp of what kinds of social groups occupied these elite compounds (for alternative models, see Webster 2002: 143–145). Whatever the precise arrangements, Webster believes that some conformed to the "house" organization defined by Claude Levi-Strauss (for a review, see Gillespie 2001). Essential features include a central core of high-ranking kin surrounded by lesser relatives, retainers, and other dependents or associates. The house as a corporate unit possesses both real material resources (e.g., land, labor) and cultural capital (e.g., access to offices and titles, rituals). Both kinds of property ensure the integrity and durability of the house, and a primary function of the organization is to maintain and augment these resources and perpetuate them through time. One or more elaborate residences provide spatial facilities for the core house personnel, and they often endure for generations, as shown by the following Copán example.

Group 9N-8

Group 9N-8 (Fig. 6) is the largest palace complex excavated and restored to date in the Copán urban core, and provides support for some of these general observations. In its overall configuration, this residential group, built largely in the 8th century, is remarkably similar to that described above by Cortés for the sixteenth-century Maya. It consists of about fifty structures, with well over one hundred individual rooms, grouped around eleven patios. Even though parts of it were washed away by the nearby Copán River, it still covers an area of about 0.8 hectares. Most buildings include the spacious interior benches that archaeologists associate with Maya residential spaces.

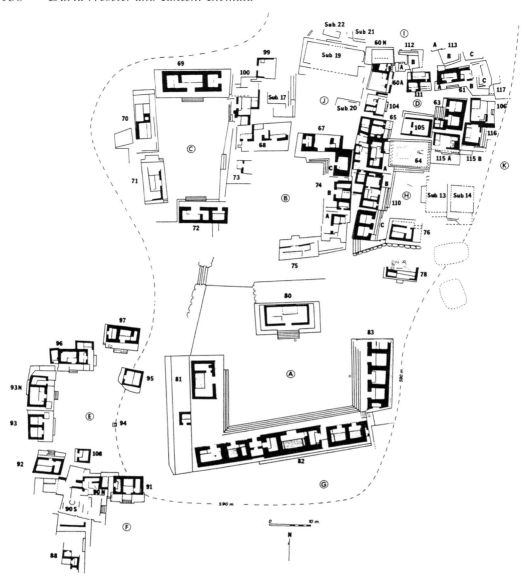

Fig. 6 Map of Group 9N-8

Just as palace groups differ from one another, so too do they differ internally. Some patio units and associated buildings at 9N-8 are more imposing than others. Patio A, for example, is dominated by the House of the Bacabs (Fig. 7). This building was probably the core residential and central political facility for the lord of the group. Its façade, as recon-structed by William Fash, Barbara Fash, and Rudy Larios, displays a complex program of sculpture that shows, among other things, scribal imagery. In the interior of the main room was a carved and inscribed bench that reveals the date—July 10, 781—when the building was erected, the names of its owner, his parents, the reigning king, and the court title of the

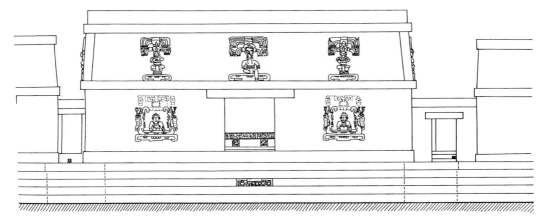

Fig. 7 Façade of Copán Structure 9N-8-82 center. Drawing courtesy of Hasso Hohmann.

resident lord. In the center of the patio stood Altar W', a kind of monument usually associated with Maya kings. Nearby are other room complexes with typical palace arrangements that probably housed close relatives of this important personage.

We are only beginning to understand what these complex symbolic programs meant to the Maya. They obviously signaled details concerning the institutionalized positions of individuals and groups in Copán society (Noble n.d.). They also probably reflect the assertions of elite factions vis-à-vis one another and the royal family. Thus they signal considerable status rivalry.

Some large patios rank just below Patio A in the quality of their buildings, but other units are much smaller, more cramped, and include structures with small rooms and comparatively slipshod construction. This variation likely means that the residents of Group 9N-8 had differing social ranks. Some were no doubt relatives of the central lord and others perhaps unrelated retainers or hangers-on. Our educated guess is that the whole group probably held between two and three hundred residents during the late eighth century. Despite this variation, however, all the patios yielded middens filled with domestic debris as well as burials, ranging from those in elaborate tombs to inhumations in simple pits or cists, the latter by far the most common.

These patio groups grew by accretion and buildings and rooms were often renovated. Walls were added, doorways blocked up, benches were subdivided, and whole buildings sometimes changed function. Such modification is to be expected in residential settings where demographic and social changes had to be accommodated by spatial reconfigurations. Certainly 9N-8 was occupied for a long time, and in fact what can reasonably be interpreted as elite activity endured into the tenth century, if not later. It thus survived Copán's dynastic collapse ca. 810 to 820.

Because we have exposed so many buildings we can detect their functional variation. In addition to residences and buildings with assumed political functions, there were also shrines, kitchens, workshops, and what appear to have been communal houses for young men.

Widmer identified a craft workshop where elite lapidary and shell items were made. A burned building in Patio A had ball court paraphernalia on its floor. This pattern is consistent with descriptions of Postclassic Maya communal houses for young men, who frequently were ballplayers. Possibly a ball court was attached to 9N-8, but we will never be certain because some of the compound has been washed away. If existence of a residential ball court had connotations of high political status (see Whittington 2001), the presence of one at 9N-8 would be extremely suggestive.

Ambient spaces in patios or adjacent to buildings often yielded in-situ features indicating that much activity, especially food preparation, took place outdoors. No doubt many other special-purpose facilities are still undetected: some possibly for production of perishable craft items and as quarters for guests and ritual feasts. Of course, in Maya fashion the use of almost any space was probably multipurpose and flexible, varying with the occasion, season, and long-term transformations of the built environment.

This variation reinforces three things. First, for the Maya what we can reasonably call *palaces* were spatially organized much differently than European ones. Second, specialized facilities that served specifically elite ends existed. Third, the social power and authority of subroyal Copán elites emanated from their residential compounds, which were potent political and religious as well as residential places. They also no doubt had courtly functions like the grander establishments of kings.

Contrary to what was believed only a short time ago, Copán is full of palaces. One strength of the research reviewed here is that we have such a comprehensive perspective on whole, laterally stripped complexes of elite buildings. Limited testing would have been much less informative and even confusing. Another is that some of these buildings project symbolic information that is explicit in epigraphic and iconographic terms. Some is even highly personalized. We can begin to name the leaders who dominated these groups and associate them with particular buildings, offices, and titles. Nowhere else, at present, are subroyal elite palaces as well understood.

There are, nevertheless, gaps in our knowledge of how palaces were used at Copán. While we can be sure that they generally had undoubted residential functions, it is often difficult to identify how individual rooms or sets of rooms were used. Only where a building burned, as in the case of the mens' house, or otherwise abruptly collapsed, like the workshop Widmer found, do we have living surfaces with functionally integrated sets of artifacts preserved on room floors. Unfortunately, such cases are rare. In most instances, buildings and rooms were abandoned slowly and their contents removed thus creating problems of interpretation.

To appreciate how thorough such removal was, let us consider for a moment one of the tiny households excavated at the site of Ceren, El Salvador, by Payson Sheets. There, ca. 590, the inhabitants abruptly abandoned their houses and possessions, which were suddenly buried by volcanic debris. Sheets has found an incredible array of materials preserved in and around these little buildings. In one tiny set of three household structures alone he recovered seventy-five whole and broken ceramic vessels. In the more than one hundred rooms of Group 9N-8, only some ninety such vessels were found in primary contexts, and postelite squatters might well have deposited some of these. Imagine what we would know about the use of space at 9N-8 had it been overwhelmed and preserved by a catastrophe as at Ceren.

Fortunately, Takeshi Inomata and his colleagues at Aguateca have provided just this kind of information.

Aguateca

Aguateca is a relatively small center located in the Petexbatun region of the southwest Peten (see Fig. 1). Ian Graham (1967) and Stephen Houston (1993, n.d.; Houston and Mathews 1985) explored the site briefly, mapped many of its features, and studied its carved monuments. Inomata originally carried out investigations from 1990 to 1993 as part of the Petexbatun Project directed by Arthur Demarest (1997; Demarest et al. 1997; Inomata 1997; Inomata and Stiver 1998). From 1996 to 1999, Inomata directed the Aguateca Archaeological Project with Daniela Triadan and Erick Ponciano (Inomata 2003; Inomata et al. 1998; Inomata et al. 2001; Inomata et al. 2002).

Survey and excavation have revealed evidence of a Late Preclassic occupation (300 B.C.–A.D. 150) followed by near abandonment during the Early Classic (i.e., 150–600). During the Late Classic period (i.e., 600–830), Aguateca rapidly became a densely occupied center. This rapid growth probably started in the middle part of the Late Classic, but peak occupation did not last long. Most excavated structures had only one major construction phase. Epigraphic study by Houston (1993, n.d.; Houston and Mathews 1985) has demonstrated that the Late Classic center of Aguateca was founded as the secondary capital of Dos Pilas. Towards the end of the Late Classic, regional warfare appears to have intensified, and the primary capital of Dos Pilas was nearly abandoned in the late eighth century (Demarest 1997; Palka 1997). The royal family and elites moved to Aguateca, where they desperately tried to defend themselves by constructing a series of stone and timber walls (Demarest et al. 1997; Inomata 1997, n.d.). Enemies probably attacked Aguateca at the beginning of the ninth century, whereupon the center was abruptly deserted.

Excavations in the central part of Aguateca revealed burned structures with numerous reconstructible objects (Inomata n.d.; Inomata and Stiver 1998; Inomata et al. 1998). Inomata has hypothesized that the residents in this area fled or were taken away during the attack by enemies, leaving most of their belongings in situ. This pattern of rapid abandonment provides an unprecedented opportunity to study the functions, meanings, and identity of the occupants of a set of Classic Maya elite residences.

To date, Inomata and his colleagues have excavated twelve burned structures extensively. These include Structures M7-22, M7-32, M7-34, M7-35, M8-2, M8-3, M8-4, M8-8, M8-10, M8-11, M8-13, and M8-17 (Fig. 8). Of these, M7-22, M7-32, M7-34, M7-35, M8-4, M8-8, M8-10, and M8-11 are large- to medium-sized range structures with three to six rooms. Excavation data suggest that M7-22 and M7-32 were a royal residence, whereas subroyal elite households occupied M7-35, M8-4, M8-8, and M8-10. Interpretation of M7-34 and M8-11 is more difficult, but they might have been communal houses.

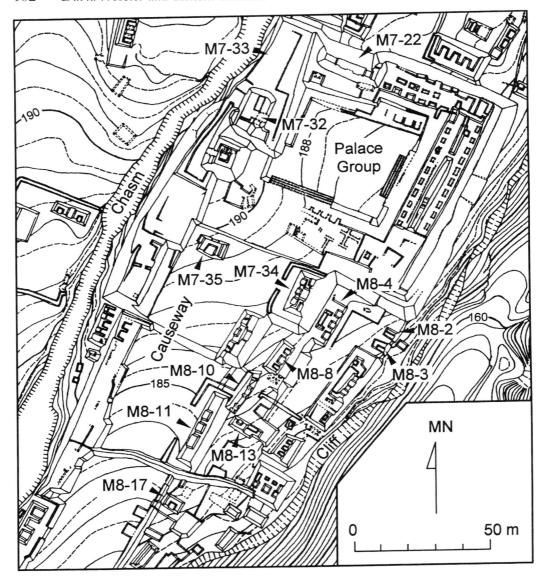

Fig. 8 Map of the central part of Aguateca

Royal Residence

Although our primary focus in this paper is on subroyal elites, a comparison with unique data from the Aguateca royal palace is instructive. Structures M7-22 and M7-32 occupy the northern and western parts of the Palace Group, which is located at the north end of the Causeway (Fig. 8). The Palace Group is the second largest architectural complex at Aguateca after the Main Plaza. The Palace Group plan, a square arrangement of buildings surrounding a plaza, is shared by other residential patio groups at Aguateca, but this compound is significantly larger. The Main Plaza was the most important public ceremonial space with open access, and the Palace Group appears to have been of a more private nature with limited access. A test excavation next to Structure M7-9 located to the north of the Palace Group yielded several limestone *manos* larger than most of those found in other residential structures. Probably Structure M7-9 or a nearby structure was a kitchen for the Palace Group. These data suggest that the Palace Group was a residential complex. Given its impressive size, it is likely that it was occupied by the royal family. The layout of defensive walls, which lie in a roughly concentric pattern, supports this interpretation. The center of this layout, that is, the most heavily defended part, is the Palace Group. A probable reason that the Aguatecans tried to defend this part rather than the Main Plaza is that it housed the ruler and his family.

Structure M7-31 to the south of M7-32 is elevated on pyramid-shaped bases and may have been a temple. Structure M7-26 on the eastern side is a long building with a series of pillars and open galleries, apparently once used for meetings or rituals. Most likely, the primary living quarters of the royal family were M7-22 and M7-32, which members of the Aguateca Project exposed almost completely.

Structures M7-22 and M7-32 had vaulted roofs that had collapsed, filling their rooms with debris. These are the only buildings at Aguateca confirmed to have had vaulted roofs. Structure M7-22 consists of five main rooms (i.e., easternmost, east, center, west, westernmost), and possibly two small front rooms that were added later (Fig. 9). The east, center, west, and westernmost rooms were nearly devoid of artifacts. The center room was large and had a spacious bench. Possibly the rulers used this chamber in a similar fashion to the center rooms of subroyal elite residences (see below; Inomata 2001a). The center room was originally connected to the east and west rooms through narrow passages. Access between the center and east rooms was later sealed. These passages remind us of the structures at Copán, and as suggested for Copán buildings (Sanders 1989; Webster 1989a), the interconnected west and center rooms might have been used by the ruler or a royal personage, while an immediate family member might have occupied the east room.

The easternmost room contained many objects in front of its bench. Its eastward-facing doorway was sealed. The wall sealing the entrance collapsed forward or was deliberately opened, and many objects were scattered over collapsed stones in front of the room. Items stored here include medium-sized jars, bowls, possible pyrite mirrors, small ceramic drums, carved bones, a carved shell, and two ceramic masks (Figs. 10–12).

Structure M7-32 was even more elaborately built than M7-22, consisting of north, center, south, and front rooms. It is probable that M7-32 was the primary residence of the ruler, and also served administrative purposes. Excavators found no reconstructible vessels. Part of the bench of the center room was deliberately destroyed, and the room floor in front of the bench was covered with sherds and other artifacts.

The abandonment pattern of Structures M7-22 and M7-32 is different from the other elite residences discussed below, and the distribution of artifacts probably does not reflect the original use-pattern of these structures. Inomata believes that this abandonment pattern is related to the unique function of these buildings, that is, as royal residences. One hypothesis holds that the royal family abandoned the Aguateca before its fall. They might

a

b

Fig. 9 Structure M7-22 after excavation (a) eastern half and (b) western half

Fig. 10 Ceramic jars and drums found in the easternmost room of Structure M7-22

Fig. 11 Carved bone found in the easternmost room of Structure M7-22. Drawing
by Stephen Houston.

a

b

Fig. 12a, b Ceramic masks found in the easternmost room of Structure M7-22

Fig. 13 Structure M7-35

have cleaned out most of their quarters but stored some possessions in the easternmost room of M7-22, hoping to come back later (Inomata 2003). The rest of the population, including most of the elite, probably remained at Aguateca and witnessed its violent end.

Subroyal Residences

Structures M7-35, M8-4, M8-8, and M8-10 contained numerous domestic objects, including storage, cooking, and serving vessels, as well as obsidian blades, various types of formal lithic tools, lithic flakes, and bone artifacts. In addition, middens associated with M8-8 and M8-10 consisted mostly of domestic refuse. Thus these buildings were likely used as residences. Their quality of construction, their proximity to the royal palace, and the presence of prestige goods such as shell and jade ornaments, indicate that their occupants were nobles (Inomata 2001b; Inomata and Triadan 2003).

There are appreciable similarities among these structures in floor plans, artifact distribution, and possibly the use of space. Main components of each structure comprised the center room and two side rooms, each of which had a high bench and a separate entrance. Buildings also had smaller chambers on the sides or at the back. Inomata calls these *annexes* or *back rooms* (Figs. 13, 14). In contrast to main rooms, these smaller chambers have no benches. Although some annexes and back rooms may have been original parts of buildings, others were clearly added later. Wide eaves likely covered the areas in front of and behind these buildings, as suggested for Ceren (Sheets 1992).

a

b

Fig. 14a, b Structure M8-8

The center room of each building appears to have been used primarily by the head of the household for official and public purposes. The presence of unique architectural features, such as the niches under the benches in Structures M7-35 and M8-10 and the side arms at both ends of the bench in M8-10, suggest the importance of these center rooms. In addition, the center room of M7-35 was larger than the side rooms. Only a few artifacts were found in the center rooms, and wide-open space seems to have been maintained for various activities, including administrative work by the household heads, social gatherings, and reception of visitors.

The center rooms of Structures M8-4 and M8-10 contained two mortars that were probably used for pigment preparation (Fig. 15). Inomata (n.d.; Inomata and Stiver 1998) has suggested that the head of the household of M8-10 was a scribe who carried out part of his duties in the center room (see below). The discovery of an extended adult male burial under the floor of the center room indicates the continuity of the room's association with the household heads through generations. Interestingly, the House of the Bacabs at Copán also shows scribal imagery in its sculptures and evidence that its lords had scribal functions for at least two generations.

Ceramic artifacts found in the center rooms include jars, small bowls, and cylinder vases, indicating the consumption of food and drink (Fig. 16). These recall the many ceramic vases excavated in the Maya area depicting gatherings, feasts, and formal receptions.

Fig. 15 Mortars found in the central and north rooms of Structures M8-4 and M8-10

Fig. 16 Ceramic vessels from the central rooms of Structures M8-4 and M8-10

Many of these events probably took place in the central rooms of elite residences. Architectural features shown on these vessels, such as benches, resemble those of elite residences. Furthermore, the assemblages of ceramic vessels excavated in the center rooms of elite residences at Aguateca are similar to those in vase paintings. Excavators also unearthed nine complete obsidian blades inside and in front of the center room of Structure M8-10 and four in M7-35. Although obsidian blades were found in various parts of most structures, complete blades were rare. Also found in M7-35 in association with obsidian blades was an imitation stingray spine made of bone (Fig. 17). These objects were likely used for ritual bloodletting. Though the residents may not have conducted ritual bloodletting in those rooms, the storage of related items points to meanings and functions for the center rooms that are somewhat outside the ordinary domestic sphere.

Chambers flanking the center rooms were probably used for domestic activities, including storage, preparation, and consumption of food, as well as child rearing and craft production. One room in each residence (i.e., the west room of M7-35, the north room of M8-4, the north room of M8-8, and the south room of M8-10) housed numerous ceramic vessels, including large ones for storage (Triadan 2000). Moreover, large limestone *metates*, probably for corn grinding, were placed inside the west room of Structure M7-35, near the

Fig. 17 Imitation sting-ray spine found in Structure M7-35

north room of M8-4, and in front of the north room of M8-8. The presence of these objects suggests food storage and preparation inside and in front of these rooms. In addition, excavators found concentrations of textile production tools, such as needles and spindle whorls, in these areas. These objects were likely used by women. Under the floor of the south room of M8-10 was an infant burial. These finds indicate that these chambers were used primarily by women, probably wives of the household heads, who were responsible for food preparation, textile production, and child rearing. The east room of M7-35 and the south room of M8-8 contained comparatively few objects and might have served as living and sleeping spaces.

Some of the side rooms were related to the work of scribes/artists and of royal courtiers (Inomata 2001c; Inomata and Triadan 1999). In the south room of Structure M8-4, excavators uncovered numerous pieces of pyrite mirrors and ceramic mirror backs. One alabaster object, also found in this room, was identified by Stephen Houston as an image of the jester god and might have been part of a royal headdress. Possibly a high courtier kept royal regalia in this room. The north room of M8-10 contained numerous scribal implements, such as mortars and pestles for pigment preparation (see Fig. 15) and halved shells used as ink pots. Other artifacts found in the room were various types of lithic tools and bone and shell ornaments. A figure depicted on a shell ornament found here exhibits characteristic items of scribal attire, and the glyphic text carved on it contains the scribal title *its'aat*. Also found in this room was a carved human skull with a glyphic text, which mentions the name of the last ruler of Aguateca. The glyphic and artifact evidence indicates that this building was a residence of a high-status scribe or artist and his family. Probably the head of this household conducted scribal work and produced bone and shell ornaments inside and in front of this room. Excavators unearthed seven polished axes, probably used for carving, inside and in front of the north room of M8-8 (Fig. 18). Eleven more polished axes were found in the north annex (Fig. 19). The use-wear analysis conducted by Kazuo Aoyama (1999) suggests that these axes were used for carving stone, possibly *stelae*.

Small annexes and back rooms appear to have been used as working and storage spaces. The presence of drainage in the north annex of Structure M8-8 and in the south annex of M8-10 points to water use here. Besides the numerous polished axes mentioned above, the north annex of M8-8 contained a large, flat limestone slab with numerous surface scratch marks. This stone was probably a working table, indicating that the residents used this room for craftwork, including carving. In the back rooms of M7-35, excavators found three polished axes, along with pounding or rubbing stones, utilitarian ceramics, and a pestle and mortar. Some kind of craft production probably took place in and in front of these back rooms. In front of the north annex of Structure M8-10, on the other hand, were a large limestone *metate* and *mano*, suggesting an association with food preparation. Some of these small rooms also probably served as storage space.

The areas behind the structures, probably protected by eaves, appear to have been important spaces for domestic activities. Behind Structures M8-8 and M8-10, investigators found several *metates* and reconstructible ceramic vessels. Figurines, bone tools, and a concentration of carbonized seeds were also unearthed behind M8-8.

Fig. 18 Polished stone axes from Structure M8-8

Fig. 19 Polished stone axes from the north annex of Structure M8-8

In summary, these elite residences were places where a wide range of essential domestic activities, such as sleeping, child rearing, and food storage, preparation, and consumption, were carried out. The residents also pursued other tasks here, including performing administrative tasks, conducting meetings, receiving visitors, and undertaking craft production. It is important to remember that at the end of the Late Classic period Aguateca was under imminent threat of enemy attack. Even so, significant continuity in use patterns of these buildings is suggested by comparisons between floor assemblages and middens, between middens found in the epicenter and outside, and between floor assemblages and burial distribution.

Possible Communal Houses

Before excavation, Structures M7-34 and M8-11 looked similar to the aforementioned subroyal elite residences, except that they faced the Causeway and were surrounded by small stone walls. Excavations, however, revealed unique architectural features. Room partitions were found only in the rear parts of these structures, and the front areas were divided by thin stone walls running parallel to the front walls. Doorways were quite wide, and the front wall segments were accordingly rather narrow, appearing almost like pillars (Fig. 20).

Fig. 20 Structure M7-34

Fig. 21 Elaborate *incensario*
from Structure M7-34

Only a small portion of Structure M8-11 was excavated, but the artifact assemblages from the completely excavated M7-34 are suggestive, in part because they were different from those found in elite residences in the following ways. First, there were fewer ceramic vessels. Second, at least eleven large, basin-shaped limestone *metates* were within and around these structures, while most residential structures appear to have only one or two such *metates*. It is likely that this type of *metate* was used for grinding corn. If so, the large number of these *metates* associated with M7-34 suggests the processing of corn in a quantity significantly larger than for consumption by one household. Third, excavators unearthed *incensarios* of elaborate shapes (Fig. 21). No similarly elaborate *incensarios* have been found in the aforementioned elite residences. Another example of an *incensario* from the central part of Aguateca came from M8-17, which was probably a shrine.

The interpretation of these structures is still problematic, but one hypothesis is that they were used by social groups larger than, or different from, ordinary households. In other words, these buildings might have been communal houses or lineage houses where gatherings and feasting took place.

Summary

In conclusion, one lesson about palaces derived from the history of Maya scholarship is that John Stephens's (1949 [1841]) comparative instincts were correct, although for many years a strange model of Maya society prevented imposing sets of structures from being appreciated as elite residences (Becker 1979). The Maya unquestionably had palaces according to our general definition, however unique or distinctive they might be. A second lesson is that drawing conclusions in the absence of effective, problem-oriented fieldwork risks many pitfalls.

We have come a long way in palace research. At Copán we now recognize most subroyal palaces by the scale and quality of surface remains, but only because we excavated a large sample of them by extensive lateral exposures. Corroboration of palace functions comes from general architectural patterns and associated artifacts. Exactly how rooms or patios were used remains unclear. By contrast, at Aguateca rich floor assemblages from rapidly abandoned structures provide much more detailed information. Some sets of rooms and buildings are indeed elite residences, while others may have been communal houses.

At Aguateca the presence of palaces remains difficult to recognize on the surface. Research there forcibly reminds us that power, wealth, and prestige are not invariably signaled by architectural scale and quality, or at least not in ways immediately apparent to the archaeologist. Range structures with three to five rooms are common throughout the site, raising many questions: Is this pattern a result of the unique circumstances of late settlement at Aguateca? How many elite residences are there, as opposed to communal structures? Were similar structures occupied by elite families of similar rank? Did nobles of different ranks live in similar houses? Or, did one elite family own more than one house inside and outside the epicenter? Because of the much more extensive excavations and surveys at Copán, it is now possible to address these issues within a larger settlement perspective.

At both sites, elite residences were used for a wide range of activities, including essential domestic work and those of more public nature, such as administrative tasks and receptions. At both evidence exists for the presence of highly ranked scribes and artists, or at least the symbolism related to these roles. Glyphic and iconographic texts, although of different kinds, are associated with elite houses. The abundant artifacts in primary contexts at Aguateca reveal consistencies among these dwellings not only in architectural features, but also in the patterned use of space.

Bibliography

ABRAMS, ELLIOT

1994   *How the Maya Built their World*. University of Texas Press, Austin.

AOYAMA, KAZUO

1999   *Analisis de las microhuellas sobre la lítica de Aguateca: Temporada de 1998–1999*. Report presented to the Instituto de Antropologia e Historia de Guatemala, Guatemala City.

ASHMORE, WENDY

1991   Site-planning Principles and Concepts of Directionality among the Ancient Maya. *Latin American Antiquity* 2 (3): 99–226.

BECKER, MARSHALL

1979   Priests, Peasants, and Ceremonial Centers: The Intellectual History of a Model. *In Maya Archaeology and Ethnohistory* (Norman Hammond, ed.): 3–20. University of Texas Press, Austin.

CORTÉS, HERNÁN

1986   *Letters from Mexico* (Anthony Pagden, trans. and ed.). Yale University Press, New Haven.

DEMAREST, ARTHUR A.

1997   The Vanderbilt Petexbatun Regional Archaeological Project 1989–1994: Overview, History, and Major Results of a Multidisciplinary Study of the Classic Maya Collapse. *Ancient Mesoamerica* 8: 209–227.

DEMAREST, ARTHUR A., MATT O'MANSKY, CLAUDIA WOOLLEY, DIRK VAN TUERENHOUT, TAKESHI INOMATA, JOEL PALKA, AND HECTOR ESCOBEDO

1997   Classic Maya Defensive Systems and Warfare in the Petexbatun Region: Archaeological Evidence and Interpretations. *Ancient Mesoamerica* 8: 229–254.

DIAMANTI, MELISSA

n.d.   Domestic Organization at Copán: Reconstruction of Maya Elite Households through Ethnographic Analogy. Ph.D. dissertation, Department of Anthropology, Pennsylvania State University, 1991.

FLANNERY, KENT

1998   The Ground Plans of Archaic States. In *Archaic States* (Gary Feinman and Joyce Marcus, eds.): 15–57. School of Americal Research Press, Santa Fe.

GERSTLE, ANDREA

n.d.   Maya-Lenca Ethnic Relations in Late Classic Period Copán, Honduras. Ph.D. dissertation, Department of Anthropology, University of California, Santa Barbara, 1988.

GILLESPIE, SUSAN

2001   Rethinking Ancient Maya Social Organization. *American Anthropologist* 102 (3): 467–484.

GONLIN, NANCY

n.d.   Rural Household Archaeology at Copán, Honduras. Ph.D. dissertation, Department of Anthropology, Pennsylvania State University, 1993.

GRAHAM, IAN

1967   *Archaeological Explorations in El Peten, Guatemala.* Middle American Research Institute, Publications 33. Tulane University, New Orleans, La.

HENDON, JULIA A.

n.d.   The Uses of Maya Structures: A Study of Architecture and Artifact Distribution at Sepulturas, Copán, Honduras. Ph.D. dissertation, Department of Anthropology, Harvard University, 1987.

HOHMANN, HASSO

1995   *Die Architekture der Sepulturas-Region von Copán in Honduras.* Academic Publishers, Graz, Austria.

HOUSTON, STEPHEN D.

1993   *Hieroglyphs and History at Dos Pilas.* University of Texas Press, Austin.

n.d.   The Inscriptions and Monumental Art of Dos Pilas, Guatemala: A Study of Classic Maya History and Politics. Ph.D. dissertation, Department of Anthropology, Yale University, 1987.

HOUSTON, STEPHEN D., AND PETER MATHEWS

1985   *The Dynastic Sequence of Dos Pilas, Guatemala.* Precolumbian Art Research Institute Monograph 1. San Francisco.

INOMATA, TAKESHI

1997   The Last Day of a Fortified Classic Maya Center: Archaeological Investigations at Aguateca, Guatemala. *Ancient Mesoamerica* 8: 337–351.

2001a   The Classic Maya Palace as a Political Theater. In *Reconstruyendo la Ciudad Maya: El Urbanismo en las sociedades antiguas* (Andres Ciudad Ruiz, Mária Josefa Iglesias Ponce de Leon, and Mária del Carmen Martínez Martínez, eds.): 341–362. Sociedad Española de Estudios Mayas, Madrid.

2001b   King's People: Classic Maya Royal Courtiers in a Comparative Perspective. In *Royal Courts of the Ancient Maya* (Takeshi Inomata and Stephen Houston, eds.): 27–53. Westview, Boulder, Colo.

2001c   The Power and Ideology of Artistic Creation: Elite Craft Specialists in Classic Maya Society. *Current Anthropology* 42 (3): 321–349.

2003   War, Destruction, and Abandonment: The Fall of the Classic Maya Center of Aguateca. In *The Archaeology of Settlement Abandonment in Middle America* (Takeshi Inomata and Ronald Webb, eds.): 43–60. University of Utah Press, Salt Lake City.

n.d.   Archaeological Investigations at the Fortified Center of Aguateca, El Petén, Guatemala: Implications for the Study of the Classic Maya Collapse. Ph.D. dissertation, Department of Anthropology, Vanderbilt University, 1995.

INOMATA, TAKESHI, ERICK PONCIANO, RICHARD TERRY, DANIELA TRIADAN, AND HARRIET F. BEAUBIEN

2001   In the Palace of the Fallen King: The Excavation of the Royal Residential Complex at the Classic Maya Center of Aguateca, Guatemala. *Journal of Field Archaeology* 28 (3/4): 287–306.

INOMATA, TAKESHI, AND LAURA STIVER

1998   Floor Assemblages from Burned Structures at Aguateca, Guatemala: A Study of Classic Maya Households. *Journal of Field Archaeology* 25: 431–452.

INOMATA, TAKESHI, AND DANIELA TRIADAN

1999   Craft Production by Classic Maya Elites in Domestic Settings: Data from Rapidly Abandoned Structures at Aguateca, Guatemala. *Mayab* 13: 57–66.

2003   Where did Elites Live?: Possible Elite Residences at Aguateca, Guatemala. In *Maya Palaces and Elite Residences* (Jessica Joyce Christie, ed.):154–183. University of Texas Press, Austin.

INOMATA, TAKESHI, DANIELA TRIADAN, AND ERICK PONCIANO (EDS.)

1996   *Informe preliminar del Proyecto Arqueologico Aguateca: La temporada de 1998.* Report presented to the Instituto de Antropologia e Historia de Guatemala. Ministerio de Cultura y Deportes, Instituto de Antropologia e Historia, and Asociación Tikal, Guatemala City.

INOMATA, TAKESHI, DANIELA TRIADAN, ERICK PONCIANO, ESTELA PINTO, RICHARD E. TERRY, AND MARKUS EBERL

2002   Domestic and Political Lives of Classic Maya Elites: The Excavation of Rapidly Abandoned Structures of Aguateca, Guatemala. *Latin American Antiquity* 13: 295–330.

INOMATA, TAKESHI, DANIELA TRIADAN, ERICK PONCIANO, RICHARD TERRY, HARRIET BEAUBIEN, ESTELA PINTO, AND SHANNON COYSTON.

1998   Residencias de la familia real y de la elite en Aguateca, Guatemala. *Mayab* 11: 23–29.

KOWALSKI, JEFFREY

1987   *The House of the Governor.* University of Oklahoma Press, Norman.

LANDA, DIEGO DE

1941   *Relación de las Cosas de Yucatan.* Papers of the Peabody Museum of Archaeology and Ethnology 18 (Alfred Tozzer, ed.). Harvard University, Cambridge, Mass.

LEVENTHAL, RICHARD

n.d.   Settlement Patterns at Copán, Honduras. Ph.D. dissertation, Department of Anthropology, Harvard University, Cambridge, Mass., 1979.

MORGAN, LEWIS HENRY

1876   A Review of Native Races of the Pacific States, by Hubert Howe Bancroft. *Civilized Nations* 2: 265–308.

NOBLE, SANDRA E.

  n.d.   *Maya Seats and Maya Seats-of-Authority.* Ph.D. dissertation, Department of
            Anthropology, University of British Columbia, Vancouver, 1998.

PALKA, JOEL W.

  1997   Reconstructing Classic Maya Socioeconomic Differentiation and the Collapse at
            Dos Pilas, Petén, Guatemala. *Ancient Mesoamerica* 8: 293–306.

SANDERS, WILLIAM T.

  1989   Household, Lineage, and State at Eighth-Century Copán, Honduras. In *The House of
            the Bacabs, Copán, Honduras* (David Webster, ed.): 89–105. Studies in Pre-Columbian
            Art & Archaeology 29. Dumbarton Oaks, Washington, D.C.

SANDERS, WILLIAM T. (ED.)

  1986-90   *Excavaciones en el area urbana de Copán*, vols. 1–3. Secretaria del Estado en el
            Despacho de Cultural y Turismo, Tegucigalpa, Honduras.

SHEEHY, JAMES

  1991   Structure and Change in a Late Classic Maya Domestic Group at Copán, Honduras.
            Ancient Mesoamerica 2: 1–19.

SHEETS, PAYSON D.

  1992   *The Ceren Site: A Prehistoric Village Buried by Volcanic Ash in Central America.* Harcourt
            Brace Jovanovich, Fort Worth, Tex.

STEPHENS, JOHN LLOYD

  1949   *Incidents of Travel in Central America, Chiapas, and Yucatan.* Rutgers University Press,
  [1841]   New Brunswick, N.J.

TRIADAN, DANIELA

  2000   Elite Household Subsistence at Aguateca, Guatemala. *Mayab* 13: 46–56.

TOURTELLOT, GAIR

  1993   A View of Ancient Maya Settlements in the Eighth Century. In *Lowland Maya
            Civilization in the Eighth Century A.D.* (Jeremy Sabloff and John Henderson, eds.):
            219–242. Dumbarton Oaks Research Library and Collection, Washington, D.C.

WEBSTER, DAVID

  1989a   The House of the Bacabs: Its Social Context. In *The House of the Bacabs, Copán,
            Honduras* (David Webster, ed.): 5–40. Studies in Pre-Columbian Art and Archaeology
            29. Dumbarton Oaks, Washington, D.C.

  1999   The Archaeology of Copán. *Journal of Archaeological Research* 7 (1): 1–53.

  2002   *The Fall of the Ancient Maya.* Thames and Hudson, London.

WEBSTER, DAVID (ED.)

  1989b   *The House of the Bacabs, Copán, Honduras.* Studies in Pre-Columbian Art and
            Archaeology 29. Dumbarton Oaks, Washington, D.C.

WEBSTER, DAVID, AND ELLIOT M. ABRAMS

1983   An Elite Compound at Copán, Honduras. *Journal of Field Archaeology* 10 (3): 285–296.

WEBSTER, DAVID, BARBARA FASH, RANDOLPH WIDMER, AND SCOTT ZELEZNIK

1998   The Skyband House: Investigations of a Classic Maya Elite Residential Complex at Copán, Honduras. *Journal of Field Archaeology* 29 (3): 319–344.

WEBSTER, DAVID, NANCY GONLIN, AND PAYSON SHEETS

1997   Copán and Ceren: Two Perspectives on Ancient Mesoamerican Households. *Ancient Mesoamerica* 8: 43-61.

WEBSTER, DAVID, AnnCORINNE FRETER, AND NANCY GONLIN

2000   *Copán: the Rise and Fall of an Ancient Maya Kingdom*. Harcourt Brace, Fort Worth, Tex.

WHITTINGTON, MICHAEL E.

2001   *The Sport of Life and Death: The Mesoamerican Ballgame*. Thames and Hudson, London.

WILLEY, GORDON R., AND RICHARD M. LEVENTHAL

1979   Prehistoric settlement at Copán. In *Maya Archaeology and Ethnohistory* (Norman Hammond, ed.): 57–102, University of Texas Press, Austin.

WILLEY, GORDON. R., RICHARD M. LEVENTHAL, ARTHUR DEMAREST, AND WILLIAM L. FASH, JR.

1994   *Ceramics and Artifacts from Excavations in the Copán Residential Zone*. Papers of the Peabody Museum of Archaeology and Ethnology 80. Harvard University, Cambridge, Mass.

The Concept of the Palace in the Andes

Joanne Pillsbury

University of Maryland and Dumbarton Oaks

When Susan Toby Evans and I began planning a symposium on palaces of the New World, we noted considerable resistance to the term *palace* on the part of Andeanists. A number of scholars felt that the term was both burdened with a Western bias and inadequate for addressing the unique qualities of ancient American elite residential architecture. Among the residual effects of the revolutions of New Archaeology in the 1960s and 1970s has been a clear discomfort in concentrating on elite residences. Palaces bring to mind the earlier history of our disciplines, when there was widespread use of Western terminology and models. Such models were indeed problematic. The roots of this avoidance may lie still deeper, however, and the legacy of Lewis Henry Morgan (1974 [1877]) may be more prevalent in contemporary archaeology than we realize. Evolutionary approaches such as Morgan's demanded a strict avoidance of the term *palace*, as it would imply that some of these New World societies were states, a position that Morgan and his followers actively rejected.

The effect of this avoidance, however, has meant that we have neglected a key aspect of rulership in the ancient New World. Simply defined, a *palace* is the official residence of a sovereign or paramount religious leader. Few would deny that there were kings and paramount religious leaders in the New World, and even the most ardent historical particularists would admit that kings needed to rule, eat, and sleep somewhere. Setting aside semantics, it is clear that a closer study of these architectural forms, their contexts and functions, would contribute to better understanding of rulership and cultural development in the ancient New World.

The concept of the palace in the Andean region was embraced by chroniclers in the sixteenth and seventeenth centuries and by explorers in the nineteenth century, only to be abruptly dropped as a focus of inquiry for most of the twentieth century. The earliest accounts by Spanish historians, administrators, and clergy contain scattered references to the residences of sovereigns, both those of the Inca and those of other earlier or peripheral groups. Nineteenth-century explorers happily searched for and "identified" specific building groups as appropriate palace candidates. With certain exceptions, however, the topic has been almost completely ignored in recent Andean scholarship.

Perusal of major works on the Inca shows that the word *palace* was rarely used.[1]

---

[1] For example, the term *palace* does not appear in the index of one of the major works on Inca architecture that of Gasparini and Margolies (1980).

The avoidance of palace discussion was not simply a semantic issue; the topic of elite residential architecture and its role in the development and maintenance of political authority is rarely addressed. This lacuna in the field can be attributed to problems in the historical sources themselves, the history of archaeology in the region, and finally, as has been noted, to the perspectives of twentieth-century investigators.

In contrast with Mesoamerica, scholars of the Pre-Hispanic Andes enjoy no counterpart to the rich Pre-Hispanic indigenous texts and thus have no correlative to an important emic view of palace life. This absence of a scribal tradition is also connected to the relatively abundant production of early colonial texts on topics of indigenous life in Mesoamerica. For the Andean region, illustrated documentary sources are comparatively scarce. A number of early sources, however, are of interest to our subject, if only for an examination of the terminology they used. Almost without exception, however, most of the descriptions are woefully brief, a direct result of the early (i.e., 1536) destruction of much of Inca Cuzco through systematic burning (Protzen and Rowe 1994: 240).

Pedro Cieza de León, considered to be one of the more thorough, and, relatively speaking, one of the more objective of the early chroniclers, writes in some detail of the residences of sovereigns, using the term *palace* for Tomebamba, as well as *aposentos principales de los reyes ingas* in a general reference to the houses of lords in Cuzco (1984 [ca. 1551]: chaps. 41–44: 191–211; chap. 92: 337). The term *palace* also appears in some of the earliest dictionaries for the region. For example, Diego de González Holguín (1989 [1590–1600]: 613) defined *çapay ccapakpa huacin* as a royal palace.

The two most important illustrated sources concerning Inca life were compiled at least sixty or so years after the arrival of the first Europeans in Peru (Guaman Poma de Ayala 1936 [1615]; Murúa 1946 [1590–1609]). By this time, life in the former Inca royal residences had changed drastically, with many of the finest structures occupied, rebuilt, or destroyed by new ruling authorities in Cuzco. A vision of what a palace must have been like at the height of the empire was probably only a dim memory by the time Felipe Guaman Poma de Ayala and Martín de Murúa wrote, which may in part explain their regrettably abbreviated comments on the subject: Guaman Poma de Ayala included one relatively simple drawing of the Inca royal palace (Fig. 1; 1936 [1615]: 329), and Murúa included what has become one of the most important detailed textual descriptions of an Inca palace in the Loyola manuscript (1946 [1590–1609]: 165–166; see Morris, this volume). There is no illustration of a palace in this edition, but his textual description bears the closest resemblance to what we know archaeologically of palace remains.

Other references are less useful. Garcilaso de la Vega, El Inca—the son of a Spanish soldier and an Inca princess—left Peru in 1560. He wrote his account of the Incas over forty years later, in his old age (for palace descriptions, see 1966 [1609]: bk. 6, chaps. 1–4; bk. 7, chaps. 8–10, 26, 27; bk. 8, chap. 5). His descriptions of palaces are more extensive than those of Murúa, but they are filled with the sort of generalizing superlatives that characterize the rest of his writings and cast doubt on the usefulness of his observations: "[Inca] palaces surpassed those of all the kings and emperors that have ever existed" (313). Although Garcilaso wrote about various palace courtiers, he acknowledged that by his time

329

Fig. 1 An Inca palace. From Felipe Guaman Poma de Ayala (1936 [1615]: 329).

the palaces had already been razed or reconfigured to suit new purposes (1966 [1609]: 425–427).

Other seventeenth-century writers, including Antonio de la Calancha (1974–82 [1638]: 1226) and Bernabé Cobo (1990 [1639–53]) also mentioned Inca palaces. Cobo's *Historia del Nuevo Mundo*, while written somewhat later than de Garcilaso's work, is a more measured and specific account of Inca life. Unfortunately, his comments on palaces were very brief. Cobo (1990 [1639–53]: bk. 2, chap. 12, 227) described the basic appearance of temples, fortresses, and palaces: palaces were encircled by a great wall, and contained rooms and lodgings; their interior walls, and sometimes their exterior ones, contained niches.

Comparatively little was written about the culture or archaeology of the Inca and other Pre-Hispanic cultures in the eighteenth century. One exception was the work of Baltasar Martínez Compañón, bishop of Trujillo, who commissioned the earliest plan of the site of Chan Chan, on the north coast of Peru (see Pillsbury and Leonard, Figs. 3, 4, this volume). The Martínez Compañón manuscript contains details of a structure, now commonly referred to as a *ciudadela*, with an inscription clearly identifying it as a royal palace.

Numerous European writers and explorers visited the Andean region in the nineteenth century, and wrote of the Pre-Hispanic remains still visible. Although many explorers claimed that they wished to break free of the biases inherent in the early historical texts and view the sites for themselves, many traveled with copies of the sixteenth- and seventeenth-century Spanish chronicles, and sought out the palaces named in those works. Most continued to use the term *palace*, and often tried to associate specific buildings with palaces known from the early colonial sources (e.g., see Rivero y Ustariz and Tschudi 1971 [1854]; Squier 1973 [1877]). It should be pointed out that there was in general a great interest in the aggrandizement of the ancient remains, both in terminology and in graphic documentation. Numerous scholars through the years have noted particularly Ephraim George Squier's tendency to introduce Lilliputian figures in front of monuments to "inflate" the size of structures (Sawyer 1980: 64).

By the turn of the twentieth century, however, scholars were abandoning the term palace. Adolph Bandelier (1969 [1910]), one of the most important writers on Andean archaeology in the late nineteenth and early twentieth century, began to speculate on the social complexity of Andean societies. Bandelier was influenced deeply by Lewis Henry Morgan, who had clear ideas about the level of development of Native American groups (Lange and Riley 1996). Arguing for a unilinear evolution of social complexity from savagery to civilization, Morgan maintained that no indigenous American population had ever advanced to the level of a state society. In his published writings, Bandelier steadfastly avoided the term *palace* when considering Andean architecture (1969 [1910]: 213, 230). Part of his reluctance to use the term may also have had to do with his interest in developing indigenous American models, rather than relying on European parallels. Whether or not it was widely seen or accepted by other scholars, Bandelier's distancing of himself from the term *palace* prevailed in Andean studies through the twentieth century.

There have been few archaeological studies of palaces in the Andes in the twentieth century. Following the systematic burning of Cuzco in 1536, little remained above ground beyond the portions of Inca walls that now serve as foundations for colonial and modern structures. The paucity of architectural evidence of the Inca palaces and the inaccessibility of what does remain have hindered study of such structures. They are clearly difficult to identify archaeologically (e.g., more so than administrative centers with storage facilities), and, therefore, as a category or class of structure, they have been overlooked. The few references to palaces of specific rulers in the historical sources are often vague and conflicting, and so provide little additional evidence to support identification.

In contrast with Mesoamerica, where a comparatively greater number of archaeological projects were conducted in the twentieth century, Andean archaeology received less attention in general, and the emphasis was on settlement pattern surveys, rather than site-specific projects. Beginning with Gordon Willey's (1953) Virú Valley Project in the 1940s, investigations focusing on valleywide surveys were the prevailing model for archaeological research. When specific sites were analyzed, the term *palace* was strictly avoided, and archaeologists favored terms such as *pyramid- dwelling- construction complexes*. One of the few exceptions to this was the work of José Alcina Franch (1976; see also Nair n.d.), whose identification of a palace at Chinchero was bolstered by a detailed historical record for the site. In other instances, archaeologists who tentatively identified structures as palaces were greeted with a surprising amount of criticism.[2]

Until recently, in Andean studies there has been a tendency to focus on the distinctive characteristics of Andean sociopolitical organization. Some scholars have felt that it was both fruitless and inappropriate to consider Andean traditions in any sort of comparative fashion. Part of this avoidance is a resistance to the idea of using Western paradigms to consider Andean phenomena; the idea that *palace* as an interpretative term is loaded with Western ideas about form and function. It is tempting to consider that this avoidance is also born of a desire to stress the uniqueness of Andean civilization, and how and why it was different from complex societies elsewhere. Furthermore, as William Isbell (this volume) points out, there is preference among Andeanists to consider the Pre-Hispanic past in light of present-day folk traditions. By assuming a continuity of consensus-based and acephalous social organization, palaces were not at the forefront of research design.

New research is changing this perspective, however. The authors in this volume and scholars such as Peter Eeckhout (1999–2000), Ian Farrington (1995), Vincent Lee (1989), Susan Niles (1993, 1999), and others, armed with a variety of interpretive tools, are revisiting the subject. These new studies range from identifications and detailed descriptions of "lost" Inca palaces to reconsiderations of familiar forms, previously thought to be indicative of other functions. Farrington and Niles have been able to work with the historical sources to identify with considerable certainty the palaces and country estates of Inca rulers. Their work on sites such as Quispiguanca has contributed to our understanding of the historical and social functions of a specific type of elite residential and landscape architecture. In contrast, at Pachacamac, an important pilgrimage site, Eeckhout studied a type of structure

---

[2] For example, see Geoffrey Conrad (1981; 1982), Kent Day (1982, n.d.), and arguments against by John Rowe (1995).

known as "Pyramid with Ramp," a form relatively well-known in the archaeological literature. Once thought to be embassies of regional polities, Eckhout argues such buildings were actually sequentially erected royal palaces.

It is a good moment to reconsider the use of the term palace and its applicability to the ancient Andean material. As we learn more about Inca and other Pre-Hispanic societies, we are in a better position to understand not only the unique qualities of ancient Andean life, but also the characteristics that the cultures of this region share with other societies elsewhere in the world. Considerations of Inca and Chimú attitudes about definitions of royalty, rulership, and especially states of being and definitions of personhood, have, in turn, changed our assumptions about our understandings of the European royal body and rulership.

So too, as we learn more about European and other non-Andean cultures, the Inca traditions are perceived as more universal. For example, the peripatetic nature of the Inca royal court and its concomitant material correlates (see Houston and Cummins this volume) seem far less unusual when we consider that many royal courts, including those of sixteenth-century Britain and Spain, as well as nineteenth-century Morocco, were often on the move (Elliott 1963; Geertz 1977: 161–167; Thurley 1993). A new focus on Andean palaces, therefore, promises to expand and enhance our understanding of an architectural type and its inherent social ideas.

Acknowledgments The author would like to thank Susan Evans for sparking initial interest in this topic, and for her scholarly insights and good humor throughout the entire process. I am also indebted to Terence D'Altroy, James Fitzsimmons, Edward Harwood, William Isbell, Mary Pye, Jeffrey Quilter, and David Webster for their excellent questions and observations on the subject of palaces.

Bibliography

ALCINA FRANCH, JOSÉ

1976   Arqueología de Chinchero. *Memorias de la Misión Científica Española en
        Hispanoamérica* 2–3. Junta para la Protección de Monumentos y Bienes Culturales en
        el Exterior, Dirección General de Relaciones Culturales, Ministerio de Asuntos
        Exteriores, Madrid.

BANDELIER, ADOLPH F.

1969   *The Islands of Titicaca and Koati.* Kraus Reprint, New York.
[1910]

CALANCHA, ANTONIO DE LA

1974–82   *Crónica moralizada del Orden de San Augustín en el Perú*, 6 vols. Transcription, critical
  [1638]   study, notes, bibliography, and indexes by Ignacio Prado Pastor. Crónicas del Perú 4–
           9. Universidad Nacional Mayor de San Marcos, Lima.

CIEZA DE LEÓN, PEDRO

1984   *Crónica del Perú: Primera parte.* With an introduction by Franklin Pease G. Y. Fondo
[ca. 1551] Editorial, Academia Nacional de la Historia, Pontificia Universidad Católica del
            Perú, Lima.

COBO, BERNABÉ

1990   *Inca Religion and Customs* (Roland B. Hamilton, ed. and trans.). University of Texas
[1639–53] Press, Austin.

CONRAD, GEOFFREY W.

1981   Cultural Materialism, Split Inheritance, and the Expansion of Ancient Peruvian
        Empires. *American Antiquity* 46(1): 3–26.

1982   The Burial Platforms of Chan Chan: Some Social and Political Implications. In *Chan
        Chan: Andean Desert City* (Michael E. Moseley and Kent C. Day, eds.): 87–117.
        School of American Research Advanced Seminar Series. University of New Mexico
        Press, Albuquerque.

DAY, KENT C.

1982   Ciudadelas: Their Form and Function. In *Chan Chan: Andean Desert City* (Michael E.
        Moseley and Kent C. Day, eds.): 55–66. School of American Research Advanced
        Seminar Series. University of New Mexico Press, Albuquerque.

n.d.   Architecture of Ciudadela Rivero, Chan Chan, Peru. Ph.D. dissertation. Harvard
        University, 1973.

EECKHOUT, PETER

1999–2000   The Palaces of the Lords of Ychsma: An Archaeological Reappraisal of the Function
             of Pyramids with Ramps at Pachacamac, Central Coast of Peru. *Revista de Arqueología
             Americana* 17–19: 217–254. Instituto Panamericano de Geografía e Historia, México,
             D.F.

ELLIOTT, J. H.

    1963   *Imperial Spain, 1469–1716.* Edward Arnold, London.

FARRINGTON, IAN S.

    1995   The Mummy, Estate and Palace of Inka Huayna Capac at Quispeguanca.
            Tawantinsuyu 1: 55–65.

GARCILASO DE LA VEGA, EL INCA

    1966   *Royal Commentaries of the Incas and General History of Peru,* pt. 1. With an introduction
    [1609] by Harold V. Livermore (trans.). University of Texas Press, Austin.

GASPARINI, GRAZIANO, AND LUISE MARGOLIES

    1980   *Inca Architecture* (Patricia J. Lyon, trans.). Indiana University Press, Bloomington.

GEERTZ, CLIFFORD

    1977   Centers, Kings, and Charisma: Reflections on the Symbolics of Power. In *Culture and
            Its Creators: Essays in Honor of Edward Shils* (Joseph Ben-David and Terry Nichols
            Clark, eds.): 150–171. University of Chicago Press, Chicago.

GUAMAN POMA DE AYALA, FELIPE

    1936   *Nueva crónica y buen gobierno (Codex péruvien illustré).* Travaux et Mémoires 23. Institut
    [1615] d'Ethnologie, University of Paris, Paris.

GONZÁLEZ HOLGUÍN, DIEGO DE

    1989   *Vocabulario de la lengua general de todo el Perú, llamada lengua qquichua o del Inca* (3rd
    [1590–1600] ed.). With a presentation by Ramiro Matos Mendieta and prologue by Raúl Porras
               Barrenechea. Universidad Nacional Mayor de San Marcos, Lima.

LANGE, CHARLES H., AND CARROLL L. RILEY

    1996   *Bandelier: The Life and Adventures of Adolph Bandelier.* University of Utah Press, Salt
            Lake City.

LEE, VINCENT R.

    1989   *Chanasuyu: The Ruins of Inca Vilcabamba.* Sixpac Manco Publications, Wilson, Wyo.

MARTÍNEZ COMPAÑÓN, BALTASAR JAIME

    1978–94 *Trujillo del Perú,* 13 vols. Ediciones Cultura Hispánica, Madrid.
    [1781–89]

MORGAN, LEWIS HENRY

    1974   *Ancient Society or Research in the Lines of Human Progress from Savagery through
            Barbarism to Civilization.* With an introduction by Eleanor Burke Leacock (ed. and
            ann.). P. Smith, Gloucester, U.K.

MURÚA, MARTÍN DE

    1946   *Historia del origen y genealogía real de los reyes incas del Perú.* With an introduction,
    [1590–1609] notes, and arrangement by Constantino Bayle. Biblíoteca "Missionalia Hispanica" 2.
               Consejo Superior de Investigaciones Científicas, Instituto Santo Toribio de
               Mogrovejo, Madrid.

NAIR, STELLA

    n.d.   Of Remembrance and Forgetting: The Architecture of Chinchero, Peru, from Thupa Inka to the Spanish Occupation. Ph.D. dissertation. University of California, Berkeley, 2003.

NILES, SUSAN A.

    1993   The Provinces in the Heartland: Stylistic Variation and Architectural Innovation near Inca Cuzco. In *Provincial Inca: Archaeological and Ethnohistorical Assessment of the Impact of the Inca State* (Michael A. Malpass, ed.): 145–176. University of Iowa Press, Iowa City.

    1999   *The Shape of Inca History: Narrative and Architecture in an Andean Empire*. University of Iowa Press, Iowa City.

PROTZEN, JEAN-PIERRE, AND JOHN H. ROWE

    1994   Hawkaypata. The Terrace of Leisure. In *Streets: Critical Perspectives on Public Space* (Zeynep Çelik, Diane Favro, and Richard Ingersoll, eds.): 235–246. University of California Press, Berkeley.

RIVERO Y USTARIZ, MARIANO EDUARDO DE, AND JOHANN JACOB VON TSCHUDI

    1971   *Peruvian Antiquities* (Francis L. Hawks, trans.) Kraus Reprint, New York.
    [1854]

ROWE, JOHN H.

    1995   Behavior and Belief in Ancient Peruvian Mortuary Practice. In *Tombs for the Living: Andean Mortuary Practices* (Tom D. Dillehay, ed.): 27–41. Dumbarton Oaks, Washington, D.C.

SAWYER, ALAN R.

    1980   Squier's "Palace of Ollantay" Revisited. *Ñawpa Pacha* 18: 63–80.

SQUIER, EPHRAIM G.

    1973   *Peru: Incidents of Travel and Exploration in the Land of the Incas*. AMS Press, New York.
    [1877]

THURLEY, SIMON

    1993   *The Royal Palaces of Tudor England: Architecture and Court Life, 1460–1547*. Yale University Press for the Paul Mellon Centre for British Art, New Haven, Conn.

WILLEY, GORDON R.

    1953   Prehistoric Settlement Patterns in the Virú Valley, Peru. *Bureau of American Ethnology Bulletin* 155. Smithsonian Institution, Washington, D.C.

Palaces and Politics in the Andean Middle Horizon

William H. Isbell

BINGHAMTON UNIVERSITY, STATE UNIVERSITY OF NEW YORK

> I venture that some Wari rulers used the name Pachacutec, and that Cusi Yupanqui chose a name that reminded him of the ancient greatness of that past culture. Possibly he felt himself heir to the legendary Wari lords and wished to emulate them (see the long list of rulers, who may be Wari lords, provided by Montesinos). (Rostworowski de Diez Canseco 1988: 60; 1999: 35)

In 1999, the members of the Conchopata Archaeological Project excavated what might be a pictorial list of kings from the Middle Horizon (Fig. 1; Isbell 2001c, Fig. 16; Isbell and Cook 2002, n.d.; Ochatoma Paravicino and Cabrera Romero 2002).[1] The figures were painted on oversize urns found at Conchopata, an early Middle Horizon city located in Peru's central highland valley of Ayacucho, ca. 10 km from Huari. (Locations of sites mentioned in this text are provided in Fig. 2.) Conchopata, Huari's major early ally, has long been famous for its spectacular polychrome urns decorated with icons that also grace the celebrated Gate of the Sun at Tiwanaku (see, for example, Cook 1987; Isbell 1987; Menzel 1964). But the new discovery is different, for it represents human faces with no mythical attributes. The themes so carefully repeated on urn after urn are the profiles of seven men, always in the same sequence, each with his characteristic skin color, face paint, headdress, nose ring, or ear ornaments. These men must have been influential paramount leaders. Because of their special garb and consistent repetition, I suggest that they represent a list of rulers: the kings of Conchopata. A radiocarbon date for the cache confirms its placement in the first half of the Middle Horizon (1270 ± 60 B.P. or A.D. 680 ± 60; cal 1 sigma A.D. 675 to 795).

As recently as a decade ago, archaeologists would undoubtedly have dismissed the argument that Middle Horizon ceramic decorations represent a pictorial list of Huari kings. But today, Andeanists are aware of painted boards and other visual representations of royal history used by the Incas as well as the possibility that narrative was recorded on *khipus* (Ascher and Ascher 1981; Pärssinen 1992: 26–51; Primeglio 1992; Quilter and Urton 2002; Urton 1997: 30–31). Juha Hiltunen (1999) argues persuasively that the dynasty of forty-six

---

[1] This project was directed by William H. Isbell, Anita G. Cook, José Ochatoma Paravicino, and Martha Cabrera Romero.

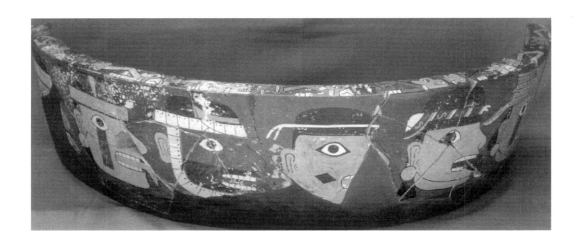

Fig. 1 Male faces (*detail*) on ceramic urns, Conchopata

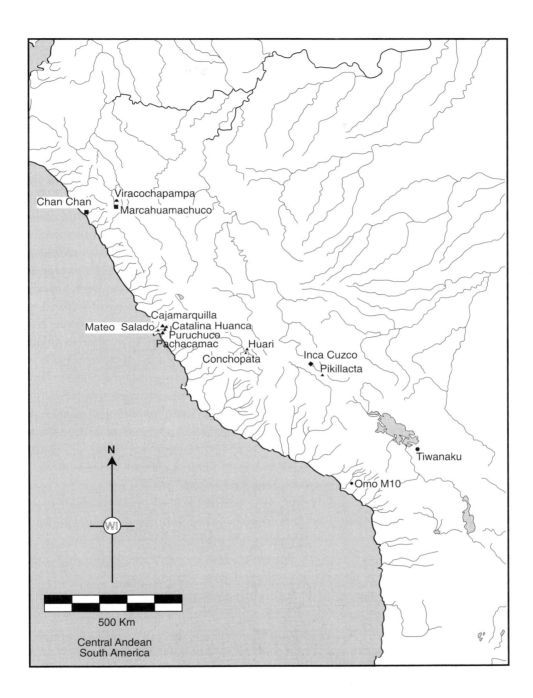

Fig. 2 Central Andean South America, labeled with sites discussed in text

Amauta kings listed in Fernando de Montesinos's notorious chronicle stretches back to Huari monarchs, whose memory was preserved in official courtly accounts of those who considered themselves their heirs: the Incas of Cuzco (see also Rostworowski de Diez Canseco [1988: 60]). Historically based scholars are cautiously exploring the possibility of a tradition of royal monarchs descending into the Andean past as far as Huari and the Middle Horizon. Archaeologists have been much less adventuresome. The best material evidence for royal power and its organization are the architectural remains of royal palaces, but, with a few exceptions, nothing has been written about royal palaces in the great Andean capitals prior to the Incas and their immediate north coast predecessors (e.g., Chimú, Sicán).

As a scholar who once preferred the term *administrative architecture* to *palace*, I identify three primary reasons for avoiding the concept of *palace* in the recent past: First is the popularity of processual evolution among North American archaeologists. This theoretical perspective represents government as adaptive and generally beneficial. Consequently, its practitioners think of rulers as servants of the people, and their architectural installations are imagined to have been centers for collecting and processing information, places where informed bureaucrats made rational policy decisions. Some scholars have attributed a passive legitimization of authority role to palatial monuments, but the necessarily active relation between the *palace* and the construction of privilege and power has been almost deliberately overlooked. Second, many Andeanists insist on describing Andean things in Andean terms, avoiding universalizing, cross-cultural categories. Since it is not clear how *palace*, a European concept, should be translated into Andean culture, the term and concept have been avoided. And, third, there exists a popular tendency to interpret the Pre-Hispanic Andean past in terms of the institutions present in modern Andean folk culture. This promotes a conceptualization of consensus-based, acephalous politics as the timeless Andean norm. Instead of palaces, archaeologists identify consensus-building temples and shrines that have parallels in the civil-religious hierarchies of modern peasant communities.

Given this absence of studies about palaces in the pre-Inca Andean past, the goal of this article is to present and evaluate evidence for earlier royal palaces, particularly those of the Middle Horizon. If there is to be verification of identifications based on independent information, however, I must develop an explicit list of palace diagnostics traced back from the time of European contact. The list of diagnostics is based largely on Inca and Chimú examples, but I also consider Pachacamac and the central coast, as these sites are indispensable links in a temporal chain. *Palace* refers to the residence of a sovereign, not simply elite housing. My set of diagnostic traits relies on other studies, including the work of Craig Morris and Joanne Pillsbury and Banks Leonard in this volume; the colonial description of Inca palaces by Martín de Murúa (1985 [1611–16]: 58–59); Santiago Agurto Calvo (1980); Manuel Chávez Ballón (1970); Graziano Gasparini and Luise Margolies (1977, 1980); John Hemming and Edward Ranney (1982); John Hyslop (1985, 1990); Ramiro Matos Mendieta (1994); Craig Morris and Donald Thompson (1985); John Rowe (1947, 1967, 1985); Dwight Wallace (1998); and Tom Zuidema (1986, 1989a, b; 1990a, b; n.d.).

My list of diagnostic attributes of a palace is as follows: (a) a walled enclosure of the entire complex; (b) a sequence of two or more sizable courtyards or patios that decline in size as access becomes more restricted; (c) impressive portals or defensible gateways controlling entrance to at least the first courtyard and second patio; (d) administrative and possibly residential buildings about the first courtyard as well as the second patio; (e) a proliferation of elaborate and relatively private buildings associated with or beyond the second courtyard (i.e., royal residence), probably including a water source and bath; (f) superior architecture as well as artifacts, especially within the relatively private rooms in the rear of the complex (the royal residence); (g) space for a garden and zoo beyond the area of private rooms, probably with its own water supply; (h) emphasis on spatial location within the complex, particularly inside versus outside, for the construction of social differences; (i) curation of the king's mummy in the palace after his death, at least in the case of palaces within and around the royal capital of Cuzco (more generally, royal palaces became mortuary monuments in their later history);[2] and (j) one or more large roofed halls in front of or within the palace. Known as *carpahuasi* in Cuzco, they were also called *kallanka*. Great celebrations were conducted in *kallanka*, but it appears that on a more regular basis, they housed enormous contingents of splendidly dressed soldiers, who guarded the Inca.

Pachacamac and the Central Coast

Another locus of palaces informs our inquiry into Middle Horizon palaces. Pachacamac was one of the most important Pre-Hispanic cities of the Andean coast, occupied from A.D. 300 or 400 through the Spanish invasion. It included several great temples as well as a building type that was repeated as many as fifteen times across the site (Figs. 3, 4). At the turn of the century, Max Uhle (1991 [1903]: 57–58) called these buildings terraced houses and identified them as the residences of chiefs and nobles. For several decades now, the building type has been called "Pyramid with Ramp" (Pirámide con Rampa; Bueno Mendoza 1974–75, 1982, 1983a, b; Burger 1988; Jiménez Borja 1985; Jiménez Borja and Bueno Mendoza 1970; Patterson 1985; Rostworowski de Diez Canseco 1972, 1989, 1992 [1977]; Shimada 1991) and identified as a religious embassy.

The Pachacamac Religious Embassies Model can be summarized as follows. The influential deity of a successful shrine such as Pachacamac would be an attractive object of veneration for neighboring peoples, who might petition for a representative of the deity in their homeland. If the petition was accepted, an image and a priest would be sent. The recipient community would then construct a temple facility and provide it with economic resources—probably lands and/or herds as well as labor to develop them for the benefit of the image and cult. Of course, the new image would be associated with the principal deity, probably by kinship (younger brother, son, wife, or some other relative), so that the products of the minor image's lands and herds would belong to the principal deity as well. Some of these products would be passed on to the ceremonial center of the principal shrine, where members of the new community would establish a presence, working for the benefit of the principal image and participating in its rituals. This would require the new community to construct itself an inn or "embassy" at the shrine center. At this embassy compound,

---

[2] Unlike Inca examples, Chimú palaces contain burial platforms.

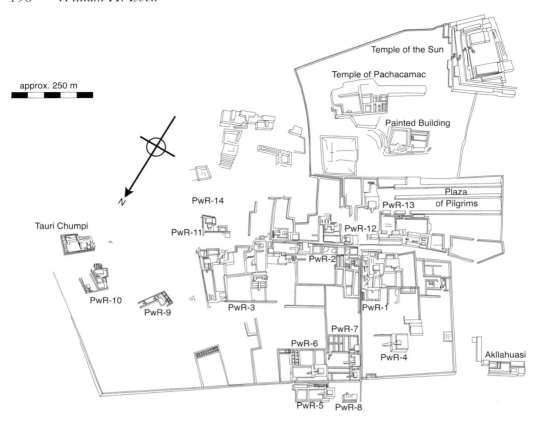

Fig. 3 Architectural core, Pachacamac. This sketch map notes "Pyramid with Ramp" (PwR) palaces, 1–14, and other major structures. After Régulo Franco Jordán (1998: fig. 6) and Peter Eeckhout (1998b).

representatives of the community, or its clergy, would receive and store tribute, promote community participation in rituals, house community workers involved in sanctioned projects at the capital, perhaps conduct economic exchanges, and carry out other activities. The model emphasizes the adaptive complementarity of the ecology as well as the goods from diverse communities that participated in Pachacamac's (and other shrines') politico-religious spheres. The embassy-like compound constructed by each subsidiary community was a "Pyramid with Ramp."

Peter Eeckhout (1997; 1999a, b; 2000) challenges this model, arguing that the three "Pyramid with Ramp" complexes excavated so far at Pachacamac do not seem to have included the kind of storage space or housing facilities for visitors that would be required by a religious embassy, as described above. But, more significantly, he reviews a wealth of evidence supporting his argument that the complexes were occupied rather briefly, perhaps for an average of about thirty years. They were then formally abandoned, a process that involved deliberately filling ceremonial spaces, blocking doorways, and burying the bodies of elites under floors at particular places. In light of the popular interpretation of Chan

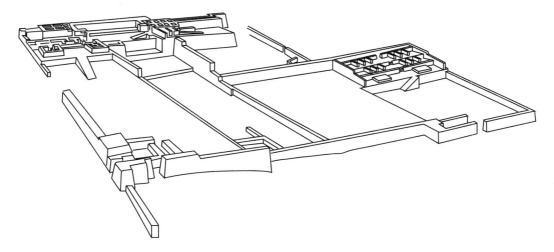

Fig. 4 "Pyramid with Ramp" no. 3, Pachacamac. After Peter Eeckhout (1998a: fig. 3b).

Chan as a capital city composed of palaces constructed sequentially by a dynasty of kings, Eeckhout argues that Pachacamac's "Pyramid with Ramp" complexes were also palaces, each one built for the reign of a single king and then abandoned or converted into a mortuary monument at his death.

I believe Eeckhout is correct, although the situation at Pachacamac may have been more complex. In some cases, a "Pyramid with Ramp" palace was rebuilt several times. "Pyramid with Ramp" no. 3 (see Fig. 4), where Eeckhout (1997; 1998a, b; 1999b; 2000) has excavated, reveals an original construction phase, a later rebuilding that almost obliterated the first, and a third remodeling that involved the construction of a new courtyard, elevated stage, and access ramp with rooms and facilities partially overlapping the abandoned, second-phase complex. Were all these enlargements conducted by one king during his lifetime, or do they represent a succession of several kings? If the latter, when and why was a "Pyramid with Ramp" palace remodeled instead of abandoned? Did remodeling require resanctification rites for royal residential space? If the palace was rebuilt instead of abandoned, could it also have functioned as a mortuary monument for a deceased king? Could it be that a "Pyramid with Ramp" palace was abandoned and converted into a mortuary monument when there was something like a dynasty change, such that the new king no longer viewed himself as belonging to the lineage of his predecessor? While these questions remain to be answered, I am satisfied with the evidence showing that Pachacamac's "Pyramid with Ramp" compounds were royal palaces.

At the end of 1534, Francisco Pizarro moved from Cuzco to the coast, where he planned to establish his new capital. Until he founded Lima the following year, he appropriated and resided in the palace of the Inca governor Tauri Chumpi. Excavated by Alberto Bueno (1983b: 6–11), Tauri Chumpi's palace at Pachacamac is a "Pyramid with Ramp" located at the end of a long row of similar buildings (Figs. 3, 5; see also Franco 1998; Jiménez 1985; Paredes 1988; Paredes and Franco 1987; and Uhle 1991 [1903]: 4–7).

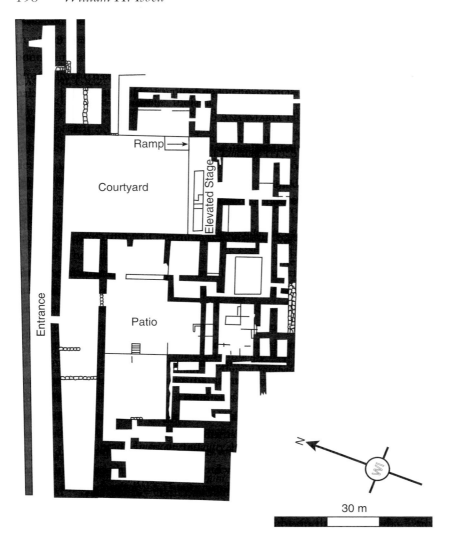

Fig. 5 Palace of the Inca governor Tauri Chumpi, Pachacamac. After Peter Eeckhout (1999b: 123).

Bueno (1983b: 10) describes the palace of Tauri Chumpi as rectangular in plan, with two sizable courtyards, around which there are rooms, habitations, halls, storerooms, and platforms, interconnected by passages, zigzags, ramps, and rectilinear portals. The north side of the walled enclosure faces a large street and had two towers that may have served for lookout and defense. A map of Tauri Chumpi's palace (see Fig. 5) supplied by Peter Eeckhout (1999b) better reveals its features. It had two courtyards, which were not related sequentially in the fashion described by Murúa, and there was no room for a garden at the rear of the complex. In fact, the entire complex is diminutive by comparison with the Inca's palace at Huánuco Pampa, but, in many respects, the form of Tauri Chumpi's compound does identify it as a palace.

The large courtyard of Tauri Chumpi appears to be the grand hallway where the king or governor held court. The south end of the courtyard is raised and accessed by a ramp, providing a stage that overlooks the rest of the hall below. This was probably the equivalent of the throne room of European palaces. Behind the stage is a complex of rooms, whose walls form a U-shaped backdrop for the stage, which could have been draped with textiles. These rooms constituted a "backstage," from which ritual officiators could emerge into public view. There is also a narrow passage from the rooms behind the stage into what appears to be the residential area associated with the second court or patio, which is lower in elevation than the courtyard and stage. So while the hall was filled with vassals, a king or governor residing in the lower, western portion of the palace could prepare for ceremonies and dress for events. Then he could slip into the courtyard section behind the U-shaped room complex to make an impressive formal appearance on the stage. Narrow rooms might have been wardrobe and treasure rooms, where valets carefully stored expensive costumes and jewelry between the governor's ritual appearances.

The west patio of Tauri Chumpi's palace probably represents domestic quarters, with rooms along the south and east for secondary wives, retainers, workers, and other low-status individuals. The rooms along the east side of the patio were surely dwellings for the governor himself.

The Tauri Chumpi palace differs from Inca palaces in much the same ways that Puruchuco does. This architectural complex was mentioned in the sixteenth century as the residence of a minor lord (*curaca*) in the Rimac Valley north of Pachacamac (Jiménez 1973). The Puruchuco ruin is a high, thick-walled rectangular enclosure, ca. 10 x 22 m.[3] Its gateway or portal consists of an ascent ramp between two walls. Upon reaching a platform, anyone entering the palace had to turn right between another pair of walls and ascend another ramp to a doorway that opened through the wall on the left. From the doorway, the visitor had to negotiate a difficult pedestal and descend into a modestly large courtyard. However, from the pedestal a ramp also ascends to the far end of the court, which is raised above the floor of the courtyard and framed by room walls to form a U-shaped stage. From the side of this stage, another ramp descends into a long hallway passing through the core of the adjoining portion of the Puruchuco compound, certainly the residential area. There is also a passage from behind the stage directly into the residential area, just as in the Tauri Chumpi palace.

A third palace reported for the Inca period on the central coast is Huaca Mateo Salado, probably the seat of Inca authority and principal palace of the Inca governor for the entire central coast region (Buse 1960: 53, 57–59; Kauffman 1983: 511, 716; Rostworowski 1978: 66); and, indeed, Huaca Mateo Salado is a first-magnitude complex. In the 1940s, before much of it was destroyed by the urban growth of Lima, Mateo Salado consisted of five earthen mounds, twelve to fifteen meters tall, enclosed within high walls. This group included one large and one medium-sized mound, two small ones, plus a fifth appended to

---

[3] Aerial photographs of Puruchuco in the 1940s show that there were outbuildings in addition to the main compound. Consequently, the 10 x 22 m enclosure may have been only part of this minor palace.

the corner of the largest mound. All of the mounds had walls and buildings on their summits, and it is clear that they supported a significant residential occupation. One of the mounds was approached by a long central ramp with reservoirs on both sides.

Although severely damaged today, the main mound was depicted in a reconstruction illustration years ago by Luis Ccosi Salas (in Buse 1960: 60). Taking this illustration into consideration as well as an aerial photograph from 1944 (Agurto 1984: 147), it appears that the largest mound had a central ramp ascending to a great courtyard that had a walled dais and/or building in the central rear, facing the entrance. This may have been reached by a ramp. Beyond this first courtyard was a smaller patio, surrounded by buildings. Another patio was located farther behind, where many more structures appear to have existed.

Lords of the late central coast seem to have had several palaces. An especially large palace may have served as a homeland capital, such as the great compound with ramped pyramid at Maranga (Canziani 1987). A second palace may have been built at the great religious center of Pachacamac. Indeed, if this were the case, the Pachacamac Religious Embassies Model is not without merit, although it was the king and court that traveled back and forth, not a religious image with its priests.

On the basis of these examples, I have abstracted a list of features for Late Intermediate period and Late Horizon central coast palaces that reveals some interesting differences from Inca palaces: (a) a securely walled compound with defensible entryway controlling access to the interior. Alternatively, some or all of the complex could be elevated on high platforms to ensure security (and enhance display). In that case, gateways were replaced by ramps, but, in many cases, walls and platforms were combined, as were gateways and ramps; (b) a sizable courtyard with one end raised to produce a prominent stage overlooking a lower assembly area. The stage is connected to the assembly area by a ramp; (c) a complex of rooms or walls on the raised stage forming a U-shaped backdrop that might have been draped with textiles; (d) a second, or small patio in the interior of the building, lower in elevation than the stage; (e) a proliferation of relatively private rooms, some quite grand and others quite modest, as well as kitchen and work areas, associated with the second, smaller patio. The floors of these rooms are often at different levels of elevation; (f) a small passageway connected the residential area to the raised stage and its U-shaped space; (g) use of variation in elevation, above and below, as the favored opposition for spatially construct-ing difference in social rank; (h) interment and abandonment of the architectural complex, usually combined with the burial of more and less elite bodies.

Like Inca palaces, central coast palaces were securely walled. However, walls could be replaced by the steep sides of mounds or platforms. In keeping with this, gateways could be replaced by ramps. Furthermore, central coast palaces appear to use higher/lower as the primary opposition for producing social difference, much as the Incas used inside/outside as the primary spatial contrast. Consequently, central coast palaces do not emphasize unilineal succession from courtyard to patio to residential area, as Inca palaces did.

Do central coast palaces of the Late Intermediate period have Middle Horizon ori-gins? Huari ceramics and textile designs appear at Pachacamac and in neighboring valleys; if "Pyramid with Ramp" palaces can be traced to the Middle Horizon, we might establish a series of links that could identify Huari palaces.

Except for the temples of Pachacamac itself, none of the architecture visible on the surface at Pachacamac seems to have originated as early as the Middle Horizon. On the other hand, there are several platform complexes, ca. 20 km up the Rimac Valley that may be Middle Horizon in date. Catalina Huanca is an elongated mound with a narrow ramp ascending one end, enclosed within a walled compound (Agurto 1984: 90–93). Huaca Trujillo is squarer but also had a long ascending ramp. Unfortunately, there has been very little investigation of these early "Pyramid with Ramp" complexes.

Close to Catalina Huanca and Huaca Trujillo are the ruins of the central coast's largest Middle Horizon city: Cajamarquilla (Agurto 1980; Bueno 1974–75, 1983a, b; Kosok 1965: 36–37; Sestieri 1964, 1971). At least one component of its occupation shows prominent Huari influence, so if "Pyramid with Ramp" palaces were forms shared with Huari, they should appear at Cajamarquilla. Disconcertingly, they do not. What Cajamarquilla does possess is a remarkably orthogonal layout composed of securely walled cells with a strong overtone of Huari influence (Isbell 1977: 47–48; 1991). Several of the larger cellular enclosures do contain a prominent pyramid as well as spacious courts and patios, but ramp ascents are nowhere apparent. Perhaps royal residences were built atop these pyramids, but their ramps were removed in later rehabilitation projects, for there seems to have been a later occupation of the Cajamarquilla city.

Another scenario is possible. Perhaps Cajamarquilla's compound with pyramid complexes do represent Middle Horizon palaces, but without ramps. Perhaps the ramp was added to central coast pyramid palaces under influence from north coast Moche culture. Huaca Grande is a very large pyramid located within a securely walled enclosure at Pampa Grande in the north coastal Lambayeque Valley. It is broadly contemporary with the Middle Horizon occupations at Cajamarquilla and Pachacamac. It almost surely had a palace residence on its summit (Haas 1985; Shimada 1994), and it was approached by an especially long and complex ramp. In fact, many north coast pyramids of this general time are classified as T-shaped for their great ramps.

We seem to be on the trail of a tradition of central coast palaces that may have roots in Huari and the Middle Horizon, but there is so little information. Especially troubling for Andean prehistory and the central coast archaeological record is their rapid destruction from the expansion of metropolitan Lima. In a few years, the crucial culture historical links among Huari, Cajamarquilla, and Pachacamac may disappear.

Identifying an Early Palace at Huari

Royal palaces have never been identified at Huari or any of its provincial installations, but archaeologists have never searched the ruins of Huari informed by lists of diagnostic features for later palaces. Huari was one of the greatest cities in the world during the eighth and ninth centuries of our era, and today it is the largest archaeological zone in the Peruvian highlands. Its ruins are located in the arid Ayacucho Valley of Peru's central highlands (see Fig. 2). For the modern visitor, the most prominent aspects of the Pre-Hispanic ruins are huge rough stone walls. Some tower more than 10 m high, and many are considerably

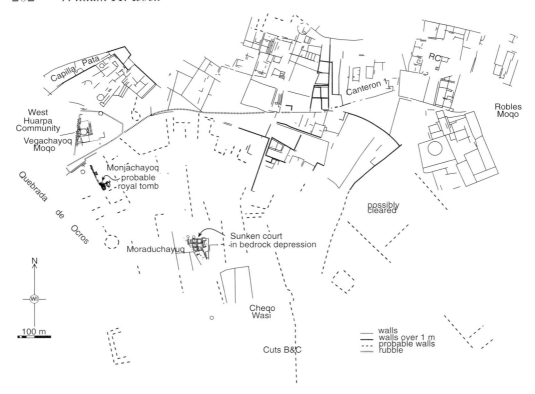

Fig. 6 Architectural core, Huari

more than 1 m thick. The most conspicuous walls are freestanding, seeming to define huge rectangles and trapezoids many hectares in area (Fig. 6). The masonry of the walls consists of rough quarried stones set in strong clay mortar. Floors are usually of hard white gypsum. Many of the walls have a thick clay coating and shiny white plaster. If all the walls were originally whitewashed in this fashion, the city must have presented a dazzling impression in the bright tropical sunlight.

Huari also has huge retaining walls of masonry similar to its freestanding walls, creating vast terraces, but the site was never divided into horizontal surfaces, as the Incas so frequently organized their space. Rather, Huari building compounds flowed over irregularities, often including rooms on different levels. Sometimes the floor of a single room was divided into distinct elevations by rounded steps. Many buildings had more than one floor, and upper stories, too, were variable in their organization. When Huari was densely occupied, its shiny white buildings of multiple stories sprawling across irregular surfaces and huge terraces must have presented a perplexing image, like a great jagged-toothed pyramid of fantastic dimensions. Internally, the flow of traffic through the city must have been convoluted and confusing.

An inventory of the standing walls and a survey of pottery sherds as well as other prehistoric trash littering the ground show that the remains of buildings cover ca. 2.5 sq km

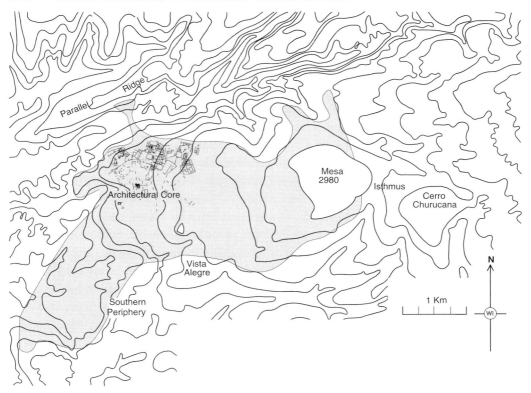

Fig. 7 Archaeological zone at Huari; depicted at maximum occupation during the
Moraduchayuq phase, ca. 700–800

(Fig. 7), constituting what I call Huari's architectural core. Lesser traces of masonry as well
as pottery fragments spread over that great an area again. Across much of another 10 sq km,
ceramic sherds and other broken items discarded by prehistoric residents can be found
where erosion has been modest. Of course, Huari's 15 sq km archaeological zone represents
centuries of occupation, beginning soon after the start of the first millennium B.C. and
continuing through today. Recent additions include hacienda houses, peasant huts, field-
stone walls, a paved highway, and a tourist museum. Even at its peak around A.D. 800, the
area in its entirety was never occupied simultaneously. Conservative techniques for estimat-
ing prehistoric population suggest ten to twenty thousand inhabitants at its peak, and more
liberal techniques imply as many as thirty-five to seventy thousand (Isbell 1984, 1985,
1997b, 2001a; Isbell, Brewster-Wray, and Spickard 1991; Isbell and McEwan 1991). I suggest forty thousand inhabitants as a likely maximum.

The largest archaeological excavation at Huari is in a sector known today as Vegachayoq
Moqo (Bragayrac 1991, n.d.; González and Bragayrac 1986; González et al. 1996, 1997;
Pérez Calderón 1999; Solano and Guerrero 1981). It has been identified as ceremonial and
named El Templo Mayor, but I will show that it is best understood as a royal palace.

Vegachayoq Moqo lies on the eastern edge of the oldest part of the Huari city, known as the West Huarpa community (see Fig. 6; Isbell 1997b, 2001a). This suggests that its construction began early in the history of Huari, but the archaeology is not well documented. Many of the excavation notes were destroyed and the collections mixed when the Instituto Nacional de Cultura's Ayacucho facilities were bombed and burned during the 1980s. Several facts do stand out. At least parts of Vegachayoq Moqo were deliberately covered with fill when it was abandoned, apparently a form of interment (Bragayrac 1991). Many burials had been placed in the complex, some late and intrusive, others, such as secondary bundle burials in a great wall niche, probably while the architectural complex was still in use (González et al. 1996).

Vegachayoq Moqo consisted of a courtyard or plaza (Figs. 8–10), with a U-shaped platform mound rising, ca. 8 m, in two terraces on the east end—the only volumetric construction currently defined at Huari. The "body and two arms" of the mound are of slightly different elevations. The main body bordering the courtyard on the east was the largest, about 70 to 80 m long on its axis, that was ca. 9 degrees west of north. This section seems to have been ca. 40 m wide and may have had a stairway or ascent on its back, east side. At the south end, a smaller and lower section projects some 30 m toward the west. In the north, where the least excavation has been conducted, it seems that another mound projected west to complete the three-lobed, U-shaped volume.

Vegachayoq Moqo appears to have been enclosed by walls and bordered by streets. In the northeast corner of the enclosure was a D-shaped building about 13 m in diameter. At the opposite, southeastern edge of the enclosure is a great worked stone, flat except for its raised edges. Analogy with Tiwanaku suggests that it was an architectural model, representing a sunken ceremonial court, although analogies with modern folk religion suggest that it might have been a *mesa*, where ceremonial objects were arranged during the observation of religious rituals.

Vegachayoq Moqo's deep courtyard was probably an early feature of the architecture, although it was probably remodeled many times. Deep below its plastered floor was an earlier floor and pottery belonging to what I call the Vista Alegre phase, a period that ended about A.D. 550. The central mound bordering the court is probably as old as the courtyard, although it, too, was surely reshaped in later eras. It rose in two terraces and had a freestanding megalithic wall on the top (Fig. 11).

At the base of the platform, long, narrow rooms were constructed, and stone corbels projecting from the high wall imply a roof. The first terrace is ca. 5 m tall. Its surface was 6.1 m wide and originally more than 35 m long—perhaps as much as 60 m in length. It is surmounted by a second terrace, originally probably 2 m high, which reached the top of the mound. The surface of this lower terrace has huge masonry blocks, a little more than two meters square, with pairs of small niches in their sides, abutting the wall of the second terrace. Named altars during excavation, they were too tall to have fulfilled this function. More likely, they were support pilasters for a roof. Furthermore, these pilasters are slightly trapezoidal, making them narrower at the rear where they stand against the terrace wall, so that they create enormous niches, ca. 2 sq m, 20 to 30 cm wider in the back than at their front openings.

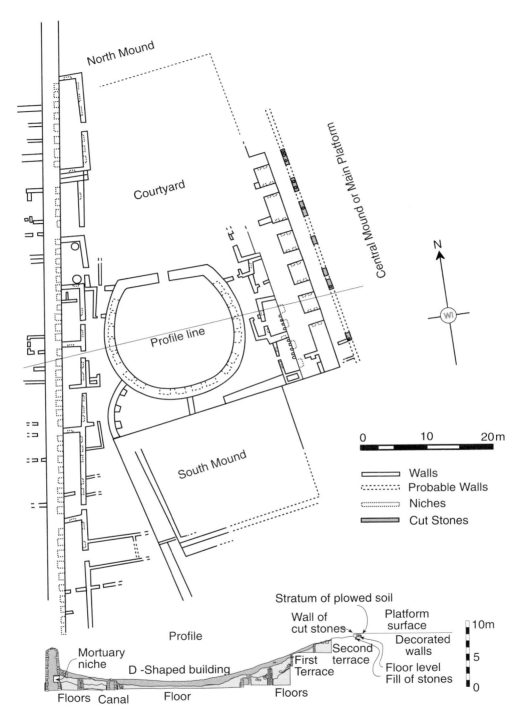

North Mound

Courtyard

Central Mound or Main Platform

Profile line

South Mound

N

W

0   10   20 m

☐ Walls
⋯⋯ Probable Walls
⋯⋯ Niches
▨ Cut Stones

Stratum of plowed soil

Wall of
cut stones

Platform
surface

Decorated
walls

Profile

Mortuary
niche

Second
terrace

First
Terrace

Floor level
Fill of stones

D -Shaped building

Floors   Canal   Floor   Floors

10 m

5

0

Fig. 8 Plan, Vegachayoq Moqo

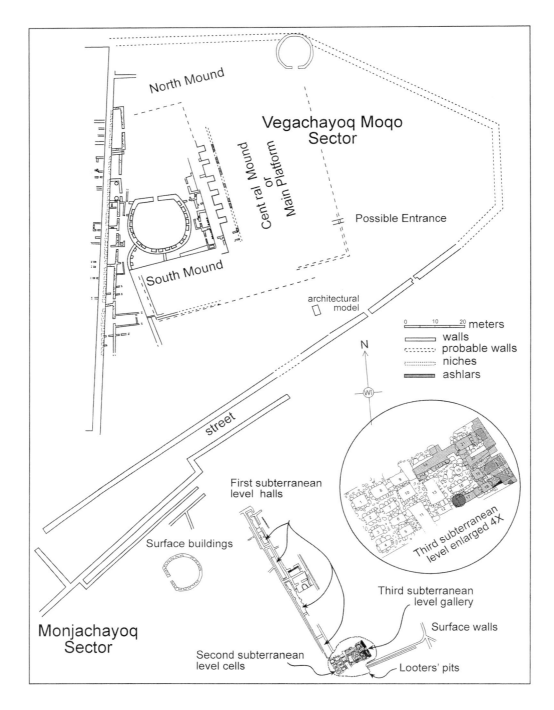

Fig. 9 Vegachayoq Moqo (*above*) and Monjachayoq (*below*) sectors. Architecture of the third subterranean level (*circle, lower right*) has been enlarged four times.

Fig. 10 Aerial view, Vegachayoq Moqo

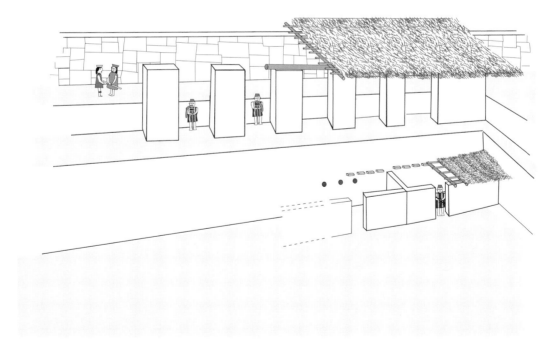

Fig. 11 Hypothetical reconstruction of the palace courtyard, Vegachayoq Moqo

Today, the freestanding wall atop the Vegachayoq Moqo platform consists of discontinuous groups of stone ashlars. Rough-stone masonry fills several spaces where expertly fitted blocks were probably removed late in the history of this building. Some of the ashlars have holes cut in their top edge, resembling mortises, which probably anchored upper courses of similarly shaped blocks. At some time in the history of Huari, almost all of the dressed stones of this wall were removed. Furthermore, many examples of beautifully finished blocks appear reused in walls of rough-stone masonry. Wendell Bennett (1953: 24–25) observed this reuse of ashlars at Huari and, on that basis, argued that dressed-stone masonry preceded rough-stone construction, a conclusion with some merit, although it oversimplifies the situation. At any rate, I believe this megalithic wall is a remnant of particularly fine buildings that once graced the summit of the Vegachayoq Moqo platform.

Only two small excavations were conducted behind the ashlar wall atop the Vegachayoq Moqo mound. One, against the east side of the wall, revealed a stratum disturbed by cultivation that apparently included an ancient floor level. The second excavation was located about 10 m east of the wall. It revealed clay wall decorations, modeled and painted in red, green, and yellow. The unit was quickly filled to prevent destruction of these wall decorations (González et al. 1996: 35–37), and excavation has never been resumed. As with the ashlars mentioned above, the cut confirms the presence of exceptionally fine buildings on the Vegachayoq Moqo platform.

The next most salient feature of Vegachayoq Moqo is a massive rough-stone wall with immense niches that encloses the courtyard on the west (Fig. 8). There is little doubt that this wall was a late addition to Vegachayoq Moqo, and I suspect that originally the courtyard continued to the west far beyond it. This great west wall does not align with the other buildings, and nowhere is it bonded to the mound architecture. Each of the twenty-five large niches measures ca. 98 x 98 cm, and one unlooted example contained the bones of four secondary burials with deformed skulls, bound into bundles. Elongated rooms abut the great west wall at the foot of the courtyard, though their masonry was consistently inferior to the rooms on the east side of the court, further implying that they were very late additions to the building complex.

The other conspicuous construction at Vegachayoq Moqo is a D-shaped building, located between the east wall and the central platform, measuring ca. 19.8 m across, with eighteen huge niches (see Fig. 8). Unfortunately, the building's excavators did not explore the stratigraphy of its foundations, so we do not know if it was part of the original architecture or one of the later rebuilding programs. Its floor is slightly elevated above the rest of the courtyard, so perhaps the D-shaped building is relatively late in the history of Vegachayoq Moqo.

In architectural form, Vegachayoq Moqo relates to both Inca and central coast palaces—more to the latter than the former. First, as in both palace traditions, Vegachayoq Moqo appears to have been securely walled with a gateway access (Fig. 9). Second, it had a large courtyard with a raised platform or stage-like complex at one end. There is no evidence for a ramp, but there are two possible explanations. Vegachayoq Moqo's ramp may have been removed when a D-shaped building was constructed in front of the pyramid platform. Alternatively, a prominent ramp may never have been part of the Huari-Middle

Horizon palace tradition, appearing on the central coast under influence from T-shaped palace platforms of the north coast.

Third, Vegachayoq Moqo's platform mound does not have a U-shaped backdrop on a stage-like summit. The entire pyramid volume, however, forms a U-shaped backdrop around the east end of the courtyard. If roofed, as I suppose, the first and second terraces of the platform would have been an excellent location for courtly activities, useful even in the highland rainy season. Fourth, we can identify a large primary courtyard, although there is no second, smaller patio at a lower elevation than the ritual stage. We know nothing about the top of the south mound, nor, for that matter, the north mound; however, it is possible that patios existed on these mounds.

Fifth, we know that there was a fine ashlar wall, as well as other buildings whose walls were decorated with red, green, and yellow paint, on the summit of Vegachayoq Moqo's main mound. Excavation was terminated before determining the form and function of the summit buildings, but palace residential and kitchen facilities may have existed.

Sixth, there is little doubt that difference in elevation was a primary means of constructing social difference in Vegachayoq Moqo architectural space. Seventh, and finally, we know that Vegachayoq Moqo was abandoned relatively early in the history of Huari and that at least some of it was deliberately interred. Furthermore, it became a focus for burials and perhaps ancestor rituals. Small wall niches in the late rooms at the foot of the courtyard were stained from burning, an indicator of ritual activity.

Few material remains verify the identification of a royal palace more convincingly than a royal tomb. Across the street bordering the south side of Vegachayoq Moqo is the Monjachayoq sector of Huari (Pérez Calderón 1999; Solano and Guerrero 1981). Surface architectural remains are poorly preserved, at least in part because of intensive looting. Near the north edge of the area are some elongated constructions and a sizable D-shaped building with eighteen big niches (see Fig. 9). Toward the south was a large building, but only a few walls and a rounded corner have been identified.[4] Between these extremes are huge looters' holes exposing truly spectacular chamber vaults deep below the surface.

The uppermost subsurface complex consists of four halls, end to end, of well-made rough-stone masonry, with massive dressed-stone slabs for roofs (Fig. 12; see also Fig. 9). Originally, these halls seem to have been ca. 1.6 m high x ca. 1.4 m wide. There is also an annex of small rooms and what may have been another complex of halls north of this annex. These halls were opened long ago, but they still contained many human remains in 1976–77, when archaeologist Abelardo Sandoval supervised their official removal.

At the south end of the hall complex is a colossal looters' hole that was reopened in 1998 by Ismael Pérez Calderón (1999). He revealed a second level of subterranean construction that must originally have been covered by the hall complex. This second subterranean level, 3 m below the hallways, consists of an architectural block containing twenty-one

---

[4]   Thick-walled halls with rounded corners occur in later royal palaces at Huari's provincial capitals. Perhaps this rounded corner identifies a palace complex at Monjachayoq, but without additional excavations there is very little on which to base an inference.

Fig. 12 Subsurface hall Monjachayoq

cells or small chambers (Fig. 13; see also Fig. 9). It was constructed of rough stonework combined with dressed-stone blocks and capped by huge ashlars, ca. 50 cm thick. Many of these capping blocks have disappeared, and others show evidence of having been recut with iron chisels, implying colonial looting.

Accessible only by means of a shaft, and 4 m below the complex of cells, is the third subterranean level: a large megalithic gallery of complex shape (Fig. 14; see also Fig. 9). In profile, this gallery resembles a llama, with the entry at the mouth of this symbolic animal (Pérez Calderón 1999). At the tip of the llama's tail is a still deeper element that might be considered a fourth subterranean level. This is a circular shaft, like a cyst tomb, lined with rough stonework, 3.7 to 4 m deep and 1.2 m in diameter, with a flat stone lid that once sealed its opening.

Today, the llama-shaped gallery is partially filled with rocks and earth, material that must have fallen in after the chamber was looted. Fragmentary human bones lie among this rubble. I believe that Monjachayoq represents a royal tomb. In fact, its subterranean architecture is reminiscent of the royal burial platforms of Chan Chan (Conrad 1982; Pillsbury and Leonard this volume), consisting of a grand chamber and numerous secondary cells. But, of course, the Huari example is completely underground: a royal catacomb, with a difference in depth and size expressing status.

Fig. 13 Cells, Monjachayoq

Fig. 14 Llama gallery, Monjachayoq

It would be attractive to argue that the royal tomb at Monjachayoq is the grave where the king who reigned from the Vegachayoq Moqo palace was buried, but it is possible that the Monjachayoq llama gallery postdates Vegachayoq Moqo by a century or so. I suspect that Vegachayoq Moqo functioned as a palace during the Quebrada de Ocros phase, A.D. 550 to 700. Well before the end of this phase, Vegachayoq Moqo seems to have been converted into a mortuary complex, perhaps by A.D. 650. The llama gallery has a wooden lintel in one of its leg-shaped sections, with a radiocarbon date of 1230 ± 60 B.P. (A.D. 720 ± 60, calibrated 1 sigma A.D. 700–880). Now this lintel serves no true structural purpose, supporting only fragments of rough-stone construction, so it might have been part of later renovation.[5] However, I suspect that the Monjachayoq tomb was built for a king who ruled Huari sometime after the death of the Vegachayoq Moqo monarch.

Niched Halls and Provincial Huari Palaces

Vegachayoq Moqo participated in a greater field of emerging political complexity. Spectacular monumental architecture was developing in conjunction with an important tradition of government in Peru's north highland Huamachuco region. Just as the "Pyramid with Ramp" embodied political power at Pre-Hispanic Pachacamac, the "niched hall" seems to have been the architectural form associated with power at the northern capital of Marcahuamachuco (see Fig. 2).

Marcahuamachuco is a remarkable collection of monumental buildings spread across a series of high ridges and walled mountaintops. John and Theresa Topic (J. Topic 1986, 1991; J. and T. Topic 1992; T. and J. Topic 1984) define the niched hall and recognize twenty examples at the site (Fig. 15). Other specimens are found at the neighboring sites of Cerro Sazón and Viracochapampa. Linked to the Vegachayoq Moqo palace by their huge niches, these halls are likely the architectural element that best identifies north highland palaces. These long narrow buildings (from 6 or 7 to 15 m wide and up to 50 m or more in length) were among the largest structures ever roofed in the northern highlands. They resemble the great *kallanka* of Inca palaces. The Topics, however, present a very different argument.

They associate niched halls with lineage-based organization that emphasized principles of consensus rather than centralization and hierarchy. Their argument considers archaeological evidence for wealth distribution, but focuses on the association of Marcahuamachuco's niched halls with defleshed bones and secondary burials. John and Theresa Topic (1992) infer that niched halls were places of assembly for political and religious activities. But rather than venerating royal mummies, lineage members honored communal ancestral remains, explicitly made mutual by reducing them to bones. The Topics go

---

[5] I have recently shown that many of Huari's tombs were designed to be re-opened so that bones of the dead could be added and/or removed (Isbell 2004). If this is the case for the llama gallery, material objects as well as architecture may have been refurbished and replaced. Perhaps the wooden lintel belongs to a late rebuilding phase.

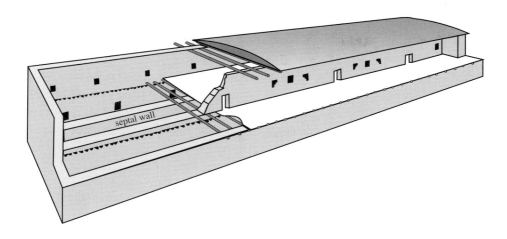

Fig. 15 Niched hall in the classic style, Marcahuamachuco. After John Topic (1986: fig. 6).

on to propose that each niched hall was the assembly place for the members of a lineage, clan, or kin grouping, and every kin group with a niched hall at Marcahuamachuco participated in a regional confederacy integrated around the great political and ceremonial center. Approximate equality in niched-hall architecture implies that lineages shared power. Even if they may have been ranked for ritual events, decisions must have been consensual, and thus relatively egalitarian.

As pointed out above, emphasis on wall niches links Huamachuco's niched halls with Vegachayoq Moqo. However, similarities between the political architecture of Huari and Huamachuco increased in the decades that probably witnessed the interment of Vegachayoq Moqo. John Topic (1991) is correct that niched halls became one of Huari's most popular building types, at least in its provincial centers. Consequently, John and Theresa Topic (1992) infer that Marcahuamachuco-style political organization—confederations of lineages—must have become the organizational basis for Huari integration.

Since consensus-based confederations require neither sovereigns nor their royal palaces, the Topic's proposal has clear implications for the built environment of Huari capitals. The presence or absence of royal palaces in subsequent Middle Horizon centers should therefore confirm the nature of Huari political structure: Was it centralized and hierarchical, united under a king or great lord (*curaca*, to use an Andean term), or was it a coalition of approximately equal kin groupings, who managed regional political affairs through some sort of league? The latter model assumes that governmental functions were located in monumental ceremonial centers where each kin group constructed its assembly halls and conducted ritual events that were more or less equivalent to those of other groups.

These halls are very long and narrow buildings, with numerous large niches in their interior walls. Generally, the niches are wider at the back than at their opening. The masonry of the halls often has defleshed human bones within it and secondary burials placed in wall tombs. At Marcahuamachuco and other Huamachuco centers, niched halls have been targets of looting, so nothing has ever been found in any niches to reveal their original function. Probably very significantly, many niched halls were part of extensive architectural complexes that included a courtyard and smaller rooms, especially during the middle of their history of popularity.

John Topic (1986) proposes a four-phase sequence for niched hall development in Huamachuco. Early, Transitional, and Classic niched halls were more or less contemporary with the Andean middle Early Intermediate period, the late Early Intermediate period and onset of the Middle Horizon, and the remainder of the Middle Horizon. Late niched halls probably postdate Huari, so they will not concern us here.

Early niched halls may have developed from local antecedents, particularly Marcahuamachuco's double defensive walls that gave rise to very long, narrow galleries. Although poorly preserved, early niched halls were 7 to 8 m wide and 26 to 30 m long. They were single storied. Wooden roof beams were supported on long rows of corbels projecting inward from both long walls. This roof must have been more or less flat with a parapet, ca. 1 m high, to counterbalance its weight. Slots through the walls allowed water to drain off the roof. None of the early niched halls is well enough preserved to demonstrate that their walls had niches or to determine the number and location of doorways.

Marcahuamachuco's transitional niched halls, which probably temporally overlap the Vegachayoq Moqo palace, tend to increase in size while playing with form. One was 12 m wide and 42 m long, though others are no more than 7 to 9 m wide. They usually have large niches on the interior of both long walls: up to 65 cm wide and 85 cm tall. Some were set on terraces or the interiors were partially filled to raise the floor level. A multistoried hall runs down a hill, so the lower part has two stories. Perhaps difference in elevation as a means of constructing social rank began to influence Huamachuco's transitional niched halls.

Complex two- and even three-storied niched halls characterize the classic group (Fig. 15), although techniques for constructing the upper floors seem experimental. Some classic niched halls have an elongated building in front, or a filled terrace. Others are on slopes, so part of the complex has a second story. Fully multistoried niched halls use thick septal walls to sustain their upper floors. These are walls constructed to the level of the wooden beams of an upper-floor level and on which the centers of the beams rested. Running under central portions of a floor, septal walls permit room floors that support the weight of great assemblies, which were much broader than would have been possible had the beams spanned the entire width of the room.

I suspect that septal walls became important in the subsequent architecture of Huamachuco and Huari. We must reconsider the organization of the buildings we study in light of the fact that second-floor room plans may not have corresponded with the organization of walls at ground level. Some of the narrow corridors and small chambers that abound in Huari architecture were probably septal walls, supporting floor beams and creating capacious halls on upper floors.

Important formal similarities emphasize the interrelatedness of power and built environments at Huari and Marcahuamachuco, even if the political institutions were different. Emphasis on vertical differentiation of space seems to have had an impact on both traditions at more or less the same time, with the builders of the Vegachayoq Moqo platform employing solutions different from those of the Huamachuco engineers, but to similar ends. Vegachayoq Moqo and Marcahuamachuco architects both preferred long narrow ceremonial space, perhaps so they could be roofed for rainy season celebrations in the highlands. Both constructed elongated annexes on the front of long ceremonial buildings.

Emphasis on immense niches is striking. Furthermore, the pilaster niches on Vegachayoq Moqo's first terrace are wider in the rear, like those of Huamachuco's niched halls. But niches also occur in Huari's D-shaped structures and in the great west wall of Vegachayoq Moqo. (Might D-shaped structures have been an early Ayacucho equivalent of the niched hall?) Finally, both the Huari and the Huamachuco political leaders manipulated human bones. At Vegachayoq Moqo, secondary bundle burials were found in one of the niches, and other human remains were placed in wall tombs. At Marcahuamachuco, defleshed human bones were included in building masonry and remains were placed in wall tombs.

Soon after Vegachayoq Moqo was ritually interred, a new architectural style appeared at Huari and in its provinces. This new style is called orthogonal cellular for its rigid rectilinear outlines and repetition of a few basic architectural forms, as though they were standardized modules (Isbell 1991). I believe that orthogonal cellular architecture was invented by Huari military commanders. To me, it expresses the imagination of victorious war chiefs, able to construct an entirely new built environment in the image of their ideal army. The vigorously outlined rectangular whole was divided into nested and equivalent rectangular units. Based on rigid discipline, the superiority of functional order reigned supreme. Orthogonal cellular architecture could only have been created by architects who began on open land, had unparalleled ambition, and commanded unimaginable labor reserves.

Huari built two great provincial centers in the orthogonal cellular style and, subsequently, numerous smaller compounds. In the Huamachuco Valley, 700 km northwest of Ayacucho, Huari constructed Viracochapampa (Fig. 16; see Fig. 2) in full view of Marcahuamachuco. Its great rectangular enclosure measured 580 x 565 m, although its landscape included a highway, aqueduct, and other built features. The second center is about 300 km southeast of Ayacucho. Pikillacta (Fig. 17; see Fig. 2), located at the south end of the Cuzco Valley, had a primary rectangular enclosure measuring 745 x 630 m (McEwan 1991, 1996, 1998), although it was probably constructed in two episodes. Pikillacta, too, was part of a total landscape transformation.

One of the most popular modular architectural forms at both Viracochapampa and Pikillacta was the niched hall. While they were easy to recognize, niched halls at Viracochapampa and Pikillacta do differ in certain respects from those at Marcahuamachuco. They are relatively wider and shorter. Characteristically, they have rounded interior corners. Their walls are very thick, and they have either one large niche near each corner or numerous large niches across entire interior walls. Without obvious prototypes at Huari, John and Theresa Topic (1992; J. Topic 1986, 1991) are probably correct that the antecedents must be in Marcahuamachuco architecture. They may also be correct that niched halls were key architectural forms in the political co-option of local authority by Huari intruders.

John Topic (personal communication, March 1999) points out that there are about the same number of niched halls at Marcahuamachuco and Viracochapampa, probably twenty at each site. He argues that Huari's leaders constructed Viracochapampa to transfer the regional lineages' ritual activities to the new site. Presumably, this would also relocate the confederacy decision-making apparatus, placing it under Huari supervision.

Niched halls were equally popular at Pikillacta, where Gordon McEwan (1987, 1991, 1996, 1998; McEwan et al. n.d.) reports a total of eighteen. He agrees with the Topic's association of this building type with lineage rituals, but infers that Huari imposed strong centralized government upon regional kin-based units. Except in its homeland of Huamachuco, the niched hall does not exist outside Huari architectural installations.

Viracochapampa and Pikillacta were not likely to have been provincial installations intended for consensus-based federation government. I believe they were probably immense palaces, royal or vice-regal, equipped with facilities for centralized government. Here are my reasons. At Marcahuamachuco, the numerous niched halls appear to have been more or less equivalent, but architectural equivalence was decidedly not a goal at Viracochapampa and Pikillacta. The very center of each of these great rectangular enclosures is occupied by an orthogonal cellular compound with a central plaza that is significantly larger than any other at the site. At Viracochapampa, the central cell, spreading over a full hectare, has two niched halls. Other niched halls occur only one to a compound. Furthermore, these are the largest niched halls in the north highlands, measuring 19 x 46 m and 18 x 48 m (Topic 1986).

At Pikillacta, the central and grandest cell, at least three quarters of a hectare, is also bordered by two exceptionally large niched halls. But Pikillacta differs from Viracochapampa in having a second orthogonal cell, located a short distance north of the central cell, which is also larger than normal and provided with two huge niched halls flanking its courtyard (McEwan 1996; McEwan et al. n.d.). It repeats the main compound, only slightly more modestly.

Viracochapampa and Pikillacta have a similar number of secondary niched halls. Although the actual count depends on what is classified as a niched hall, some twelve to eighteen seems likely. Both sites have a somewhat exceptional niched hall opening onto an empty area within the great rectangular enclosure. Perhaps these halls were part of a reception area for the central complex. The other niched halls were located within normal-sized orthogonal cells and have only one hall per cell. If niched halls accommodated public celebrations where power was negotiated, then the central complexes had the grandest facilities. But Viracochapampa and Pikillacta contained numerous secondary niched-hall complexes. I suspect that these secondary facilities were employed by the king's close relatives, lords who were his vassals.

When inferring the palatial functions of Viracochapampa and Pikillacta, we must remember the importance of septal walls as supports for upper floors. McEwan (1996, 1998) found fragments of upper floors collapsed into the first floor while excavating Pikillacta,

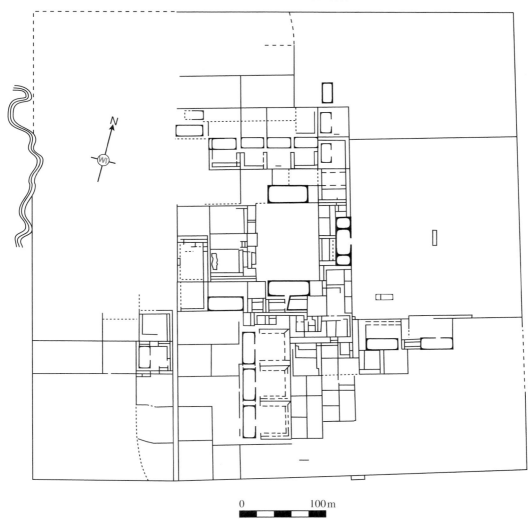

Fig. 16 Plan, Viracochapampa. After John Topic (1991: fig. 2).

but our maps (see Figs. 16, 17) represent only ground plans. I believe that where we saw a labyrinth of walls forming narrow corridors and tiny chambers at ground level, we should infer septal walls, supporting capacious upper-story quarters, intended for elite activities.

Pikillacta has been better preserved and more intensively investigated than Viracochapampa. McEwan's (1996, 1998; McEwan et al. n.d.) maps show that the plaza of the central orthogonal cell is bordered by three, and even four narrow, parallel-walled halls, about 2 m wide. Today, these inner walls are preserved to a height that implies their function as septal walls supporting floors of *kallanka*-like halls, 6 to 8 m wide, that encircled the great courtyard.

The second largest orthogonal cell, also provided with two large niched halls, has even more echelons of narrow halls and diminutive chambers surrounding its courtyard.

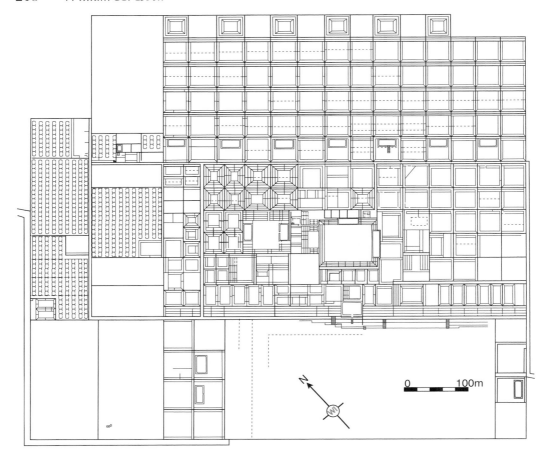

Fig. 17 Plan, Pikillacta. After Gordon McEwan et al. (n.d.: figs. 4–7).

On its northwest side, they are five rows deep. Certainly, these architectural remains also imply an elite upper story of open-roomed apartments. Finally, this entire section of Pikillacta, and especially from the central orthogonal cell to the north, is distinguished by its cramped hallways and chambers. No other cellular compounds in this sector have niched halls, but many have parallel, thick-walled corridors appropriate for expansive upper stories. I believe that these compounds were royal residential quarters adjacent to courtyards with pairs of niched assembly halls.

Viracochapampa is less well preserved than Pikillacta, but narrow halls and tiny chambers are concentrated about its central orthogonal cell. Consequently, this site also appears to have had a central palace courtyard, with assembly halls, that was surrounded by governmental facilities and residential quarters in spacious second-floor apartments.

Generally, how do Viracochapampa and Pikillacta score in terms of my lists of diagnostics for Pachacamac and Inca palaces? First, Viracochapampa and Pikillacta were very securely walled, and at least Pikillacta had an impressive entry complex. Each had a sizable courtyard, but unlike the Pachacamac or Inca examples, it was located at the center of the enclosure. Today, we have no direct evidence for a raised stage and ascending ramp, but it is increasingly apparent that extensive upper-floor compartments surrounded and adjoined the central orthogonal cell.

Both Viracochapampa and Pikillacta have smaller courtyards near the central cell that may have included kitchen and residential facilities, although neither site has been investigated sufficiently to confirm this interpretation. Furthermore, we have numerous great assembly halls and strong indications that elevation was used to construct social difference. Finally, archaeology at Pikillacta reveals that numerous rooms were deliberately closed by filling the doorways. Perhaps this was equivalent to ritual interment at the time of abandonment.

Much about Viracochapampa and Pikillacta has of necessity been inferred, so we are far from confirming the royal palace interpretation. Our examination of formal features shows the palace interpretation to be at least plausible. From an alternative perspective, it is difficult to imagine the construction of such vast centers with anything less than conscripted labor under centralized, hierarchical management. Their planning required astonishing authority. McEwan (McEwan et al. n.d.) believes that Pikillacta was built in two great construction epochs, with the second never concluded. In the initial construction phase, the great rectangle, which includes what I consider to have been the core of the royal palace, was built. McEwan estimates nearly 4 million man days of labor to have been required. Labor invested in the second construction phase totaled ca. 1.8 million man days; another 2 million man days would have been required to complete the project. Could any authority except a powerful king or viceroy have undertaken such a Herculean construction program, and for anything but his own royal palace?

What should be concluded from the apparently unfinished condition of both Viracochapampa and Pikillacta? John Topic (1991; see also T. Topic 1991) argues that Huari's scheme to move Marcahuamachuco's lineage ancestor rituals to Viracochapampa failed. Marcahuamachuco was not abandoned and Viracochapampa was never completed, so whatever Huari intended to achieve by constructing Viracochapampa must have failed. Consequently, the Huamachuco region apparently liberated itself from Huari's political program. Pikillacta was also unfinished, although McEwan (1998; McEwan et al. n.d.) feels that the section I judge to the have been the core of the royal palace was built first and occupied for numerous generations. Other areas, including sectors with secondary niched halls, remained incomplete.

Generally, Huari provincial architecture seems to have been characterized by great rectangular enclosures with numerous empty spaces and unfinished buildings. Does this mean that Viracochapampa and Pikillacta never fulfilled their intended roles, or is it that our Western conception of the built environment has failed to appreciate the "timescape" of Huari provincial architecture: Was empty space required for encampments of numerous visitors during ceremonial occasions? Were empty sectors included for the emergence of new vassals who needed to build and occupy cells with secondary niched halls? Was open space included within enclosures because the royal palace would be interred and abandoned at the death of the monarch and a new one built?

If open space was left for the construction of new palace complexes each time a king died, the explanation of Pikillacta is obvious. Its two oversize orthogonal cells, each with a pair of assembly halls to identify it as a primary palace, must represent the construction of a second palace compound at the death of the first lord. The largest orthogonal cell, at the true center of the site, appears to have been the initial royal compound. The other court-yard, with twin niched halls, to its north must have been the second royal compound. When the king of the central cell died, his heir had his palace interred, but first he built himself a new royal palace on land left vacant for that purpose a short distance to the north.[6]

Viracochapampa appears to have had but one royal facility, so it was probably in service for less time than Pikillacta, but Viracochapampa does have about as many niched halls as Marcahuamachuco. If the goal of the Huari paramount was to provide each of Marcahuamachuco's social units with a niched hall, it seems that this part of Viracochapampa's plan was complete as built. I suspect that empty spaces were not left haphazardly by un-timely failure; open spaces represent a timescape for Huari's built environments that we do not fully understand. I believe at least one factor was royal succession and the replacement of palaces.

If niched halls were central political facilities in the royal compounds of Huari's pro-vincial palaces, they may reveal additional royal palaces at Huari. In 1973, when I mapped the standing architecture of Huari with Patricia Knobloch and Katharina Schreiber, we recorded a building with thick walls, rounded corners, and a niche near its two preserved corners (Fig. 18). A second building, with thick walls and rounded corners, was mapped ca. 500 m east, although no niches were observed in these ruins. Perhaps these buildings were royal palaces, with central orthogonal cells that had a pair of niched halls bordering their spacious plazas and royal quarters located on adjacent upper floors. This proposal certainly stretches the information we have now. No excavations have been conducted and pub-lished for these sectors of Huari. Of course, the idea establishes interesting research priori-ties for the future. Each building lies more or less at the center of a large area of orthogonal cellular architecture in the part of Huari that I (Isbell 1997b, 2001) date to the Moraduchayuq phase, when Vegachayoq Moqo had already been abandoned and the provincial capitals of Pikillacta and Viracochapampa were occupied. Huari political institutions continued changing, however, and, before the end of the Moraduchayuq phase, the niched hall was discarded. The orthogonal cellular architecture of Middle Horizon II employed symmetrical patio groups, so the rituals conducted in niched halls were apparently abandoned.

Palaces of Tiwanaku

No discussion of Middle Horizon Andean palaces can ignore the *altiplano* capital of Tiwanaku, even though so little is known about its archaeology. Surprisingly, a search of

---

[6] We should remember that palace construction and reconstruction at Pachacamac imply a new palace for each royal generation, although this may oversimplify reality. At least some palaces were remodeled imply-ing two or more successive rulers occupying a palace before it was abandoned. Perhaps palaces were associated with something more like a European dynasty.

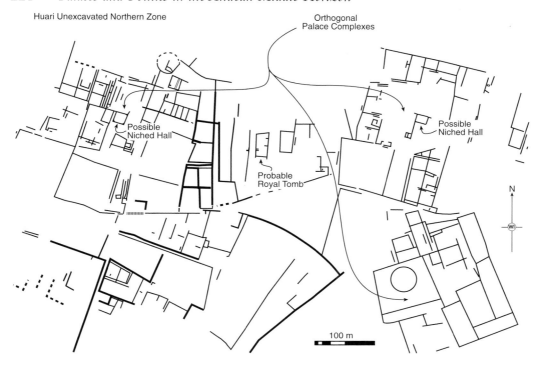

Fig. 18 Unexcavated northern zone, Huari. This sector included two possible orthogonal palace complexes (see *arrows*).

Tiwanaku architecture using the diagnostic attributes of Inca and Pachacamac palaces identifies not the megalithic monuments of Tiwanaku itself, but the rather modest and unique example of provincial Tiwanaku architecture.

Located in the coastal Moquegua Valley (see Fig. 2), the Omo M10 Temple has been classified as a ceremonial building, not a palace (Fig. 19; Goldstein n.d., 1989, 1993). Paul Goldstein (1993: 28), however, also asserts that "the height of this architectural and ceremonial tradition clearly coincides with the apogee of Tiwanaku's political growth." A radiocarbon date for the wall post from a domestic structure dates 1120 ± 60 B.P. (calibrated A.D. 897, 1 sigma range, A.D. 880–986; Goldstein 1993: 32). Perhaps politics and religion were little differentiated in Middle Horizon times, but we must also remember that archaeologists tend to be influenced by theoretical convictions in favor of temples and against palaces.

The Omo M10 Temple is heavily eroded, but it appears to have been securely walled, probably with a single entrance. Like Inca palaces, it consisted of a large outer court, a smaller inner patio, and a cluster of buildings that probably included residences beyond the inner patio. At Omo, these three sectors were constructed on a northwest to southeast axis (see Fig. 19). The first court was an artificially leveled, adobe-walled enclosure, 42 x 57 m. Except for a circular depression, it appears to have been an open space. The second smaller court or patio, 37 x 20 m, was surrounded by more substantial adobe walls and had elon-

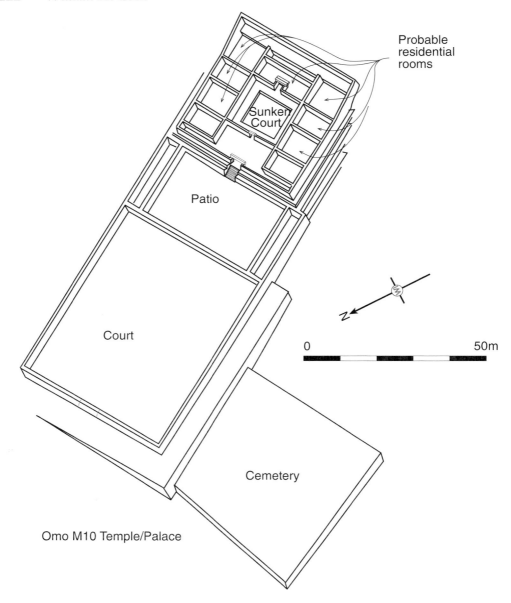

Fig. 19 Omo M10 Temple. After Paul Goldstein (1993: figs. 5, 9).

gated halls on either side. It was paved with red clay. The third sector was raised above the other courts and separated from the inner patio by a fine dressed-stone wall. As with the "Pyramid with Ramp," a steep flight of steps led to a U-shaped stage atop a platform overlooking a court below. But Omo differs from the "Pyramid with Ramp" in employing a stairway instead of a ramp and crowning the stairway with an impressive triple-jamb gateway.

Behind the U-shaped atrium, lies not a modest secret entry, but another elaborate portal complex. Beyond it is a lower and smaller court around which a proliferation of rooms is nested. This at least was how Goldstein (1993) proposed to reconstruct Omo M10 after combining topographic field data with information from a volcanic-tuff architectural model recovered from the site by earlier investigators. Minor discrepancies between the two are a bit confusing, but the third enclosure is represented as an artificial terrace, 34 x 36 m. Beyond the U-shaped atrium, the second gateway, and the sunken court, a substantial roofed edifice lay on the site axis, which in turn was surrounded by a complex of smaller rooms on a low platform. These buildings may have served as residences for a petty king or governor (*curaca*) with his court. An open area was located in the far rear of this palace complex, although it seems too small to have been a garden of the kind described for Inca palaces.

Excavations in the Omo M10 Temple yielded a large quantity of luxury goods, especially in the third, residential area. They came not only from contexts suggesting offerings but also scattered refuse. Omo M10 also has a terrace annex attached to the southwest side of the compound. This appears to have been a cemetery. No royal burials have been discovered, but the association of palaces with mortuary monuments, or perhaps more accurately, the transformation of palaces into mortuary monuments seems to be a prominent Andean pattern.

Useful generalizations about Huari provincial palaces came from comparisons among several examples. Unfortunately, Omo M10 is unique. No other Tiwanaku administrative facility has been identified beyond the city's hinterland. Consequently, if I want to use royal architecture of the provinces to illuminate the architecture of Tiwanaku, I am limited to the single example from Omo. At least the Omo palace shares important features with Inca palaces and Pachacamac's "Pyramid with Ramp," such as emphasis on difference in elevation and the U-shaped stage or atrium. But Omo has distinctive elements as well. This almost certainly means that Tiwanaku palaces differed in significant ways from both Inca and "Pyramid with Ramp" palaces. As with Huari, identifying Tiwanaku palaces requires keeping the attributes of other royal palaces firmly in mind, along with the exercise of great flexibility and imagination.

Tiwanaku, located 20 km southeast of the southern shore of Lake Titicaca (see Fig. 2), consists of a monumental civic center surrounded by a vast residential area (Fig. 20). The size and density of the habitation area at Tiwanaku is yet to be convincingly demonstrated.

Are there any royal palace compounds in Tiwanaku's architectural core? The preliminary answer is that none of Tiwanaku's buildings corresponds sufficiently with models based on Inca, Pachacamac, or Huari palaces to be identified securely as royal palaces. On the other hand, most of Tiwanaku's monumental buildings, or building groups, have some formal features that resemble later Andean palaces. Consequently, several of them may have been a royal palace during part of their history.

The determination of architectural forms and functions at Tiwanaku is complicated by several issues. First, there has been a long history of severe destruction at Tiwanaku, confusing basic descriptive information about buildings and their relationships. Second,

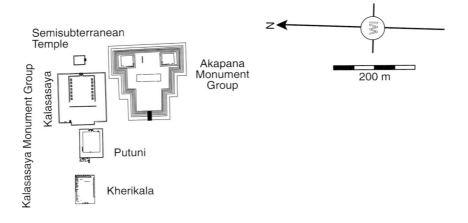

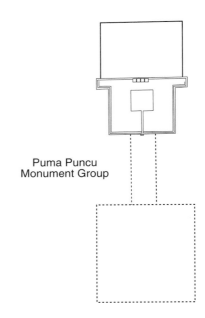

Fig. 20 Tiwanaku civic center, simplified plan. After Jorge Arellano López (1991: figs. 2, 20); Javier Escalante Moscoso (1993: figs 113, 143, 187, 189, 194, 200); Alan Kolata (1993: figs. 5.3, 5.5a, 5.36a, b); Linda Manzanilla (1992: fig. 4); Arthur Posnansky (1945: pl. 1); and Alexei Vranich (n.d.: figs. 6.3, 7.1).

fantastic ideas about Tiwanaku, promulgated by travelers and amateur archaeologists of the past, continue to shape some thinking about Tiwanaku.

The complex chronology of Tiwanaku is still poorly understood (Isbell and Burkholder 2002). This situation has been exacerbated by Tiwanaku's role in modern Bolivian nationalism. Patriotic enthusiasm strongly favors interpretations of great antiquity, as well as autochthonous origins for all that has been classified as Tiwanaku. With relatively few of the excavations at Tiwanaku published as more than summary conclusions, erroneous assumptions are too easily repeated, while thoughtful reevaluations are rare. Furthermore, archaeologists are guilty of thinking about Tiwankau's past in terms of ideal types and homogeneous stages. Individual buildings are imagined as though there was one form and one function and upon achieving this, the building was "finished." But as Joanne Pillsbury and Banks Leonard (this volume) show for Chan Chan, great building complexes were intended to have different forms and different functions at different times. If there was an Andean tendency to convert royal palaces into mortuary monuments—and mortuary monuments developed in relation to political negotiations in ways we still do not understand—we must imagine that palaces were dynamic, changing in form and function. We may not recognize them by the configurations of their final construction epochs.

The map of Tiwanaku (see Fig. 20) reveals no central focus or great ceremonial plaza— as in Cuzco—around which royal palaces might have been located. Rather, Tiwanaku seems more like Chan Chan, and, perhaps to a lesser degree, like Pachacamac and Huari, in consisting of distinct building complexes with spatial organization relatively independent of one another. But Tiwanaku differs from Chan Chan, Pachacamac, and even Huari in another way: Its monumental buildings are volumetric platforms, with massive walls sustaining earthen terraces. There are few or no walled compounds securely defended by freestanding ramparts.

In this essay, I have shown that careful enclosure within walled precincts was the key attribute of Andean palaces. The only exceptions occur when part or all of the palace is elevated on high, steep-sided platforms. Only one building at Tiwanaku has a platform mound tall enough to securely defend a palace, and that is the Akapana. It may be, however, that Tiwanaku's enclosure walls have disappeared because they were made of adobe. At Chan Chan and other coastal capitals, adobe precinct walls have endured for centuries. Certainly, they were massive and well-built, but the primary reason they have survived is because of the desert climate. At Huari, enclosure walls were constructed of stone set in clay mortar. The rainy highland climate has demolished an unknown number, but at least some perimeter enclosures and massively walled streets survive to show that much of Huari was divided into securely walled compounds.

Rain at Tiwanaku is as heavy as at Huari. Walls built a millennium ago exclusively of adobe might have disappeared entirely. Several recent excavators at Tiwanaku have reported discovering parallel rows of stones that they interpret as wall foundations. They argue that adobe walls constructed on the stone foundations enclosed *barrios* or compounds (Janusek n.d., 1999; Kolata 1993: 164). However, Wendell Bennett (1934: 375–377) found similar remains and interpreted them as stone-paved pathways. This issue of walls, enclosed compounds, and perhaps even walled *barrios* requires renewed research. If the buildings of Tiwanaku lay as open as popular reconstructive drawings imply, Tiwanaku certainly was an unusual city for the Andes. And, to the degree that it may have been unique, we cannot understand Tiwanaku with analogies from other Andean urban traditions.

Without resolving the problem of walled compounds, Alan Kolata (1993: 149–162; Sampeck n.d.) identified a palace at Tiwanaku, which he named the Palace of the Multicolored Rooms. The archaeological remains consist of evidence for floors and building walls, several burials, and numerous pits and hearths along the exterior west side of the Putuni building (Fig. 21). This palace is represented as 8 x 22 m in size, and a fragment of a decorated stone architrave was found near what is inferred to have been its entrance. On the floors were many fragments of wall plaster painted in diverse colors, providing the building's name. In front of the palace, there may have been an open patio with paved floor extending west, perhaps the entire distance to the building known as the Kherikala. Excavations in what may be a similar palace have been completed by Nicole Couture, but further information is not yet available (Couture 2002; Couture and Sampeck 2003).

On formal grounds, it seems improbable that Kolata's Palace of the Multicolored Rooms represents a Tiwanaku ruler's royal residence. There was no evidence for secure enclosure, gated courtyard, or progression to an inner patio. There were no capacious roofed buildings, raised platform, ramps or stairs, garden area, or bath. The fragment of a megalithic portal may or may not be from this building. Furthermore, the Palace of the Multicolored Rooms is a tiny complex, comparable in size with the Puruchuco palace (ca. 10 x 22 m), the rural home of a third- or fourth-level *curaca*, who was subject to a regional king at Pachacamac as well as an Inca governor over Peru's central coast. If the Palace of the Multicolored Rooms does represent Tiwanaku's royal residence, then the power of this monarch hardly qualifies him to be called king.

While I doubt that the Palace of the Multicolored Rooms was a royal residence, it could have been part of a royal palace. Perhaps it was a compartment or section within a royal palace, and, in view of the hearths and food refuse it contained, it may have related to the preparation and consumption of food.

If the Palace of the Multicolored Rooms was a kitchen within a greater Tiwanaku royal palace, we might reconsider an interpretation that has been popular since E. George Squier's (1877: 278–280) visit to Tiwanaku in the mid-nineteenth century. He imagined that the entire Putuni had been Tiwanaku's palace compound. Javier Escalante (1993: 231–243; see also Arellano 1991; Ponce 1969, 1972) discusses this argument, pointing out that the Putuni was a raised platform measuring ca. 69 x 55.2 m, constructed around a central sunken courtyard. Interestingly, this vision of the Putuni resembles the third sector of the Omo M10 Temple, composed of residential buildings raised on a platform around a rectangular sunken court.

The Putuni's sunken interior courtyard measures approximately 48 x 40 m. The surrounding terraces of the raised platform are about 6.5 m wide on the north and south and about 6.8 m wide on the east. As at Omo, the rear or western terrace was the widest, measuring 12.2 m across. This seems to have been the preferred location of the cardinal

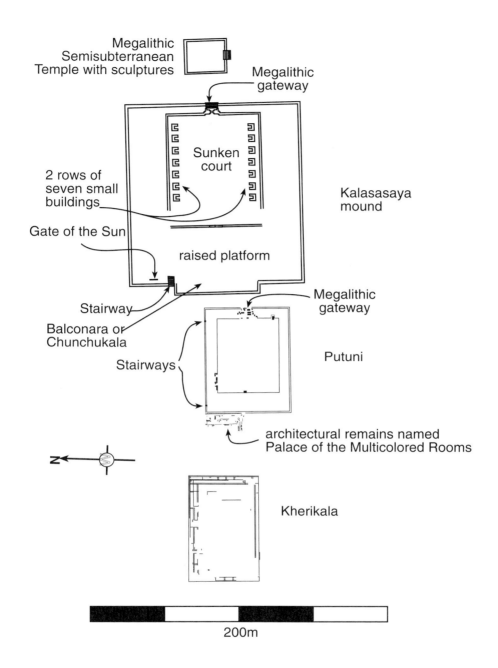

Megalithic Semisubterranean Temple with sculptures

Megalithic gateway

Sunken court

2 rows of seven small buildings

Kalasasaya mound

Gate of the Sun

raised platform

Stairway

Balconara or Chunchukala

Megalithic gateway

Stairways

Putuni

architectural remains named Palace of the Multicolored Rooms

N

Kherikala

200m

Fig. 21 Kalasasaya monument group, a possible palace complex at Tiwanaku. After Jorge Arellano López (1991: figs. 2, 20); Javier Escalante Moscoso (1993: figs 113, 143, 187, 189, 194, 200); Alan Kolata (1993: figs. 5.5a, 5.36a, b); and Arthur Posnansky (1945: pl. 1).

building; the Palace of the Multicolored Rooms is built against the outside of this segment of the Putuni. Also as at Omo, an impressive gateway provided access through the east body of the Putuni platform into the sunken courtyard. In the Putuni, this was a megalithic, multijamb portal painted in diverse colors. If the comparisons hold, the Omo reconstruction implies that the surface of the Putuni platform was covered with the residential buildings of the royal palace, much as Escalante asserts. Presumably, these were adobe structures that have melted into a homogeneous fill that archaeologists have excavated from within and without the Putuni platform.

Two small stairways in the north face of the Putuni platform provide access to its upper surface, ca. 1.2 m above the apparent ground level. Kolata believes that the Putuni was intended to appear much as it does today, as a raised platform from which important spectators viewed activities in the courtyard below. Indeed, at the center of the courtyard is a statue, and in its walls are several chambers that have been interpreted as sarcophagi, even though human remains were not found in them. Did these chambers really contain human burials? Do they imply a special function for the Putuni that involved spectators on the platform, or do they enhance the identification of the Putuni as a royal palace that subsequently became a mortuary monument?

The Omo M10 Temple and its formal correspondences with Inca as well as "Pyramid with Ramp" palaces stimulate me to push the analogy with Tiwanaku's Putuni. At Omo, the Putuni-like sector of the palace followed two rectangular enclosures located in an access sequence. At Tiwanaku, the megalithic entrance to the Putuni faces the back (i.e., west) wall of the Kalasasaya, a great rectangular platform with megalithic portal on the opposite, east side.

To have oriented the Putuni's spectacular gateway to a blank wall seems inconsistent, so perhaps the back wall of the Kalasasaya did not exist when the Putuni was a royal residence. This is not as fantastic as it may sound. The west wall of the Kalasasaya, now reconstructed for touristic purposes, is also known as the *balconara* or *chunchukala*. Its masonry and alignment are inconsistent with the rest of the Kalasasaya. Furthermore, when Father Bernabé Cobo (1956–64 [1653]: 2:196) described these architectural remains in the seventeenth century, the walls of the *chunchukala* were much better preserved than the north, south, and east walls of the Kalasasaya.[7] Consequently, I suggest that the rear of the Kalasasaya represents a late remodeling of a larger royal palace complex.

Once we accept the possibility that the western portion of the Kalasasaya was rebuilt, many fascinating possibilities present themselves. The Kalasasaya is a low pyramid. Its east-

---

[7] After our discussion (personal communication, March 1999), Alexei Vranich restudied Bernabé Cobo's description of architectural remains to the north of the Akapana and realized that Cobo may not have been describing the entire Kalasasaya but only the west part of it. The remainder of the Kalasasaya was described as a "fence" extending to the east. Apparently Cobo saw the north, south, and east walls of the Kalasasaya in such poor condition that only the great upright stones were visible, resembling a fence. However, the walls of the *chunchukala* were so much better preserved that he was able to describe the masonry of large uprights and smaller blocks, sometimes called *post and infill*, in considerable detail. It is quite reasonable to conclude that the *chunchukala* was constructed significantly later than the other Kalasasaya walls.

facing portal provides access into a large sunken court surrounded on the north, south, and west by a raised platform. The west end is by far the widest, so broad that it could have contained a smaller sunken patio, from which one might have passed to the Putuni. This would produce a formal structure remarkably similar to Inca royal palaces as well as the palace at Omo M10. Of course, today there is no evidence for a second sunken court or an impressive gateway complex to transit between the courts. But the famous Gate of the Sun lies isolated on the northwest corner of the Kalasasaya platform. It is not in its original location, and its sculptural details were refurbished at some moment in its history (Protzen and Nair 2002), adding more crudely carved profile winged figures.

The hypothesis that the Kalasasaya and Putuni might have constituted one royal palace implies a dynamic picture of Tiwanaku architecture, along with new insights that can be investigated in the future. Could the semisubterranean temple in front of the entrance to the Kalasasaya be compared with the great halls (*kallanka*) of Inca palaces? Tiwanaku's semisubterranean temple might have served the ritual functions of Cuzco's *carpahuasi*, although it seems unlikely that it was roofed to protect celebrants during bad weather, as the *carpahuasi* and other *kallanka* presumably did. Furthermore, the semisubterranean temple does not seem to replace the *kallanka* in its ability to double as a guardhouse for an entourage of splendidly dressed troops defending the palace.

Of course, there are problems with the Kalasasaya-Putuni palace hypothesis. Traditional dating at Tiwanaku places these buildings in different construction epochs, although this may not have much basis in reality. Furthermore, the Putuni is not on the central axis of the Kalasasaya, but is significantly displaced to the south. Perhaps this displacement permitted another compound on the north, although there is no evidence for such a building. On the other hand, a compound that aligns well with the central axis of the Kalasasaya is the Kherikala, 70 m farther west than the Putuni. Could this complex, sometimes considered an elite residential compound and at other times a market (Arellano López 1991), have been the residential portion of a royal palace at some other moment in Tiwanaku's history? Perhaps the Kalasasaya palace was refurbished several times, with some residential areas abandoned and interred as others were built and occupied.

The Puma Puncu is the other low pyramid complex at Tiwanaku, about a kilometer from the Putuni. It is 167.36 m north-south and 116.7 m east-west, with projections, 27.6 x ca. 20 m, on the corners of the east side. As reconstructed by Vranich (n.d.; Fig. 22), it consisted of two great courtyards, one to the east and another to the west of a four-terrace platform that had an inner court sunken into the center of its flat summit. As I have argued for the Kalasasaya-Putuni complex, Vranich (n.d.: 234) emphasizes that the Puma Puncu was "a dynamic center of ritual activity that was intentionally and substantially transformed over time." Three major building epochs, in addition to small repairs and remodelings, are documented. A radiocarbon date from the earliest construction epoch places it at 1510 ± 25 B.P. (A.D. 440; calibrated, A.D. 536–600).

Throughout most of the history of archaeological investigation at the Puma Puncu, only the mound has been recognized as architecturally significant, meaning that this building complex has been seriously misunderstood. Vranich (n.d.: 197) identifies a huge court

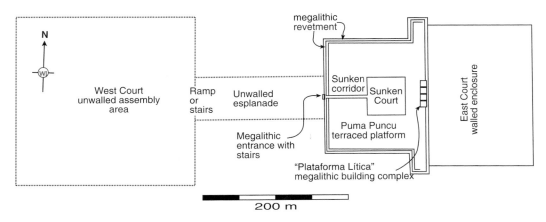

Fig. 22 Puma Puncu monument group. After Alexei Vranich (n.d.: fig. 6.3).

on the east side, measuring 192.5 x 143.5 m, enclosed by twenty-six upright megaliths that probably had smaller stones between. Perhaps the fact that the walls of this enclosed court were overlooked by so many researchers shows that walled enclosures did exist at Tiwanaku.

On the east edge of the Puma Puncu mound is the greatest megalithic construction at Tiwanaku. Known as the Plataforma Lítica (Ponce et al. 1971), it is a terrace, 6.75 x 38.72 m in area, paved with enormous stone blocks, about which are many other megalithic fragments, including portions of several great gateways similar to the Gate of the Sun. Apparently, this Plataforma Lítica was a megalithic building of undetermined form, with spectacular doorways. For centuries, it was assumed that the Plataforma Lítica was the principal gateway entering the Puma Puncu from the east, but recent excavations have revealed a heavily worn stairway, as well as remains of gates, on the west side of the mound. From there, a passageway conducted visitors through the body of the platform mound to its central, inner court. As no stairways have been found from the Plataforma Lítica down to the east courtyard, it seems that this was the rear of the complex, not its grand entryway. From the inner court, the route to the buildings on the Plataforma Lítica and into the east court remains unknown. This new understanding of the orientation illuminates features the Puma Puncu shares with Inca palaces, namely, the positioning of the most exquisite building in the rear of the complex and a great enclosure beyond this building.

Vranich (n.d.) identifies a projection to the west of the Puma Puncu as a ramp or stairway, on which one ascended, ca. 7 m, from a west courtyard before entering the Puma Puncu platform. I consider this west courtyard to be the most speculative of Vranich's Puma Puncu reconstructions, even though it accords very well with the form of Inca palaces moderated by features of Pachacamac's "Pyramid with Ramp." One problem is that this west court has no defining walls.

It is premature to identify Tiwanaku's Puma Puncu as a royal palace. Conversely, as we learn more about this great architectural complex, it is increasingly apparent that the Puma Puncu shares more features with Inca and Pachacamac palaces than anyone anticipated. It may have functioned as a palace at least for some time in its history. Excavations about the

Puma Puncu's inner court have revealed a stone "table" with massive legs that might have been either an altar or a throne. If future excavations reveal the Plataforma Lítica to have housed an elite residence, accompanied by bath and similar facilities, with the east court-yard containing kitchens, lesser residences, and perhaps a fine garden, then there would be ample reason to count the Puma Puncu among the royal palaces of the Middle Horizon.

Located next to the Kalasasaya, 1 km east of the Puma Puncu, is the Akapana, a more or less cross-shaped pyramid at platform 257 m long, 197 m wide, and about 16.5 m high (Manzanilla 1992). As pointed out above, it is the only building at Tiwanaku tall enough to have been a secure location without walls, and, even considering its terraced sides and irregular shape, it furnished enough upper surface space for an ample palace complex.

In the top of the Akapana is a great looters' hole that extends to the east face of the pyramid and from which excavated material was discharged over the side of the building, covering much of the eastern façade. This crater has been interpreted as the enlargement of what was originally a great sunken court. Inferences about the size and form of this hypo-thetical court are based on electronic resistivity (Manzanilla 1992), but I remain skeptical until further research is published.[8] We must try to discover how much was destroyed before making inferences about the Akapana. We must also determine how the structure was transformed throughout its architectural history.

Linda Manzanilla (1992; Manzanilla and Woodard 1990), who excavated on the Akapana, found a great stairway, perhaps originally double, ascending the west façade (Fig. 23). At the summit of these stairs was a single flat expanse that may have functioned like a courtyard. Manzanilla (1992: 46–53) found remains of a cut-stone room about 10 m wide, on both its north and south sides. The other dimensions cannot be determined, so Manzanilla inferred two relatively small rooms on the edge of a great sunken court. But perhaps the sunken court was not so extensive, and the two were actually one long building of the *carpahuasi* or *kallanka* type.

Farther northeast, a residential area was discovered, separated from the cut-stone rooms by a strong wall. A megalithic portal, fragments of which were discovered on the Akapana by Protzen and Nair (2002), may once have controlled the route to these build-ings.

The Akapana's northeast residential complex consists of remains of an L-shaped dis-tribution of rooms, but it may originally have been a rectangular or U-shaped compound enclosing a patio (Manzanilla 1992: 54–70). The better-preserved side of the patio group-ing contained at least eight rooms; on the shorter side, traces of at least three rooms were preserved. The rooms were small, measuring only about 2 x 2 m. They probably had adobe walls placed on a foundation composed of a double row of stone blocks. A cut-stone paving covered the surrounding surface within and outside the patio. At some moment, the rooms were partially dismantled, and an offering was spread over the corner room that yielded an uncalibrated radiocarbon date of A.D. 830 ± 140.

---

[8] Research published recently by Alexei Vranich (2002) shows that many traditional ideas about the Akapana are probably in error. However, his investigations focused on the form of the Akapana's megalithic façade, and on dating the monument, not on the form and presence of a central sunken court.

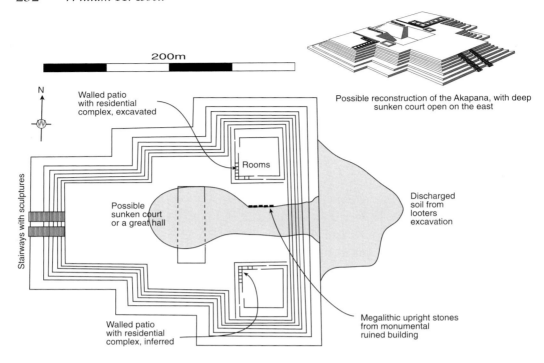

Fig. 23 Akapana platform. After Javier Escalante Moscoso (1993: 140 and fig. 113) and Linda Manzanilla (1992: fig. 4).

Excavations in the Akapana residential area revealed numerous burials, many with luxury goods and ceremonial objects. One man, probably the central interment, had been buried holding a puma incense vessel in his hands. None of the burials possessed sufficient offerings to suggest a royal tomb, and Manzanilla concluded that the residents were priests. Of course, we must not forget that the center of the pyramid was looted years ago, and its original contents remain unknown.

There are no reports of a courtyard controlling admission to the west entrance of the Akapana, and we know very little of the eastern façade of this important platform mound. As in the case of the Puma Puncu, it is too early to determine the functions of the Akapana. It surely could have served as a royal palace at some moment in its history.

I do feel that the Putuni should be counted among the royal palaces of the Middle Horizon. One of its precincts was Kolata's (1993) Palace of the Multicolored Rooms. It would be worth investigating the hypothesis that the Kalasasaya and Gate of the Sun were part of this same royal palace. Perhaps even the Kherikala was one of the residential compounds constructed during the history of this large and dynamic palace complex. We need more research at Tiwanaku to determine the architectural history of individual buildings and building complexes. If Tiwanaku's buildings all have long and complex histories, it may well be that several of them served as royal palaces during some phase of their development.

Conclusions

Royal palaces are the best material remains to document kings and regal authority in the prehistoric past. Not only did the royal palace represent monarchical power, it was also one of the most important means and media for the construction of power. Careful study of palace forms and functions can provide key information about the nature of political power, its structure, experience, and its social production. Of course, we must first identify royal palaces. In the Central Andean culture area, the concept of *palace* has not been popular. Its use has been rare and unsystematic.

Scholars do not agree about the political organization of Central Andean polities before the Incas. Some believe that kings ruled at least as far back as Huari and Tiwanaku. They have suggested that Inca kings might have legitimized their authority by reference to these kings, an ancient knowledge kept alive by means we do not understand. Many archaeologists have spoken of centralization and hierarchy without referring to kings or lords. Others have championed theocratic organization associated with ceremonial centers and religious embassies. John and Theresa Topic have presented another argument, based on archaeological remains, that lineage-like kin groupings, organized into more or less consensual confederations, dominated the political organization of Marcahuamachuco, Huari, and much of the Middle Horizon.

If royal palaces existed within Middle Horizon cities, there can be no doubt of monarchical government. Investigation of Middle Horizon capitals must be informed by an explicit list of material attributes that identify ethnographically known palaces. I conclude that there were several Andean palace traditions; palaces of the central coast share many attributes with Inca palaces, but there are important differences as well. Ideally, a study of palaces should begin with Cuzco and the royal palaces of the Inca capital and then work backward. But Cuzco continues to confuse scholars, and no one seems able to resolve the important questions about the way Cuzco and its principal buildings actually functioned. What of dual kingship? And what of the argument asserting that each Inca monarch built his own palace, which was subsequently inherited by his heirs (i.e., the one-king/one-palace model; Conrad 1981)? But, in Cuzco, it is impossible to identify one palace for each king, and several of the buildings consistently referred to as palaces are assigned to different kings by different authorities (Isbell 1981). If one-king/one-palace was really a prominent structural ideal, why is there such disagreement and confusion about Cuzco's royal palaces?

Another difficulty in the study of royal palaces of the Middle Horizon springs from the scarcity of excavation information from all kinds of habitation sites, from common to elite. There is little basis for determining the social status of residences atop Tiwanaku's Akapana without significant comparative material. Only in the last few years have these basic data begun to appear in print. Burials and mortuary patterns are almost as poorly understood.

In spite of numerous difficulties, the accumulated sum of evidence indicates the presence of royal palaces during the Andean Middle Horizon. Conversely, no single example from Huari, Tiwanaku, or Pachacamac is irrefutably confirmed as a royal palace. But I have developed systematic lists of explicit criteria and shown that most of those criteria co-occur in select Middle Horizon architectural complexes. This has permitted highly probable identification of palaces. At least one—Vegachayoq Moqo at Huari—seems confirmed by a royal tomb nearby.

This preliminary study of the palaces of the Middle Horizon significantly expands our general understanding of Andean palaces, perhaps paving the way for scholars to translate the European concept into Andean contexts for more productive comparative studies of Andean politics and power. We have found that palaces in the Andean past were variable, with differences in ideal designs. Innovation seems to have been common as well. Huari lords invented a virtually new palace design at Pikillacta and Viracochapampa, one that was subsequently introduced into their urban capital. Perhaps some of this innovation was related to new architectural technology: the construction of capacious second floors, combined with enthusiasm for producing social difference in vertical space.

Innovation and variation appear to have been frequent in palace architecture, and it is clear that the built environment played a key role in constructing power, royal or otherwise. The repetition of certain building types in Cuzco, Pachacamac, Marcahuamachuco, and Huari demonstrates that power and authority were produced within the built environment. These buildings furnish archaeologists with dazzling insights into how Andean peoples created leadership. Furthermore, interregional architectural similarities show that the social construction of power was a vast multiregional process. Even at Marcahuamachuco, where a confederation of lineages may have been the supreme political authority, political architecture developed interdependently with processes taking place hundreds of kilometers away.

In Huamachuco, the ancient inhabitants constructed numerous niched halls, within which regional government was produced. Most of the sites where niched halls were the mediators of power—Marcahuamachuco, Viracochapampa, and Pikillacta—had similar numbers of these buildings. A safe estimate is between ten and twenty. Now that we understand the niched hall and take this concept to Huari, where preliminary indications suggest their existence, will we find a similar total? Significantly, Pachacamac has about this same number of "Pyramid with Ramp" palaces. Chan Chan has about this number of *ciudadelas*. Is there an important insight here, yet to be understood?

I hesitate to conclude that niched halls show that centralized authority never crystallized at Marcahuamachuco. During the middle of the niched-hall sequence, these buildings were associated with courtyards, large rooms, and a building known as El Castillo. I wonder if, at least during this time, the *curacas* of Huamachuco's ranking lineages did not gain the power of kings, concentrating niched halls around a palace-like compound?

An important aspect of Andean palaces, which archaeologists have underestimated, is their dynamic quality. This may be true of other building types. There probably never was a form for royal palaces, but a "timescape" through which they changed size, shape, and function. Archaeologists must learn to deal with major Andean buildings in terms of their timescape and give up homogeneous models that are attached to conceptualizations of culture change that always have the trajectories of cannonballs. What was the metronome of royal Andean timescapes? Was it generational succession, dynastic change, or was it driven by the chaotic events of history?

A critical question about Middle Horizon and other Andean palaces is their relationship to mortuary monuments. There seems to have been a popular if not universal Andean ideal that the royal palace was eventually converted into a cemetery or mortuary monument. Was the one-king/one-palace model an Andean ideal? The palaces of Pachacamac might be consistent with such a model. If Vegachayoq Moqo, two orthogonal cellular complexes in the northern portion of the Huari city, and perhaps the round-cornered buildings at Monjachayoq were palaces, then Huari may also have been a capital composed of numerous palaces. Even Tiwanaku could be interpreted as a collection of at least three royal palaces that were subsequently converted into mortuary and religious monuments. This issue requires a great deal more investigation. It lies at the very heart of Andean state government and city formation. But we must be very careful not to allow a model to shape our information. If such a model is first used to interpret the archaeological data, and then we turn around and employ our interpretations to confirm the model, we are guilty of circular reasoning. We impose our conceptions onto the Andean past (Isbell 1995).

I believe we have already begun to impose an Inca pattern of founder mummy worship onto the political orders of the Middle Horizon—an interpretation closely associated with the one-king/one-palace issue. Mummies of Inca emperors, and the mummified founders of individual clanlike *ayllu*, were the primary religious objects of most Andean people at the time of the Spanish invasion (Isbell 1997a). In the sixteenth century, it is clear that the mummy of a group's apical ancestor was the focus of religious ritual for all who considered themselves descendants and beneficiaries of that individual.

We have found no evidence for royal mummies in Middle Horizon palaces. While we cannot deny their existence, what is documented in the archaeological record is the veneration of defleshed human bones. While there is much to learn, this seems different from Inca adoration of a mummified ancestor. Defleshed bones and human ossuaries are not described as a significant part of sixteenth-century Inca religion. This probably means that during the Middle Horizon, Andean politico-religious ideology was different from that of the Incas. John and Theresa Topic (1992) may simplify too much when they argue that defleshed bones imply consensus-based political organization, but they are right to seek to understand Middle Horizon ideological phenomena in their own terms and not as timeless institutions forever identical to Inca practices.

As we learn more about prehistoric Andean palaces, we can evaluate questions of continuity between Huari and later imperial organizations. Just as royal palaces show how power was socially produced, continuity in palace form implies the protraction of institutions and knowledge. It seems possible that succession was unbroken from the Huari capital to southern Lucre's Pikillacta, then to Chokepukio (see McEwan et al. 1995; McEwan n.d.), and finally to Cuzco's royal city. Furthermore, if Conchopata's vase painters did paint an official succession of royal monarchs, early narrative history would be documented. Attached to visual representations, narrative accounts might have survived almost a millennium from Huari to Inca times. Perhaps archaeologists will agree with the adventuresome historians that Inca kings knew of their Huari predecessors, but first we must learn a great deal more about royal palaces.

Acknowledgments I thank Peter Eeckhout, whose work is the single most important contribution to my discussion of royal palaces on Peru's central coast. He corresponded with me and shared his exhaustive study of central coast "Pyramid with Ramp" buildings, including his unpublished manuscripts and original research. Having independently concluded that these buildings were palaces, Eeckhout made available many of his data and interpretations. I also thank Alexei Vranich, who verified my suspicion that the *chunchukala* (i.e., west wall) of the Putuni may have been added to the Kalasasaya building complex late in its history, and Monica Barnes, who introduced me to Eeckhout's work. I also wish to acknowledge Susan Evans and Joanne Pillsbury for organizing this volume on Pre-Hispanic palaces and seeing it through publication. They have been a constant source of inspiration.

Bibliography

AGURTO CALVO, SANTIAGO

1980   *Cusco: La traza urbana de la ciudad inca.* Proyecto Per 39, United Nations Educational, Scientific, and Cultural Organization, Cusco.

1984   *Lima prehispánica.* FINANPRO, Empresa Financiera, Lima.

ARELLANO LÓPEZ, JORGE

1991   The New Cultural Contexts of Tiahuanaco. In *Huari Administrative Structure: Prehistoric Monumental Architecture and State Government* (William H. Isbell and Gordon F. McEwan, eds.): 259–280. Dumbarton Oaks, Washington, D.C.

ASCHER, MARCIA, AND ROBERT ASCHER

1981   *Code of the Quipu: A Study in Media, Mathematics and Culture.* University of Michigan Press, Ann Arbor.

BENNETT, WENDELL C.

1934   Excavations at Tiahuanaco. *Anthropological Papers of the American Museum of Natural History* 34 (3): 359–494.

1953   *Excavations at Wari, Ayacucho, Peru.* Yale University Publications in Anthropology 49. Yale University Press, New Haven, Conn.

BRAGAYRAC DÁVILA, ENRIQUE

1991   Archaeological Excavations in the Vegachayoq Moqo Sector of Huari. In Huari Administrative Structure: Prehistoric Monumental Architecture and State Government (William H. Isbell and Gordon F. McEwan, eds.): 71–80. Dumbarton Oaks, Washington, D.C.

n.d.   Wari: Excavaciones en el sector Vegachayoq Moqo, temporada 1982. Informe al Instituto Nacional de Cultura, Filial Ayacucho, Perú, 1982.

BUENO MENDOZA, ALBERTO

1974–75   Cajamarquilla y Pachacamac: Dos ciudades de la Costa Central del Perú. *Boletín Bibliográfico de Antropología Americana* 37 (46): 171–211.

1982   El Antiguo valle de Pachacamac: Espacio, tiempo y cultura [1º parte]. *Boletín de Lima* 4 (24): 10–29.

1983a   El Antiguo valle de Pachacamac: Espacio, tiempo y cultura [2º parte]. *Boletín de Lima* 5 (25): 5–27.

1983b   El Antiguo valle de Pachacamac: Espacio, tiempo y cultura [conclusión]. *Boletín de Lima* 5 (26): 3–12.

BURGER, RICHARD L.

1988   Unity and Heterogeneity within the Chavín Horizon. In *Peruvian Prehistory* (Richard W. Keatinge, ed.): 99–144. Cambridge University Press, Cambridge.

BUSE DE LA GUERRA, HERMANN

    1960   *Guía arqueológica de Lima: Pachacamac.* [Self-published], Lima.

CANZIANI A., JOSÉ

    1987   Análisis del complejo urbano Maranga Chayavilca. *Gaceta Arqueológica Andina* 4 (14): 10–17.

CHÁVEZ BALLÓN, MANUEL

    1970   Ciudades incas: Cuzco, capital del imperio. *Wayka* 3: 1–14.

COBO, BERNABÉ

1956–64   *Obras del P. Bernabé Cobo* (Francisco Mateos, ed.). Biblioteca de Autores Españoles
[1653]   91–92. Ediciones Atlas, Madrid.

CONRAD, GEOFFREY W.

    1981   Cultural Materialism, Split Inheritance, and the Expansion of Ancient Peruvian Empires. American Antiquity 46 (1): 3–26.

    1982   The Burial Platforms of Chan Chan: Some Social and Political Implications. In *Chan Chan: Andean Desert City* (Michael E. Moseley and Kent C. Day, eds.): 87–117. School of American Research Advanced Seminar Series. University of New Mexico Press, Albuquerque.

COUTURE, NICOLE

    2002   Construction of Power: Monumental Space and Elite Residences at Tiwanaku, Ph.D. dissertation. Department of Anthropology, University of Chicago.

COUTURE, NICOLE, AND KATHRYN E. SAMPECK

    2003   Putuni: A History of Palace Architecture at Tiwanak. In *Tiwanaku and its Hinterland: Archaeology and Paleoecology of an Andean Civilization*, vol.2: *Urban and Rural Archaeology* (A. L. Kolata, ed.): 226–263. Smithsonian Institution Press, Washington, D.C. and London.

COOK, ANITA G.

    1987   The Middle Horizon Ceramic Offerings from Conchopata. *Ñawpa Pacha* 22/23: 49–90.

EECKHOUT, PETER

    1997   *Pachacamac (Côte Centrale du Pérou). Aspects de fonctionnement, du développement et de l'influence du site durant l'Intermédiare récent.* Université Libre de Bruxelles, Brussels, Belgium.

    1998a   Offrandes funéraires à Pachacamac et Pampa de Las Flores. Exemples des relations entre les côtes nord et centrale du Pérou à l'époque pré-inca. *Baessler-Archiv,* Band 46 (Neue Folge), Heft 1: 165–229.

    1998b   Le Temple de Pachacamac sous l'empire inca. *Journal de la Société des Américanistes* 84: 9–44.

1999a   *Pachacamac durant l'Intermédiaire récent: Etude d'un site monumental préhispanique de la côte centrale du Pérou.* BAR International Series 747. Oxford.

1999b   Pirámide con rampa no. 3, Pachacamac: Nuevos datos, nuevas perspectivas. *Bulletin de l'Institut Français d'Études Andines* 28 (2): 169–214.

2000   The Palaces of the Lords of Ychsma: An Archaeological Reappraisal of the Function of Pyramids with Ramps at Pachacamac, Central Coast of Peru. *Revista de Arqueología Americana* 17–19: 217–254

ESCALANTE MOSCOSO, JAVIER F.

1993   *Arquitectura prehispánica en los Andes bolivianos.* CIMA, La Paz, Bolivia.

FRANCO JORDÁN, RÉGULO

1996   Arquitectura monumental en Pachacamac. *Arkinka* 1 (11): 82–94.

1998   *La pirámide con rampa no. 2 de Pachacamac: Excavaciones y nuevas interpretaciones.* R. Franco Jordán, Trujillo, Perú.

GASPARINI, GRAZIANO, AND LUISE MARGOLIES

1977   *Arquitectura Inka.* Centro de Investigaciones Históricas y Estéticas, Facultad de Arquitectura y Urbanismo. Universidad Central de Venezuela, Caracas.

1980   *Inca Architecture* (Patricia J. Lyon, trans.). Indiana University Press, Bloomington.

GOLDSTEIN, PAUL S.

1989   The Tiwanaku Occupation of Moquegua. In *Ecology, Settlement and History in the Osmore Drainage, Peru* (Don S. Rice, Charles Stanish, and Phillip R. Scarr, eds.): 219–255. BAR International Series 545 (1). Oxford.

1993   Tiwanaku Temples and State Expansion: A Tiwanaku Sunken-Court Temple in Moquegua, Peru. *Latin American Antiquity* 4 (1): 22–47.

n.d.   *Omo, a Tiwanaku Provincial Center in Moquegua, Peru.* Ph.D. dissertation. University of Chicago, 1989.

GONZÁLEZ CARRÉ, ENRIQUE, AND ENRIQUE BRAGAYRAC DÁVILA

1986   El Templo Mayor de Wari: Ayacucho. *Boletín de Lima* 8 (47): 9–20.

GONZÁLEZ CARRÉ, ENRIQUE, ENRIQUE BRAGAYRAC DÁVILA, C. VIVANCO POMACANCHARI, V. TIESLER BLOS, AND M. LOPEZ QUISPE

1996   *El Templo Mayor en la ciudad de Wari: Estudios arqueológicos en Vegachayoq Moqo-Ayacucho.* Oficina de Investigaciones, Laboratorio de Arqueología, Facultad de Ciencias Sociales, Universidad Nacional de San Cristóbal de Huamanga, Ayacucho, Perú.

GONZÁLEZ CARRÉ, ENRIQUE, JAIME URRUTIA CERUTI, AND JORGE LÉVANO PEÑA

1997   *Ayacucho: San Juan de la frontera de Huamanga.* Colección de arte y tesoros del Perú. Banco de Crédito del Perú, Lima.

HAAS, JONATHAN

1985   Excavations on Huaca Grande: An Initial View of the Elite of Pampa Grande, Peru. *Journal of Field Archaeology* 12 (4): 391–409.

HEMMING, JOHN, AND EDWARD RANNEY

1982   *Monuments of the Incas.* Little, Brown, Boston, for the New York Graphic Society.

HILTUNEN, JUHA J.

1999   *Ancient Kings of Peru: The Reliability of the Chronicle of Fernando de Montesinos, Correlating the Dynasty Lists with Current Prehistoric Periodization in the Andes.* Bibliotheca Historica 45. Suomen Historiallinen Seura, Helsinki, Finland.

HYSLOP, JOHN

1985   *Inkawasi, the New Cuzco: Cañete, Lunahuaná, Peru.* BAR International Series 234. Oxford.

1990   *Inka Settlement Planning.* University of Texas Press, Austin.

ISBELL, WILLIAM H.

1977   *The Rural Foundation for Urbanism: Economic and Stylistic Interaction between Rural and Urban Communities in Eighth-Century Peru.* Illinois Studies in Anthropology 10. University of Illinois Press, Urbana-Champaign.

1981   Comment on Conrad. *American Antiquity* 46 (1): 27–30.

1984   Huari Urban Prehistory. In *Current Archaeological Projects in the Central Andes: Some Approaches and Results* (Ann Kendall, ed.): 95–131. BAR International Series 210. Oxford.

1985   El origen del estado en el valle de Ayacucho. *Revista Andina* 3 (1): 57–106.

1987   Conchopata: Ideological Innovator in Middle Horizon IA. *Ñawpa Pacha* 22/23: 91–126.

1991   Conclusion: Huari Administration and the Orthogonal Cellular Architecture Horizon. In *Huari Administrative Structure: Prehistoric Monumental Architecture and State Government* (William H. Isbell and Gordon F. McEwan, eds.): 293–315. Dumbarton Oaks, Washington, D.C.

1995   Constructing the Andean Past, or "As You Like It." In *Current Research in Andean Antiquity* (Ari Zighelboim and Carol Barnes, eds.): 1–12. Journal of the Steward Anthropological Society 23 (1–2). University of Illinois, Urbana-Champaign.

1997a   *Mummies and Mortuary Monuments: A Postprocessual Prehistory of Central Andean Social Organization.* University of Texas Press, Austin.

1997b   Reconstructing Huari: A Cultural Chronology for the Capital City. In *Emergence and Change in Early Urban Societies* (Linda Manzanilla, ed.): 181–227. Plenum, New York.

2001a   Huari: Crecimiento y desarrollo de un capital imperial. In *Wari: Arte Precolombino Peruano* (Martha Cabrera Romero et. al.): 99–172. Fundación El Monte, Seville.

2001b   Huari y Tiahuanaco, Arquitectura, Identidad y Religion. In *Los Dioses del Antiguo Peru*, vol. II (K. Makowski): 1-37. Colección Arte y Tesoros del Peru, Banco de Credito del Peru, Lima.

2001c   Repensando el Horizonte Medio: el caso de Conchopata, Ayacucho, Perú. In *Boletín de Arqueología PUCP, No. 4, 2000. Huari y Tiwanaku: Modelos vs. Evidencias, Primera Parte* (P. Kaulicke and W. H. Isbell, eds.): 9–68. Departamento de Humanidades, Especialidad de Arqueología, Pontífica Universidad Católica del Perú, Lima.

2004   Mortuary Preferences: A Huari Case Study from Middle Horizon Peru. *Latin American Antiquity* 15(1): 3–32.

ISBELL, WILLIAM H., CHRISTINE BREWSTER-WRAY, AND LYNDA E. SPICKARD

1991   Architecture and Spatial Organization at Huari. In *Huari Administrative Structure: Prehistoric Monumental Architecture and State Government* (William H. Isbell and Gordon F. McEwan, eds.): 19–53. Dumbarton Oaks, Washington, D.C.

ISBELL, WILLIAM H., AND JOELLEN BURKHOLDER

2002   Iwawi and Tiwanaku. In *Andean Archaeology*, vol. 1: *Variations in Sociopolitical Organization* (William H. Isbell and Helaine Silverman, eds.): 199–241. Kluwer Academic/Plenum, New York.

ISBELL, WILLIAM H., AND ANITA G. COOK

2002   A New Perspective on Conchopata and the Andean Middle Horizon. In *Andean Archaeology*, vol. 2: *Art, Landscape and Society* (William H. Isbell and Helaine Silverman, eds.): 249–305. Kluwer Academic/Plenum, New York.

n.d.   Report of the Proyecto Arqueológico Conchopata for the Instituto Nacional de Cultura del Perú, Lima. Binghamton University, State University of New York, and Catholic University of America, Washington, D.C., 1999.

ISBELL, WILLIAM H., AND GORDON F. MCEWAN (EDS.)

1991   *Huari Administrative Structure: Prehistoric Monumental Architecture and State Government.* Dumbarton Oaks, Washington, D.C.

JANUSEK, JOHN W.

1999   Craft and Local Power: Embedded Specializations in Tiwanaku Cities. *Latin American Antiquity* 10 (2): 107–131.

n.d.   State and Local Power in a Prehispanic Andean Polity: Changing Patterns of Urban Residence in Tiwanaku and Lukurmata, Bolivia. Ph.D. dissertation, University of Chicago, 1994.

JIMÉNEZ BORJA, ARTURO

1973   *Puruchuco.* Editorial Jurídica, Lima.

1985   Pachacamac. *Boletín de Lima* 7 (38): 40–54.

JIMÉNEZ BORJA, ARTURO, AND ARTURO BUENO MENDOZA

1970   Breves notas acerca de Pachacamac. *Arqueología y Sociedad* 4: 13–25.

KAUFFMAN DOIG, FEDERICO

1983   *Manual de arqueología peruana.* Ediciones Peisa, Lima.

KOLATA, ALAN L.

1993   *The Tiwanaku: Portrait of an Andean Civilization.* Blackwell, Cambridge, Mass., and Oxford.

KOSOK, PAUL

1965   *Life, Land and Water in Ancient Peru.* Long Island University Press, New York.

MANZANILLA, LINDA

1992   *Akapana: Una pirámide en el centro del mundo.* Instituto de Investigaciones Antropológicas, Universidad Nacional Autónoma de México, México, D.F.

MANZANILLA, LINDA, AND ERIC WOODARD

1990   Restos humanos asociados a la pirámide de Akapana: Tiwanaku, Bolivia. *Latin American Antiquity* 1 (2): 133–149.

MATOS MENDIETA, RAMIRO

1994   *Pumpu: Centro administrativo inka de la puna de Junín.* Arqueología e Historia 10. Editorial Horizonte, Lima.

McEWAN, GORDON F.

1987   *The Middle Horizon in the Valley of Cuzco, Peru: The Impact of the Wari Occupation of the Lucre Basin.* BAR International Series 372. Oxford.

1991   Investigations at the Pikillacta Site: A Provincial Huari Center in the Valley of Cuzco. In *Huari Administrative Structure: Prehistoric Monumental Architecture and State Government* (William H. Isbell and Gordon F. McEwan, eds.): 93–119. Dumbarton Oaks, Washington, D.C.

1996   Archaeological Investigations at Pikillacta, a Wari Site in Peru. *Journal of Field Archaeology* 23 (2): 169–186.

1998   The Function of Niched Halls in Wari Architecture. *Latin American Antiquity* 9 (1): 68–86.

n.d.   The Selz Foundation Excavations at Chokepukio, Cuzco, Peru: Report of the 1999 Excavations. Unpublished report, Department of Sociology and Anthropology, Wagner College, Staten Island, N.Y.

McEWAN, GORDON F., ARMINDA GIBAJA O., AND MELISSA CHATFIELD

1995   Archaeology of the Chokepukio Site: An Investigation of the Origin of the Inca Civilization in the Valley of Cuzco, Peru. A Report on the 1994 Field Season. *Tawantinsuyu* 1: 11–17.

McEWAN, GORDON F., A. VALENCIA ZEGARRA, M. GLOWACKI, J. W. VERANO, AND H. LECHTMAN

n.d.   *Pikillacta: The Wari Empire in Cuzco.* Manuscript in review by the University of Iowa Press, Iowa City.

MENZEL, DOROTHY

1964   Style and Time in the Middle Horizon. *Ñawpa Pacha* 2: 1–106.

MORRIS, CRAIG, AND DONALD E. THOMPSON

1985   *Huánuco Pampa: An Inca City and Its Hinterland*. Thames and Hudson, London.

MURÚA, MARTÍN DE

1985   *Historia general del Perú* (Manuel Ballesteros Gaibrois, ed.). Crónicas de América 35.
[1611–16] Historia 16. Madrid.

OCHATOMA PARAVICINO, JOSÉ, AND MARTHA CABRERA ROMERO

2002   Religious Ideology and Military Organization in the Iconography of a *D*-Shaped
        Ceremonial Precinct at Conchopata. In *Andean Archaeology*, vol. 2: *Art, Landscape and
        Society* (William H. Isbell and Helaine Silverman, eds.): 225–247. Kluwer Academic/
        Plenum, New York.

PAREDES BOTONI, PONCIANO

1988   Pachacamac: Pirámide con rampa no. 2. *Boletín de Lima* 10 (55): 41–58.

PAREDES BOTONI, PONCIANO, AND RÉGULO FRANCO JORDÁN

1987   Pachacamac: Las pirámides con rampa, cronología y función. *Gaceta Arqueológica
        Andina* 4 (13): 5–7.

PÄRSSINEN, MARTTI

1992   *Tawantinsuyu: The Inca State and Its Political Organization*. Studia Historica 43. Societas
        Historica Finlandiae, Helsinki, Finland.

PATTERSON, THOMAS C.

1985   Pachacamac—An Andean Oracle under Inca Rule. In *Recent Studies in Andean
        Prehistory and Protohistory: Papers from the 2nd Annual Northeast Conference on Andean
        Archaeology and Ethnohistory* (D. Peter Kvietok and Daniel N. Sandweiss, eds.): 159–
        176. Latin American Studies Program, Cornell University, Ithaca, N.Y.

PÉREZ CALDERÓN, ISMAEL

1999   *Huari: Misteriosa Ciudad de Piedra*. Facultad de Ciencias Sociales, Universidad
        Nacional San Cristóbal de Huamanga, Ayacucho.

PONCE SANGINÉS, CARLOS

1969   La Ciudad de Tiwanaku: A propósito del último libro sobre planeamiento urbano
        precolombino de Jorge Hardoy. *Arte y Arqueología* 1: 81–108.

1972   *Tiwanaku: Espacio, tiempo y cultura. Ensayo de síntesis arqueológica*. Publicación 30.
        Academia Nacional de Ciéncias de Bolivia, La Paz.

PONCE SANGINÉS, CARLOS, A. CASTAÑOS ECHAZU, W. AVILA SALINAS, AND F. URQUIDI BARRAU

1971   *Procedencia de las areniscas utilizadas en el templo precolombino de Pumapunka (Tiwanaku)*.
        Publicación 22. Academia Nacional de Ciéncias de Bolivia, La Paz.

POSNANSKY, ARTHUR

1945   *Tihuanacu, the Cradle of American Man* (James Francis Shearer, trans.). Augustin, New
        York.

PRIMEGLIO, C. R. D.

1992   La Interpretación de los quipus. In *Los reinos preincaicos y los incas* (Cecilia Bákula, Laura Laurencich Minelli, and Mireille Vautier, eds.): 189–192. Lunwerg, Barcelona.

PROTZEN, JEAN-PIERRE, AND STELLA NAIR

2002   The Gateways of Tiahuanaco: Symbols or Passages? In *Andean Archaeology*, vol. 2:*Art, Landscape and Society* (William H. Isbell and Helaine Silverman, eds.): 189–223. Kluwer Academic/Plenum, New York.

QUILTER, JEFFREY, AND GARY URTON (EDS.)

2002   *Narrative Threads: Accounting and Recounting in Andean Khipu.* University of Texas Press, Austin.

ROSTWOROWSKI DE DIEZ CANSECO, MARÍA

1972   Breve ensayo sobre el señorío de Ychma o Ychima. *Arqueología PUC* 13: 37–51. Instituto Riva Agüero, Pontífica Universidad Católica del Perú, Lima.

1978   *Señoríos indígenas de Lima y Canta.* Historia Andina 7. Instituto de Estudios Peruanos, Lima.

1988   *Historia del Tahuantinsuyu.* Historia Andina 13. Instituto de Estudios Peruanos, Lima.

1989   *Costa peruana prehispánica.* Edición augmentada y corrigida de *Etnía y sociedad.* Instituto de Estudios Peruanos, Lima.

1992   *Pachacamac y el señor de los milagros: Una trayectoria milenaria.* Historia Andina 19.
[1977]   Instituto de Estudios Peruanos, Lima.

1999   *History of the Inca Realm* (Harry B. Iceland, trans.). Cambridge University Press, Cambridge.

ROWE, JOHN H.

1947   Inca Culture at the Time of the Spanish Conquest. In *Handbook of South American Indians*, vol. 2: *The Andean Civilizations* (Julian H. Steward, ed.): 183–330. *Bureau of American Ethnology Bulletin* 143. Smithsonian Institution, Washington, D.C.

1967   What Kind of a Settlement Was Inca Cuzco? *Ñawpa Pacha* 5: 59–76.

1985   La constitución inca del Cuzco. *Histórica* 9: 35–73.

SAMPECK, KATHRYN E.

n.d.   Excavations at Putuni, Tiwanaku, Bolivia. Master's thesis, Department of Anthropology, University of Chicago, 1991.

SESTIERI, PELLIGRINO C.

1964   Excavations at Cajamarquilla, Peru. *Archaeology* 17 (1): 12–17.

1971   The Necropolis of the Huaca Tello, Cajamarquilla, Peru. *Archaeology* 24 (2): 101–106.

SHIMADA, IZUMI

1991   Pachacamac Archaeology: Retrospect and Prospect. In *Pachacamac: A Reprint of the 1903 Edition by Max Uhle* (Izumi Shimada, ed.): 15–66. University Museum Monograph 62. University Museum of Archaeology and Anthropology, University of Pennsylvania, Philadelphia.

1994   *Pampa Grande and the Mochica Culture.* University of Texas Press, Austin.

SOLANO RAMOS, F. F., AND V. P. GUERRERO ANAYA

1981   Estudio arqueológico en el sector de Monqachayoq, Wari. Tésis para optar el grado
            de bachiller en ciencias sociales: Antropología, Universidad Nacional San Cristóbal
            de Huamanga, Ayacucho, Perú.

SQUIER, E. GEORGE

1877   *Peru: Incidents of Travel and Exploration in the Land of the Incas.* Harper, New York.

TOPIC, JOHN R.

1986   A Sequence of Monumental Architecture from Huamachuco. In *Perspectives on
            Andean Prehistory and Protohistory* (D. H. Sandweiss and D. P. Kvietok, eds.): 63–83.
            Latin American Studies Program, Cornell University, Ithaca, N.Y.

1991   Huari and Huamachuco. In *Huari Administrative Structure: Prehistoric Monumental
            Architecture and State Government* (William H. Isbell and Gordon E. McEwan, eds.):
            141–164. Dumbarton Oaks, Washington, D.C.

TOPIC, JOHN R., AND THERESA L. TOPIC

1992   The Rise and Decline of Cerro Amaru: An Andean Shrine during the Early
            Intermediate Period and Middle Horizon. In *Ancient Images, Ancient Thought: The
            Archaeology of Ideology: Proceedings of the 23rd Annual Conference of the Archaeological
            Association of the University of Calgary* (A. Sean Goldsmith, et al., eds.): 167–180.
            University of Calgary Archaeological Association, Calgary, Alberta.

TOPIC, THERESA L.

1991   The Middle Horizon in Northern Peru. In *Huari Administrative Structure: Prehistoric
            Monumental Architecture and State Government* (William H. Isbell and Gordon F.
            McEwan, eds.): 233–246. Dumbarton Oaks, Washington, D.C.

TOPIC, THERESA L., AND JOHN R. TOPIC

1984   *Huamachuco Archaeological Project: Preliminary Report on the Third Season, June–August
            1983.* Occasional Papers in Anthropology 1. Trent University, Peterborough, Trent,
            Canada.

UHLE, MAX

1991   *Pachacamac: A Reprint of the 1903 Edition by Max Uhle* (Izumi Shimada, ed.).
[1903]   University Museum Monograph 62. University Museum of Archaeology and
            Anthropology, University of Pennsylvania, Philadelphia.

URTON, GARY

1997   *The Social Life of Numbers: A Quechua Ontology of Numbers and Philosophy of Arithmetic.*
            University of Texas Press, Austin.

VRANICH, ALEXEI

2002   La Piramide de Akapana: Reconsiderando el Centro Monumental de Tiwanaku. In *Boletín de Arqueología PUCP, No. 5, 2001. Huari y Tiwanaku: Modelos vs. Evidencias, Segunda Parte* (P. Kaulicke and W. H. Isbell, eds.): 295–308. Departamento de Humanidades, Especialidad de Arqueología, Pontífica Universidad Católica del Perú, Lima.

n.d.   Intepreting the Meaning of Ritual Spaces: The Temple Complex of Pumapunku, Tiwanaku, Bolivia. Ph.D. dissertation, University of Pennsylvania, 1999.

WALLACE, DWIGHT T.

1998   The Inca Compound at La Centinela, Chincha. *Andean Past* 5: 9–33.

ZUIDEMA, R. TOM

1986   Inka Dynasty and Irrigation: Another Look at Andean Concepts of History. In *Anthropological History of Andean Polities* (John V. Murra, Nathan Wachtel, and Jacques Revel, eds.): 177–200. Cambridge University Press, Cambridge.

1989a   At the Kings' Table: Inca Concepts of Sacred Kingship in Cuzco. *History and Anthropology* 4: 249–274. [Special issue: Kingship and the Kings, Jean-Claude Galey, ed.]

1989b   The Moieties of Cuzco. In *The Attraction of Opposites: Thought and Society in the Dualistic Mode* (David Maybury-Lewis and Uri Almagor, eds.): 255–275. University of Michigan Press, Ann Arbor.

1990a   Dynastic Structures in Andean Culture. In *The Northern Dynasties: Kingship and Statecraft in Chimor* (Michael A. Moseley and Alana Cordy-Collins, eds.): 489–505. Dumbarton Oaks, Washington, D.C.

1990b   *Inca Civilization in Cuzco* (Jean-Jacques Decoster, trans.). University of Texas Press, Austin.

n.d.   Cuzco de los incas. Manuscript in author's possession.

Identifying Chimú Palaces: Elite Residential Architecture in the Late Intermediate Period

Joanne Pillsbury

UNIVERSITY OF MARYLAND AND DUMBARTON OAKS

Banks L. Leonard

CENTER FOR INDIGENOUS STUDIES IN THE AMERICAS

This chapter examines elite residential architecture of the Chimú empire of the Peruvian north coast from the tenth to the fifteenth centuries A.D. and its most important local antecedents.[1] Recent archaeological, art historical, and ethnohistorical research allows comparison between the capital, Chan Chan, and elite architecture in other parts of the empire. Inherent to this analysis is the way in which elite residential structures reflected changing social relations in the north coast sphere. The development of the *ciudadela*, or monumental enclosure type, from earlier residential and monumental platforms reflects the increased centralization of power at the capital compared to earlier state organizations of the north coast. Here we trace the development of the *ciudadela* from previous north coast architectural traditions where activity spaces were sometimes collected together in roughly analogous combinations, but not in the *ciudadela* configuration, where the functions were gathered into singular, highly restrictive enclosures.

We first consider the role of the *ciudadela* as palace, defined as the official residence of a sovereign. In this sense the *ciudadela* was a private residence with a public role—a manifestation of political authority and its center of operations. The functional attributes of rulership are analyzed against the formal morphologies of the *ciudadelas* and related north coast structures. Central to this discussion is the relationship of ancestors and funerary traditions to concepts of authority, legitimacy, and rulership in Chimú culture.

The study of architecture can shed light on specific cultural traditions and illuminate aspects of social processes. We argue that, while sharing traits with palace forms known

[1] The authors would like to thank the following institutions and individuals for assistance in the field research and writing of this paper: the American Association of University Women, Dumbarton Oaks, the Fulbright Commission, the Samuel H. Kress Foundation, Metropolitan Museum of Art, Center for Indigenous Studies in the Americas, Christopher Attarian, Genaro Barr, Brian Billman, Jamie Brindley, Lisa DeLeonardis, Peter Eeckhout, Ana María Hoyle, William Isbell, Carol Mackey, Jean-François Millaire, Jerry Moore, Magali Morlion, Michael Moseley, Glenn Russell, Lucia Santistevan-Alvarez, Flora Vilches, and Colleen Winchell.

elsewhere in the ancient Americas, *ciudadelas* remain a unique form in several key aspects. This unique quality, particularly the prominence of a funerary aspect, has hampered clear understanding of these complex forms. In specific Andean contexts, palace and funerary architecture were not mutually exclusive; they were part and parcel of the same thing. The worlds of the dead and the living were constantly interpenetrating in the complex maintenance of rulership. Though it seems important for us to separate them out, it was important for them not to. During their use histories, the *ciudadelas* were dynamic architectural forms that underwent transformations from active administrative, ritual, and residential centers to mausolea and places of periodic veneration. As archaeologists seeing the final phase, we confront the accumulated result of these transformations.

We first examine the historical evidence on Chimor and related traditions of Andean rulership. Thus establishing a set of expected features, the *ciudadelas* are analyzed alongside other structures from surrounding areas of the north coast.

Chan Chan

The Historical Record

Chimor, the late Pre-Hispanic empire of early Colonial documents, is identified archaeologically with the Chimú culture. Chimor flourished on the north coast between the tenth and fifteenth centuries A.D., until conquered by the Inca ca. 1462–70 (Rowe 1948: 40). At its height, it extended approximately 1,000 km along the Peruvian coast, from near the present Ecuadorian border south to the Chillón Valley north of modern Lima (T. Topic 1990: 177).

Available information indicates that the imperial capital was located at the site now known as Chan Chan (Fig. 1), on the west flank of the modern city of Trujillo in the Moche Valley. The monumental core of Chan Chan covers 6 sq km, with associated buildings extending to another 12 to 14 sq km (Fig. 2) (Moseley and Mackey 1974: intro.). Topic and Moseley (1983: 157) have estimated the peak population at 20,000 to 40,000. The core consists of nine major monumental enclosures, or *ciudadelas*,[2] platform structures known as *huacas*, "elite compounds," and small, irregularly agglutinated rooms (SIAR) and plazas (Klymyshyn n.d.; Moseley 1990; Moseley and Day 1982; J. Topic 1990).

Spaniards conquered the Inca roughly a half-century after the Inca conquered the Chimú. Partly because of this sequence, historical references to Chan Chan and the Chimú are brief and few in number. By the time of the first written accounts, Chan Chan was largely abandoned, and the city and its ruling lineages no longer functioned as they had at the height of the Chimú empire.

---

[2] The term *ciudadela* (citadel) has been applied to the monumental compounds at Chan Chan since the nineteenth century. In general, it is used to refer to the nine monumental compounds at the core of the city. They are characterized by high perimeter walls, restricted access (usually a single entrance at the north), interior courts, and an internal or attached burial structure. A tenth monumental structure, Tello, is classified as a compound, rather than a formal *ciudadela*, as it lacks a burial platform and other features common to the other nine.

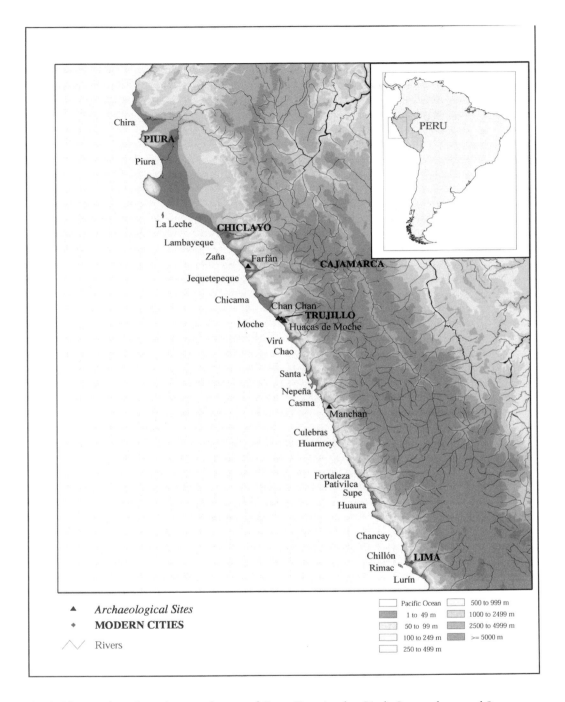

Fig. 1 The north and north-central coast of Peru. Drawing by Gisela Sunnenberg and Jean-François Millaire.

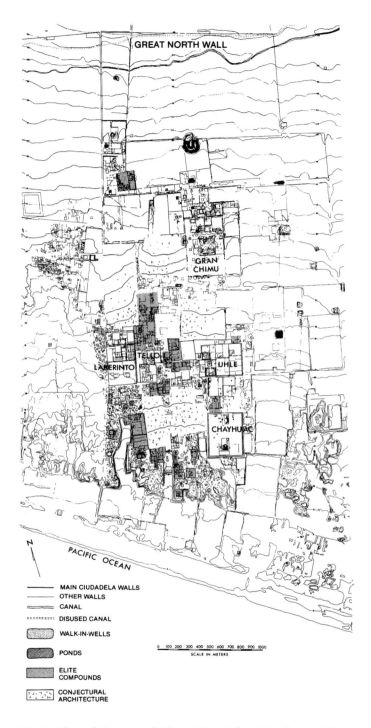

Fig. 2 Plan of the city of Chan Chan (after Moseley and Day 1982: fig. 4.6)

Documentary sources suggest sharp social stratification in Chimor. For example, commoners and elites supposedly descended from different sets of stars, or different eggs (Calancha 1974–82 [1638]: bk. 3, chap. 2, 1244; Netherly n.d.: 101–124). A king list written in 1604 delineates a ruling dynasty founded by a personage called Tacaynamo (Vargas Ugarte 1936). Zevallos Quiñones (1992a) has since fleshed out the rather skeletal framework of the rulers that succeeded him.

Early seventeenth-century accounts refer to the residences of the kings of Chimor in the area of the colonial city of Trujillo, but specific references to the Chimú capital are limited. For example, Antonio de la Calancha (1974–82 [1638]: bk. 3, chap. 1, 1226) notes only that "the Chimú [king] had his seat [*asiento*] or his palace [*palacio*], in what is now called Trujillo." Neither Chimor nor Chan Chan figure prominently in eighteenth-century accounts, although a set of watercolor maps of the city was commissioned by Bishop Martínez Compañón (Figs. 3, 4). In the Martínez Compañón plans, "palaces" were separated from other structures and what is now known as Ciudadela Rivero (Fig. 4) was rendered in detail (1978–81 [1781–89]: vol. 9, ill. 6).

Nineteenth-century visitors to Chan Chan also generally referred to the *ciudadelas* as palaces (Rivero and Tschudi 1971 [1854]: 265–266; Squier 1973 [1877]: 135–164), but by the twentieth century Adolph Bandelier (1942) and others began to turn away from the term "palace" (see Pillsbury, this volume). Though his thoughts on Chan Chan were incompletely published (Pillsbury n.d.: 24–25), Bandelier was among the first to move away from regarding *ciudadelas* as palaces and toward identifying them as generalized compounds for corporate groups (Bandelier 1942: 248). Whether widely seen or accepted by other scholars, interpretations similar to Bandelier's prevailed on into the mid-twentieth century (e.g., Horkheimer 1944: 61; Kimmich 1917: 453; Mason 1957: 97; Schaedel 1967: 232).

The concept of *ciudadela*-as-palace was not revived until the Chan Chan-Moche Valley Project of 1969–74, directed by Michael Moseley and Carol Mackey. Project members argued that the *ciudadelas* were occupied by the kings of Chimor and that they combined the functions of elite residence, centralized storage, administered redistribution, and royal entombment (see, e.g., Andrews 1974; Conrad 1981; Moseley and Day 1982). Noting that the *ciudadelas* were apparently initiated at different times, Conrad (n.d., 1981, 1982) proposed that they were the palaces of rulers during their lifetimes and at death became their mausolea. Conrad followed an Inca model of kingship, whereby a new ruler was obliged to construct his own palace rather than inherit his predecessor's. Although Inca palaces contained no burial platforms, they had a funerary component in the larger sense, as Inca mummies continued to inhabit the palaces and were venerated during periodic ceremonies (Niles 1999: 75).

The idea of *ciudadela*-as-palace has been challenged (most recently by Rowe 1995: 29–30; see also Paulsen 1981). One objection was that most areas in them were remarkably clear of habitation refuse or other indicators of residence. Examples are known from other cultures, however, where elite residences can have little domestic debris, as buildings of such status are often exceedingly well-maintained and serviced (see, e.g., Evans 1991). Nonetheless, several lines of evidence suggest that these complex structures served as elite residences in the early portion of their individual use histories.

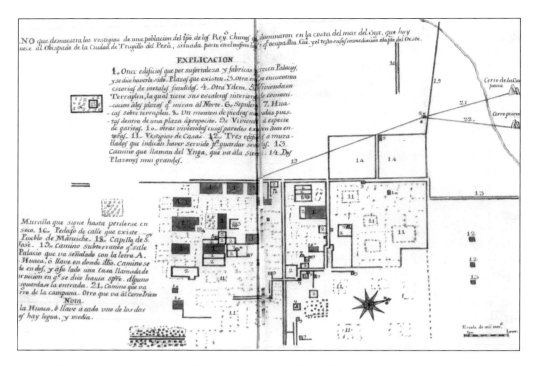

Fig. 3 Plan of the city of Chan Chan commissioned by Baltasar Martínez Compañón in the last quarter of the eighteenth century (after Martínez Compañón 1978–81 [1781–89])

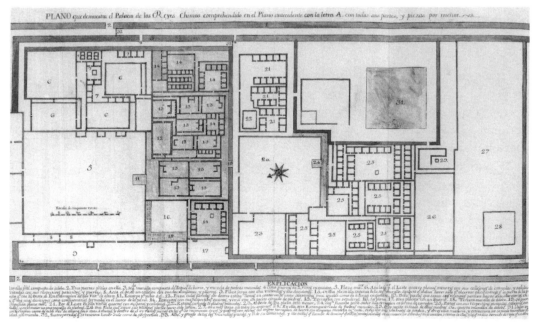

Fig. 4 Plan of Ciudadela Rivero commissioned by Baltasar Martínez Compañón in the last quarter of the eighteenth century (after Martínez Compañón 1978–81 [1781–89])

Susan Ramírez's account (1996) of a court case in Trujillo twenty-six years after the Spanish Conquest provides insight about the character and significance of *ciudadelas*. It involved the looting of a chambered structure located behind high adobe walls at Chan Chan—clearly one of the burial structures in a *ciudadela*.

Whereas Spanish writers of the sixteenth century referred to sacred or important native structures with the term *huaca* (a generic Hispano-Quechua term for a sacred location), the Chimú litigants were more specific about the disputed structure, repeatedly insisting that it was not just a *huaca*. Rather, according to court papers, it was the burial place of ancestors of the current *curaca principal* (paramount leader) of the Chimú, don Antonio Chayhuaca. Don Antonio himself consistently referred to the structure as a "house." He said that within the houses (*cassas*) "of my dead grandfather there is a burial and a tomb" (Ramírez 1996: 144; see also Zevallos Quiñones 1994: 90). Furthermore, such was the significance of the structure that when faced with its impending depredation, the Chimú litigants testified that disaster could result and all their people could die. Ramírez argues that the structure represented the origins, history, survival, and prosperity of the followers of don Antonio Chayhuaca: "the living and the dead were all related and interdependent" (1996: 135).

As Ramírez (1996: 147) further noted, functional distinctions between palace, temple, and tomb may have held little practical meaning. A structure may have originally been constructed as a palace with a burial precinct. Over time, and depending on the greatness of the individual(s) interred, these structures could gradually become templelike monuments.

It is useful to consider the general morphological features indicated in sixteenth- and seventeenth-century accounts of Andean palaces. These descriptions are drawn from both the north coast (Cieza de León 1984 [ca. 1551]: 160; Ruiz de Arce 1933 [ca. 1547]: 358) and the Cuzco region (Murúa 1987 [1611–16]: 58–59). They speak of palaces as the largest structures in a community, impressive for their scale and luxury. Five other specific features are consistently mentioned: (1) ornament, in the form of metal revetment, textiles, painting, or stone carving; (2) restricted and regulated access to a compound, via limited portals, high perimeter walls, and guards; (3) series of successive courts or plazas; (4) storage areas for valuables; and (5) gardens and/or pools and wells. Feature for feature, Murúa's description of a Cuzco palace suggests an intriguing correspondence with what is known archaeologically from the *ciudadelas* at Chan Chan:

> The royal palace . . . had two magnificent gateways, one at the entrance to the palace, and another farther inside where the finest and most impressive of these portals made its appearance. . . . In the entrance of the first doorway there were 2,000 indian guards . . . [and this first gateway] opened into a plaza. Here all those who accompanied the Inca from the outside entered and remained there. The Inca and the four *orejones* of his cabinet entered the second gate, where there was another guard [composed of kinsmen] . . . Beside the second gateway was the armory . . . [and] another great plaza or patio for the officials of the palace, and

those who had regular jobs were there conducting tasks assigned them according to their responsibilities. Continuing on, one enters the quarters, apartments, and buildings where the Inca lived that were filled with pleasures and delights for there were trees, gardens with a thousand varieties of birds that went about singing; lions, tigers, and pumas; and every species of beast and animal found in this kingdom. The buildings were large and spacious and worked with great skill. . . . Within the house of the Inca was a treasure room . . . where the jewels and gold and silver of the king were kept. (Murúa 1987 [1611–16]: bk. 2, chap. 2, 345–348)[3]

Jerry Moore (n.d.) has discussed the historical descriptions of the palace of Chilimassa, near Tumbes on the far north coast. It is unclear when the palace was built, and its cultural affiliation has yet to be established, although it is possible that it was the home of a Chimú lord. The descriptions of this palace, such as the following early description by Ruiz de Arce (1933 [ca. 1547]: 358), stress the ornamentation of the architecture, as well as the sequence of doorways: "In this town there was a fortified house, made with great skill. There were five doorways before arriving at the inner apartments [*aposentos*], with more than 100 paces between them. It has many terraces, all made from adobes. It has many inner spaces, with many murals. In the middle there was a plaza of good size, and further on more rooms and a patio. In the middle of this patio was a garden, and next to the garden was a fountain."[4] The interior gardens and wells must have been a remarkable spectacle in the context of the extremely arid north coast setting. Such features bespeak the power of the ruler to harness scarce resources and to position himself symbolically and metaphorically as one who controls access to sources of fertility and abundance.

Archaeological Evidence

The central features of a palace described in the historical sources are found at the site

---

[3] "Tenía el Palacio Real . . . dos soberbias puertas, una a la entrada dél y otra de más adentro, de donde se parecía lo mejor y más digno de estas puertas. . . . A la primera puerta, en la entrada della, había dos mil indios de guarda . . . [a esta puerta primera] se seguía una plaza hasta la cual entraban los que con el Ynga venían acompañándole de fuera y allí paraban, y el gran Ynga entraba dentro con los cuatro *orejones* de su consejo, pasando a la segunda puerta, en la cual había también otra guarda. . . . Junto a esta segunda puerta estaba la armería. . . . Más adelante de esta puerta, estaba otra gran plaza o patio para los oficiales del Palacio, y los que tenían oficios ordinarios dentro dél, que estaban allí aguardando lo que se les mandaba, en razón de su oficio. Después entraban las salas y recámaras, y aposentos, donde el Ynga vivía, y esto era todo lleno de deleite y contento, porque había arboledas, jardines con mil género de pájaros y aves, que andaban cantando; y había tigres y leones, y onzas y todos los géneros de fieras y animales que se hallaban en este reino. Los aposentos eran grandes y espaciosos, labrados con maravilloso artificio. . . . Había en el Palacio del Ynga una cámara de tesoro . . . done se guardaban las joyas y piedras [y oro y plata] del Ynga."

[4] "En este pueblo estava una casa fuerte, hecha por el mas lindo arte que nunca se vido tenian çinco puertas Antes que llegasen A los aposentos De puerta a puerta avia mas de cient pasos tenia muchas çercas todas de tierra. hechas a mano, tenia muchos aposentos. De muchas pinturas En el mº Estava una plaça. De buen tamaño, mas adelante estavan otros aposentos los quales tenian un patio, En medio de este patio estava un jardin y junto al jardin estava una fuente."

of Chan Chan. Separation, controlled access, ornament, and other aspects of the descriptions of palaces accord well with what is known archaeologically from the site.

The social stratification apparent in the documentary sources is reiterated in the architecture. Members of the Chan Chan–Moche Valley Project proposed a three-tiered hierarchy for Chimor, with the different strata associated with distinct architectural forms. The upper nobility or royalty, associated with the *ciudadelas*; the lesser nobility, linked with "elite compounds"; and the commoners, inhabiting the SIAR (Fig. 2; Moseley and Day 1982). Craft production, an important activity at the site, was located primarily in the last area (J. Topic 1990; Topic and Moseley 1983).

The *ciudadelas* are distinguished by their central location, monumental scale, high degree of formal planning, extreme control of access, and architectural complexity. They contain features that, prior to Chan Chan, were not found enclosed together within such simultaneously extensive and restricted spaces. Although the layouts vary, the features include large interior courts or plazas, storage areas, wells, retainer areas, and funerary platforms (Figs. 5–7). In most *ciudadelas*, the features are distributed in different combinations among three major sectors, parts of a complex chain (or "tree" in the terminology of Hillier and Hanson 1984) of restricted access. The combination of formal traits shared by the *ciudadelas* implies a shared constellation of functional correlates.

Scale. The *ciudadelas* are the largest architectural complexes at the site, with internal spaces from 87,900 to 221,000 sq m (Day 1982a: 55). Formally, they each represent such large labor investments that the functional involvement of multiple social units and strata is implied.

Ornament. The *ciudadelas* share the formal trait of ornamentation, implying types of symbolic function that sheer labor investment alone cannot carry. The interiors, particularly of the plazas, courts, corridors, U-shaped structures, and even entrances to wells and burial platforms, were elaborately ornamented with sculpted adobe reliefs (Fig. 8) (Pillsbury n.d.). Occasionally painted, the reliefs are often skeuomorphic representations of textile patterns. The compositions are made up of repeated geometric, zoomorphic, and anthropomorphic images, contained within borders. Rather than creating hierarchical compositions emphasizing large, brightly painted human and deity figures, such as those found in earlier periods on the north coast, Chan Chan friezes seem more closely related to decorative traditions like those seen in late Pre-Hispanic Andean tapestries.

Restricted access. The *ciudadelas* are enclosed by perimeter walls that were originally up to 9 or 10 m high. Access to the interior is through a single entrance in the north wall. The exteriors of the perimeter walls are unornamented.

The perimeter walls lack features consistent with military defense, such as bastions, parapets, towers, or openings for missile fire (see Topic and Topic 1987). Though restricted access would still assist nonmilitary security functions, it is doubtful that such massive walls would be necessary for this purpose alone (see Conklin 1990). Rather, monumental

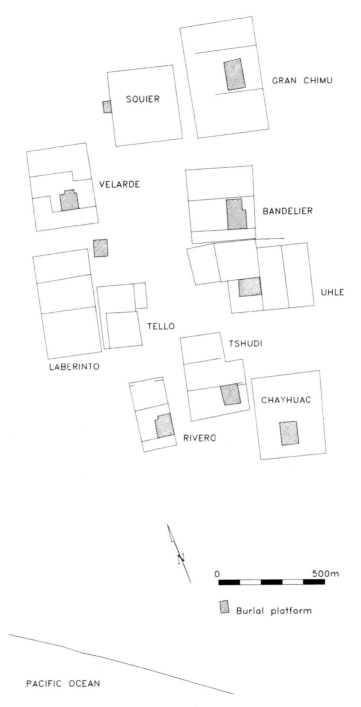

Fig. 5 Location of the *ciudadelas* in Chan Chan (after Topic
and Moseley 1983: fig. 28)

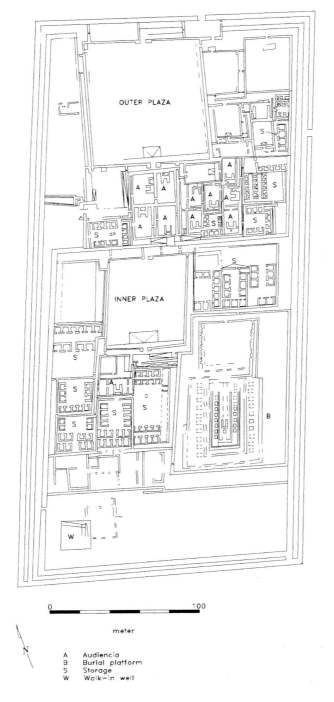

OUTER PLAZA

INNER PLAZA

B

W

0   100

meter

A   Audiencia
B   Burial platform
S   Storage
W   Walk-in well

Fig. 6   Plan of Ciudadela Rivero (after Uceda 1999: fig. 3)

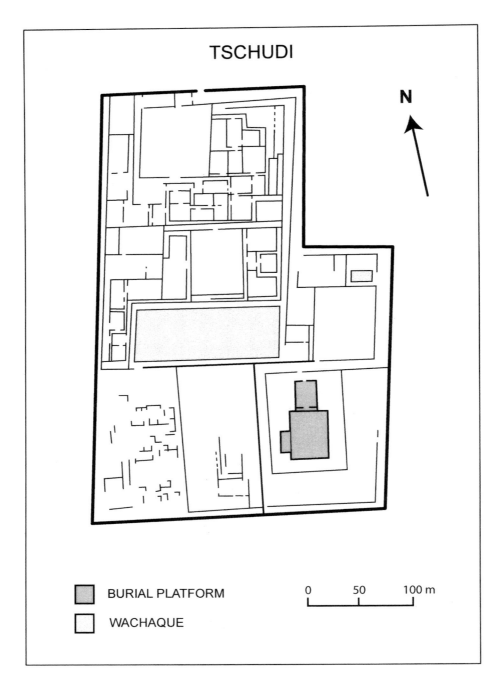

TSCHUDI

N

BURIAL PLATFORM

WACHAQUE

0   50   100 m

Fig. 7 Plan of Ciudadela Tschudi (after Moseley and Mackey 1974)

Fig. 8 Section of a wall ornamented with adobe reliefs, Ciudadela Squier

perimeter walls may have served primarily to express profound social distance between ruler and ruled (Day 1982a: 65; Kolata 1990: 140–142). The use of restricted access to royal precincts for functions other than defense or security can be found in stratified societies throughout the world.[5] Thus the formal trait of restricted access probably implies chiefly a function of social separation, as much visual (see Moore 1996: 92–120) as physical, and only secondarily a concern for security.

Once inside the main entry, other features imply the regulation of access and internal movement (Day 1982a; Moore 1996: 179–219). Progress is impeded by baffled entries between sectors. Distinctive U-shaped features—variously called *audiencias*, *trocaderos*, *arcones*, or *auxilios* depending on their exact configurations—are frequently located at junctures in

[5] For example, we may consider the case of the *afins* or palaces of the Yoruba kingdoms of West Africa. The *afin*, or official residence of the Oba, or ruler, was always an extensive walled compound, usually on elevated land at the center of a settlement (Ojo 1966). Filled with many courtyards and buildings, it was a repository of treasure, a place of ritual devotion, and a site for assembly and entertainment. A portion of the *afin*, the *ojú osi*, was designated as a burial ground for the ancestors of the Oba, and was a place where he sought the consultation of his ancestors and offered annual sacrifices. The *afin* is characterized by restricted access, with one main entrance, and perhaps two or three "secret" exits elsewhere in the palace to allow the Oba to leave or enter the palace secretly. The imposing perimeter walls of the *afin* were, in Ojo's (1966: 56) description, essential "to keep townspeople from their 'divine' ruler, who must be unseen and unheard except on special ceremonial occasions." Although speculative, it could be suggested that the institution of divine kingship on the north coast may have occurred earlier than has been suggested (Kolata 1990: 140–141), and indeed developed in concert with walled, restrictive enclosures.

Fig. 9 Wooden figure found at the entrance to Ciudadela Rivero. Photograph courtesy of Michael Moseley.

the bifurcation, flow, or gathering of interior movement (Andrews 1974; Cornejo n.d.; Kolata 1982). Many, especially the *audiencia* types, sat atop low platforms or were ornamented, and some were underlain by dedicatory burials containing high-status artifacts. The special treatment afforded to them implies a degree of vested authority (Keatinge 1977: 232), and their seemingly strategic locations suggest a relationship to access among the architectural subdivisions (see, however, Moore n.d., 1992, 1996: 210).

Social factors were also probably important in controlling access and internal movement. One is reminded of Murúa's description of the guards at the palace gate by two wooden sculptures found at the entrance to Ciudadela Rivero (Fig. 9) (Day n.d.: 140–147). The figures, about 60 cm tall, resemble guardians, and may have had some sort of weapon or standard (now missing) in their right hands.

Internal plazas. The *ciudadelas* have enclosed plazas or courts, implying that those granted access to them could be exposed in groups to such activities as ceremonies and displays, or to group organization for still other activities. The plazas often have ancillary features consistent with display functions, such as raised platforms or stages (generally on the south side) and perimetral benches (Topic and Moseley 1983: 154). Furthermore, many internal plazas are quite large. For example, the entry plaza of Ciudadela Rivero, the smallest of the *ciudadelas*, is 75 by 80 meters (Day n.d.: 149). By conservative estimates, such a plaza could hold hundreds of people at one time. In most *ciudadelas*, at least two such very large plazas are found at graduated distances along the restricted access system.

The appearance of reciprocity was central to the exercise of Andean rulership. This principal was articulated most prominently in ritual feasting hosted by paramount and lesser leaders. Several *ciudadela* plazas have adjacent kitchens (Day n.d.: 165–171). As mentioned above, many plazas are ornamented, undoubtedly enhancing the ability of activities in these grand spaces to reiterate the royal rhetoric of the state.

Storage areas. The *ciudadelas* have the formal trait of bulk storage facilities, consisting of repetitively grouped, similar-sized bins or chambers (see Day 1982b; Klymyshyn 1987). These storage units are generally reached from the main entrance after passing through restricted access points, through one or more interior plazas, and sometimes past *audiencias* and the like.[6] This configuration implies both that access to storage units was monitored and that the acquisition and distribution of stored goods were regulated. The second function would have been fulfilled by both backward and forward movement through the access system, and in whatever combination of whatever goods or people.

Direct evidence of what was stored in the *ciudadelas* is remarkably scarce (Day 1982a: 60; Klymyshyn 1987: 100). Worldwide, however, storage facilities are generally cleaned when emptied, and are usually not abandoned while full. Furthermore, those at Chan Chan would have been looted eventually by the Inca and/or Spaniards had they not been left empty. In any case, whatever they contained—foodstuffs, raw materials, finished craft products, ritual paraphernalia, weaponry, etc.—the context of the storage units implies not only a need for storage, but a function of tight regulation over collection and redistribution. The form of the access system emphasizes that whatever the relationship was between the activities of the plaza and the storage areas, communication between these areas was tightly controlled. Both the absence of any sort of remains and the strict control over access imply that highly valued items, rather than staple goods, were stored in these areas.

By far the majority of formal storage capacity at Chan Chan is located in the *ciudadelas* (Day 1982b),[7] implying that they were the dominant locus of controlled exchange within

---

[6] Recently, Jerry Moore (1996: 205–210) convincingly refuted an oft-repeated assertion that U-shaped structures regularly served to regulate access to storage areas in the *ciudadelas*. Moore analyzed access patterns in compounds with both U-shaped structures and formal storage areas and found insufficient association between these feature types to support the notion that U-shaped structures were located primarily between storage areas and precincts closer to the main entries of compounds. Nonetheless, we would point out that U-shaped structures still may have been related to storage access in some cases and to the regulation of internal movement in general. Moreover, other factors, including the sheer complexity of *ciudadela* access hierarchies, still imply that access to interior parts of the compounds, and therefore to formal storage units, was restricted in general. Indeed, the plazas, too, may have served a regulatory role.

[7] Formal bulk storage facilities concentrated on this scale are unknown from elsewhere on the north coast for any time period, although far larger bulk storage facilities were constructed elsewhere, especially by the Inca state (D'Altroy n.d., 1992; D'Altroy and Earle 1985; D'Altroy and Hastorf 1984; Earle and D'Altroy 1982; LeVine n.d., 1992; Morris n.d., 1972, 1981). This concentration of formal storage within the *ciudadelas* seems to support the impression of the unprecedented degree of power centralization achieved by the Chimú rulers.

the capital. Further, the quantity of formal storage capacity at Chan Chan far exceeds all that reported in the provinces (Klymyshyn 1987), emphasizing the degree of centralized control focused in the *ciudadelas* at the level of the Chimú empire. Storage facilities are often a feature of palace architecture elsewhere in the world (see, e.g., premodern Islamic palaces [Necipoğlu 1993]), and their abundance in the *ciudadelas* reinforces the idea that they encompassed functions beyond those of simple royal residences.

Burial platforms. Eight *ciudadelas* contain one or more mortuary platforms, at least as deeply imbedded in the access system as the storage features, and each contains multiple tombs (Conrad n.d., 1978, 1982).[8] The ninth, Ciudadela Laberinto, has a mortuary platform, Huaca Las Avispas, located outside its perimeter walls, but access to this platform is also tightly restricted. All these structures were heavily looted, but it is apparent that they contained one principal chamber and multiple smaller chambers. In his study of Huaca Las Avispas, Thomas Pozorski (1979) excavated one of these smaller chambers and found the remains of thirteen young women in it. Pozorski estimated that perhaps three hundred individuals were buried in Las Avispas. No evidence was found to indicate that the principal burial chamber was sealed; indeed it is possible that the occupants (mummies) were brought out periodically. Eight of the nine principal burial platforms had additional cells added to the original structure, and in several *ciudadelas* a later, second burial platform was constructed, which was also sometimes expanded. These patterns indicate that more interments were made at occasions that postdated the interment of the original principal corpse (Conrad n.d., 1978; Verano 1995: 199, note 1). Both the secondary cells in the original platform and the later, additional burials could have held relatives or other associates of the ruler, his retinue, or of descendants, as well as sacrifices. These various additions may have been part of periodic observances of the death of the ruler or of ritual renewals of the platform. Such later acts of veneration may in part explain difficulties in the ceramic chronology of the *ciudadelas*. The ceramics often appear to bias late, that is, the ceramics date later than other morphological features of the compounds. For example, a small number of Inca and Chimú-Inca ceramics have been recovered at Ciudadelas Tschudi (Conrad n.d.: 62; Narváez and Hoyle 1985) and Gran Chimú (Conrad n.d.: 632–636), which are both solidly pre-Inca in other respects.

The post-principal-occupation venerations in the *ciudadelas* may have also involved architectural activities beyond the addition of new cells. In Ciudadela Uhle, there is an apparent funerary platform known as "El Muestrario" (also known as the "Plataforma de las Vírgenes," Fig. 10; Pillsbury n.d.: 145–151). On its north side is a small courtyard with an

---

[8]   Several of the *ciudadelas*, particularly the earlier ones such as Uhle, contain more than one burial platform. Conrad (1981) has argued that the pattern of "one king—one palace" may have developed over time in the history of Chan Chan, and only became rigidly standardized later in the history of the site. The situation is indeed complex, and not necessarily straightforward at any point in the history of Chan Chan. For example, Ciudadela Velarde may have a secondary (and distinct type of) burial platform in addition to the principal platform previously recognized (Pillsbury n.d.). Such evidence, however, may not negate the model, as additional burials in the *ciudadelas* may represent interments of important relatives of the king.

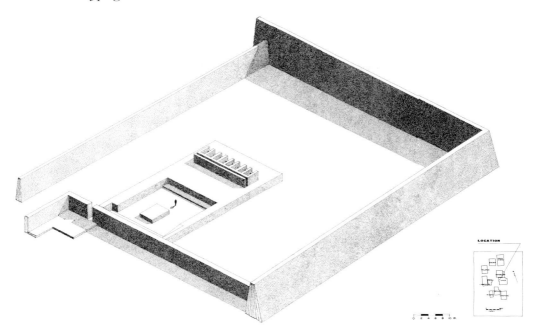

Fig. 10 Simplified isometric reconstruction of the "El Muestrario" platform, Ciudadela Uhle, Chan Chan. Drawing by Alberto Barba, based on measurements by Alberto Barba and Peter Kvietok.

Fig. 11 Reconstruction drawing of the "El Muestrario" relief, Ciudadela Uhle. Drawing by Alberto Barba.

elaborate sculpted relief composed of two sets of diagonal bands with anthropomorphic, zoomorphic, and geometric forms joined at the center by a vertical band (Fig. 11). The relief was created at the same time as part of the first stage of construction of the platform, which was later remodeled. Possibly at the same time as the remodeling, the relief was remade, with an apparently identical relief constructed directly over the face of the original. Fragments of this second layer are visible along the top margin of the first (Fig. 12). Judging from archival photographs from the 1950s, the original relief was in relatively good shape when covered over. This suggests that reconstruction of the same image in the same spot may have been directed to ends other than enlargement of the platform or repair of the original relief (Pillsbury n.d.: 119, 146–147).

Fig. 12 Detail of the "El Muestrario" relief in 1990

Also, we note that Ciudadela Squier—probably the last to be initiated (Pillsbury n.d.; Topic and Moseley 1983)—has a less complex internal configuration. It either lacks or has fewer of certain features common to the others, including *audiencia*-type features (Andrews 1974: 262), storage units (Conrad n.d.: table 4), and access restrictions (Moore 1996: 200). Moreover, its burial platform sector is much less elaborate and apparently had fewer tomb cells. Because of these patterns, Squier has sometimes been regarded as an incomplete *ciudadela* (e.g., Moore 1996: 79). But these patterns are also consistent with the idea that Squier had fewer transformations in its use history by the time Chan Chan was abandoned, and did not have an extensive post-principal-occupation mortuary stage (Conrad n.d.: 81).

Some of the best data on funerary activities in the *ciudadelas* come from a three-dimensional Chimú architectural model (Fig. 13) excavated in 1995 by Santiago Uceda (1997, 1999) at the Huaca de la Luna. The architectural model and associated figures were found in an intrusive Chimú tomb on Platform 1 of this Moche structure. The tomb was probably quite late (C-14 dates A.D. 1440–1665), and Uceda suggested that it may have been placed at Huaca de la Luna during the late Inca occupation of the north coast, a time when Chan Chan was abandoned and perhaps partially destroyed (Zevallos Quiñones n.d.).

The model clearly represents a ritual gathering in a plaza. Details including the layout and ornamentation suggest that it represents the first plaza of one of the late *ciudadelas*, either Rivero or Tschudi. The figures include musicians, a *chicha* (maize beer) server, and apparent funerary bundles. Two of the three bundles were found in the back corridor of the model, located beyond a doorway from the plaza. This scene may well depict the bringing

Fig. 13 Drawing of an architectural model (as seen from above) with figures excavated at Huaca de la Luna (after Uceda 1999: fig. 4b). The mummy bundle figures are not shown here.

forward of bundles to the first plaza as part of periodic rituals held after the death of the principal individual.

The funerary function was clearly integral to the *ciudadela*, but does not preclude an earlier role as residence for a ruling monarch. Part of the difficulty in recognizing *ciudadelas* as palaces for the living lies in the fact that we see them in their final incarnation—as mausolea. What is visible today is the final phase of the metamorphosis from thriving residence and administrative center to burial structure and place of veneration. For later observers, accustomed to European traditions where the dead are separated from everyday activities of the living, this amalgam of functions is counterintuitive. It is important to bear in mind, however, that in the ancient Andes the realms of the quick and the dead, in a conceptual as well as spatial sense, were not strictly divided (Salomon 1995). Indeed it was politically advantageous to have the dead close at hand. For a descendant sodality, the ancestors would have been essential to clarifying and reiterating their own powerful role in the world of the living.

Retainer areas. We noted that one criticism of the identification of *ciudadelas* as palaces is the apparent lack of domestic debris related to elite residential occupation (Rowe 1995: 30). That such important structures were "swept clean" might be expected given their importance and their later transformation into mortuary complexes; the *ciudadelas* were not abandoned directly after their use as palaces of the living. In seeming contradiction, the clearest evidence of domestic habitation in *ciudadelas* seems to reflect the remains of commoner residence, including communal kitchen areas (McGrath n.d.). Within the compound perimeters, such remains are usually embedded even more deeply in the access system than the enclosed plazas, storage units, or even the burial platforms, in areas that would rarely be observed by visitors admitted to the *ciudadelas* from outside. These embedded commoner quarters and communal kitchens have been identified as belonging to attached, low-status retainers or possibly also to personnel involved in ongoing construction and remodeling (see also Conrad n.d.; Klymyshyn n.d.). Such retainers and workers might have served either living or dead royal occupants, or both during the use histories of the *ciudadelas*.

Wells. Large walk-in wells were made possible by the rather high prehistoric water table at Chan Chan, and many of these were also located deep within the access systems of the *ciudadelas* (Day 1974, 1982a). Whereas the wells provided secure and independent water sources, they also may have fulfilled important religious and ceremonial prerequisites. In Ciudadela Tschudi, archaeologists from the Instituto Nacional de Cultura in Trujillo found quantities of *Spondylus* in an offering at its large walk-in well (Pillsbury 1996: 323; Arturo Paredes, personal communication, 1991). These offerings suggest that the wells played an important symbolic role in the hyper-arid north coast. The enormous well at Tschudi was perhaps as clear a statement of luxury and control over resources as anything else.

Two other formal traits related to the *ciudadelas* can only be evaluated at the scale of the city as a whole. First, they are intimately surrounded by lesser forms of architecture that contain evidence of activities that supported the functioning of the *ciudadelas*. These include habitation precincts with areas devoted to specialized craft production and transport (Klymyshyn n.d., 1980, 1982; J. Topic n.d., 1982, 1990). Additional retainer precincts were located atop platforms built adjacent to all the *ciudadelas* (Klymyshyn n.d.; Topic and Moseley 1983). In other words, the monumental/palatial/mortuary precincts of the *ciudadelas* were linked with residences and specialized activities carried out in the immediate vicinity.

Some of the elite compounds seem to replicate the characteristics of the *ciudadelas* on a smaller, simpler scale. A few examples contain burial structures (Conrad n.d.: 114–128; Klymyshyn n.d.: 59–65, 73–107), which have been interpreted as the residences or palaces of minor nobles or mid-level elites (Klymyshyn 1982).

Finally, many Chan Chan-Moche Valley Project scholars have observed that the initial construction of the various *ciudadelas* apparently occurred at different times and possibly sequentially (see especially Conrad n.d.; Narváez n.d.; Kolata n.d., 1982, 1990; Topic and Moseley 1983). As a corollary, some have ventured that, at least in the later part of Chan Chan's imperial history, each *ciudadela* was particular to a given ruler, his reign, and his mortuary sodality (see especially Conrad n.d., 1981, 1982). If this interpretation is correct, then the dynastic succession of individual rulers has been played out horizontally across the landscape. Therefore, although the function of each *ciudadela* was transformed during its particular use history, and although the phases of construction, remodeling, and transformation overlapped temporally among them, each one potentially represents the same sequence of transformations in spatial segregation from the others.

Synchronic and Diachronic Comparisons with the Chan Chan Ciudadelas

Evaluating *ciudadelas* in the immediate context of Chan Chan, we go far toward understanding them as symbolic and material seats of power for the Chimú apical rulers. Evidence from this context enables us to argue that *ciudadelas* encompassed the functional equivalents of palaces in the configuration of the Chimú state. Further, this context allows us to address why it has been problematic to fit them into such a nonindigenous category as palace; chiefly, the *ciudadelas* served as more than palaces in the Western sense during their complex use histories.

As argued, several functions are reflected in the formal characteristics of *ciudadela* architecture and use history. Still, the precise combinations and transformations of ideological, social, and political functions remain perhaps unique and impenetrable without comparisons to sites and structures in broader contexts of the Chimú world. Such comparisons can be fruitful in both synchronic and diachronic dimensions. In the synchronic dimension, we compare the *ciudadelas* to known contemporaneous structures and sites outside Chan Chan to evaluate whether formal or functional equivalents exist away from the capital. On the diachronic dimension, we search for antecedents of the same functional complex reflected in the *ciudadelas*, even if the formal characteristics and their combinations and transformations changed.

Synchronic Comparisons

To simplify comparison, we limit our synchronic examination to known sites and structures with clear Chimú associations along the coast from the Casma Valley in the south to the Jequetepeque Valley in the north. We exclude the Lambayeque region of the far north coast as it was the core area of its own particularly elaborate and distinct legacy of kingship, with attendant forms and configurations, in the period prior to Chimú conquest (see especially Shimada 1987, 1990). Prior to the rather late Chimú conquest of Lambayeque in the mid-to-late fourteenth century (Donnan 1990a, b; Shimada 1990), Lambayeque and the Chicama-Moche-Virú cradle of the Chimú culture were apparently each the core areas of the two most dominant statehood traditions that developed during and after late Moche times on the north coast. Because of these strong and different local legacies, comparisons with Lambayeque sites may be complicated by the overlay of intrusive Chimú forms on native traditions more than would be the case in the areas we are including in our analysis.

Temporally, we include sites dating to the period when Chan Chan was the foremost Chimú center, from approximately A.D. 950 into the period of Inca control, beginning in approximately A.D. 1470 (Rowe 1948: 40) and ending with the Spanish Conquest. Chan Chan was evidently largely abandoned before the Spanish Conquest (Zevallos Quiñones n.d.), but at least some of its *ciudadela*s apparently continued to function in a reduced fashion into the first decades of Inca control (Conrad n.d.; Narváez n.d., 1989; Narváez and Hoyle 1985; Ramírez 1990). Given continued use and transformation of Chan Chan after Inca conquest, clearly separating pre-Inca and post-Inca aspects of the late occupation of Chan Chan is difficult. The same difficulty is present in the provinces as well. Of course, as with the Chimú conquest of Lambayeque, the overlay of local traditions by the Inca remains a consideration, but the Inca conquered the entire region, and therefore we have no simple means for sorting away Late Horizon components by simple geography.

Outside Chan Chan and within the area from Casma to Jequetepeque, only four contemporaneous sites are preserved with structures that possess almost all the formal traits reflected in the massive Chan Chan enclosures (Fig. 14). These are Compound II at Farfán (Fig. 15, Conrad n.d.: 177–181, 1990; Keatinge and Conrad 1983) and El Algarrobal de Moro in the Jequetepeque Valley (Carol Mackey, personal communication 1998, 1999), Manchan in the Casma Valley (Fig. 16, Klymyshyn 1987; Mackey and Klymyshyn 1981, 1990), and the Chimú-Inca site of Chiquitoy Viejo in the Chicama Valley (Fig. 17, Conrad n.d.: 153–177, 1977, 1981; Leonard n.d.c; Leonard and Russell n.d.c). These four sites have large walled enclosures with areas between approximately 40,000 and 100,000 sq m, overlapping the size of the smallest Chan Chan *ciudadela*, Rivero (Day n.d.). These compounds share several other formal characteristics with the *ciudadelas*, and also with the more elaborate and formal examples of the lesser elite compounds at Chan Chan.

Ornamentation was documented at both compounds in the Jequetepeque Valley (Keatinge and Conrad 1983: 271; Carol Mackey, personal communication 1998), although none has been clearly identified at the others.[9] All four have restricted access features and *audiencias* or similar U-shaped features. All have enclosed plazas entered only through restricted access points. Still, at all four sites the access system is generally less complex and tortuous than in the *ciudadelas* (see also Moore 1996: 188–205).

All have storage units, although their numbers and the space they occupy are considerably less than those of the individual *ciudadelas*. Further, at least the structures at Chiquitoy Viejo, El Algarrobal de Moro, and Farfán clearly have less storage capacity than some of the elite compounds at Chan Chan. Thus, in terms of storage capacity, El Algarrobal de Moro,

---

[9] Evidence of ornamentation is scarce in general in the provinces. This may be due in part to the reduced level of renovation and rebuilding, which often preserves reliefs or paintings that would otherwise have been destroyed by exposure to the elements. This aside, the quantity and degree of architectural ornamentation are far less than at the capital.

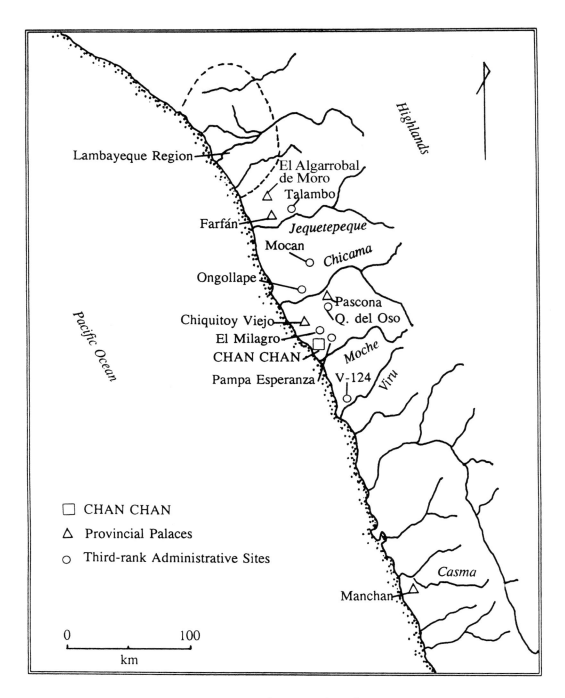

Fig. 14 Late Intermediate period north coast sites

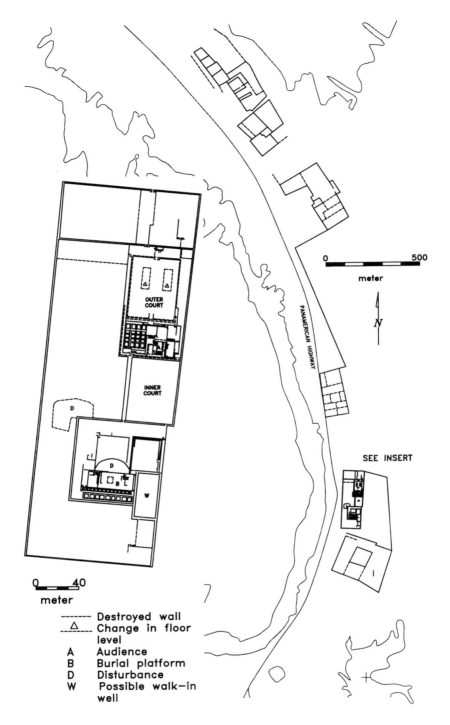

OUTER
COURT

INNER
COURT

D

D

B

W

SEE INSERT

PANAMERICAN HIGHWAY

0   500
meter

N

0   40
meter

------- Destroyed wall
--△-- Change in floor
level
A   Audience
B   Burial platform
D   Disturbance
W   Possible walk—in
well

Fig. 15 Plan of Farfán, Jequetepeque Valley (after Keatinge and Conrad 1983: fig. 8)

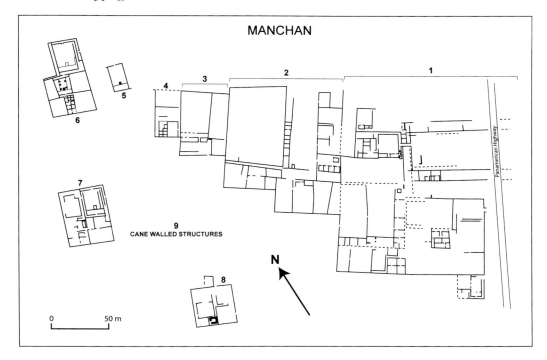

Fig. 16 Simplified plan of Manchan, Casma Valley (after Mackey and Klymyshyn 1981: fig. 1)

Farfán, Chiquitoy Viejo, and perhaps Manchan rank lower than some non-*ciudadela* compounds at the capital. On the other hand, the lack of storage at the hybrid Chimú-Inca compound at Chiquitoy Viejo may only reflect the altered nature of state economic strategies under the Inca (Conrad n.d.: 175–177; Leonard n.d.c; Leonard and Russell n.d.c).

At least three (all except El Algarrobal de Moro) have one or more burial structures of some form, which are less imposing than those in the *ciudadelas*, but generally more elaborate than those in the handful of lesser elite compounds that possess them at Chan Chan. Thus, in terms of evidence for mortuary function, three of the four sites rank intermediate between the two highest-ranked categories of architecture at the capital. To date, no burial structure has been clearly identified at El Algarrobal de Moro, suggesting that this site may rank somewhere below the other three with respect to mortuary function (Carol Mackey, personal communication, 1999).

Low-status habitation areas are known to be associated with two of the sites (Manchan and Chiquitoy Viejo), with a strong possibility that they exist in the others (Conrad n.d., 1977; Mackey and Klymyshyn 1981, 1990; Leonard n.d.c; Leonard and Russell n.d.c; Carol Mackey, personal communication,1999). At Chiquitoy Viejo, a large zone of apparent commoner retainer dwellings is more deeply embedded in the access system than the burial platform, as was the usual case with the *ciudadelas* (Conrad n.d.: 156–157). Commoner habitation has not yet been clearly identified at El Algarrobal de Moro, although the analysis is still ongoing (Carol Mackey, personal communication, 1998).

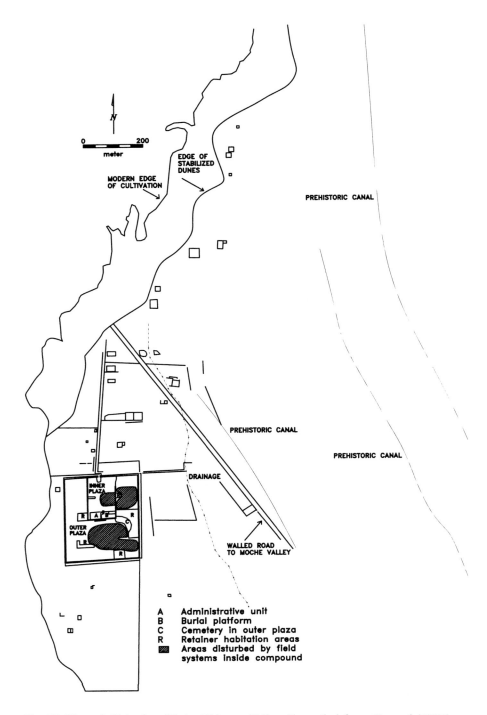

Fig. 17 Plan of Chiquitoy Viejo, Chicama Valley. Compiled from Conrad (1977) and unpublished drawings by Banks Leonard.

Only one of the four sites, Farfán, contains a feature that resembles a walk-in well, but the absence of wells at the other three may reflect only lack of a high water table. Still, the apparent well at Farfán is located deep in the access system like many of those at Chan Chan.

To date, the immediate surroundings of the four compounds have been studied to different degrees, most completely at Manchan and Chiquitoy Viejo and perhaps least at Farfán. Nonetheless, evidence is seen for a range of middle- and lower-status residents involved in support activities in the immediate vicinities, and other, less elaborate compounds are found at Chiquitoy Viejo, Farfán, and Manchan that may be analogs to the lesser elite compounds at Chan Chan.

Overall, the formal characteristics of these four compounds more or less imply a replication of the same set of functions seen in the *ciudadelas* and a few of the more formal elite compounds at the capital. As at Chan Chan, Chiquitoy Viejo and the Farfán compound, at least, show some evidence of remodeling consistent with the idea that they underwent functional transformations during their use histories (Conrad n.d.: 154–173; Keatinge and Conrad 1983: 274). If the Chan Chan *ciudadelas* and elite compounds encompassed the Chimú version of palaces, then we may infer that these four sites encompassed that function along the same model. Because of their location in the provinces, the interpretation that these were the seats of power for local lords or provincial governors seems reasonable. Remarkably, aside from these four sites, no other well-preserved compounds outside Chan Chan from Casma to Jequetepeque are reported that fit well into a *ciudadela*-based model of Chimú palace. There are sites, however, with architecture that conforms partially to the same canons.

Carol Mackey (1987) has developed a model for ranking formal Chimú state compounds in a hierarchy based on total area, area of the largest internal plaza, and presence or absence of architectural feature types. In this model, *ciudadelas* occupy the primary rank, and the large compounds at Farfán and Manchan occupy the second rank, with areas of 40,250 and 86,400 sq m, respectively. With approximate areas of 66,000 and 95,000 sq m respectively, we could argue that Chiquitoy Viejo and the more recently studied El Algarrobal would also fit into this second rank. In Mackey's model, aside from large size, the first- and second-rank compounds all have at least one internal plaza in excess of 1,000 sq m. They also have *audiencias*, storage units, and, with the possible exception of El Algarrobal de Moro, burial features and evidence of domestic habitation in perishable structures in their vicinities.

The third rank in Mackey's hierarchy includes six other compounds. These include V-124 in the Virú Valley, H-360485 and El Milagro de San José in the Moche Valley (Fig. 18), Pampa de Mocan in the Chicama Valley, and Talambo in the Jequetepeque Valley. The sizes range from 1,479 sq m (Pampa de Mocan) to 7,504 sq m (V-124) and plazas from 150 sq m (H-360485 in Moche) to 816 sq m (Talambo). We could add at least one other well-preserved Chimú compound to this list. It is an intrusive construction located atop Huaca Ongollape in the lower Chicama Valley, and has an area of 3,300 sq m and a formal plaza measuring 750 sq m (Fig. 19).

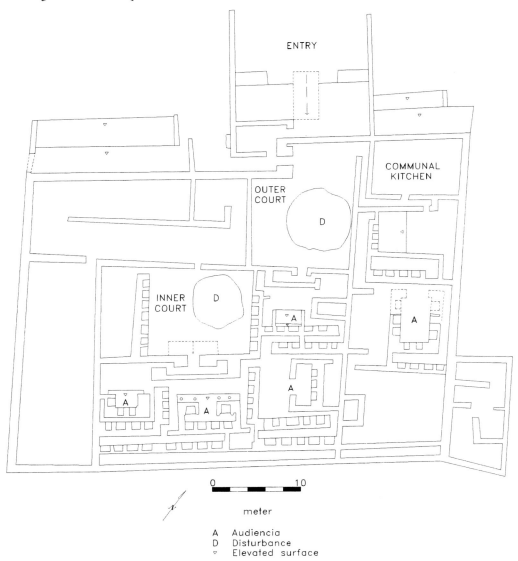

ENTRY

COMMUNAL
KITCHEN

OUTER
COURT

D

INNER
COURT   D

A

A

A

A

A

0   10

meter

A   Audiencia
D   Disturbance
▽   Elevated surface

Fig. 18 Plan of El Milagro de San José, a third-rank compound in the Moche Valley (after
Keatinge and Conrad 1983: fig. 4)

The fourth rank in Mackey's original formulation contains four other compounds, all
in the Moche Valley, ranging from 204 to 950 sq m, and with plazas from 45 to 100 sq m.
Whereas all possess restricted accesses and at least one *audiencia*-type structure, however, the
compounds in the third and fourth ranks of the hierarchy lack storerooms, burial platforms
(except V–124 [Mackey and Klymyshyn 1990: 216]), and habitation areas with perishable
structures. Thus the lower-ranked compounds conform to a degree to architectural canons
that otherwise are combined rarely outside Chan Chan and the four apparent provincial
palaces. Notably, however, they lack formal traits that imply storage and mortuary functions

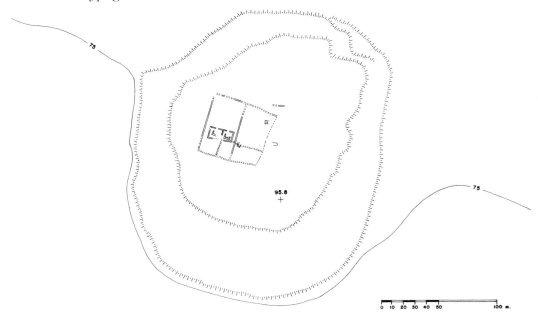

Fig. 19 Plan of compound atop Huaca Ongollape, Chicama Valley

(except for the burial structure at V-124), or the presence of resident populations.[10] In other words, despite some formal resemblance, they are apparently something other than palaces of the *ciudadela* pattern.

Indeed, all the third- and fourth-rank compounds in this list in the Moche, Chicama, and Jequetepeque Valleys except the one atop Huaca Ongollape are situated adjacent to Chimú canals or field systems. This has led to the interpretation that they served as rural administrative centers (Keatinge 1974, 1975; Keatinge and Conrad 1983; Keatinge and Day 1973; Pozorski 1987).

In the past few years, more than 30 percent of the lower Chicama Valley below Sausal has received complete pedestrian survey coverage, and virtually all potential Chimú walled compounds visible on aerial photos have been field inspected (Leonard n.d.a, b, c; Leonard and Russell n.d.a, b, c; Russell n.d.; Russell and Leonard 1990). Thus we might focus for the moment on the Chicama and examine whether any smaller versions of palaces can be identified that appear to conform to the *ciudadela*-type configuration.

In the Chicama, several less well preserved Chimú compounds exist that may represent third- or fourth-rank compounds, based on their modest sizes and lack of burial platforms. Most of these are also located along Chimú canals or among field systems, although one is an intrusive construction atop Huaca Sonolipe.[11] One other poorly preserved Chimú

10 At least three of these third- and fourth-ranked compounds—at El Milagro de San José (Moche Valley), Quebrada del Oso (Chicama Valley), and Quebrada Katuay (Moche Valley)—do appear to have internal kitchen areas (see Keatinge and Day 1973).

11 As far as we know, this structure and the one atop Huaca Ongollape are the only Chimú compounds built atop monumental adobe mounds south of Lambayeque, where others are known (Donnan 1990a; Reindel 1993; Shimada 1990).

compound deserves special mention. At a site in the Pampa de Pascona on the south margin of the Chicama Valley, three compounds are present, one of which is unusually large. Although over half this compound has been destroyed by modern construction, it appears mostly intact in a 1943 aerial photograph, allowing its original size to be measured and some of its features to be discerned (Fig. 20). Its internal area was approximately 22,000 sq m—about half the size of the smallest palace in Mackey's second rank, but roughly three times larger than any of the third-rank compounds. It had numerous internal subdivisions, including multiple internal plazas. The still-undestroyed portion of the compound appears to be a Chimú construction and is associated with middle and late Chimú ceramics. But this is the closest thing to a palace compound on the *ciudadela* model among the less well preserved examples in the lower Chicama.

Numerous better-preserved Chimú compounds have also been recorded in the lower Chicama. Most of these, too, are located adjacent to canals or among field systems, but none has sufficient size or evident burial platforms, and they individually contain nothing approaching the full complement of formal attributes of palaces on the *ciudadela* pattern. At the same time, their layouts or feature combinations do not resemble the Chan Chan-like rural administrative compounds that compose the third and fourth ranks of Mackey's site hierarchy, even though they have restricted access, internal plazas, *audiencia*-like features, and/or repetitive, formal storage units in various combinations.

If we can find only four or five sites outside Chan Chan with compounds that resemble the *ciudadelas*, or even the "elite compounds" of Chan Chan, then where are the lower provincial elites living? Unless the "missing" elites are at Chan Chan, perhaps occupying parts of the *ciudadelas* and elite compounds, they must be living and being buried in places that do not resemble the *ciudadelas* and their lesser variants and that do not combine the same suite of residential, ceremonial, redistributive, and mortuary functions.

At the better-preserved Chimú residential sites recorded in the lower Chicama survey, status differences between habitation structures is sometimes evident in relative size, symmetry, and construction quality of the architecture, and in the proportion of finer ceramics present. Such variation is perhaps most evident at the two large, late Chimú fortified sites of Cerro Azul and Cerro Facalá on the north side of the valley. But these higher-status residential units resemble the architectural forms of Chan Chan *ciudadelas* even less than do the apparent rural administrative centers of Mackey's third- and fourth-ranked compounds. They lack significant access restrictions such as high perimeter walls or convoluted passages. Sizable internal plazas, *audiencia*-type features, formal storage units, and burial platforms are entirely absent, and they usually lack any evidence of mortuary use. These residences seem only like larger, nicer houses, built of relatively imperishable materials, and occupied by people with access to better-quality possessions.

Thus, in the provinces, the vast majority of contemporaneous structures with architectural characteristics reminiscent of the *ciudadelas* were apparently not palaces. Even in the rural parts of the Moche Valley and in nearby Chicama, no elite residential architecture analogous to that of Chan Chan has been identified clearly with the exception of the Chimú-Inca compound at Chiquitoy Viejo. Instead, the vast majority of sites with combi-

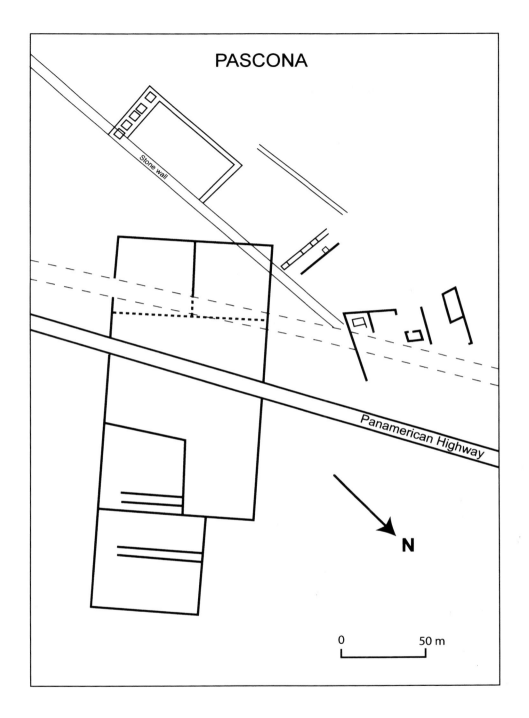

PASCONA

Stone wall

Panamerican Highway

N

0   50 m

Fig. 20 Plan of compounds in the Pampa de Pascona, Chicama Valley

nations of traits that are common at Chan Chan—restricted access, internal plazas, and U-shaped features—appear to be intrusive administrative facilities that are mostly located away from residential sites (Keatinge 1974, 1975; Keatinge and Conrad 1983; Keatinge and Day 1973; Pozorski 1987), apart from the four or five possible provincial palaces. An exception to this, the compound atop Huaca Ongollape in the central part of the lower Chicama Valley, is perhaps even more intrusive in nature; it was built on the summit of the largest pre-imperial Chimú monumental structure, after the top of the mound was cleared of its original summit architecture. A similarly intrusive but poorly preserved Chimú compound is located atop another nearby giant pre-imperial mound—Huaca Sonolipe.

Rather than seeing numerous lesser rural versions of *ciudadelas* that would imply some continuum between rural and Chan Chan elites, including the apical royalty of the *ciudadelas*, the distribution and configuration of architectural forms and implied functional combinations that replicate those of Chan Chan appear as imposed patterns emanating from the capital. The impression is that these configurations coalesced at Chan Chan as part of the unprecedented centralization of power by the Chimú rulers in imperial times. Once this power was consolidated, its form was extended out from the capital. So, lacking any contemporaneous analog in the Chimú world, perhaps we may find antecedents for the *ciudadela* configuration in preceding periods. Where else in the preceding periods can we find the formal traits that imply similar functions, and in what contexts and combinations?

Diachronic Comparisons

To simplify our brief diachronic analysis, we limit our examination to the Chimú core region, specifically the Chicama and Moche Valleys. The cultural traditions of these two valleys, along with the Virú, manifest great similarities and a deep continuity that imply that they participated in a single variety of north coast culture from the first millennium B.C., or earlier.

We focus our comparison on the elite/ceremonial centers that were the major foci of power in these two adjacent valleys in the seven or eight centuries before the coalescence of the Chimú state. In the Chicama Valley these were the earlier Gallinazo and Moche center of Mocollope, the Moche center at El Brujo, and the early Chimú mound complex at Sonolipe (Fig. 21). In the Moche Valley these were the Huaca del Sol/Huaca de la Luna complex and the late Moche center at Galindo in the Moche Valley. As with the site of Cerro Orejas in the Moche Valley, the Mocollope complex was the first political center of a unified lower valley polity. In the case of the Chicama Valley, the centralization of power occurred at about the onset of the first century A.D., in the late Gallinazo period (Leonard and Russell n.d.a, b, c; Russell n.d.). Unlike Cerro Orejas, which was replaced by the prime center at the site of Moche in the early Moche period (Billman n.d.), Mocollope continued to function as the focus of political and ceremonial power in its valley well into Moche times. The monumental structures at the site are thus the cumulative result of more than five centuries of construction and remodeling (see also Reindel 1993: 82–106, 286–292).

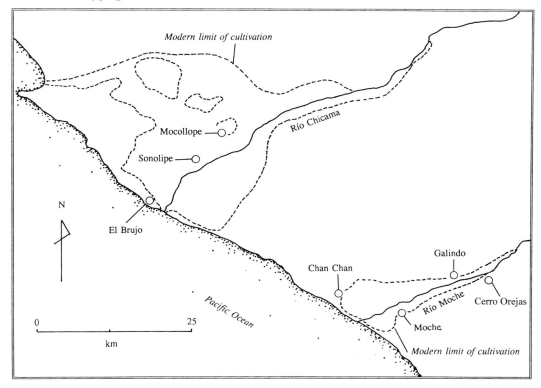

Fig. 21 Early Intermediate–Late Intermediate period sites in the Moche and Chicama valleys

The main precinct at Mocollope occupies approximately 40 ha on the southwest base of a dry, rocky hill, located almost exactly in the geographic center of the lower valley alluvial fan (Fig. 22). The dominant architecture consists of two large, parallel platforms with a large plaza between them. In front of these major platforms are smaller constructions including compounds and platforms, among which is a series of minor plazas. Cemeteries and zones with evidence of habitation and craft production are found within the complex, surrounding it, and at nearby sites (Attarian n.d.; Leonard and Russell n.d.a; Russell, Leonard, and Briceño 1994a, b). The complex has been heavily looted, but ironically the looting has exposed important details about the sequence of construction and remodeling and the types of architectural features.

With the exception of *audiencia*-like features and wells, formal analogs for all the major functions represented in the Chan Chan *ciudadelas* can be identified buried within the many layers of construction or near the major monuments at Mocollope. The major constructions are larger than any earlier monuments in the valley and represent a greatly concentrated labor investment. Interior ornamentation is present, both polychrome murals and relief friezes. Walled enclosures and narrow passages reflect restricted access. Enclosed plazas of various sizes represent controlled group activities. One and possibly two areas of repetitive storage rooms have been identified within one of the major platforms. High-

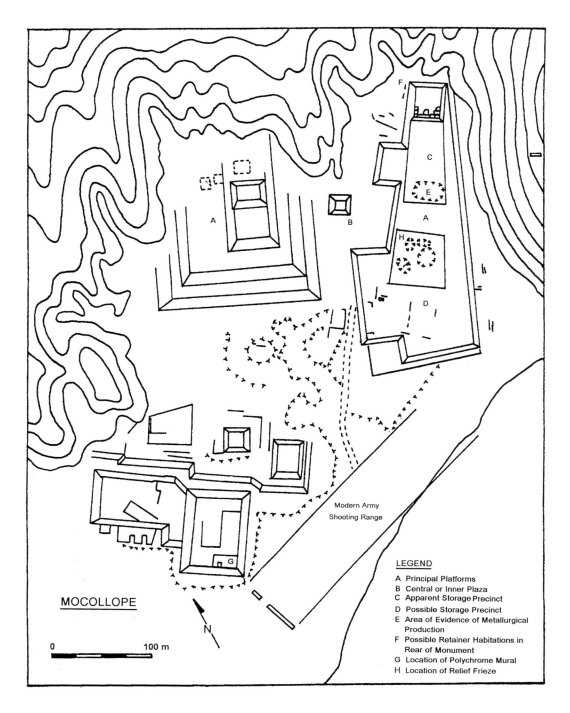

MOCOLLOPE

N

0   100 m

Modern Army
Shooting Range

LEGEND

A Principal Platforms
B Central or Inner Plaza
C Apparent Storage Precinct
D Possible Storage Precinct
E Area of Evidence of Metallurgical
  Production
F Possible Retainer Habitations in
  Rear of Monument
G Location of Polychrome Mural
H Location of Relief Frieze

Fig. 22 Plan of Mocollope complex, Chicama Valley. Drawing by Christopher Attarian.

status cemeteries surround the monuments, and some now-looted, high-status tomb chambers are located within the monumental zones. Evidence of ceramic and metal production and apparent retainer habitations are found both within and near the monuments. Interestingly, apparent low-status retainer habitation has been identified in the rearward part of one of the major platforms, yet detailed inspection of the site has failed to identify clearly elite habitation quarters.

As we see them archaeologically, the formal traits of Mocollope do not resemble their Chimú functional analogs. As best we can discern, the layout of functions is not integrated or articulated in the singular fashion of the *ciudadelas*. Nonetheless, we are tempted to see the structures at Mocollope as encompassing the functions of an Andean palace, but, unlike Chan Chan, they did so repetitively within the irregular "onion skin" of its centuries of remodeling and alteration. The same architectural complex presumably served as a seat of power for succeeding generations of religiopolitical leaders. It is significant that the remodeling, unlike that in the *ciudadelas*, involved the complete filling in and building over of earlier configurations at Mocollope.

Recent studies at the younger Moche center at El Brujo near the Chicama River mouth have revealed a few of the same patterns seen at Mocollope. Again, two major monuments are present—Huaca El Brujo and Huaca Cao Viejo.[12] Recent excavations have focused on the north side of the latter mound (Franco, Gálvez, and Vásquez 1994; Gálvez and Briceño 2001). Some seven phases of construction and remodeling have been reported to date. The various phases each apparently consisted of corridors, ramps, and exterior façades, the last two of which, at least, were decorated with reliefs. The imagery is dominated by themes of combat, prisoners, and sacrifice, with the decorated façades bearing images related to decapitation of human victims by superhuman or supernatural beings.[13] In Huaca Cao Viejo, we see a repetition of the general principal of superimposed but functionally equivalent constructions that was implied by the evidence at Mocollope.

Research at the more intensively studied site of Moche paints a similar picture. Like Mocollope and El Brujo, there are two major monuments, the largest of which, Huaca del Sol, was probably the largest freestanding monument built in prehistoric South America (Hastings and Moseley 1975). Recent excavations in the smaller Huaca de la Luna have revealed particularly interesting patterns within the mass of the monument (Uceda 2001; Uceda et al. 1992, 1994; Uceda and Morales 1993; Uceda, Mujica, and Morales 1997; Uceda and Paredes 1994). Like Mocollope, successive generations apparently constructed the monument anew, in a sequence of repetitive remodeling and building over of large enclosed spaces entered through restricted passages. Both interior and exterior space were ornamented with bright polychrome friezes, the exterior ones certainly visible from considerable distances as was the case at El Brujo, if not also at Mocollope. Like both Mocollope and the *ciudadelas*, the major constructions are associated with habitation and craft produc-

---

[12]   These mounds are also known as Huaca Partida or Cortada and Huaca Blanca, respectively.

[13]   In an interesting parallel, virtually identical depictions of one image—lines of standing figures, rendered frontally, with arms outstretched and hands clasped one to the other—have been found at both Cao Viejo and Mocollope (Franco, Gálvez, and Vásquez 1994: 171-172, lám. VI; Reindel 1993: Abb. 106).

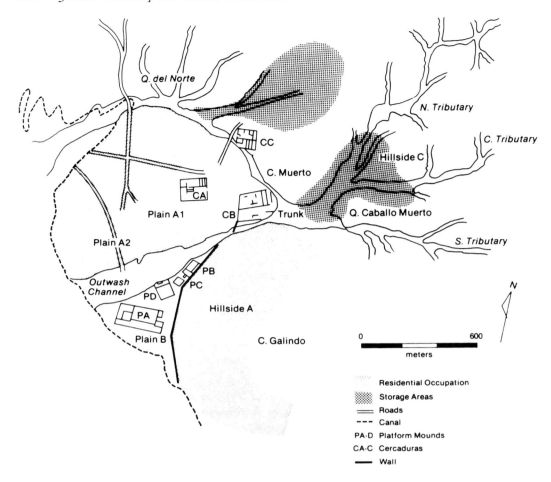

Fig. 23 Plan of Galindo, Moche Valley (after Bawden 1982a: fig. 12.1)

tion areas in the vicinity (T. Topic n.d.; Chapdelaine 1998, 2001; Tello 1998; Uceda and Chapdelaine 1998). Still, whatever functional analogs the site may have had with the Chimú palaces, the formal traits do not occur in the same singular configuration, and the transformation sequences were apparently repeated periodically in the same monument and superimposed (see especially Montoya 1998).

Mocollope, El Brujo, and Moche were abandoned as civic-ceremonial centers by the late Moche period (Chapdelaine 2001; Gálvez and Briceño 2001; Uceda 2001). In late Moche times, the focus of political power in the Moche Valley apparently shifted inland to the site of Galindo (Bawden n.d., 1978, 1982a). Scholars have recognized that this extensive site has perhaps more formal resemblance to Chan Chan than do the earlier centers (Fig. 23) (Bawden 1983, 1994; Conklin 1990; Conrad n.d.; Keatinge 1982). Large walls seem to separate the site into precincts of different status inhabitants, which include at least some evidence for craft and transport specialists (Bawden n.d., 1982b, 1990; but see also Topic and Topic 1987). Rather than being dominated by very large paired monuments, each the result of repeated episodes of construction and remodeling in the same spot, the site is spread out horizontally to encompass roughly 5 sq km (Bawden 1978, 1982a). Walled compounds of various sizes predominate over large platforms, and much of the space around them is filled with dense concentrations of small rooms (Bawden 1982a, b, 1990). All these characteristics are generally reminiscent of the larger, later city of Chan Chan. Furthermore, as at Chan Chan, the importance of visual and physical barriers seems emphasized over visually accessible elevated monuments (Bawden n.d., 1983; Conklin 1990).

One compound in particular has been seen as a *ciudadela* precursor (Conrad n.d.: 217–233). Called Huaca Galindo (Platform A: PA), it has an area of approximately 33,000 sq m, small by *ciudadela* standards, with three major subdivisions analogous to internal plazas. The largest is adjacent to the compound's single formal entrance and has interior wall surfaces lined with benches and decorated with polychrome murals. The most rearward enclosure contains a tiered platform that cannot be accessed directly from the first enclosure. The platform has evidence of both habitation and mortuary use and was interpreted by Conrad as a burial platform precursor. The entire compound shows comparatively little evidence of remodeling; certainly it was not filled in and built over repeatedly like the inner spaces of Huaca de la Luna, the façade of Huaca Cao Viejo, or the major platforms at Mocollope. Though it lacks many formal traits of the *ciudadelas*—formal storage areas and U-shaped features are absent, and the restriction of access is far less elaborate—Huaca Galindo may present something more readily recognized as a palace. Perhaps significantly, it is the only such structure at the site.

In the Chicama Valley during the period immediately before the rise of Chan Chan, an entirely new monumental center was constructed on the open alluvial fan several kilometers southwest of Mocollope in an area historically known as Sonolipe (Zevallos Quiñones 1992a: 20). The early Chimú[14] Sonolipe complex consists of five enormous adobe mounds

[14] The authors prefer to describe the cultural affiliation of the Sonolipe complex as early Chimú (as characterized in Donnan and Mackey 1978). An appropriate alternative description would be pre-imperial Chimú, as the construction of the mounds apparently predates the rise of Chan Chan as a city. Other than in samples collected from looted intrusive tombs, the ceramic assemblages from the Sonolipe monuments chiefly consist of early Chimú types and wares—San Nicolás Molded, San Juan Molded, Rubia Plain, Tomaval Plain, Virú Plain, and Queneto Polished Plain (Strong and Evans 1952; Collier 1955)—with very few fine-paste, Moche-like sherds and a notable lack of Moche-associated Valle Plain utilitarian wares (Strong and Evans 1952; Leonard and Russell n.d.a, b). Several considerations leave the degree of Lambayeque influence or presence open to question. The ceramic forms used to define a Lambayeque or Sicán tradition are mostly fine blackwares (Shimada 1995; Zevallos Quiñones 1992b), distinguished from early Chimú types by a particular set of stylistic attributes. Lambayeque-style ceramics have been recovered at many sites in the lower Chicama, generally from mortuary contexts (Leonard and Russell n.d.a, b; Franco, Gálvez, and Vásquez 1994). At the Sonolipe complex, as in surface collections from mounds throughout the valley, few large sherds were recovered except from graves disturbed by looting. Because the forms and design elements considered to typify the Lambayeque tradition are observed only in larger fragments or whole vessels, it is difficult to ascertain whether Lambayeque-style ceramics are present in the samples collected from the mounds. In the Sonolipe mounds, samples from looted intrusive graves generally date to middle and late Chimú times (see Leonard and Russell n.d.a). Petrographic analysis and similar sourcing techniques could reveal whether imported Lambayeque ceramics were present at Sonolipe, but unfortunately the identification of locally made Lambayeque-style vessels would be difficult. Pending future study, the relationship of the Sonolipe complex to a Lambayeque phenomenon remains unresolved. Nonetheless, evidence of a connection is presently lacking.

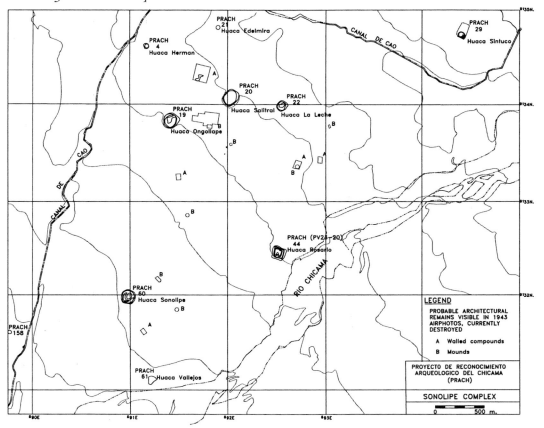

Fig. 24 Plan of the Sonolipe Complex, Chicama Valley

and an incomplete mound or monumental enclosure within an area approximately 3 km across (Fig. 24) (Kosok 1965: 108; Leonard n.d.a, c; Leonard and Russell n.d.a, c; Reindel 1993: 252–253, 297, 345–349, 375–377). Aerial photographs from 1943 show that small platforms and walled enclosures were present in the area between the *huacas* which have since been destroyed by mechanized sugar cane cultivation. The four largest mounds range in volume from 190,000 to 350,000 cu m each, and the total volume of construction approached 1,000,000 cu m (Leonard and Russell n.d.c).

Unlike the mound centers at Mocollope, Moche, and El Brujo, but like Galindo and Chan Chan, there is no obvious pairing of the major structures at Sonolipe. Independent seriations of monuments in the valley based solely on architectural data (Reindel 1993: 82–106) and on combined ceramic and architectural data (Leonard and Russell n.d.a) both agree that these mounds were each built in single episodes, very close together in time, and probably sequentially, between the eighth and early tenth centuries A.D. This represents an unparalleled rate of monumental construction in the Chicama Valley (Leonard and Russell n.d.c) and apparently surpasses the rate of construction at the earlier site of Moche. Though of course the Sonolipe complex in no way resembles Chan Chan in formal attributes, two of its characteristics may be seen as predecessors to Chan Chan.

First, though they are adobe mounds like earlier monuments, they were each apparently built as single constructions in a sequence, played out in a horizontal dimension, like the Chan Chan *ciudadelas*. Here we may see the first manifestation of the sort of kingship manifested at Chan Chan. This principal can be seen as the other thread that combined with the form of urban patterning at Galindo to lead to the unique form of Chan Chan with its sequential palace enclosures.

Second, the unprecedented flurry of mound building in Sonolipe represents the greatest mobilization of mass labor ever seen in the Chimú core area, prior to the even larger labor expenditures by the Chimú state at Chan Chan and in the enormous Chimú irrigation projects. This implies an unprecedented concentration of political power in the hands of the rulers who presumably oversaw the erection of these mounds, whether they served as royal residences or not; only the Chimú kings would surpass this degree of manifested power. Perhaps this is why the Chimú leaders later saw fit to build intrusive walled compounds atop two of these *huacas*.

Conclusions

The Chan Chan *ciudadela* is in several respects a unique form of palace architecture. The walled compound model, where various activities are gathered within highly restrictive spaces, was a Chimú experiment that grew out of developments in the Moche and Chicama valleys. Earlier architectural complexes of the Moche contain evidence of activities commensurate with palace functions, yet these were formed over centuries of remodeling and rebuilding on the same spot, suggesting a greater interest in maintaining a strong association with a particular sacred spot or landscape, over the dramatic statement of creating an entirely new palace with each generation.

The repeated building sequences across horizontal space rather than vertical accumulation developed at Galindo and Sonolipe and signaled a profound shift in the interaction spheres of the north coast populations. Although monumental architecture on the north coast nearly always had restrictive features at some level, the enclosing of space, of visual access, was complete in the *ciudadelas*. The tradition of large, brightly painted friezes present on the exteriors of monuments, which had persisted on the north coast since the time of Huaca de los Reyes in the Initial period through Moche times (see Moore 1996; Moseley and Watanabe 1974; Pozorski 1975), had become by the Late Intermediate period largely an interior characteristic of ornament, reserved for those allowed in the walled compounds.

At the same time, the subject matter of decoration and ornamentation changed. The earlier tradition dramatically emphasized hierarchical representations of supernatural beings and violent themes involving warriors, prisoners, and sacrifices. This iconography seems to express the roles of earlier rulers and leaders as wielders of violent worldly power and as mediators with supernatural beings that were superior even to themselves. In striking contrast, the extensive and repetitive Chimú friezes seem relatively devoid of either narrative iconography of sacrifice or veristic representations of warriors, rulers, or threatening supernaturals.[15] Perhaps at Chan Chan it was no longer necessary to emphasize the agencies of power or to depict gods when the ruler himself had become the very embodiment of power; the king *was* God and did not need pictures of himself.

The cardinal features of this new architectural manifestation, centralization and separation—centralization of activities and separation of the ruling elite from the commoner populations—suggest the development of dynastic power and divine kingship on the north coast prior to the foundation of Chan Chan. This centralization of power is reflected not only in the gathering together of previously disparate activity centers into single walled complexes, but also in the relatively intense concentration and elaboration of complex elite architecture at the capital city of Chan Chan, as opposed to the provinces. Chan Chan demonstrates a level of architectural complexity, scale, and elaboration not closely approximated by any of the provincial sites. Again, this signals a profound shift away from earlier traditions on the north coast where there were a number of centers of comparable size.

Central to the development and functioning of the *ciudadela* is the presence of burial platforms. Various lines of evidence indicate that the living continued to interact with tomb occupants long after their death. Though a similar pattern has been attributed to Inca palaces and royal estates, in this respect the *ciudadelas* diverge most from a Western concept of palace, and even from their Mesoamerican equivalents in the transformation from palace to mortuary structure. This unique function bears the critical implication that the form in which we see the *ciudadelas* archaeologically is not that of royal residence inhabited by living rulers when abandoned. Therefore, formal traits that we might expect for royal living quarters may no longer be apparent because they have been transformed by the later functions related to the mortuary phase of the use history.

The *ciudadela* represents a centralization of activities, a centralization of power unseen on the north coast prior to the rise of the Chimú state. In many ways, this gathering together of activities within highly restrictive spaces is a model that is not repeated following the demise of Chimor. The Inca opted for architectural configurations that in several key respects are substantially different from the *ciudadelas*, particularly in their choice of central and more open spaces for public ritual, at least in Cuzco and at highland provincial centers such as Huánuco Viejo (Morris 1972, this volume), Pumpu (LeVine n.d; Matos Mendieta 1994), and Hatun Xauxa (D'Altroy n.d; LeVine n.d.). Ultimately it may have been the Inca penchant for integrative and adaptive solutions, in architecture as in other social conventions, that made the later empire the victorious one of the two.

---

[15] Depictions of anthropomorphic figures (human or supernaturals) are more common in other media such as precious metals or shell mosaic, items closely associated with elite individuals (Mackey and Pillsbury n.d.). Supernaturals are also present on the walls at Chan Chan, but they tend to be small in scale and repeated in textilelike "infinity" patterns across walls, therefore muting the impact or power of the symbol. The reliefs, in some ways, seem to be designed more as backdrop to human (be they alive or dead) performance.

Bibliography

ANDREWS, ANTHONY P.

1974   The U-Shaped Structures at Chan Chan, Peru. *Journal of Field Archaeology* 1(3): 241–264.

ATTARIAN, CHRISTOPHER J.

n.d.   Plant Foods and Ceramic Production: A Case Study of Mochica Ceramic Production Specialists in the Chicama Valley, Peru. Master's thesis, Department of Anthropology, University of California, Los Angeles, 1996.

BANDELIER, ADOLPH F.

1942   Adolph F. Bandelier to His Friend, Thomas Janvier. In *Indians of South America* by Paul Radin: 242–250. Doubleday, Doran & Company, Garden City, N.Y.

BAWDEN, GARTH

1978   Life in the Pre-Columbian Town of Galindo, Peru. *Field Museum of Natural History Bulletin* 49 (3): 16–23.

1982a   Galindo: A Study in Cultural Transition during the Middle Horizon. In *Chan Chan: Andean Desert City* (Michael E. Moseley and Kent C. Day, eds.): 285–320. School of American Research Advanced Seminar Series. University of New Mexico Press, Albuquerque.

1982b   Community Organization Reflected by the Household: A Study of Pre-Columbian Social Dynamics. *Journal of Field Archaeology* 9: 165–181.

1983   Cultural Reconstitution in the Late Moche Period: A Case Study in Multidimensional Stylistic Analysis. In *Civilization in the Ancient Americas: Essays in Honor of Gordon R. Willey* (Richard M. Leventhal and Alan L. Kolata, eds.): 211–235. University of New Mexico Press, Albuquerque.

1990   Domestic Space and Social Structure in Pre-Columbian Northern Peru. In *Domestic Architecture and the Use of Space: An Interdisciplinary Cross-Cultural Study* (Susan Kent, ed.): 153–171. Cambridge University Press, Cambridge.

1994   La paradoja estructural: La cultura Moche como ideología política. In *Moche: Propuestas y Perspectivas* (Santiago Uceda and Elias Mujica, eds.): 389–412. Actas del Primer Coloquio sobre la Cultura Moche, Trujillo, 12 al 16 abril de 1993. Travaux de l'Institut Français d'Études Andines 79. Trujillo and Lima.

n.d.   Galindo and the Nature of the Middle Horizon in Northern Coastal Peru. Ph.D. dissertation, Department of Anthropology, Harvard University, Cambridge, Mass., 1977.

BILLMAN, BRIAN R.

n.d.   The Evolution of Prehistoric Political Organizations in the Moche Valley, Peru. Ph.D. dissertation, Department of Anthropology, University of California, Santa Barbara, 1996.

CALANCHA, ANTONIO DE LA

1974–82   *Corónica moralizada del Orden de San Augustín en el Perú.* Transcription, critical study,
[1638]   notes, bibliography and indexes by Ignacio Prado Pastor. 6 vols. Crónicas del Perú 4–
9. Universidad Nacional Mayor de San Marcos, Lima.

CHAPDELAINE, CLAUDE

1998   Excavaciones en la zona urbana de Moche durante 1996. In *Investigaciones en la
Huaca de la Luna 1996* (Santiago Uceda, Elías Mujica, and Ricardo Morales, eds.):
85–115. Proyecto Arqueológico Huacas del Sol y de la Luna. Facultad de Ciencias
Sociales, Universidad Nacional de La Libertad, Trujillo.

2001   The Growing Power of a Moche Urban Class. In *Moche Art and Archaeology in Ancient
Peru* (Center for Advanced Study in the Visual Arts, Symposium Papers 40, Joanne
Pillsbury, ed.): 69–87. Studies in the History of Art 63, National Gallery of Art,
Washington, D.C.

CIEZA DE LEÓN, PEDRO DE

1984   *La crónica del Perú* (Manuel Ballesteros Gaibrois, ed.) Crónicas de América, Historia
[ca. 1551]   16, Madrid.

COLLIER, DONALD

1955   *Cultural Chronology and Change as Reflected in the Ceramics of the Virú Valley, Peru.*
Fieldiana: Anthropology 43. Chicago Natural History Museum, Publications, 779.
Field Museum of Natural History, Chicago.

CONKLIN, WILLIAM J

1990   Architecture of the Chimu: Memory, Function, and Image. In *The Northern Dynasties:
Kingship and Statecraft in Chimor* (Michael E. Moseley and Alana Cordy-Collins, eds.):
43–74. Dumbarton Oaks, Washington, D.C.

CONRAD, GEOFFREY W.

1977   Chiquitoy Viejo: An Inca Administrative Center in the Chicama Valley, Peru. *Journal
of Field Archaeology* 4: 1–18.

1978   Royal Burials of Ancient Peru. *Field Museum of Natural History Bulletin* 49(2): 6–7,
10–11, 21–23, 26.

1981   Cultural Materialism, Split Inheritance, and the Expansion of Ancient Peruvian
Empires. *American Antiquity* 46: 3–26.

1982   The Burial Platforms of Chan Chan: Some Social and Political Implications. In *Chan
Chan: Andean Desert City* (Michael E. Moseley and Kent C. Day, eds.): 87–117.
School of American Research Advanced Seminar Series. University of New Mexico
Press, Albuquerque.

1990   Farfan, General Pacatnamu, and the Dynastic History of Chimor. In *The Northern
Dynasties: Kingship and Statecraft in Chimor* (Michael E. Moseley and Alana Cordy-
Collins, eds.): 227–242. Dumbarton Oaks, Washington, D.C.

n.d.   Burial Platforms and Related Structures on the North Coast of Peru: Some Social
and Political Implications. Ph.D. dissertation, Department of Anthropology, Harvard
University, Cambridge, Mass., 1974.

CORNEJO GARCÍA, MIGUEL

n.d.   Estudio de los recintos ceremoniales en forma de U del Palacio Tschudi en Chan Chan: Una hipótesis de interpretación. Professional thesis, Escuela Profesional de Arqueología, Facultad de Ciencias Sociales, Universidad Nacional de Trujillo.

D'ALTROY, TERENCE N.

1992   *Provincial Power in the Inka Empire.* Smithsonian Institution Press, Washington, D.C.

n.d.   Empire Growth and Consolidation: The Xauxa Region of Peru under the Incas. Ph.D. dissertation, Department of Anthropology, University of California, Los Angeles, 1981.

D'ALTROY, TERENCE N., AND TIMOTHY K. EARLE

1985   Staple Finance, Wealth Finance, and Storage in the Inka Political Economy. *Current Anthropology* 26(2): 187–206.

D'ALTROY, TERENCE N., AND CHRISTINE A. HASTORF

1984   The Distribution and Contents of Inca State Storehouses in the Xauxa Region of Peru. *American Antiquity* 49(2): 334–349.

DAY, KENT C.

1974   Walk-in Wells and Water Management at Chanchan, Peru. In *The Rise and Fall of Civilizations, Modern Archaeological Approaches to Ancient Cultures: Selected Readings* (C. C. Lamberg-Karlovsky and Jeremy A. Sabloff, eds.): 182–190. Cummings, Menlo Park.

1982a   Ciudadelas: Their Form and Function. In *Chan Chan: Andean Desert City* (Michael E. Moseley and Kent C. Day, eds.): 55–66. School of American Research Advanced Seminar Series. University of New Mexico Press, Albuquerque.

1982b   Storage and Labor Service: A Production and Management Design for the Andean Area. In *Chan Chan: Andean Desert City* (Michael E. Moseley and Kent C. Day, eds.): 333–349. School of American Research Advanced Seminar Series. University of New Mexico Press, Albuquerque.

n.d.   Architecture of Ciudadela Rivero, Chan Chan, Peru. Ph.D. dissertation, Department of Anthropology, Harvard University, Cambridge, Mass., 1973.

DONNAN, CHRISTOPHER B.

1990a   The Chotuna Friezes and the Chotuna-Dragon Connection. In *The Northern Dynasties: Kingship and Statecraft in Chimor* (Michael E. Moseley and Alana Cordy-Collins, eds.): 275–296. Dumbarton Oaks, Washington, D.C.

1990b   An Assessment of the Validity of the Naymlap Dynasty. In *The Northern Dynasties: Kingship and Statecraft in Chimor* (Michael E. Moseley and Alana Cordy-Collins, eds.): 243–274. Dumbarton Oaks, Washington, D.C.

DONNAN, CHRISTOPHER B., AND CAROL J. MACKEY

1978   *Ancient Burial Patterns of the Moche Valley, Peru.* University of Texas Press, Austin.

EARLE, TIMOTHY K., AND TERENCE N. D'ALTROY

1982   Storage Facilities and State Finance in the Upper Mantaro Valley, Peru. In *Contexts for Prehistoric Exchange* (Jonathon E. Ericson and Timothy K. Earle, eds.): 265–290. Academic Press, New York.

EVANS, SUSAN T.

1991   Architecture and Authority in an Aztec Village: Form and Function of the Tecpan. In *Land and Politics in the Valley of Mexico: A Two Thousand-Year Perspective* (H. R. Harvey, ed.): 63–92. University of New Mexico Press, Albuquerque.

FRANCO, RÉGULO, CÉSAR GÁLVEZ, AND SEGUNDO VÁSQUEZ

1994   Arquitectura y decoración Mochica en la Huaca Cao Viejo, Complejo El Brujo: Resultados preliminares. In *Moche: Propuestas y perspectivas* (Santiago Uceda and Elías Mujica, eds.): 147–180. Actas del Primer Coloquio Sobre la Cultura Moche, Trujillo, 12 al 16 abril de 1993. Travaux de l'Institut Français d'Études Andines 79. Trujillo and Lima.

GÁLVEZ MORA, CÉSAR, AND JESÚS BRICEÑO ROSARIO

2001   The Moche in the Chicama Valley. In *Moche Art and Archaeology in Ancient Peru* (Center for Advanced Study in the Visual Arts, Symposium Papers 40, Joanne Pillsbury, ed): 141–157. Studies in the History of Art 63, National Gallery of Art, Washington, D.C.

HASTINGS, CHARLES M., AND MICHAEL E. MOSELEY

1975   The Adobes of Huaca del Sol and Huaca de La Luna. *American Antiquity* 40(2): 196–203.

HILLIER, BILL, AND JULIENNE HANSON

1984   *The Social Logic of Space.* Cambridge University Press, Cambridge.

HORKHEIMER, HANS

1944   *Vistas arqueológicas del noroeste del Perú.* Librería e Imprenta Moreno, Trujillo.

KEATINGE, RICHARD W.

1974   Chimu Rural Administrative Centres in the Moche Valley, Peru. *World Archaeology* 6(1): 66–82.

1975   Urban Settlement Systems and Rural Sustaining Communities: An Example from Chan Chan's Hinterland. *Journal of Field Archaeology* 2: 215–227.

1977   Religious Forms and Secular Functions: The Expansion of State Bureaucracies as Reflected in Prehistoric Architecture on the Peruvian North Coast. *Annals of the New York Academy of Sciences* 293: 229–245.

1982   The Chimú Empire in a Regional Perspective: Cultural Antecedents and Continuities. In *Chan Chan: Andean Desert City* (Michael E. Moseley and Kent C. Day, eds.): 197–224. School of American Research Advanced Seminar Series. University of New Mexico Press, Albuquerque.

KEATINGE, RICHARD W., AND GEOFFREY W. CONRAD

1983   Imperialist Expansion in Peruvian Prehistory: Chimu Administration of a
        Conquered Territory. *Journal of Field Archaeology* 10(3): 255–283.

KEATINGE, RICHARD W., AND KENT C. DAY

1973   Socio-Economic Organization of the Moche Valley, Peru, during the Chimu
        Occupation of Chan Chan. *Journal of Anthropological Research* 29(4): 275–295.

KIMMICH, JOSÉ

1917   Etnología Peruana. Origen de los Chimus. Pruebas paleográficas y arquitecturales.
        Boletín de la Sociedad Geográfica de Lima 33: 441–462.

KLYMYSHYN, ALEXANDRA M. ULANA

1980   Inferencias sociales y funcionales de la arquitectura intermedia. In *Chanchán:
        Metrópoli Chimú* (Rogger Ravines, ed.): 250–266. Instituto de Estudios Peruanos,
        Lima.

1982   Elite Compounds in Chan Chan. In *Chan Chan: Andean Desert City* (Michael E.
        Moseley and Kent C. Day, eds.): 119–143. School of American Research Advanced
        Seminar Series. University of New Mexico Press, Albuquerque.

1987   The Development of Chimu Administration in Chan Chan. In *The Origins and
        Development of the Andean State* (Jonathan Haas, Shelia G. Pozorski, and Thomas G.
        Pozorski, eds.): 97–110. Cambridge University Press, Cambridge.

n.d.   Intermediate Architecture, Chan Chan, Peru. Ph.D. dissertation, Department of
        Anthropology, Harvard University, Cambridge, Mass., 1976.

KOLATA, ALAN L.

1982   Chronology and Settlement Growth at Chan Chan. In *Chan Chan: Andean Desert
        City* (Michael E. Moseley and Kent C. Day, eds.): 67–85. School of American
        Research Advanced Seminar Series. University of New Mexico Press, Albuquerque.

1990   The Urban Concept of Chan Chan. In *The Northern Dynasties: Kingship and Statecraft
        in Chimor* (Michael E. Moseley and Alana Cordy-Collins, eds.): 107–144. Dumbarton
        Oaks, Washington, D.C.

n.d.   Chan Chan: The Form of the City in Time. Ph.D. dissertation, Department of
        Anthropology, Harvard University, Cambridge, Mass., 1978.

KOSOK, PAUL

1965   *Life, Land and Water in Ancient Peru.* Long Island University Press, New York.

LEONARD, BANKS L.

n.d.a   Moche through Late Horizon Settlement Patterns, Chicama Valley, Peru. Paper
        presented at the 55th Annual Meeting of the Society for American Archaeology, Las
        Vegas, 1990.

n.d.b   Chimu Agricultural Projects in the Chicama Valley, Peru: New Observations. Paper
        presented at the 58th Annual Meeting of the Society for American Archaeology, St.
        Louis, 1993.

n.d.c   Public Works in the Lower Chicama, North Coast of Peru. Paper presented at the
        60th Annual Meeting of the Society for American Archaeology, Minneapolis, 1995.

LEONARD, BANKS L., AND GLENN S. RUSSELL

n.d.a   *Informe preliminar: Proyecto de reconocimiento arqueológico del Chicama, resultados de la primera temporada de campo, 1989.* Chicama Survey Project. Submitted to the Sección de Patrimonio Cultural-Monumental de la Nación, Instituto Nacional de Cultura, Lima. Copies available from the Instituto Nacional de Cultura, Lima.

n.d.b   Coalescence and Transformation in the Early Intermediate Period: From Horizon to Horizon in the Chicama Valley, Peru. Paper presented at the 59th Annual Meeting of the Society for American Archaeology, Anaheim, 1994.

n.d.c   The Politics of Settlement in the Lower Chicama Valley, North Coast of Peru. Paper presented at the 61st Annual Meeting of the Society for American Archaeology, New Orleans, 1996.

LEVINE, TERRY Y.

n.d.   Inka Administration in the Central Highlands: A Comparative Study. Ph.D. dissertation, Archaeology Program, University of California, Los Angeles, 1985.

LEVINE, TERRY Y. (ED.)

1992   *Inka Storage Systems.* University of Oklahoma Press, Norman.

MACKEY, CAROL J.

1987   Chimu Administration in the Provinces. In *The Origins and Development of the Andean State* (Jonathan Haas, Shelia G. Pozorski, and Thomas G. Pozorski, eds.): 121–129. Cambridge University Press, Cambridge.

MACKEY, CAROL J., AND ALEXANDRA M. ULANA KLYMYSHYN

1981   Construction and Labor Organization in the Chimu Empire. *Ñawpa Pacha* 19: 99–114.

1990   The Southern Frontier of the Chimu Empire. In *The Northern Dynasties: Kingship and Statecraft in Chimor* (Michael E. Moseley and Alana Cordy-Collins, eds.): 195–226. Dumbarton Oaks, Washington, D.C.

MACKEY, CAROL J. AND JOANNE PILLSBURY

n.d.   Chimú Silverwork. Manuscript in authors' possession.

MARTÍNEZ COMPAÑÓN, BALTASAR

1978–81   *Trujillo del Perú en el siglo XVIII.* Facsimile edition. Ediciones Cultura Hispánica del
[1781–89]   Centro Iberoamericano de Cooperación, Madrid.

MASON, J. ALDEN

1957   *The Ancient Civilizations of Peru.* Penguin Books, Harmondsworth.

MATOS MENDIETA, RAMIRO

1994   *Pumpu: Centro administrativo Inka de la puna de Junín.* Editorial Horizonte; Lima.

MCGRATH, JAMES E.

n.d.   The Canchones of Chan Chan, Peru: Evidence for a Retainer Class in a Preindustrial Urban Center. Master's thesis, Department of Anthropology, Harvard University, Cambridge, Mass., 1973.

MONTOYA, MARÍA

1998   Excavaciones en la Unidad 11, Plataforma I de la Huaca de La Luna, durante 1996. In *Investigaciones en la Huaca de La Luna 1996* (Santiago Uceda, Elías Mujica, and Ricardo Morales, eds.): 18–28. Proyecto Arqueológico Huacas del Sol y de La Luna. Facultad de Ciencias Sociales, Universidad Nacional de La Libertad, Trujillo.

MOORE, JERRY D.

1992   Pattern and Meaning in Prehistoric Peruvian Architecture: The Architecture of Social Control in the Chimu State. *Latin American Antiquity* 3: 95–113.

1996   *Architecture and Power in the Ancient Andes: The Archaeology of Public Buildings*. New Studies in Archaeology. Cambridge University Press, Cambridge.

n.d.   The Palace of Chilimassa: A Late Prehistoric Complex in the Lower Tumbes Valley, Peru. Manuscript in authors' possession.

MORRIS, CRAIG E.

1972   State Settlements in Tawantinsuyu: A Strategy of Compulsory Urbanism. In *Contemporary Archaeology: A Guide to Theory and Contributions* (Mark P. Leone, ed.): 393–401. Southern Illinois University Press, Carbondale and Edwardsville.

1981   Tecnología y organización incaica del almacenamiento de víveres en la sierra. In *Runakuna Kawsayninkupaq Rurasqankunaqa, Tecnología del mundo Andino* (Heather Lechtman and Ana María Soldi, eds.) 1: 327–374. Universidad Nacional Autónoma, México, D.F.

n.d.   Storage in Tawantinsuyu. Ph.D. dissertation, Department of Anthropology, University of Chicago, 1967.

MOSELEY, MICHAEL E.

1990   Structure and History in the Dynastic Lore of Chimor. In *The Northern Dynasties: Kingship and Statecraft in Chimor* (Michael E. Moseley and Alana Cordy-Collins, eds.): 1–41. Dumbarton Oaks, Washington, D.C.

MOSELEY, MICHAEL E., AND KENT C. DAY (EDS.)

1982   *Chan Chan: Andean Desert City*. School of American Research Advanced Seminar Series. University of New Mexico Press, Albuquerque.

MOSELEY, MICHAEL E., AND CAROL J. MACKEY

1974   *Twenty-Four Architectural Plans of Chan Chan, Peru: Structure and Form at the Capital of Chimor*. Peabody Museum Press, Harvard University, Cambridge, Mass.

MOSELEY, MICHAEL E., AND LUIS WATANABE

1974   The Adobe Sculpture of Huaca de los Reyes. *Archaeology* 27(3): 154–161.

MURÚA, MARTÍN DE

1987   *Historia general del Perú* (Manuel Ballesteros, ed.). Crónicas de América 35, Historia
[1611–16] 16, Madrid.

NARVÁEZ VARGAS, [LUÍS] ALFREDO

   1989   Chan Chan: Chronology and Stratigraphic Contexts. *Andean Past* 2: 131–174.
           Cornell University Latin American Studies Program, Ithaca, N.Y.

   n.d.   Chan Chan: Crecimiento de la ciudad. Professional thesis, Escuela Profesional de
           Arqueología, Facultad de Ciencias Sociales, Universidad Nacional de Trujillo, 1986.

NARVÁEZ VARGAS, [LUÍS] ALFREDO, AND ANA MARÍA HOYLE MONTALVA

   1985   Evidencias Inca en Chan Chan, Palacio Tschudi. *Boletín del Instituto Nacional de
           Cultura, Departamental La Libertad* 1(1): 51–61.

NECIPOĞLU, GÜLRU (ED.)

   1993   Pre-Modern Islamic Palaces. A special issue of *Ars Orientalis* (vol. 23).

NETHERLY, PATRICIA J.

   n.d.   *Local Level Lords on the North Coast of Peru.* Ph.D. dissertation, Cornell University,
           Ithaca, N.Y.; University Microfilms International, Ann Arbor, Mich, 1977.

NILES, SUSAN

   1999   *The Shape of Inca History: Narrative and Architecture in an Andean Empire.* University of
           Iowa Press, Iowa City.

OJO, G. J. AFOLABI

   1966   *Yoruba Palaces: A Study of Afins of Yorubaland.* University of London Press, London.

PAULSEN, ALLISON C.

   1981   The Archaeology of the Absurd: Comments on "Cultural Materialism, Split
           Inheritance, and the Expansion of Ancient Peruvian Empires" (by Geoffrey W.
           Conrad, *American Antiquity* 46(1): 3–26). *American Antiquity* 46(1): 31–37.

PILLSBURY, JOANNE

   1996   The Thorny Oyster and the Origins of Empire: Implications of Recently
           Uncovered *Spondylus* Imagery from Chan Chan, Peru. *Latin American Antiquity* 7(4):
           313–340.

   n.d.   Sculpted Friezes of the Empire of Chimor. Ph.D. dissertation, Columbia University,
           New York; 1993.

POZORSKI, THOMAS G.

   1975   El complejo Caballo Muerto: Los frisos de barro de la Huaca de los Reyes. *Revista
           del Museo Nacional* 41: 211–251.

   1979   The Las Avispas Burial Platform at Chan Chan, Peru. *Annals of the Carnegie Museum
           of Natural History* 48(8): 119–137.

   1987   Changing Priorities within the Chimu State: The Role of Irrigation Agriculture. In
           The Origins and Development of the Andean State (Jonathan Haas, Shelia G. Pozorski,
           and Thomas G. Pozorski, eds.): 111–120. Cambridge University Press, Cambridge.

RAMÍREZ, SUSAN E.

   1990   The Inca Conquest of the North Coast: A Historian's View. In *The Northern
           Dynasties: Kingship and Statecraft in Chimor* (Michael E. Moseley and Alana Cordy-
           Collins, eds.): 507–537. Dumbarton Oaks, Washington, D.C.

1996   *The World Upside Down: Cross-Cultural Contact and Conflict in Sixteenth-Century Peru.* Stanford University Press, Stanford, Calif.

REINDEL, MARKUS

1993   *Monumentale Lehmarchitektur an der Nordküste Perus: Eine Repräsentative Untersuchung nach-formativer Großbauten vom Lambayeque-Gebiet bis zum Virú-Tal.* Bonner Amerikanistische Studien 22. Holos, Bonn.

RIVERO Y USTARIZ, MARIANO EDUARDO DE, AND JOHANN JACOB VON TSCHUDI

1971   *Peruvian Antiquities* (Francis L. Hawks, trans.). Kraus Reprint Co., New York.
[1854]

ROWE, JOHN H.

1948   The Kingdom of Chimor. *Acta Americana* 6(1/2): 26–59.

1995   Behavior and Belief in Ancient Peruvian Mortuary Practice. In *Tombs for the Living: Andean Mortuary Practices* (Tom D. Dillehay, ed.): 27–41. Dumbarton Oaks, Washington, D.C.

RUIZ DE ARCE, JUAN

1933   Relación de servicios en Indias de don Juan Ruiz de Arce (Antonio del Solar y
[ca. 1547] Taboada and José de Rújula y Ochotorena, transcribers). *Boletín de la Academia de la Historia* 102: 327–384.

RUSSELL, GLENN S.

n.d.   Preceramic through Moche Settlement Pattern Change in the Chicama Valley, Peru. Paper presented at the 55th Annual Meeting of the Society for American Archaeology, Las Vegas, 1990.

RUSSELL, GLENN S., AND BANKS L. LEONARD

1990   Chicama Valley Archaeological Settlement Survey, Peru. *Backdirt: Newsletter of the Institute of Archaeology, UCLA.* Spring: 1, 7–8.

RUSSELL, GLENN S., BANKS L. LEONARD, AND JESÚS BRICEÑO ROSARIO

1994a   Cerro Mayal: Nuevos datos sobre la producción de cerámica Moche en el Valle de Chicama. In *Moche: Propuestas y perspectivas* (Santiago Uceda and Elías Mujica, eds.): 181–206. Actas del Primer Coloquio Sobre la Cultura Moche, Trujillo, 12 al 16 abril de 1993. Travaux de l'Institut Français d'Études Andines 79. Trujillo and Lima.

1994b   Producción de cerámica Moche a gran escala en el Valle de Chicama, Perú: El taller de Cerro Mayal. In *Tecnología y organización de la producción de cerámica prehispánica en los Andes* (Izumi Shimada, ed.): 201–227. Fondo Editorial, Pontificia Universidad Católica del Perú, Lima.

SALOMON, FRANK

1995   "The Beautiful Grandparents": Andean Ancestor Shrines and Mortuary Ritual as Seen through Colonial Records. In *Tombs for the Living: Andean Mortuary Practices* (Tom D. Dillehay, ed.): 315–353. Dumbarton Oaks, Washington, D.C.

SCHAEDEL, RICHARD P.

1967   Major Ceremonial and Population Centers in Northern Peru. In *The Civilizations of Ancient America: Selected Papers of the XXIXth International Congress of Americanists* (2d ed., Sol Tax, ed.): 232–243. University of Chicago Press, Chicago.

SHIMADA, IZUMI

1987   Horizontal and Vertical Dimensions of Prehistoric States in North Peru. In *The Origins and Development of the Andean State* (Jonathan Haas, Shelia G. Pozorski, and Thomas G. Pozorski, eds.): 130–144. Cambridge University Press, Cambridge.

1990   Cultural Continuities and Discontinuities on the Northern Coast of Peru, Middle–Late Horizons. In *The Northern Dynasties: Kingship and Statecraft in Chimor* (Michael E. Moseley and Alana Cordy-Collins, eds.): 297–392. Dumbarton Oaks, Washington, D.C.

1992   The Late Prehispanic Coastal States. In *The Inca World: The Development of Pre-Columbian Peru A.D. 1000–1534* (Laura Laurencich Minelli, ed.): 49–110. University of Oklahoma Press, Norman.

1995   *Cultura Sicán: Dios, riqueza y poder en la Costa Norte del Perú*. Fundación del Banco Continental para el Fomento de la Educación y la Cultura, Lima.

SQUIER, EPHRAIM GEORGE

1973   *Peru: Incidents of Travel and Exploration in the Land of the Incas*. Reprint of the 1877 ed.
[1877] AMS Press, New York.

STRONG, WILLIAM D., AND CLIFFORD EVANS, JR.

1952   *Cultural Stratigraphy in the Virú Valley, Northern Peru*. Studies in Archaeology and Ethnology 4. Columbia University Press, New York.

TELLO, RICARDO

1998   Los conjuntos arquitectónicos 8, 17, 18, y 19 del centro urbano Moche. In *Investigaciones en la Huaca de La Luna 1996* (Santiago Uceda, Elías Mujica, and Ricardo Morales, eds.): 117–135. Proyecto Arqueológico Huacas del Sol y de La Luna. Facultad de Ciencias Sociales, Universidad Nacional de La Libertad, Trujillo.

TOPIC, JOHN R.

1982   Lower-Class Social and Economic Organization at Chan Chan. In *Chan Chan: Andean Desert City* (Michael E. Moseley and Kent C. Day, eds.): 145–175. School of American Research Advanced Seminar Series. University of New Mexico Press, Albuquerque.

1990   Craft Production in the Kingdom of Chimor. In *The Northern Dynasties: Kingship and Statecraft in Chimor* (Michael E. Moseley and Alana Cordy-Collins, eds.): 145–176. Dumbarton Oaks, Washington, D.C.

n.d.   The Lower Class at Chan Chan: A Qualitative Approach. Ph.D. dissertation, Department of Anthropology, Harvard University, Cambridge, Mass., 1977.

TOPIC, JOHN R., AND MICHAEL E. MOSELEY

1983   Chan Chan: A Case Study of Urban Change in Peru. *Ñawpa Pacha* 21: 153–182.

Topic, John R., and Theresa Lange Topic

1987   The Archaeological Investigation of Andean Militarism: Some Cautionary
Observations. In *The Origins and Development of the Andean State* (Jonathan Haas,
Shelia G. Pozorski, and Thomas G. Pozorski, eds.): 47–55. Cambridge University
Press, Cambridge.

Topic, Theresa Lange

1990   Territorial Expansion and the Kingdom of Chimor. In *The Northern Dynasties:
Kingship and Statecraft in Chimor* (Michael E. Moseley and Alana Cordy-Collins, eds.):
177–194. Dumbarton Oaks, Washington, D.C.

n.d.   Excavations at Moche, Ph.D dissertation, Department of Anthropology, Harvard
University, Cambridge, Mass., 1977.

Uceda, Santiago

1997   Esculturas en miniatura y una maqueta en madera. In *Investigaciones en la Huaca de la
Luna 1995* (Santiago Uceda, Elías Mujica, and Ricardo Morales, eds.): 151–176.
Proyecto Arqueológico Huacas del Sol y de La Luna. Facultad de Ciencias Sociales,
Universidad Nacional de la Libertad, Trujillo.

1999   Esculturas en miniatura y una maqueta en madera: El culto a los muertos y a los
ancestros en la época Chimú. *Beiträge zur Allgemeinen und Vergleichenden Archäologie* 19.
Philipp Von Zabern, Mainz.

2001   Investigations at Huaca de La Luna, Moche Valley: An Example of Moche Religious
Architecture. In *Moche Art and Archaeology in Ancient Peru* (Center for Advanced
Study in the Visual Arts, Symposium Papers 40, Joanne Pillsbury, ed.): 47–67. Studies
in the History of Art 63, National Gallery of Art, Washington, D.C.

Uceda, Santiago, and Claude Chapdelaine

1998   El centro urbano de las huacas del Sol y La Luna. *Arkinka* 3(33): 94–103.

Uceda, Santiago, and Ricardo Morales (eds.)

1993   *Informe segunda temporada 1992, Proyecto de investigación y conservación Huaca de La
Luna.* Facultad de Ciencias Sociales, Universidad Nacional de Trujillo, Trujillo.

Uceda, Santiago, and Arturo Paredes

1994   Arquitectura y función de la Huaca de La Luna. *Masa* 6(7): 42–46. Revista cultural
del INDES (Instituto Norperuano de Desarrollo Económico Social, Trujillo).

Uceda, Santiago, Elías Mujica, and Ricardo Morales (eds.)

1997   *Investigaciones en la Huaca de La Luna 1995.* Proyecto arqueológico Huacas del Sol y
de La Luna. Facultad de Ciencias Sociales, Universidad Nacional de la Libertad,
Trujillo.

Uceda, Santiago, Ricardo Morales, José Canziani, and María Montoya

1992   *Informe técnico financiero, Proyecto de investigación y conservación relieves Huaca de La Luna.*
Facultad de Ciencias Sociales, Universidad Nacional de Trujillo, Trujillo.

1994   Investigaciones sobre la arquitectura y relieves polícromos en la Huaca de La Luna,
valle de Moche. In *Moche: Propuestas y perspectivas* (Santiago Uceda and Elías Mujica,
eds.): 251–303. Actas del Primer Coloquio Sobre la Cultura Moche, Trujillo, 12 al 16
abril de 1993. Travaux de l'Institut Français d'Études Andines 79. Trujillo and Lima.

VARGAS UGARTE, RUBÉN

  1936   La fecha de la fundación de Trujillo. *Revista Histórica* 10(2): 229–239.

VERANO, JOHN W.

  1995   Where Do They Rest? The Treatment of Human Offerings and Trophies in Ancient Peru. In *Tombs for the Living: Andean Mortuary Practices* (Tom C. Dillehay, ed.): 189–227. Dumbarton Oaks, Washington, D.C.

ZEVALLOS QUIÑONES, JORGE

  1992a   *Los cacicazgos de Trujillo.* Fundación Alfredo Pinillos Goicochea, Trujillo.

  1992b   Decoraciones extras en el ceramio "rey" de Lambayeque. *Revista del Museo de Arqueología, Universidad Nacional de Trujillo* 3: 75–88.

  1994   Huacas y huaqueros en Trujillo durante el Virreinato (1535–1835). Editora Normas Legales, Trujillo.

  n.d.   Supervivencia de Chan Chan (Chan Chan después de la fundación de Trujillo): Notas para su estudio. Manuscript on file, Museo de Arqueología, Antropología e Historía, Universidad Nacional de Trujillo, Trujillo, 1989.

Enclosures of Power: The Multiple Spaces of Inca Administrative Palaces

Craig Morris

THE AMERICAN MUSEUM OF NATURAL HISTORY

Our common conception, confirmed by the dictionaries, of a palace is that of a place where a ruler resides. But from a social and political point of view, the residential functions are clearly secondary to the symbolic and ritualistic importance of palaces as the focus of power and authority. When a subject is in a palace, or even sees one from a distance, there is, or at least should be, the sense of awe that is the crux of the behavior of civic obedience. This awe is certainly increased by the presence of the ruler with the attendant sumptuary goods that surround him or her, but it is not entirely dependent on that presence—at least if the palace is sufficiently monumental.

The edifice of the palace can be seen as a physical, permanent incarnation of authority, and its architectural permanence is designed to endure well beyond the life of the ruler who built it. The institution of the palace transcends the ruler, eventually evolving into the bureaucratic structures that enable a state to function. In the process, a palace building is often transformed into a seat of government, becoming literally and symbolically the seat of the state, with the monumentality of palace buildings signifying and perpetuating the state. Even though there may be multiple palaces, built at the initiatives of various rulers, individually and collectively they become *the* permanent symbol of state power and the center of its governing structure.

The Inca boasted a state society with powerful rulers who obviously had royal residences. The Spanish conquerors who destroyed the state and killed its last ruler, Atawallpa, in 1532 left little doubt that there were palaces that compared favorably in wealth to those of Europe. Unfortunately, no Spaniard ever saw the Inca court living and governing in a palace. Most of the many references to palaces were vague, giving us little description that allows us to relate the references to given architectural remains, to pinpoint the activities they housed, or to determine the meanings they had for the functioning of the state. We thus have only fragmentary written evidence tied still rather tenuously to an archaeological record not systematically studied. That makes it very difficult to identify a palace, much less analyze its place in the state where it, by definition, was a key element. Any recognition of an Inca palace, life in and around it, and its sociopolitical functions is thus still speculative, and what I offer here must be considered tentative.

The Account of Martín de Murúa

By far the most complete account of an Inca palace is that offered by Martín de Murúa (1946 [1590–1609]: 165–166) of a palace in Cuzco, probably that of Huayna Capac. Murúa's description, written in the late sixteenth and early seventeenth centuries, was a late account, and we do not know the source of his information. His account, however, is sufficiently full to provide clues for identifying the architectural remains of palace buildings. His descriptions of the palace guards and the access of people into various parts of the palace also give us evidence on the spatial hierarchy of the parts of the palace. This allows us to propose interpretations of aspects of both the structure of the Inca court and the political role of palaces in forming and maintaining the state.

What we learn from Murúa is that the palace, at least as it was seen by an outsider, was a complex of buildings divided into two parts, each entered through elaborate doors or gateways and each containing a spacious courtyard:

> This great palace has two large principal doors, one at the entrance of the complex and the other, farther inside, from which the most meritorious of the famous stonework could be seen; at the entrance of this [first] door there were two thousand soldiers, on guard with their captain; and they guarded [for] one day, and later came another [captain] with another two thousand; and these were from the multitudes of Cañaris and Chachapoyas who . . . were certain warriors who guarded the person of the Inca; . . . Between this door and the other farther in was a great and wide plaza, into which all of those who accompanied the Inca entered, and the Inca and the principal *orejones*, the four of his council, who were the most privileged, passed to the second door; at the second door there were also guards; they were men of this city of Cuzco and relatives of the Inca, those in whom he had greatest trust, and it was those who had the charge of raising and teaching the sons of the principal leaders of all this realm, who went to serve the Inca and be with him in his court when they were young men . . . by this [second] door were the armor and arrows of the royal palace of the Inca, and at the door of the palace were a hundred captains proven in war; and a little farther on was another great plaza or patio for the officials of the palace and the regular service, and then, going farther in, were the salons and rooms where the Inca lived. And this was all full of delights, since various areas were planted with trees and gardens, and the royal lodgings were spacious and built with marvelous artistry. (1946 [1590–1609]: 165–166)[1]

[1] "Tenía este gran palacio dos grandes puertas principales, una a la entrada del zaguán y la otra más adentro, de donde se veía lo más digno de obra tan famosa de cantería; a la entrada desta puerta había dos mil indios soldados, de guarda, con su capitán, y guardaba un día, y después entraba otro con otros dos mil; y así de la multitud de los cañares y chachapoyas, que era cierta gente de guerra . . . se hacía la guarda a la persona del Inga; . . . En medio desta puerta y de la otra más interior había una grande y extendida plaza, hasta la que entraban todos los que acompañaban al Inga, y pasaba el Inga y los señores principales orejones, los cuatro de su consejo, que eran muy privados, hasta la segunda puerta; en la segunda puerta había también guarda, y era

There are a few additional details on the sumptuous nature of the residence, but the most useful information in Murúa's text is his description of the basic pattern of spatial arrangement. This gives us a spatial scheme that we can compare to physical remains and perhaps identify Inca palaces archaeologically, providing the basis for obtaining additional information and further understanding of the nature of the palaces and their role in the functioning of Tawantinsuyu (literally, "the land of the four quarters," or the Inca realm).

Murúa's description suggests the following schematic paradigm for a palace complex with three principal parts. (1) The first part consisted of a door or gateway, guarded by trusted non-Inca soldiers, beyond which was a spacious plaza. The Inca and all who accompanied him were permitted in this area, but some were permitted to move on to the second door. (2) The second part of the palace complex was marked by this second door at which one hundred proven captains were stationed. Those who were permitted to pass to this door included the Inca and the principal "*orejones*, the four of his council." The guards were natives of Cuzco and trusted relatives of the Inca. They were charged with teaching the sons of the leaders of the realm. There was a plaza beyond the door in this second part which, according to Murúa, was used by palace officials and service personnel. (3) The third and final part of this elaborate palace compound was the residential buildings used by the Inca. It is interesting that Murúa does not mention a door or gateway here that served as a strict boundary as in the other cases, and in a sense this final, residence section can be considered a subunit of the previous sector with its spacious plaza.

Given the impossibility, due to lack of preservation, of seeing and describing the actual buildings in Cuzco described in Murúa's account, we must look to other, better-preserved urban centers to see if we can identify architectural complexes that seem to fit Murúa's information. If we can succeed in that, we can then use the new architectural and archaeological data to expand on the written evidence and gain a better perspective of the nature, use, and political context of palaces in Tawantinsuyu.

This essay is thus essentially an archaeological exposition and looks at three examples of architectural complexes that I have studied with varying degrees of thoroughness. While they are far from identical, their general similarity to each other in architectural organization, and to my reading of Murúa's description, is such that we may have identified the material remains of at least one class of architectural complex associated with Inca rulers—architectural units thought, at least by Murúa, to have been in some sense equivalent to the European notion of "palace."

---

de indios naturales desta dicha ciudad del Cuzço y parientes del Inga, y de quien él se fiaba más, y eran los que tenían a cargo de criar y enseñar a los hijos de los principales de todo este Reino, que iban a servir al Inga y a estar con él en su Corte cuando muchachos. . . . Junto a esta segunda puerta estaba la armería y flechas del palacio real del Inga, y a la puerta della estaban cien capitanes aprobados en guerra; poco más adelante estaba otra gran plaza o patio para los oficiales del palacio y servicio ordinario, y despúes entraban más adentro, donde estaban las salas y piezas a donde el Inga vivía. Y esto era todo lleno de deleites, porque tenían diversas arboleadas y jardines, y los aposentos eran muy grandes y labrados con maravilloso artificio."

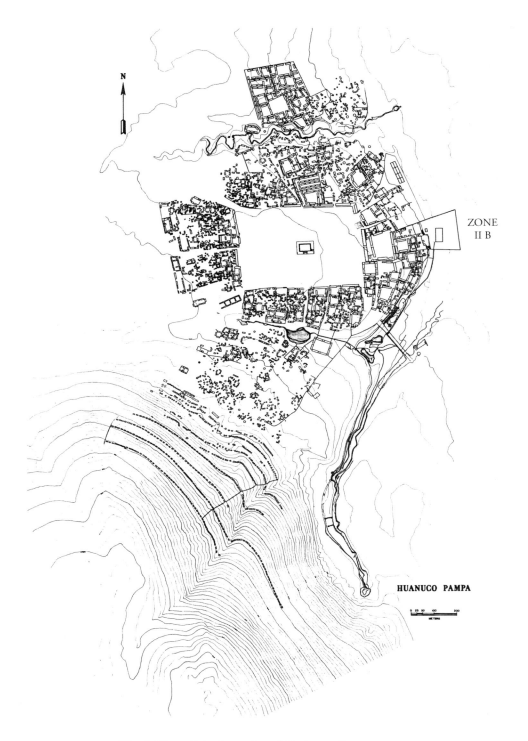

ZONE
II B

HUÁNUCO PAMPA

0 25 50 100 200
METERS

Fig. 1 Plan of the Inca city of Huánuco Pampa

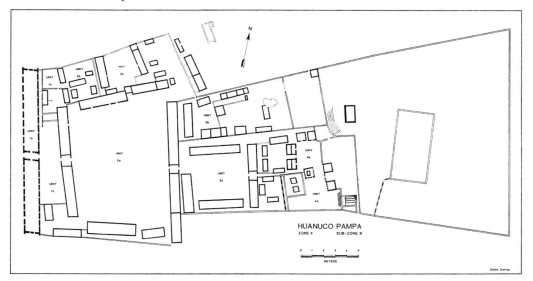

Fig. 2 Plan of the administrative palace, Zone IIB, on the eastern side of Huánuco Pampa

Huánuco Pampa: An Administrative Capital in a Region of Many Small Polities

The first of the three examples comes from Huánuco Pampa where I worked extensively during much of the 1970s and early 1980s. It has been touched on in different analytical contexts in several previous publications (Morris 1982, 1987; Morris and Thompson 1985). The second is from La Centinela in the Chincha Valley where I have been working intermittently with a series of colleagues since 1983. The third is from Tambo Colorado where I first surveyed in 1983 and am currently conducting a detailed architectural study.

Huánuco Pampa is perhaps the best-preserved of any large Inca city. It was built by the Inca on a site with little pre-Inca evidence at about 3,700 m above sea level. It is about 700 km north of Cuzco on the principal Inca highland road from Cuzco to Quito. That road runs through the city's principal plaza. The map (Fig. 1) shows about 3,300 structures, both circular and rectangular, in a great variety of sizes. Some buildings have been completely destroyed by modern construction, but in general the site plan is remarkably complete, and the original number of structures probably was around 4,000.

The part of the city in which I am interested here is that labeled Zone II, Sector B (Fig. 2), which I believe coincides with the outline from Murúa, presented above. As I have remarked on other occasions (Morris 1982, 1987), I feel this part of the city was inextricably linked to many of the ritual-administrative functions for which Huánuco Pampa was built. Although there are no written records to prove it, I think we can assume that this complex was associated with the Sapa Inca (paramount ruler) himself. Part of this complex served as his lodgings on the very rare occasions when he was present in Huánuco, and in his absence his officials and substitutes used it to represent and symbolize the ruler and his office.

Fig. 3 Structures of dressed stone thought to have been royal lodgings in Sector IIB4 at Huánuco Pampa

On architectural grounds alone, the easternmost part of Zone II, called IIB4, was the most elite residential compound in the city. Its finely dressed stone masonry, rare at Huánuco, implies an official or elite building. Indeed, architect Emilio Harth-Terré (1964) called the six-structure unit in this compound (Fig. 3) the "palacio real" in his early publication on the site. Students of Inca architecture have understood, ever since Rowe's (1944) pioneering work, that the basic unit of Inca architecture was an enclosure (called a *kancha* in Quechua), surrounding relatively small rectangular buildings that usually opened into a small interior courtyard. This form was used for common houses, many official buildings, palaces, and even the famous temple of the sun. Much of the common construction in Huánuco is of irregular circular and rectangular structures without clear groupings, but most of the formally planned buildings follow the vocabulary of rectangular structures around an open courtyard within some kind of enclosure. The enclosure may be an actual enclosure wall or it may be formed by the buildings themselves.

Rather than concentrate immediately on this group of six beautifully constructed buildings referred to as "the palace" by Harth-Terré, let us try to follow Murúa's paradigm of divisions through this zone of the city. The IIB complex is linked together by a series of cut stone gateways that lie on an east-west axis extending from the great main plaza and ending in the easternmost compound just mentioned. The first gateway, on the eastern perimeter of the main plaza in Huánuco, is not really a gateway in the sense that the others

Fig. 4 Entrance to the area of the Huánuco Pampa administrative palace, passing between two large *kallankas* that face the main plaza

are, but rather the space between the two long, so-called *kallanka* buildings that open onto
the main plaza (Figs. 1, 4). The buildings are of a type of masonry made of rather large
stones roughly dressed on one face only, and the extremities of the buildings are not modified by cut stone. In all respects the long *kallanka* buildings and the entrance passage between them, leading toward the gateways, are architecturally identified with the main plaza.
They do not form part of the palace complex. The logical beginning point of that complex
is the pair of dressed stone gateways (Fig. 5) immediately to the east, just behind the passage
between the two *kallankas*. These well-constructed gateways are decorated with relief figures of animals, perhaps pumas. The dressed stone and the relief figures set the architecture
of this unit apart from the much cruder passageway between the buildings on the main
plaza.

Let us now follow the Murúa description in Huánuco's architecture: "at the entrance
of this door there were two thousand soldiers, as guards with their captains; and they guarded
one day, and later another two thousand took their place; and these were from the multitudes of Cañaris and Chachapoyas who ... were certain warriors who guarded the person
of the Inca." Of course I do not mean to imply that Cañaris or Chachapoyas were necessarily stationed in Huánuco. What is important is that the people assigned to this position just
at the entrance of the palace were special groups of non-Inca, who somehow had privileged relations to the state.

Fig. 5 Cut-stone gateways at the entrance to IIB2

Beyond the main entrance "between this door and the other one, farther in, was a great and wide plaza, into which all of those who accompanied the Inca entered." This first plaza (IIB2), east of the first dressed stone gateways, is spacious and surrounded by six large *kallanka* type structures and two smaller buildings. As we will see below, excavations in these buildings produced enormous quantities of pottery, most of it from large jars and plates. The area was one of communal food and beverage service on a lavish scale. We have interpreted it as space used for drinking and feasting by large numbers of people. We do not need to take Murúa's version of the personages who might have gone into such a space in Cuzco as a literal or precise account, to come to the conclusion that these were people important to the state. Besides the guards and functionaries, who were those primarily associated with this area, the higher officials who went on to the second "door" likely participated in certain ritual events in this area as well. My interpretation of the primary social association of this plaza and its surrounding buildings is that it was linked to those non-Inca who were related to the Inca themselves by marriage or some other special alliance. They occupied an intermediate status between the outsiders, who were excluded from the administrative palace, and the Inca relatives from Cuzco. They were probably the group so essential to the actual administration of Tawantinsuyu, often referred to as Incas-by-privilege by ethnohistorians such as Tom Zuidema (1983).

At the back of the first plaza of the palace compound was a second set of gateways (Fig. 6) of dressed stone with relief figures which led into another plaza, smaller than the first. Murúa (1946 [1590–1609]: 165–166) says:

Fig. 6 Cut stone gateway at the entrance to IIB3, looking west from the IIB3 plaza toward IIB2

the Inca and the principal *orejones*, the four of his council . . . passed to the second door; at the second door there were also guards; they were men of this city of Cuzco and relatives of the Inca, those in whom he had greatest trust, and it was those who had the charge of raising and teaching the sons of the principal leaders of all this realm, who went to serve the Inca and be with him in his court when they were young men . . . by this [second] door were the armor and arrows of the royal palace of the Inca, and at the door of the palace were a hundred captains proven in war; and a little farther on was another great plaza or patio for the officials of the palace and the regular service.

The identification of the people who used this second, smaller plaza is even less specific than before. But from the nature of its guards and the reference to the officials of the palace, it seems likely that the primary association is with the Inca themselves. Once again the excavated evidence shows communal feasting.

On the backside of this second plaza was yet a third set of dressed stone gateways which led to the compound of dressed stone structures (IIB4) mentioned at the beginning of the description of the Huánuco compound (Fig. 3). Murúa notes: "and then, going farther in, were the salons and rooms where the Inca lived. And this was all full of delights, since various areas were planted with trees and gardens, and the royal lodgings were spacious and built with marvelous artistry." In addition to the six dressed buildings that were presumably the lodgings themselves, this compound contained five more rustic buildings. Water from a spring about 1.5 km away was brought into the compound and fed into a large pool and a smaller basin, usually called a bath, lined with dressed stone. At its eastern extreme was a high platform overlooking a small, shallow artificial pond.

It is important to point out that while the second plaza area (IIB3) and the fine buildings that supposedly constituted the royal lodgings (IIB4) were separated by the third set of gateways, not unlike those at the entrances of the two previous plazas, they were probably conceptually part of the same section of the palace as the second plaza. If we examine the plan closely (Fig. 2), we can see that the second plaza is contained within the larger semi-trapezoidal compound that also includes the lodgings and the aforementioned pools and basin. To the north, it also incorporates a small, very fine, incomplete building that was probably intended to become a religious structure, as well as a compound of smaller structures in a rather poor state of preservation. Visualizing the area of the lodgings as part of the same unit as the second plaza also fits with Murúa's assignment of the "arms and arrows" of the Inca at the door before the second plaza, and his assignment of "palace officials" to that area. In other words, what we have called IIB3 and IIB4 were in a sense linked as the public and private sectors of the same overall architectural unit.

On the basis of this evidence and interpretation, one might suggest that this last semi-trapezoidal compound (IIB3 and IIB4) with its multiple components might better be called the palace proper. It appears to have contained the royal lodgings and the areas for the officials and was probably associated with the royal group itself. Murúa's inclusion of the first plaza and the first gateway or "door" (IIB2) might simply have been an interpretation of the whole complex adjoining the main plaza in Cuzco as the "palacio real." Had he seen a plan with the sets of trapezoidal enclosing walls in place, as we have here, he might have used his terms differently. But in terms of the political functioning of the spaces, I think Murúa's conception of the two spaces together is important: he ties the Incas, per se, and those referred to as Incas-by-privilege together as the essence of the governmental structure in relation to the non-Inca and their ritual space centered in the main plaza (Zone I), as discussed below.

The Ceramics of the Public Areas of the Administrative Palace

It is worth a short digression to evaluate the ceramic evidence from the two plaza areas. That evidence, though still preliminary, is the basis for the conclusion that the area as a whole was the scene of elaborate feasting. Enormous numbers of jars and plates demonstrate the large-scale preparation and serving of food and drink. The data also generally support the arguments drawn here for a two-part administrative palace with notable differences between the parts.

Pat H. Stein of the Huánuco Pampa Project team made sampling excavations in the interiors and around the exteriors of six buildings in the outer plaza (IIB2) and the five buildings of the inner plaza (IIB3). Although comprising less than 5 percent of the total area of these parts of the administrative palace, these excavations yielded more than 3 metric tons of ceramics. The material was coded by Stein, entered into the project database by Delfín Zúñiga, and is currently being analyzed with the assistance of Alan Covey.

While the overall use of both plazas for public consumption of food and drink seems clear, functional distinctions among the buildings of each plaza are suggested, and a series of important differences between the two plaza areas is emerging. The details of building function are beyond the scope of this essay and must await a full discussion of the ceramic evidence at the conclusion of the study, but the distinctions between the two plaza areas are directly pertinent to the present argument.

About 75,000 sherds were recovered from similar volumes of excavation in each of the two plaza groups. This unusually high density of ceramics, along with significant quantities of botanical and faunal remains, argues for intensive use of both areas. Large numbers of people almost certainly used both plaza areas; however, it is impossible to determine if the intensive use was on a continuing basis or was periodic.

The data show that decorated ceramics are more common in the palace area than in any other part of the site. They also demonstrate a significantly stronger presence of Cuzco-style imperial decorative motifs, the locally produced varieties of Cuzco Red and White, Cuzco Polychrome A and Cuzco Polychrome B (Rowe 1944). More than 35,500 sherds were analyzed from each of the two plaza areas. Comparison of these two large samples shows that the distribution of specific decorative motifs between them is quite distinct. The large plaza area (IIB2) included more local incised designs and other non-Cuzco designs, while the smaller plaza to the east (IIB3) had more decorated sherds, including 36 percent more imperial Inca designs. Probably the most intriguing aspect of the ceramic distribution, however, are the comparisons between Polychrome A and Polychrome B. Only 13 percent of the decorated sherds in IIB2 were Polychrome A, while in IIB3 Polychrome A accounted for more than twice that proportion, 27 percent, of the decorated sherds. Polychrome B, on the other hand, is represented by 57 percent of the decorated sherds in IIB2 and 35 percent of those in IIB3. Looked at in terms of the distributions of decorative types, 73 percent of the Polychrome A sherds from the two plaza areas were from the smaller IIB3 area, and only 27 percent were found in IIB2; in contrast the majority of Polychrome B, 55 percent, came from IIB2. The local version of Cuzco Red and White tracks rather closely the distribution of Polychrome A. Just over 70 percent of those sherds came from IIB3.

These data thus suggest a strong tendency for Polychrome A and Red and White to associate predominately with the inner plaza area, IIB3. While Polychrome B is common in both plaza areas, it shows a slightly higher tendency to associate with IIB2. If our suggestions based on the Murúa account are correct, this would imply that Polychrome A and Red and White were somewhat more restricted in their use, at least in the palace complex, than Polychrome B. There are a number of caveats. First, although sample sizes are large, we must remember that many of these sherds come from large vessels, so that a very large sample of sherds does not necessarily mean a large sample of vessels. In addition, the palace complex, because of its fine architecture and large buildings, was used during the Spanish occupation. This use is demonstrated by a sizable quantity of Old World domesticates among the faunal remains. We would expect a non-Inca use to pay little attention to Inca design distinctions on functionally similar vessels; thus if the distribution of vessels was modified from that of Inca times, we would expect the two plaza areas to become more homogeneous, not less so.

Although it seems safe to assume that these distributions reflect patterns of use during the Inca occupation of the site, we still need to reflect on the extent to which they indicate a principle that essentially required people in the various plaza areas to use a ceramic assemblage decorated with particular motifs. If this were the case, the less than absolute distinction between the distributions in the two areas might be attributed to either the less than fully rigid enforcement of the principle or a tendency for the vessels to be moved about indiscriminately in the years following the Spanish Conquest.

Alternatively, the decorative motifs might relate to social groups rather than to specific spaces per se. For example, Polychrome A might have been associated with the strictly Inca ruling group, whatever the spatial position of its members at any point in time. Likewise, Polychrome B might have been associated with the so-called Incas-by-privilege. If this were the case, distributions would likely have been the result of use and discard patterns related both to primary spatial associations of the group and their movement within and between spaces. I suspect this latter scenario to have been the more likely one. Ritual occasions in both spaces would have involved the participation of both groups, and the ceramic vessels with the appropriate motifs may either have been brought with the various participants or kept in both spaces for their use. Obviously, we need additional research in other contexts to confirm and clarify these points—as well as a closer reading of the Spanish accounts with these questions in mind.

The Administrative Palace and the Central Plaza in the Context of Reciprocal Administration

Returning to architectural and textual information to conclude discussion of the Huánuco Pampa administrative palace, it is interesting to take Murúa's description of the palace with its two plazas and sumptuous residential buildings a step further and examine the relationship of the palace to the main plaza. Plazas were obviously the primary ritual spaces of the city. The excavated evidence at Huánuco Pampa demonstrates that quite clearly. From the combination of the architecture, ceramics, and Murúa's text, I have posited an association of the easternmost plaza and its adjoining royal lodgings with the royal groups, the larger plaza just off the main plaza with Incas-by-privilege. The third major ceremonial or ritual space, of course, is the main plaza, the most evident and important architectural element in the city as a whole. With large *kallanka* buildings opening onto it from all sides, this was probably the public space of the non-Inca outsiders and was associated with the various non-Inca groups who were housed (mostly on a part-time basis) in the various zones of the city. I suspect that this tripartite division of the three ceremonial plazas relates to the terms *collana, payan,* and *cayo* as major social divisions within Tawantinsuyu as outlined in analyses by Zuidema (1964) and Wachtel (1973), among others. This notion requires further study, including a careful analysis of the ceramics and other excavated remains from the area of that plaza (Zone I). If this notion is correct, we can begin to see how the royal lodgings and their associated ritual spaces are part of a concentric organization of space and society, an organization that linked the Inca in the easternmost part of the administrative palace (IIB3) with the outsiders they ruled in the main plaza. The intermediate plaza area was the space of the mediating groups that helped create ties between the rulers and the non-Inca. Ritual spaces and the gateways that connected them provided both the symbolic armature and the real architectural spaces and buildings that shaped the human interactions necessary for forging links between rulers and ruled.

La Centinela: Capital of the Chincha Kingdom under Inca Rule

The Chincha kingdom was one of the principal polities incorporated into Tawantinsuyu. The lord of Chincha was a major ally of the Inca and was accompanying Atawallpa in a nearby litter during the fateful encounter with the Spaniards at Cajamarca. La Centinela, the modern name of the Chincha capital, is an unusual site in that it is one of the very few places where the Incas incorporated a major state installation into a preexisting, and still functioning, non-Inca capital.

The Inca compounds at La Centinela are clearly distinguished in both style and construction techniques from local Chincha construction. The building of these imperial compounds was complemented by the modification of several of the earlier Chincha areas as part of a strategy of alliance and indirect rule (Morris and Santillana n.d.).

The Inca installation at La Centinela is executed in adobe bricks, but in terms of its spatial patterns, including its relationship to a large main Inca-built plaza, it is closely analogous to Murúa's description of the palace in Cuzco and the one discussed above in Huánuco Pampa. It is much smaller than the palace in Huánuco Pampa, probably in part because a much smaller Inca presence was required in Chincha than in Huánuco, since the Incas could count on a loyal local nobility to accomplish their goals. But there are other substantial differences. These differences reflect the very different political strategies of the Inca in the two areas.

Putting the differences aside for the moment, I argue that the basic division of the palace into two major parts, corresponding to different social groups, is present. We can also see the subdivision of the second part of the palace into a public space and structures reserved as royal lodgings. The palace area is the prominent feature of Zone II at La Centinela (Fig. 7), the part of the site constructed almost exclusively in Inca times. Its prominence is shown by the quality of its construction in comparison to the rest of the Inca sector and by its height in relation to the surrounding structures in the zone (Fig. 8). The representation of sociopolitical hierarchy in architecture had both a horizontal and vertical expression at La Centinela; hierarchy could be expressed in elevations as well as horizontal space.

It is fruitful to focus on how the differences in palace architecture between Huánuco Pampa and La Centinela relate to differing political strategies in the two regions. I have said elsewhere (Morris 1987) that in the Huánuco region the Inca were trying to fashion a new political hierarchy from the many fragmented local groups with themselves unambiguously placed at the top. Huánuco Pampa was both a map of the new organization and a way of channeling human activities through ritual to direct its creation. In Chincha, the Inca

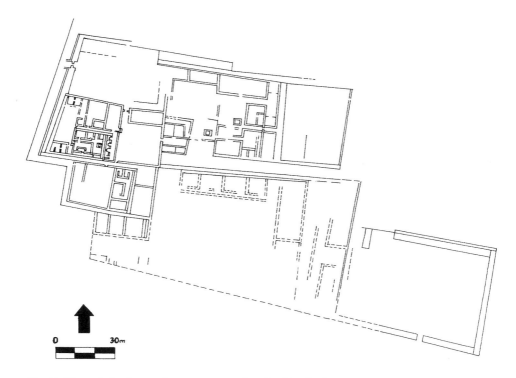

Fig. 7 Plan of the Inca palace compound at La Centinela

Fig. 8 The Inca administrative palace at La Centinela, capital of the Chincha kingdom

encountered a complex social and political structure already in place. They opted to graft an imperial administrative operation onto a functioning kingdom, incorporating their own palace and other administrative buildings into La Centinela, the Chincha capital.

If my reading of the architecture is correct, what we see in La Centinela is not heavy-handed Inca domination, but a more subtle form of control based on alliance and apparent mutual respect. The unusual fusion of Inca and Chincha design elements in the Inca-Chincha ceramic style (Menzel 1959) can also be seen in architecture. The aim was to obtain the collaboration of Chincha, in part by creating an architectural scheme that positioned them as seeming near equals.

In doing this, the palace structure at La Centinela differs from that at Huánuco Pampa in two notable ways. First is the placement of the palace. The Inca built what appears to have been a main plaza as part of their installation at La Centinela, in this case very much smaller than at Huánuco and near the site's periphery. But in the Chincha case the palace is not entered directly from the main plaza. Instead an architectural unit in the form of a small truncated pyramid—which borrows Chincha formal ideas, but is executed in Inca adobe brick construction—sits just off-center at the plaza's north end (Fig. 7). It is separated from the palace complex by a long narrow passageway that runs north at the level of the main plaza's eastern periphery.

The pairing of the two-part palace complex with a structure that seems to have Chincha affinities is notable, as is the placement of the palace off-center from the main plaza. Both of these features subtly soften the hierarchical superiority of the Inca. The entry of the palace is from the dividing corridor, not from the plaza itself. Its location is thus much less prominent in relation to the main plaza than is that of the palace at Huánuco Pampa, and the plaza itself is also smaller, less central, and of presumably less public importance than at Huánuco and many other Inca centers. Perhaps what is implied in this architectural scenario is a pairing of near equals on either side of a passageway, with the Inca palace discreetly to the side, leaving a more prominent and visible position for the structure the Inca had built with apparent reference to local architectural traditions. This subtle play of representations and perspectives at La Centinela is not surprising in light of the importance the lord of Chincha was apparently accorded in the Inca court.

The second striking difference between the Chincha palace and those of Huánuco and, as we will see below, Tambo Colorado, is in the size of the space in the plaza area between what Murúa would have referred to as the first and second doors of the complex (the equivalent to IIB2 at Huánuco Pampa). In both of those latter sites that space is much larger than the total space beyond the second door, in what is equivalent to IIB3 and IIB4 at Huánuco Pampa. In La Centinela the relationship is reversed; the outer compound is barely half the size of the inner compounds of the royal lodgings and their associated open spaces. In addition, there is but a single structure in that outer plaza, and our test excavations suggest that it was barely used—a far cry from the dense ceramic and organic remains found in the apparently equivalent IIB2 at Huánuco Pampa. I suspect that the group of Incas-by-privilege is much smaller in this case where the Inca were dealing with a single subservient polity that was already hierarchically structured. In addition, the platform mound

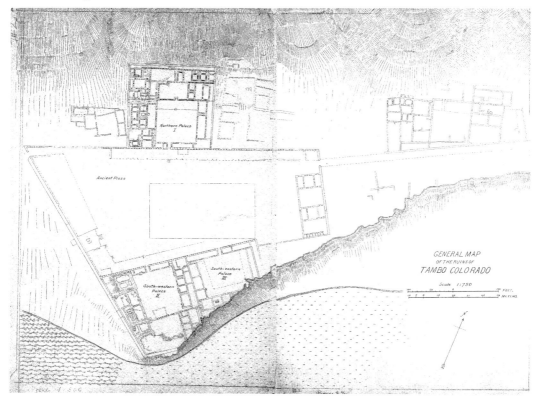

Fig. 9 General plan of the Inca center of Tambo Colorado, as drawn by Max Uhle in 1901 (see Wurster 1999)

structure across the passageway was likely the primary architectural association with the intermediate group in this particular local situation, reflecting a much more subtle relation to the Inca in terms of authority.

Tambo Colorado: An Inca Center on the Road from Cuzco to the Sea

Tambo Colorado, in the middle Pisco Valley, is one of the largest and best-preserved Inca sites on the Peruvian coast. The red, yellow, and white colors for which it is known are still visible in many areas but are far dimmer than when I first visited in the mid-1960s.

In spite of its adobe brick construction, the planning and many of the architectural details are heavily reminiscent of Inca sites in the highlands. It is one of several Inca installations that lie on a principal lateral road connecting the highland Capac Ñan with the main coastal road. The number and architectural importance of these sites are perhaps related to the symbolic importance of the road which runs almost due west (though not in a straight line) from Cuzco to the Pacific—the route of the setting sun.

Tambo Colorado is planned around a semi-trapezoidal plaza with numerous structures on its north, south, and east sides (Fig. 9). The west side overlooks the Pisco River and

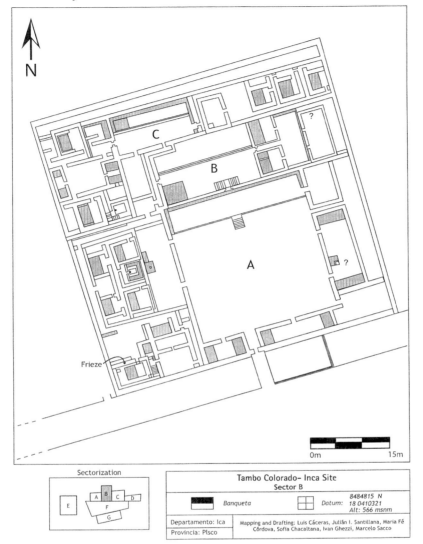

Fig. 10 Plan of the administrative palace at Tambo Colorado

is formed by a long niched wall with an *ushnu* platform in front of it. A few small structures are behind the platform and the wall. This wall and the *ushnu* platform were probably related to public ceremonies held in the plaza. Low rectangular platforms are visible along the edges of the plaza, particularly on the north side, and remains of what appears to have been columns can be seen in some of them. I suspect that these areas were roofed and may have been much more open versions of the large *kallanka* at Huánuco Pampa and other highland Inca sites. As at Huánuco, such structures probably served as temporary shelters and lodgings for visitors and participants in the site's ritual activities, although at Tambo Colorado we have no excavated evidence. We would also assume that the main plaza here was used mainly by a large non-Inca populace. This is the most public area, corresponding

Fig. 11 Tambo Colorado, general view, looking south, with palace area in foreground. Photograph by Jorge Aguilera.

Fig. 12 Tambo Colorado, looking north from the first plaza. The doorway at the right leads to the second plaza and the royal lodgings. Photograph by Jorge Aguilera.

to the main plaza at Huánuco Pampa; it would likely have served the largest group of people—those who were considered outsiders, not linked by special privilege to the Incas.

The two-part palace of the type described by Murúa is Tambo Colorado's most prominent feature (Figs. 10, 11). We can easily identify the outer plaza area (A) with two large rectangular structures and three smaller ones opening onto it (Fig. 12). The second, presumably more royal, sector (analogous to IIB3 at Huánuco Pampa) has a small open plaza (B) with three small rectangular buildings to its side. Behind and above this area is a very restricted compound (C) that probably contained the royal lodgings. The lodging area has four structures on its eastern side. The three easternmost structures have so-called bed platforms built into their floors, and each has a distinctive window treatment. One is stepped on both sides; one is stepped on one side only; and the other is not stepped. We can only speculate that these three structures might have been actual sleeping quarters used by different personages each with his/her architectural signs.

The most intriguing single feature of the Tambo Colorado palace complex is found in the southwestern corner of its southern part, just north of the main plaza. There a spacious double-room building with a "bed" platform contains a single block of what was once an apparently much larger adobe frieze (Figs. 13, 14). The frieze had two faces, and the design element on both its faces is similar to a design on a frieze fragment (Figs. 15, 16) discovered several kilometers south of La Centinela at the site of Litardo Bajo by Luis Lumbreras, as part of the survey portion of our joint Chincha Valley project. That frieze had been detached from the wall of which it was part many years ago, perhaps by an earthquake.

The exact relationship between the Chincha and Pisco valleys in immediately pre-Inca and Inca times is unclear from the written sources. Just to the east of the palace complex are the remains of *tapia* (tamped adobe) construction, which might have already been in ruins when Tambo Colorado was built. The architecture of that structure is very similar to buildings in the Chincha Valley; but I am not aware of ceramic studies that could establish a more reliable understanding of the relationships between Tambo Colorado and the next valley to the north.

Nevertheless, the evidence of a frieze fragment with elements very similar to a frieze in the Chincha Valley, executed under the control of Inca architects, is a telling presence as part of the Inca palace complex. Its position as part of the outer or first part of the architectural complex is consistent with the argument of an association of that unit with privileged persons who were not members of the Cuzco nobility. We must be cautious not to impute too much significance to this one architectural symbol, versions of which appear at other sites along the coast. But such symbols are exactly what we might expect in this position of mediation and joining of Inca and local groups. Somewhat curiously the structure with the frieze could only be reached by passing through the inner plaza (analogous to Huánuco Pampa, compound IIB3) of the complex. This has the double implication that the user of that structure was actually able to enter that inner, presumably royal, courtyard and, at the same time, that he or she did not have the liberty of easy access to the building through the outer courtyard. Perhaps the most likely reading of these features is that an important local personage was given a prestigious lodging, but its use was strictly regulated by the Inca.

Fig. 13 Adobe relief frieze at Tambo Colorado. Photograph courtesy of the Phoebe Hearst Museum of Anthropology, University of California, Berkeley.

Fig. 14 Drawing of the relief at Tambo Colorado

Fig. 15 Fragment of an adobe relief frieze at Litardo Bajo, Chincha Valley, shown fallen over

Fig. 16 Drawing of the relief at Litardo Bajo, Chincha Valley, right side up

Issues for Further Exploration

From the above archaeological exercises complemented by Murúa's information, we have identified and partially described one kind of administrative-residential complex that we may legitimately call a palace. In addition to continuing attempts to verify and amplify our understanding of these units, future research needs to address a number of issues. Prominent among these are questions of distribution and construction sequences or chronology.

There are intriguing hints of antecedents to Inca administrative palaces, but a full exploration of the origins and chronology of these kinds of architectural units would lead us into another study. As for the distribution of reciprocity-based administrative palaces, there are suggestions at several other sites of architectural complexes that may fit the three-part pattern described above. Tunsukancha (Morris 1966), one-day's travel south of Huánuco Pampa on the highland road, almost certainly did. Pumpu, on the banks of Lake Junín, described by Ramiro Matos (1994), perhaps did. Inkawasi (Hyslop 1984: 105–106), in the *puna* above the Pisco Valley, may have been a disarticulated and rarely used example. Inkaracay in the Cochabamba Valley, Bolivia, perhaps was another little used and incomplete example. Most large Inca centers are simply not well enough preserved to make a determination possible. Particularly interesting would be some of the larger urban-size centers such as Cajamarca and Hatun Xauxa, but if such units existed in these important centers they are probably destroyed beyond recovery.

There are some major Inca centers where such administrative palaces probably were never built because they were inconsistent with the use of the centers. Inkawasi (Hyslop 1985) in the Cañete Valley may be an example. Cieza (1959 [1551]: 338–339) suggests that it was a military installation and only temporarily occupied. If true, it would not have been the kind of center where we would expect an administrative palace. In that installation, however, we have to worry about what kind of structures may have been in a badly destroyed part of the site overlooking the Cañete River. Centers with specific religious, military, and other special functions probably had royal lodgings of some sort, but might not have had a need for a multicomponent administrative palace. For example, this was likely the case for the royal estates near Cuzco (Niles 1999; Salazar and Burger, this volume). As the archaeological record for the Inca progresses, we are likely to see the definition of several categories of royal residences.

Palaces, Society, and the Expansion of the State

The rulers' quarters per se cannot be studied in isolation from the larger settlement complexes of which they were a part. We have seen from both Murúa's text and the architecture that the space associated with the Sapa Inca was carefully articulated with spaces that symbolized other groups. Taken together they provided ceremonial spaces for a microcosm of Inca and non-Inca society. They were true instruments of power. Much more than merely the residences of leaders, they became the links between authority and various levels of the populace. Studying them and the activities that took place in them can show us how such links were created and maintained. Charting these hierarchical links that allow groups to be combined under powerful leaders into larger, dominating, polities is, of course, central to our understanding of how archaic states arose, grew, and functioned. Furthermore, as the cases presented here suggest, palace architecture can be a useful comparative tool for examining varying strategies of rule in different parts of a state.

Put in a slightly different way, we can see these multipart palace complexes as process and narrative, not just static architecture. They were the stage sets for the critical process of incorporation, of bringing non-Inca peoples into Tawantinsuyu, of gaining their loyalty and their economic support. In a state that still relied heavily on reciprocity and kin ties, fictive and otherwise, they enabled the ruler to be represented in rituals throughout the empire, even when he could not be present. The palace setting created a personification of the authority of the state through the ruler's lodgings and the feasting and rituals offered in his name. The role of the administrative palaces was to order, contain, and direct the ceremonial life of the state. But it was also to impress, to inspire, and to a certain extent to frighten. In rituals, the architecture combined with the clothing, and items of adornment, laden with appropriate symbols of rank and office, were issued as state gifts (Morris 1993; Murra 1962). Together they reinforced songs and other verbal messages and were essential ingredients of the way personal and group identities were imprinted and arranged into the hierarchies that formed the structure and organization of the state.

In sum these Inca administrative palaces were royal residences only in a minor sense; they were essential vehicles of state creation; they ranked with political and religious rituals and with economic reciprocity as part of the generative processes of the growing empire. Seen in their broader architectural versions, they housed not just the Sapa Inca and his personal retainers, but the body politic. The palaces were symbol and substance of the state itself.

Bibliography

CIEZA DE LEÓN, PEDRO DE

    1959   *The Incas.* Translated by Harriet de Onis. Edited, with an Introduction, by Victor
    [1551]   Wolfgang von Hagen. University of Oklahoma Press, Norman.

HARTH-TERRÉ, EMILIO

    1964   El pueblo de Huánuco-Viejo. *Arquitecto Peruano* 320/321: 1–22.

HYSLOP, JOHN

    1984   *The Inka Road System.* Academic Press, Orlando.

    1985   *Inkawasi, the New Cuzco: Cañete, Lunahuaná, Peru.* BAR International Series 234.
            Oxford.

MATOS MENDIETA, RAMIRO

    1994   *Pumpu: Centro administrativo Inka de la Puna de Junín.* Arqueología e Historia 10.
            Editorial Horizonte, Lima.

MENZEL, DOROTHY

    1959   The Inca Occupation of the South Coast of Peru. *Southwestern Journal of Anthropology*
            15(2): 125–142.

MORRIS, CRAIG

    1966   El tampu real de Tunsucancha. *Cuadernos de Investigación, Antropología* 1: 95–107.
            Universidad Nacional Hermilio Valdizán, Huánuco, Peru.

    1982   The Infrastructure of Inka Control in the Peruvian Central Highlands. In *The Inca
            and Aztec States, 1400–1800: Anthropology and History* (George A. Collier, Renato I.
            Rosaldo, and John D. Wirth, eds.): 153–171. Academic Press, New York.

    1987   Arquitectura y estructura del espacio en Huánuco Pampa. *Cuadernos* 12: 27–45,
            Instituto Nacional de Antropología, Buenos Aires.

    1993   The Wealth of a Native American State: Value, Investment, and Mobilization in the
            Inka Economy. In *Configurations of Power: Holistic Anthropology in Theory and Practice*
            (John S. Henderson and Patricia J. Netherly, eds.): 36–50. Cornell University Press,
            Ithaca, N.Y.

MORRIS, CRAIG, AND IDILIO SANTILLANA

    n.d.   Chincha and Huánuco: Contrasts in the Exercise of Inka Power. Paper presented at
            the Variations in the Expression of Inka Power symposium, Dumbarton Oaks,
            Washington, D.C., 1997.

MORRIS, CRAIG, AND DONALD E. THOMPSON

    1985   *Huánuco Pampa: An Inca City and its Hinterland.* Thames and Hudson, London.

MURRA, JOHN

1962   Cloth and Its Functions in the Inca State. *American Anthropologist* 64: 710–728.

MURÚA, MARTÍN DE

1946   *Historia del origen y genealogía real de los reyes inças del Perú.* Introduction, notes, and
[1590–1609] arrangement by Constantino Bayle. Biblioteca Missionalia Hispanica 2. Consejo
Superior de Investigaciones Científicas, Instituto Santo Toribio de Mogrovejo,
Madrid.

NILES, SUSAN A.

1999   *The Shape of Inca History: Narrative and Architecture in an Andean Empire.* University of
Iowa Press, Iowa City.

ROWE, JOHN H.

1944   *An Introduction to the Archaeology of Cuzco.* Papers of the Peabody Museum of
American Archaeology and Ethnology 27 (2). Harvard University, Cambridge, Mass.

WACHTEL, NATHAN

1973   Estructuralismo e historia: A propósito de la organización social del Cuzco. *Sociedad e
ideología:Ensayos de historia y antropología andinas*: chap. 1, 21–58. Historia Andina 1.
Instituto de Estudios Peruanos, Lima.

WURSTER, WOLFGANG W. (ED.)

1999   *Max Uhle (1856–1944): Pläne archäologischer Stätten im Andengebiet (Planos de sitios
arqueológicos en el área andina).* Materialien zur Allgemeinen und Vergleichenden
Archäologie 56. IAI PK und KAVA, Verlag Philipp von Zabern, Mainz am Rhein.

ZUIDEMA, R. TOM

1964   *The Ceque System of Cuzco:The Social Organization of the Capital of the Inca.* (Eva M.
Hooykaas, trans.). International Archives of Ethnography, Supplement to vol. 50. E. J.
Brill, Leiden.

1983   Hierarchy and Space in Incaic Social Organization. *Ethnohistory* 30(2): 49–75.

Lifestyles of the Rich and Famous: Luxury and Daily Life in the Households of Machu Picchu's Elite

Lucy C. Salazar

PEABODY MUSEUM OF NATURAL HISTORY, YALE UNIVERSITY

Richard L. Burger

YALE UNIVERSITY

It is difficult to imagine a pre-industrial state that did not express the power and authority of its rulers through the construction of impressive palaces. The images of Versailles of France's Sun King, the Escorial of Spain's Philip II, and the Ming Dynasty's Palace City of Beijing all immediately spring to mind, as do the awed accounts of medieval visitors to the great palace of Byzantium. These remarkable architectural creations not only symbolized the institutions that built them, but actively conveyed the power of their patrons. Palaces have been tools in political and social action since the emergence of powerful states, and it is tempting to think of the term *palace* as a universal phenomenon, at least among complex societies. Tawantinsuyu, the Pre-Columbian world's largest empire, would be expected to have produced palaces comparable to those of other great civilizations. Yet one looks in vain for the term *palace* in contemporary syntheses on Inca monuments such as *Inca Architecture* (Gasparini and Margolies 1980) or *Inca Settlement Planning* (Hyslop 1990).

Joanne Pillsbury and Susan Evans (this volume) defined the term *palace* as an elite residence pertaining to sovereigns that is the central locus of social, political, economic, and ritual activities in a complex society and is among the most important and imposing architectural forms. This formulation is instructive because it combines the basic functional definition, that of the ruler's residence, with a series of expectations involving other aspects of the ruler's and the society's life, as well as the assumption that these will be expressed through monumental architecture. While this combination of expectations is not unreasonable and occurs in many instances, there is no reason why these functions cannot occur in spatially separate locations. Moreover, the assumption that the structure where the ruler resides must necessarily be imposing presupposes a single view of how power is most meaningfully conceptualized and expressed.

The Western notion of *palace*, like most categories of human experience assumed to be natural, turns out on closer inspection to be closely linked with particular social and historical contexts. Inca palaces are different in some respects from the Western preconception, but there are dozens, perhaps hundreds, of complexes that can be considered to have been Inca palaces. Before focusing on one concrete example of an Inca palace complex, the famous site of Machu Picchu, it is worthwhile to examine the general reasons for the uneasy fit between Inca palaces and the term *palace* as conceptualized by many Western scholars. One problem already alluded to is the absence among the Incas of a single palace complex that could be viewed as a unitary symbol of the collective authority of the state. On the contrary, Inca palaces were considered the property of individual rulers and their descendants. Each ruler had to embark on the construction of his own palace compound, and consequently there were numerous palace complexes in the capital, each belonging to a royal corporation or *panaca* (Cieza de León 1984 [1551], pt. 1, chap. 43: 144; Conrad and Demarest 1984; Niles 1987: 12–15). Thus there was no single complex that was equivalent to Versailles, Hampton Court, or the White House.

Moreover, the construction of palaces by the king or Sapa Inca was not limited to the capital. Palace complexes also were constructed in the hinterland of Cuzco and more distant provinces as far away as Tomebamba in Cuenca, Ecuador (Niles 1988; Rostworowski 1962). These palace complexes were not equivalent to each other in their form or function. Some royal residences, like Huánuco Pampa, were large in scale and linked to administrative centers (see Morris, this volume; Morris and Thompson 1985). Others, like Tambo Machay, were smaller country palaces designed as hunting lodges to offer relief and relaxation for a weary emperor. Unlike Camp David, the modern U. S. version of the country palace, Inca country palace complexes were the individual property of the emperors and their *panaca*, and as a consequence, like the palaces in the capital, they multiplied accordingly with each new king.

The term *palace* often carries with it an assumption that the building must be of great scale, but this implies a focus on interior living that is somewhat at odds with the lifestyle of highland Andean peoples. To appreciate this discrepancy, it is necessary to consider some of the special geographic features of the high Andes from which the Inca rulers exercised their authority. The Cuzco region, like the rest of the Central Andes, is characterized by strong diurnal variation and only limited seasonal fluctuations in temperature due to its tropical latitude. As a consequence, daytime temperatures are agreeable throughout the year, and, as Cobo observed in the seventeenth century, in Inca and early Colonial times most native people spent their waking hours outdoors and showed little interest in making their houses more comfortable (Cobo 1964 [1639–53]: bk. 14, chap. 3). In the highlands, temperatures drop sharply after dark, particularly in the winter, and highland people coped with this by living in small windowless dwellings that absorbed solar heat during the day and retained it at night. These patterns, chronicled by Spaniards at the time of their arrival (Cobo 1990 [1639–53]: 193; Rowe 1947: 222–224), continue to persist in traditional Quechua highland communities. The residences of the Inca had no chimneys from which heat could escape, but rather the smoke was eliminated through the thatched roofing. This design was well adapted to the highland environment and maintained a comfortable interior temperature even during cold nights.

Fig. 1 The Coya surrounded by her attendants (Guaman Poma de Ayala 1980 [1615]: 98)

The limited importance of interior household activity was mirrored in the lack of elaboration inside the dwellings themselves. This was most conspicuously expressed by the absence of immovable furnishings, either functional or ornamental. Even the Inca ruler was said to sleep on the ground on a cotton quilt covered with woolen blankets. Descriptions of the interior decoration of the Inca's royal residence mention the elaborate textiles with which he was surrounded and the portable vessels of gold and silver metal that were set on rushes before him and held for him by his serving women while he ate (Rowe 1947: 259). In Guaman Poma's drawings of the succession of Sapa Incas and Coyas or queens, his emphasis is on the imperial costume, the personal service offered by his or her numerous attendants, and portable objects (Fig. 1). Textiles were particularly important in creating a rich and elaborate interior décor specific to the royal family (Salazar and Roussakis 2000). These portable items appear to have been more important in symbolizing royal authority than the scale of the architecture or the permanent furnishings of the royal residence itself (Guaman Poma 1980 [1615]: 76–120).

Descriptions of royal residences can be found in several early chronicles, and it is clear that the "ordinary" town palaces in Cuzco were much larger and more impressive than the country palaces. Nevertheless, despite the range of variation between them, there are some

Fig. 2 Guaman Poma's drawing of an
Inca palace (1980 [1615]: 303)

commonalities that reflect the values of the Inca nobility. Although built using fine stonework, the actual structure in which the king dwelled was modest in scale. The building in
which he slept was grouped along with a small number of other small buildings around an
open patio, echoing the domestic compound arrangement widespread in the Cuzco area
and referred to by the term *kancha*. It was in the small private patios that most domestic
activities took place. Gardens and baths figure in several of the descriptions of the royal
residences. The central loci of the most important social, political, economic, and ritual
activities, to use Pillsbury's and Evans's phrasing, were usually located not in the residences
themselves, but in large open plazas or in small special-purpose structures independent of
the king's dwelling.

The somewhat different character of the Inca notion of palace is illustrated by the
lack of a special term for the word *palace* in early Quechua dictionaries. The royal residence
is referred to as *hatun wasi* or "big house" in some chronicles, and "palace" is translated
simply as *Capay ccapakpa huacin* (House of the King) in Diego González Holguín's colonial
Quechua dictionary (1989 [1590–1600]: 613). This absence of a special Quechua term for
palace explains why Guaman Poma used the Spanish word *palacio* prominently in his illus-

Fig. 3 The Sapa Inca, Tupac Inca, and the Coya, Mama Ocllo, being carried on a bejeweled litter by members of the Callauaya ethnic group (Guaman Poma 1980 [1615]: 305)

tration of a late Inca palace complex along with the Quechua term *Inkap wasin* (House of the Inca) (Fig. 2) (Guaman Poma 1980 [1615]: 303).

In the symbolics of power, the creation of impressive palaces is merely one of many strategies that a ruler may choose. Since the Inca rulers extracted their taxes in labor rather than goods, it is perhaps not surprising that control over human labor was the focus of many of the most conspicuous displays of royal authority. One expression of Inca royal authority that figures prominently in the chronicles was the processions or royal progresses, as they are referred to in the historical literature, in which the Sapa Inca, sometimes accompanied by his queen, the Coya, were carried on a litter surrounded by thousands of soldiers and retainers. Such progresses carried the message of royal power and authority across geographical space to its subject populations throughout the empire, and the multiethnic entourage physically carrying the litter of the Inca ruler on their shoulders served as a vivid metaphor for his political domination and claims of divine kingship. The anthropologist Clifford Geertz (1983) has observed that royal processions, or courts-in-motion, are common cross-culturally and that in some societies, such as eighteenth- and nineteenth-century Morocco, imperial progresses were a more important tool in statecraft than the construction of an imposing royal palace or capital. For the Inca, the chroniclers frequently describe the lengthy journeys made by the Inca ruler by litter to the different parts of his empire.

Royal progresses are shown frequently in the drawings that illustrate the manuscripts of Guaman Poma (1980 [1615]: 305, 307) and Martín de Murúa (1946 [1590–1609]; 1985 [1611–16]) (Fig. 3).

Although processions were an important imperial strategy, perhaps underappreciated in most analyses of Tawantinsuyu, the building of monuments was another popular medium through which the Sapa Inca could demonstrate his ability to mobilize and control labor. One of the characteristics most commonly attributed to kings in Inca narrative history was that of builder, one who transforms unproductive and wild zones into economically and culturally rich regions. Many of these construction projects created temples, agricultural infrastructure, or administrative centers, but emperors also used their authority to mobilize their subjects for the construction of royal residences in Cuzco and in the lands they subjugated. The crucial link between a ruler's power and palace construction is evident from the descriptions in the earliest Spanish accounts. For example, Betanzos (1987 [1551–57], pt. 1, chap. 43: 187) writes that one of the last Inca rulers, Huayna Capac, asserted his authority shortly after becoming the Sapa Inca by raising 150,000 workers from throughout Tawantinsuyu for the building of his country palace in the Urubamba Valley. In contrast, the weakness of Atahualpa was made manifest by his difficulty in raising a workforce for the construction of his palace in Tomebamba after claiming the contested throne (Niles 1999: 79–80).

Many of the Inca rulers chose to build country palaces near Cuzco that could be used seasonally by the emperor and his family while he was alive and by his mummified body and his descendants following his death. The construction of such complexes, like all palaces, was one form of visual propaganda, effective in emitting its message long after the death of its creator. It is worth observing, however, that, unlike royal processions, such propaganda in the form of architecture reaches only those visiting the palace or residing in the area of the complex.

Symbolics of Power at the Country Palace of Machu Picchu

One of the preferred zones for the construction of country palaces was the Vilcanota-Urubamba Valley to the north of Cuzco (Fig. 4). The proximity to the capital, the gorgeous landscape, and the favorable climate account in part for this pattern. Such royal estates were used as retreats from the cold weather and political pressures in the capital, and Incas were described as enjoying the gardens and hunting in these more rural zones. Susan Niles has identified eighteen probable country palace complexes in the drainage (1999: fig. 5.1; see also Niles 1988: table 1.2) and published accounts of two: Callachaca, created by the emperor Topa Inca, and Quispiguanca, a late Inca country palace built by Huayna Capac in Yucay. Others, such as Pisac, Ollantaytambo, and Patallacta, are also well known.

But, without a doubt, the most famous of the Urubamba country palaces is Machu Picchu, located three-days' journey on foot from Cuzco (Fig. 5). Historical documents published by John Rowe (1990) indicate that the emperor Pachacuti built this royal estate, perhaps to commemorate his victory over the lowland peoples of the forested eastern

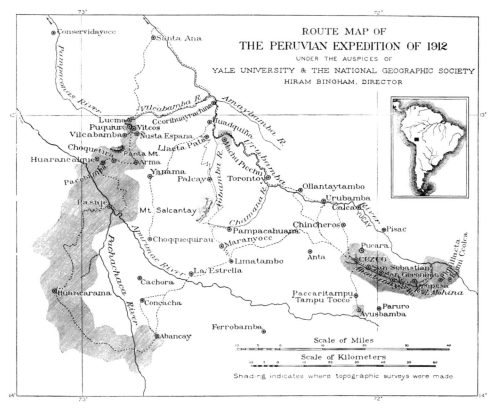

Fig. 4 Yale Peruvian Expedition map of the Urubamba River and surrounding region. Courtesy of the Peabody Museum of Natural History, Yale University.

Fig. 5 Panorama of Machu Picchu taken by Hiram Bingham III before the site was cleared. Courtesy of the Peabody Museum of Natural History, Yale University.

Fig. 6 The Inca Pachacuti (Guaman
Poma 1980 [1615]: 88)

slopes of Vitcos and Vilcabamba. Fortunately, unlike most Inca palace complexes, the architecture of Machu Picchu has been fully uncovered, meticulously documented, and preserved by the Peruvian government. The design and construction of this built environment
permit some intriguing insights into the daily life of Tawantinsuyu's elite, or, in the parlance
of contemporary U.S. culture, the "lifestyles of the rich and famous."

There is consensus among scholars that the site was largely designed and built as a
single unit, a conclusion consistent with the archaeological evidence uncovered by the
1912 Yale Peruvian Expedition and later projects. Thus Machu Picchu offers a window
into the way in which the Inca Pachacuti used the palace architecture he created as a
vehicle to express his authority, while at the same time producing man-made environments
suitable for the activities associated with royal daily life on the country estates (Fig. 6). The
power of architecture in symbolizing royal authority is widely acknowledged, and often
new architectural styles are associated with the establishment or strengthening of central
authority. According to William Coaldrake (1996: 281), architecture helps to effect the
centralization of authority by creating a pervasive image of the new order. While Coaldrake
was referring to repeated occurrences of this in early Japanese history, Pachacuti's introduction of the imperial Inca architectural style can be interpreted as an example of the same
process. The early chroniclers are explicit in attributing the vision of the new imperial

constructions to the emperor himself, and, according to Betanzos (1987 [1551–57], pt. 1, chap. 16: 75–76), Pachacuti created a clay model of his plans to renovate Cuzco and then laid out the ground plan with his own hands. Betanzos (1987 [1551–57], pt. 1, chap. 11: 50) writes:

> ... he decided to make this house of the Sun. After making this decision, he called the lords of the city of Cuzco whom he had there with him and told them his plan and how he wanted to build this house. They told him to explain the dimensions and style of the building. Such a house as that should be built by the natives of the city of Cuzco. Inca Yupanque [Pachacuti] told them that he agreed with them. Seeing the place which he thought best to build the house ... Inca Yupanque himself with his own hands took the cord, measured and laid out the plan of the temple of the Sun ... and went to a town. ... He measured the stones for building this temple ... they went to work on it just as Inca Yupanque had designed and imagined it. He always supervised the work himself along with the other lords. They watched how it was being built, and Inca Yupanque along with the others worked on the building. [Translation by Roland Hamilton (Betanzos 1996 [1551–57]: pt. 1, chap. 11: 45)][1]

Although it is likely that Pachacuti's physical involvement was probably more symbolic than real, the special importance that the Inca emperor attributed to his public constructions seems clear.

The building style that Betanzos attributes to Pachacuti was not only used at Coricancha (Temple of the Sun) and other buildings in Tawantisuyu's capital, but also at Machu Picchu and Pachacuti's other royal estates at Ollantaytambo and Pisac. The architectural features that dominate Machu Picchu, such as the trapezoidal doors and niches and the finely fitted, cut and polished stonework, constitute a distinctive and immediately recognizable style, and their presence at Pachacuti's country palace at Machu Picchu clearly signaled the settlement as part of this new world order.

Architecture has the power of communicating messages at several levels at the same time, and the imperial architectural style associated with Pachacuti can be seen as not only symbolizing a new imperial order, but also buttressing his claims to divine kingship in subtle ways. In Cuzco, many of the same conventions of masonry, architectural elements, and layout were employed both in specialized religious structures such as Coricancha and in the royal palaces. Likewise, in Machu Picchu, the architecture of the king's residence and that of his elite relatives shares many architectural conventions with the Torreón, the Prin-

---

[1] "... [él] presupuso de hacer esta casa del sol e como lo presupusiese llamó los señores de la ciudad del Cuzco que el allí consigo tenía e díjoles lo que ansi tenía pensado y que quería edificar esta casa y ellos, le dijieron que diese la orden y traza del edificio della porque tal casa como aquella ellos los naturales y propios de la ciudad del Cuzco la debían edificar e hacer e Ynga Yupangue [Pachacuti] les dijo que ansi lo tenía el pensado e visto por el sitio do a él le paresció mejor que la casa debía de ser edificada ... el mesmo por sus manos con el cordel midió e trazó la casa del sol ... y fue a un pueblo ... y midió las piedras para el edificio desta casa ... andando él siempre y los demás señores encima de la obra mirando como la edificaban y ansi él como los demás trabajaban en tal edificio."

Fig. 7 Photograph of the Temple of the Three Windows at Machu Picchu taken by Hiram Bingham III. Courtesy of the Peabody Museum of Natural History, Yale University.

cipal Temple, and other ceremonial constructions. It can be argued that the merging of religious and secular authority as embodied by the Sapa Inca was being naturalized and reinforced through the shared usage of the same architectural conventions. Analogs can be drawn to eighth-century Japan when the theocratic pretensions of the royal court led it to imitate the architectural style of Buddhist monasteries in their imperial residences and state halls (Coaldrake 1996).

This linkage between imperial rule and divine right was echoed in other aspects of the architecture at Machu Picchu. Encoded within Machu Picchu's architecture are metaphorical references to the mythical times upon which Pachacuti's legitimacy rested. For example, the design of the Temple of the Three Windows (Fig. 7) alludes to the three caves from which Pachacuti's ancestors emerged at the hill of Tambotoco at Pacaritambo. According to Sarmiento de Gamboa (1943 [1572]: 49–51), these three caves were named Maras-toco, Sutic-toco, and Capac-toco. The three caves of Inca origin are illustrated twice in Guaman Poma's *Nueva corónica y buen gobierno* (Fig. 8) (1980 [1615]: 62, 238) and, according to him, were shown on the Inca coat of arms.

Near the Temple of the Three Windows is the distinctively curved wall of the Torreón (Fig. 9). Its similarity to Coricancha, Cuzco's Temple of the Sun, would have been a constant reminder that Pachacuti claimed divine descent from the Sun. The Torreón itself was built atop a large natural boulder that was modified to form a ritual chamber suitable for

Fig. 8 The Sapa Inca and his wife wor-
shiping at the three caves of Tanbo Toco
[Tambotoco] (Guaman Poma 1980
[1615]: 238)

Fig. 9 The Torreón at Machu Picchu. Photograph by Hiram Bingham III. Courtesy of the Peabody
Museum of Natural History, Yale University.

Fig. 10 The carved exterior to the cave beneath the Torreón at Machu Picchu. Photograph by Hiram Bingham III. Courtesy of the Peabody Museum of Natural History, Yale University.

ceremonies and the storage of mummified ancestors (Fig. 10). Significantly, cut stone was used to transform this natural rock shelter into an artificial cave, thus further reiterating the Inca origin myth of Tambotoco.

While this origin myth provided the explanation for the Inca's arrival in the Valley of Cuzco, a second and complementary myth tracing Inca origins to Lake Titicaca provided an even stronger foundation for Pachacuti's imperial ambitions. According to a number of the chroniclers, the Creator of the Universe resided at Tiahuanaco, on the shores of Lake Titicaca. And it was there that the Incas originated before traveling underground to Tambotoco. Cristóbal de Molina (1916 [1576]: 7–9) provides this account.

> There was a Creator of all things. . . . They said at that time the Creator was at the Land of Huanaco [Tiahuanaco] because they said that was his principal place of residence, so there are located some magnificent buildings worthy of great admiration, within which were painted many elaborate costumes of these Indians and many stone sculptures of men and women who, for not obeying the commands of the Creator, they said that he converted them into stones; they say that it was night and there he made the Sun, the Moon, and the Stars and he commanded that the Sun, the Moon, and the Stars go to the Island of Titicaca, that is near there, and from there to rise up to the sky. And at the time the Sun wanted to rise in the form of a very resplendent man he called to the Incas and to Manco Capac, as the oldest of them, and said to him: You and your descendants will be Lords and subjugate many nations. Accept me as a father, and for being my children I will glorify you, and there you will revere me as a father . . . at that instant, Manco

Fig. 11 Photograph of the double-jambed entryway to an elite household (the Ingenuity Group) at Machu Picchu taken by Hiram Bingham III. Courtesy of the Peabody Museum of Natural History, Yale University.

Capac and his brothers and sisters, at the behest of the Creator, went down beneath the earth and came out at the cave of Pacaritambo. [Translation by the authors][2]

In addition to the myth, the largest empire in southern Peru and northern Bolivia prior to the Incas had its capital at Tiahuanaco.

Tiahuanaco had both an unparalleled mythical and historical significance for the Incas, and this was reflected by Pachacuti's imperial architectural style. Cieza de León (1924 [1551]: chap. 105: 300–302) specifically states that in formulating the Inca architectural style, Pachacuti emulated the fitted stonework at Tiahuanaco (cf. Sarmiento de Gamboa 1943 [1572], chap. 40: 111–112; Cobo 1964 [1639–53], 2: 168). Architectural elements such as ornamental windows and double-jamb doors can likewise be interpreted as coming from Tiahuanaco antecedents (Fig. 11). Despite considerable archaeological research,

[2] "auia un Hacedor de todas las cosas . . . dizen que al tiempo que el Hacedor estaua en tierra Huanaco [Tiahuanaco], porque dizen que aquel era su principal asiento, y assi alli ay unos edificios soberuios de grande admiracion, en los quales estaban pintados muchos trajes de estos indios y muchos bultos de piedra de hombres y mugeres, que no por obedecer el mandato del Hacedor dizen que los convirtio en piedras; dizen que era de noche y que alli hizo el Sol, y la Luna y estrellas y que mando al Sol, y Luna y estrellas fuesen a la isla de Titicaca, que esta alli cerca, y que desde alli suuiesen al cielo. Y al tiempo que se queria suuir el Sol en figura de un hombre muy resplandeciente llamo a los ingas y a Mancocapac como a mayor dellos, y le dijo: tu y tus descendientes auies de ser señores y aueis de sujectar muchas naciones, tenedme por padre y por tales hijos mios os jatad, y alli me reuerenciareis como a padre . . . y que luego en aquel instante Mango capac y sus hermanos y hermanas, por mandado del Hacedor se sumieron deuajo de tierra y uenieron a salir a la queba de Pacaritambo."

nothing similar to these architectural elements and masonry effects is known from the Cuzco area prior to Pachacuti's rulership. Through the intentional and archaistic imitation of the much earlier altiplano imperial style, Pachacuti and his architects produced a tangible expression of an invented history in which the Incas appear as the heirs of an early great civilization, rather than as a historically undistinguished ethnic group.

Recently Jean-Pierre Protzen and Stella Nair (1997) have cast doubt upon this relationship on the basis of their analysis of detailed differences in masonry technique between the two cultures. While Protzen and Nair's study offers many useful insights into Inca technology, their conclusions fail to take into account what has impressed the sixteenth- and seventeenth-century Spanish chroniclers, nineteenth-century travelers, and modern archaeologists: the visual impact created by much high-quality Inca masonry is strongly reminiscent of the finest buildings at Tiahuanaco, regardless of the particular masonry techniques employed. Like nineteenth-century New England wooden courthouses imitating the marble temples of the Classical Greeks, the goal was to evoke an association rather than create an exact replica and, by doing this, to create the illusion of historical linkage or continuity.

Daily Life at Machu Picchu

Machu Picchu was not created solely, or even primarily, to legitimize symbolically Pachacuti's rulership, although this is a major theme inhering in the site's architecture. The main motivation for building Machu Picchu was to provide Pachacuti, his family, and his guests with a country palace that could be used and enjoyed during the months of June, July, and August. During these months the climate at Machu Picchu was relatively warm and dry, the paved Inca roads were passable, and the surrounding cloud forest vegetation was lush. In contrast, Cuzco, a mere three or four days away from Machu Picchu, would have nightly frosts that made life far less pleasant, and the lack of rain there left the landscape parched. But what was life like for the Inca royalty when staying at a palace such as Machu Picchu? The study of visible architecture at the site can offer insights into the activities of the elite and their cultural values, particularly when combined with information from the chronicles and the excavation data available.

A good place to start is with the households of the Sapa Inca and his family. As noted, the royal family traveled with a huge entourage sometimes numbering in the thousands, and since Machu Picchu's architecture could comfortably house no more than about 750 people, it is likely that only a small portion of the subjects accompanying the royal family were permitted into the palace complex. Most of the soldiers and attendants probably encamped in cotton tents outside the palace walls, much like the arrangement witnessed by the Spaniards during the initial encounter at Inca Atahualpa's residence in Cajamarca (Xérez 1968 [1534]: 225–226).

Enough is known about Inca architecture to be able to distinguish between the areas of elite housing and that of retainers. The Inca elite lived in domestic compounds referred to as *kanchas*, while most retainers dwelled in simple rectangular buildings usually facing terrace walls (Niles 1987: 25–58). At Machu Picchu (Fig. 12), there are three elite com-

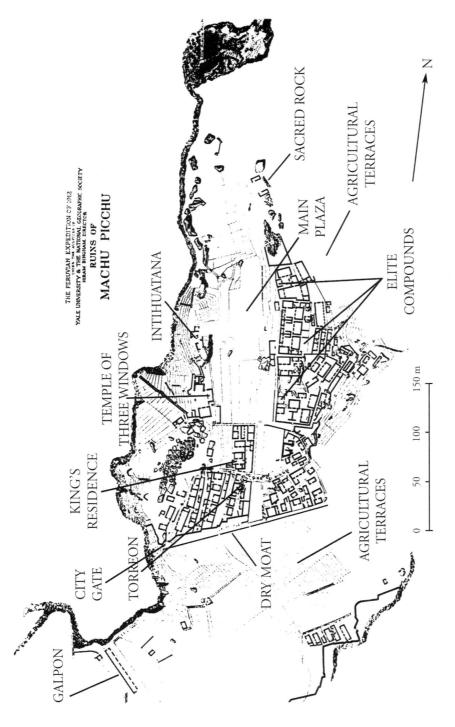

Fig. 12 Map of Machu Picchu made by the 1912 Yale Peruvian Expedition; locations of features have been added. Courtesy of the Peabody Museum of Natural History, Yale University.

pounds on terraces to the east of the central plaza which probably housed members of the Inca royal groups (*panacas*). Hiram Bingham (1930) labeled these architectural compounds Clan Groups, and he assigned names to them based on their distinctive characteristics, such as the Ingenuity Group and the Three Doors Group.

The three residential compounds, the Ingenuity Group, the Three Doors Group, and a third compound, not named by Bingham, but known as the Upper Group (Conjunto Superior; Buse de la Guerra 1978), are located adjacent to each other in the northeast sector of the site, overlooking Machu Picchu's central plaza. Each is unique, and none conforms to a simple *kancha* pattern such as that known from the elite housing at Ollantaytambo. Nevertheless, they do resemble *kanchas* in their basic components, albeit with more buildings and more complex floorplans. The distinctive layouts and construction of each complex suggested to Bingham (1930) that these corresponded to different elite families or lineages, each with its own character and composition. This idea, although difficult to test, is reasonable and worthy of future exploration.

The largest and most southern of the compounds, referred to by Bingham as the Ingenuity Group and Private Garden Groups, has eleven buildings that could have housed some fifty or sixty elite residents. In contrast, the Upper Group probably held fewer than twenty people. It is unlikely that the three elite compounds held more than 120 members of the Inca elite.

The Ingenuity Group can be divided into four sections. The entire compound, however, is surrounded by a perimeter wall with only a single entrance on its southern wall. The imposing entry by way of a double-jambed doorway was topped by a massive lintel that immediately distinguishes this as a high-status compound. Covering a zone of approximately 38 by 62 m, the interconnecting four sections extend over three different ascending land surfaces. Bingham was particularly struck by the elaborate bar-holds carved into the sides of the entryway, permitting the closure of the compound to those outside (Fig. 13). The back wall of a dual *huairona* (a rectangular structure with three walls and one side open) has been placed to obstruct vision of the compound from the entrance, thereby enhancing privacy. Within the compound, each of the sections includes roofed buildings, which may have served as living quarters, and *huaironas*, open on one side to the open air. Both the houses and *huaironas* have numerous interior trapezoidal wall niches—up to eighteen in some the larger buildings—alternating with stone cylindrical tenons projecting from the walls; these features were probably used to store and hang household goods, a necessity given the lack of freestanding furniture. Several of the houses have finely fitted cut and polished stonework, and they range in size from 32 to 80 sq m. The sections of this compound are connected by narrow stone staircases, one of which is carved from a single block of bedrock. One notable feature of this large compound is the presence of two shrines focused on natural stone outcrops, one of which is 8 m in height, framed by low stone platforms, and two unique circular mortars (Fig. 14) meticulously carved into the bedrock (Bingham 1930: 83). Six windows in the western wall of the compound provide a view of the Torreón and the Temple of the Three Windows.

The adjacent compound, the Three Doors Group, covers an area of 34 by 52 m. Entrance into it is provided by three massive stone doorways, each of which has a double

Fig. 13 Bar-holds used to block entrance to the elite compound known as the Ingenuity Group. Photograph by Hiram Bingham III, courtesy of the Peabody Museum of Natural History, Yale University.

Fig. 14 Bedrock mortars found in the courtyard of an elite compound in the eastern sector of Machu Picchu. Courtesy of the Peabody Museum of Natural History, Yale University.

jamb with carved stone bar-holds. Its layout is basically three adjacent and interconnecting *kanchas* in which houses and *huaironas* surround a central patio on four sides. The larger roofed buildings, which probably served as dwellings, are 84 sq m in area. As in the previously described compound, interior walls were provided with numerous niches and stone tenons. The few buildings with windows offer a view toward the eastern terraces and mountain landscape.

The third and final elite compound at Machu Picchu, known as the Upper Group, has two sections. It has a single entry, which like the others, features the distinctive double jamb and carved stone bar-holds. The main entrance leads into a blind corridor, insuring maximum privacy, and a secondary entrance provides access to the lower level of the compound. The most important section of this compound is a central patio flanked by *huaironas* and a roofed dwelling. The main dwelling measures 13 by 8 m and has twenty large vertical niches (*hornacinas*).

The people staying in these compounds were clearly concerned with questions of privacy. Each compound is surrounded by a high enclosure wall that would have hidden activities inside the compounds from prying eyes. In those few cases where the wall was breached by windows, the lowered exterior land surfaces would not have permitted intrusive views by outsiders. All of the compounds were isolated from prying eyes; the Upper Group was the most private, due to the absence of constructions on the northern side. Although the elite in the compounds would have had some modicum of privacy, this would have been undermined somewhat by their close proximity to each other.

As already indicated, access into the compounds was severely restricted. There were no more than four entryways into any compound complex, and in some cases there was only a single entryway. Frequently these entrances were baffled so that no clear view of life within the compound existed. Probably related to this concern is the carving of bar-holds into the jambs of the compound entryways (Fig. 13). Significantly, these bar-holds exist only in the exterior entries and are absent within the compounds themselves. This distinctive pattern of restricted visibility and accessibility led Bingham (1930: 79) to suggest: "From these facts the conclusion may be drawn that while there was common ownership within the family group which occupied the compound, and hence no desire to provide any device for securing doors to houses, there was no intention of allowing free access at all times to outsiders."

The Spanish chroniclers agree that theft was rare among the Incas and that they had neither doors nor locks. Several chroniclers do mention the placement of sticks or stones in the entryways to signal that the owners were not home, and it seems likely that the bar-holds were designed to allow the owners to close the entryway, if only symbolically, in order to prevent unwanted visitors. Bingham's speculative reconstruction of massive wooden gates closing the entryways (1930: 76–79, fig. 50b) suggests something more ambitious, but this may reflect the reality of early twentieth-century New Haven or Cuzco more closely than that of fifteenth-century Machu Picchu.

The houses in these elite compounds average about 84 sq m, which is more than twice the size of the rustic dwellings on the terraces outside the compounds which were

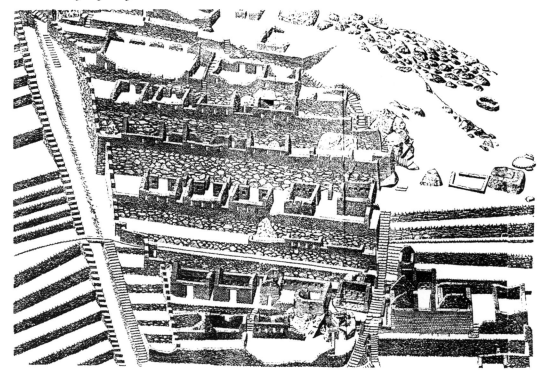

Fig. 15 Illustration by the 1912 Yale Peruvian Expedition of Machu Picchu's southwest sector including the dry moat (far left), Torreón (in lower left), and King's Group (in lower right). Illustration courtesy of the Peabody Museum of Natural History, Yale University.

occupied by the retainers. The interiors of the elite dwellings are undecorated except for some fine masonry surfaces, but it is likely that many were originally plastered and painted. Niches in the walls would have held household goods, and other items could have been hung from the projecting stone cylinders. In Bingham's excavations in the refuse adjacent to these compounds, cooking vessels were rare, making up only 6 percent of the vessels recovered. This finding, along with his failure to identify hearths, raises the possibility that food might have been prepared outside the compounds.

The elite character of the compounds is implied by their unusual size and elaboration, but it is also attested to by the presence of masonry conventions that mark high status. The double-jambed door, for example, is rare at Machu Picchu, but, as indicated, it is employed in almost all of the compound entryways. The use of well-fitted stone that has been carefully cut and polished is often viewed as a characteristic of the Incas. It is, however, rare at most Inca sites including Machu Picchu, and its presence in portions of all three of the compounds reinforces the identification of them as elite households. There are no provisions for running water, sanitary facilities, or other features that we think of today as basic amenities, but these features were likewise absent from the palaces of Western Europe at this time.

The compound of the Sapa Inca appears to have been located in the southwestern sector of the site; this royal residential complex (Fig. 15) is adjacent to the Temple of the

Fig. 16 Finely cut and polished masonry doorway with massive incised lintel from the complex interpreted as a royal residence. Photograph by Hiram Bingham III, courtesy of the Peabody Museum of Natural History, Yale University.

Sun (i.e., the Torreón). The dwelling of the sovereign is no larger than that of his elite relatives; in fact, the building in which he probably slept measures only 7 by 5 m and the interior patio covers only 28 sq m. Entrance into the Sapa Inca's compound, however, is more restricted and difficult. A large gateway is found in the compound's entryway, and another gateway limits access into the sector of the site in which the compound is located. Thus access to this complex is even more restricted than for the three compounds described above. The buildings in this complex are also set apart from the others by the care with which the white granite was selected for the walls, the superior quality of their fitted stonework, and the massive size of the stone lintels (Fig. 16). These lintels are twice the size of those used in the other residential compounds, and Bingham estimated their weight at 3 tons (Bingham 1930: 96).

Unlike the elite compounds, the residence of the Sapa Inca is set apart physically from all other domestic architecture (Fig. 17; see also Fig. 12). Above the complex to the west are broad terraces, and below it to the east is a small walled garden. Running along the north and south of the complex are the deeply inset staircases leading to the plaza below. Thus there was no housing adjacent to or even near the royal compound. This spatial isolation would have given the sovereign a degree of privacy absent from the elite compounds, and this may have been a necessary feature to maintain the myth of divine kingship.

Machu Picchu was supplied with fresh spring water brought by a stone-lined gravity canal from its source 749 m to the south (Wright, Kelly, and Valencia 1997: 838). Reaching the royal estate, it was channeled into a descending series of sixteen ritual fountains, the first

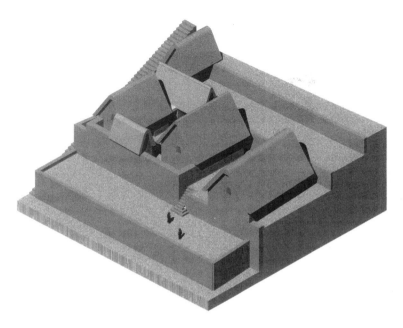

Fig. 17 Isometric reconstruction of the royal residential complex with adjacent lower garden and upper terraces. Drawing by Ana María Pavez.

of which is adjacent to the doorway of the royal compound. Thus the water reached the Sapa Inca from the spring in its pure state, uncontaminated by prior usage. The fountain of the Sapa Inca is unique at Machu Picchu in its unusual cut stone walls forming what can be interpreted as a ceremonial bath (Fig. 18). As with other fountains at Machu Picchu, a cut-stone channel delivers spring water to the top of the fountain and a sharp-lipped rectangular spout creates a falling jet of water into a small cut-stone basin at the bottom of the enclosure (Fig. 19) (Wright, Kelly, and Valencia 1997: 842). Rising 1.5 m in height, the walls of the fountain would have allowed the Sapa Inca to be bathed in privacy, a concern referred to explicitly in the early chronicle of Pedro Pizarro (1978 [1571]: 32). Although the Sapa Inca's compound does not bespeak a fondness for luxury, the privacy of it, particularly the private garden and adjacent bath, attest to the special comforts provided for the Sapa Inca and roughly match the descriptions of royal dwellings in the Spanish chronicles. For example, Xérez (1968 [1534]: 233) offers a firsthand account of Atahualpa's living quarters at the thermal baths at Cajamarca in 1532.

> The house of residence of Atabalipa [Atahualpa], that he had in the middle of his realm, although small, is the best that has been seen among the Indians. Built as four rooms with a patio in the middle, and within it [the patio] a small pool into which came very hot water by a conduit . . . cold water came from another conduit, and along the way they merge and arrive mixed together through a single conduit to the pool. . . . The pool is large and made of stone. . . . The residence where Atabalipa was during the day is a gallery in a garden, and next to this is a

Fig. 18 Inca bath (foreground) and Torreón. Photograph by Hiram Bingham III, courtesy of the Peabody Museum of Natural History, Yale University.

Fig. 19 Interior of Inca bath. Photograph by Hiram Bingham III, courtesy of the Peabody Museum of Natural History, Yale University.

chamber, were he slept, with a window opening onto the patio and the pool, and the gallery likewise gives access to the patio. [Translation by the authors][3]

In the Inca residence at Machu Picchu, there are no jewel-encrusted walls nor attempts to create a larger or more imposing dwelling that would overshadow either the neighboring ceremonial buildings or the dwellings of the Inca's family and guests. Nevertheless, the quality of the stonework and the size of the lintels do set the dwelling apart from the other residences at the site. Moreover, additional architectural distinctions may have been accomplished using perishable materials. For example, the description of the Inca residence in Cajamarca quoted above goes on to observe that the walls of the house and the wooden roofing were covered with a distinctive red bitumen-like paint (Xérez 1968 [1534]: 233).

The compounds of the Inca and the other elite residents of Machu Picchu flank the series of broad stone terraces that served as an open plaza. The proximity of these compounds to the plaza suggests the centrality of this open public space in the life of the royal estate. Much of the palace's activity was carried on outside, and the plaza, which constitutes the central axis of Machu Picchu, comprises nearly a third of the site (excluding the agricultural terracing). The few descriptions of Inca elite life in the ethnohistorical accounts tell of numerous festivals, most of which involved dancing, singing, feasting, and drinking. Of these activities, the imbibing of *chicha* or corn beer was usually signaled as the most important. One of the few eyewitness accounts of Inca court life that has survived comes from Miguel de Estete, who was among the Spaniards when Atahualpa was captured. Estete (1968 [1535]: 400–401) offers the following description of a royal banquet in an open plaza.

> Everybody was placed according to their rank; from eight in the morning until nightfall they were there without leaving the feast, there they ate and drank. . . . The wine they drank was made of roots and maize, like beer, and was enough to get them intoxicated because they are very lightheaded people. There were so many people and so much wine, and both men and women poured so much [wine] into their skins, because they are good at drinking rather than eating. It is certain without any doubt that two broad drains, more than half a *vara* wide, went under the paving to the river, which must have been made for cleanliness and to drain the rain which fell in the plaza or by chance, the most certain is for that purpose all day urine ran, from those who urinated in it in such an abundance, it was as if there were fountains issuing from it . . . to see it was marvelous and a thing never seen before. [Translation by the authors][4]

[3] "La casa de aposento de Atabalipa, que en medio de su real tenía, es la mejor que entre indios se ha visto, aunque pequeña; hecha en cuatro cuartos, y en medio un patio, y en él un estanque, al cual viene agua por un caño, tan caliente. . . . Otra tanta agua fría viene por otro caño, y en el camino se juntan y vienen mezcladas por un solo caño al estanque. . . . El estanque es grande, hecho de piedra. . . . El aposento donde Atabalipa estaba entre día es un corredor sobre un huerto, y junto está una cámara, donde dormía, con una ventana sobre el patio y estanque, y el corredor asimesmo sale sobre el patio."

[4] "Puestos todos por su orden, desde las ocho de la mañana hasta la noche estaban allí sin salir de las fiestas, que allí comían y bebían. . . . El vino, porque aunque el que ellos bebían era de raíces y maíz como cerveza,

Estete is by no means alone in contrasting the Inca elite's imbibing of large quantities of corn beer with a limited concern with more solid food. Food preparation was not elaborate, and the Inca royalty never developed a true elite food tradition analogous to that of Chinese or French cuisine (Coe 1994: 192–211). The only heavy meal of the day appears to have been in the morning, and most meals quickly gave way to drinking, which followed rather than accompanied the eating.

In considering Machu Picchu's central plaza, there are two features conspicuous in their absence: the *ushnu* and *galpones*. The *ushnu* was a freestanding terraced platform that served the king as a combination throne, reviewing stand, and altar. The *galpones* (the great halls sometimes referred to as *kallankas* in the archaeological literature) were massive rect-angular structures that border the central plazas in many Inca centers such as Cuzco and Huánuco Pampa (see Morris, this volume). The ethnohistorical and archaeological evi-dence suggests that these *galpones* served as drinking halls and perhaps shelters to large numbers of subjects while they were being feted by the Inca or his official representatives (Morris and Thompson 1985). Both the *ushnu* and the great halls seem to be linked to the official duties that the emperor carried out as part of his relationship with subject peoples. If this interpretation is correct, it is understandable why these features are missing from a country palace occupied by members of the Cuzco elite and their retainers.

Interestingly, small versions of the *galpones* exist immediately behind each of the three elite compounds at Machu Picchu; the largest of these, located adjacent to the Three Doors Group (Fig. 12), measures 23 by 10 m and has eight entryways on its long side. The pattern of small *galpones* associated with residential compounds suggests the possibility of reciprocal small-scale entertaining by the elite near their quarters. Two other small *galpones* are found just inside the city gate, perhaps to provide hospitality for recent arrivals to the palace.

In addition to the areas of elite residence and ceremonial architecture, there is a series of small roofed buildings situated on narrow terraces; many of these probably served to house the retainer population of the country palace. Although many of these individuals dedicated their efforts to food preparation, building construction and maintenance, and other mundane activities, some were brought to Machu Picchu because of their specialized metallurgical skills. The fine metal objects that they produced at the royal palace under the supervision of the elite played an important role in the political economy of Pachacuti's *panaca* (Salazar n.d.).

While much of the life of the Machu Picchu elite seems to have been focused inward, it could not be entirely isolated from the area beyond the palace walls. One of the explicit purposes of royal estates was to produce resources for the Inca and his *panaca* or royal corpo-ration. Massive terracing suitable for maize cultivation was found by Bingham immediately

---

bastaba para embeodarles porque es gente de muy flacas cabezas. Era tanta gente y tan buenos mojones, así ellos como ellas, y era tanto lo que envasaban en aquellos cueros, porque todo su hecho es beber y no comer, que es cierto, sin duda ninguna que dos vertederos anchos de hueco de más de media vara que vertían por debajo de losas en el río que debían ser hechos para la limpieza y desaguadero de las lluvias que caían en la plaza o por ventura, lo más cierto para aquel efecto, corrían todo el día orines de los que en ellos orinaban; en tanta abundancia, como si fueran fuentes que allí manaran . . . verlo es maravilla y cosa nunca vista."

Fig. 20 Agricultural terraces on the steep western slopes of Machu Picchu. Photograph by Hiram Bingham III, courtesy of the Peabody Museum of Natural History, Yale University.

adjacent to the royal complex (Fig. 20), and, more recently, additional terracing has been revealed beneath the heavy vegetation on the slopes below Machu Picchu. These terrace systems appear to cover an area far larger than the archaeological site as it is presently delimited. Agricultural production on Pachacuti's lands at Machu Picchu would have been a matter of some importance, although a recent study of the site's agricultural potential indicates that production on the terraces would not have been sufficient to support the residents, even on a seasonal basis (Wright, Witt, and Valencia 1997). It is likely that most of the maize, meat, and other foodstuffs was brought to Machu Picchu by llama caravans from the capital. This conclusion is consistent with the absence of large government storage facilities at the site, in contrast with imperial administrative centers such as Hatun Xauxa, Pumpu, or Huánuco Pampa (D'Altroy and Hastorf 1984; Matos 1994: 242–260; Morris 1992).

The elaborate terracing surrounding Machu Picchu had symbolic as well as practical importance. It served to frame visually the built landscape in which Pachacuti's country palace was created. As Ian Farrington (1995: 57) has observed during his investigations of Inca terracing in the Urubamba Valley: "The non-universal nature of such constructions [masonry terracing] in the heartland of Cuzco suggests that terracing was not only an agro-technological device to improve production and control microclimate and erosion, but also one whose architectural symbols were to be noted by the populace and whose lands needed to be distinguished from those of local communities."

Regardless of the economic importance of the terrace agriculture, its existence would have required that the Inca (or his representative) periodically entertain those working his lands with ritualized acts of generosity, especially banqueting. The absence of agricultural tools in the assemblage recovered by Bingham's 1912 excavations and the lack of requisite housing for farmers indicate that the farming population lived in the rural lands surrounding Machu Picchu. Pachacuti built the architectural facilities to carry out his obligation to these and other groups of laborers, and they can be observed on the upper terraces 120 m south of the city gate adjacent to one of the two Inca roads leading into Machu Picchu (Fig. 12). This area features a great hall measuring 44 by 7 m, which is substantially larger than any found within the city walls; it has eight entryways along its long wall. A *huairona*, an open patio area, and a massive stone altar exist in front of the great hall for carrying out the royal ceremonies associated with religious rituals, ceremonial feasting, and other activities.

Judging from the architectural evidence, the Inca royalty devoted much of their time at Machu Picchu to religious observances. As Bingham (1930: 56–66) and others have observed, the entire upper section of the royal estate west of the main plaza is dedicated to structures or features designed for ceremonial activities. The principal temple with its massive granite altar, the so-called Intihuatana, the Torreón, and the series of sixteen fountains carved in living stone all suggest the centrality of worship to the activities at the country palace (Fig. 21). Significantly, the finest stone masonry at the site is utilized in these ceremonial structures. Moreover, religious features are not limited to the ceremonial sector. Natural stone outcrops that served as the focus of shrines occur on the eastern side of the site both within and adjacent to the principal areas of elite residence (Fig. 22). Similar features are well known from sites in Cuzco, where they were interpreted as reified elements from myth or history. In Cobo's list of some 328 *huacas* or sacred spots in Cuzco's landscape, about 30 percent corresponded to natural stone formations (Cobo 1964 [1639–53]). The fine masonry platforms surrounding analogous features at Machu Picchu dispel any doubts that might exist concerning their ceremonial function. But why should religious activity be so central to a country palace where hunting and other nonurban pleasures might be expected?

It can be suggested that the claim by Inca Pachacuti and later rulers that a special relationship existed between the Inca royal lineages and the supernatural forces immanent in the landscape and the celestial sphere was so important that they had to be actively reaffirmed through daily ritual. So crucial were such ceremonial activities to Pachacuti and his *panaca* that he dedicated substantial amounts of skilled labor and prime real estate to them within the palace complex at Machu Picchu.

The conscious effort to locate the palace complex within a cosmic grid above and beyond the built landscape is pervasive (Chávez Ballón 1971). The accounts recorded by the Spanish indicate that supernatural forces associated with mountain peaks were among the most common foci of ceremonial activity. Johan Reinhard (1991) has hypothesized that the constructions at Machu Picchu are oriented in relation to such centers of power, particularly the mountain Salcantay. In some cases, as in the so-called Sacred Rock (Fig. 22), the natural stone shrine appears to replicate the form of the mountain Yanantin behind it.

Fig. 21 The Main Temple with its massive stone altar at Machu Picchu. Photograph by Hiram Bingham III, courtesy of the Peabody Museum of Natural History, Yale University.

Fig. 22 Ellwood C. Erdis standing at a shrine known as the Sacred Rock in the northeast sector of Machu Picchu. Photograph by Hiram Bingham III. Courtesy of the Peabody Museum of Natural History, Yale University.

The Temple of the Three Windows seems intentionally to direct attention to the mountain of Putucusi. Other natural features, such as the great ledge at the southern extreme of the site, seem to have been used as the focus of rituals to Pachamama (Salazar 2001: 122).

The designer of Machu Picchu intentionally left the northern end of the site open, providing an uninterrupted view of Huayna Picchu. The residential buildings appear to be oriented intentionally away from the north, as if observing a convention related to the special character of Huayna Picchu. It is significant that a natural cave occurs on the north face of Huayna Picchu, 390 m below its summit. The cave was extensively modified and contains some of the finest stonework in the Machu Picchu complex, including five niches with double jambs carved from single stone blocks. The importance of sacred geography for understanding Machu Picchu's design is underscored by the findings of David S. Dearborn, Katharina J. Schreiber, and Raymond E. White (1987) that a structure at the entrance to a cave known as Intimachay was designed for observations of the December solstice.

Although the architectural remains shed light on the pleasures and pastimes of the Cuzco elite during their stay at Machu Picchu, they also provide a clear indication of their anxieties. Located on the eastern slopes of the Andes, far from the capital and other large highland population centers, the elite apparently felt extremely vulnerable. These fears could have been of the raids by forest-dwelling Indians never fully subdued by the Inca or of sneak attacks by hostile highland ethnic groups choosing to use the Apurimac and lower Urubamba drainages as a route of entry into the Cuzco heartland. Pachacuti also may have feared rebellions by local agriculturists and *mitimaes* (contingents of people moved from conquered lands). Whatever provoked these anxieties, they were sufficient to justify exceptional expenditures of labor to insure the safety of the small elite population staying at Machu Picchu. Protected on three sides by its steep slopes and sheer cliffs, the more vulnerable southern end of Pachacuti's country palace at Machu Picchu was equipped by multiple lines of defense capable of holding off attackers until troops could arrive from the Cuzco heartland. There is an outer defensive wall at the edge of the terracing, followed by a deep dry moat bordered by the inner defensive wall (Fig. 15). Moreover, on the other side of these obstacles, a single entrance controls access into the country palace, and that entryway is flanked by a defensive platform from which the main gate could be defended. The amount of energy dedicated to the construction of these security features rivals that expended in the construction of the royal and elite residences. Significantly, analogous fortifications are lacking from country palaces such as Quispiguanca which were located closer to the capital.

Conclusions

The archaeological settlement of Machu Picchu offers a window on palace life during the reign of Inca Pachacuti. The creation of palaces in newly conquered lands responded to economic, political, and ideological motivations, as well as the desire to enjoy a rather Spartan style of rest and relaxation. Yet whatever the limitations in amenities, the wonderful climate and glorious views at Machu Picchu more than justified the journey by the Inca and his court from the capital. The palace at Machu Picchu was not designed to serve as a center of economic or political power for the state, and its constructions suggest that the elite may have been more concerned with solidifying social ties while banqueting with their friends and family than collecting tribute or governing their subjects. On the other hand, the importance of divine kingship and ceremonial activity for the occupants of the country palace is amply attested to at the site by the plethora of religious architecture (Salazar 2001: 118). Although Machu Picchu is justly famous for the quality of its architecture, its creators did not aspire to impress outsiders with the monumentality of its constructions. Rather they sought to create a beautiful and harmonious environment where the gods could be worshiped and life could be enjoyed. This patterning probably reflected the vision that Pachacuti wished to project at the time of Machu Picchu's construction and the specific role this country palace played near the edge of Tawantinsuyu's authority.

Bibliography

BETANZOS, JUAN DE

    1987   *Suma y narración de los Incas.* Transcription, notes, and prologue by María del Carmen
  [1551–57] Martín Rubio. Ediciones Atlas, Madrid.

    1996   *Narrative of the Incas,* from the Palma de Mallorca manuscript (Roland B. Hamilton
  [1551–57] and Dana Buchanan, trans. and eds.). University of Texas Press, Austin.

BINGHAM, HIRAM

    1930   *Machu Picchu: A Citadel of the Incas.* Memoirs of the National Geographic Society.
            Yale University Press, New Haven, Conn.

BUSE DE LA GUERRA, HERMANN

    1978   *Machu Picchu* (3d ed.). Librería Studium, Lima.

CHÁVEZ BALLÓN, MANUEL

    1971   Cusco y Machupijchu. *Wayka* 4: 4–5. Universidad Nacional San Antonio de Abad,
            Cusco.

CIEZA DE LEÓN, PEDRO DE

    1924   *La crónica general del Perú,* vol. 1. Annotations and concordances by Horacio H.
  [1551]   Urteaga. Colección Urteaga: Historiadores Clásicos del Perú 7. Gil, Lima.

    1984   *Crónica del Perú: Primera parte.* Introduction by Franklin Pease G. Y. Fondo Editorial,
  [1551]   Academia Nacional de la Historia, Pontificia Universidad Católica del Perú, Lima.

COALDRAKE, WILLIAM H.

    1996   *Architecture and Authority in Japan.* Routledge, London.

COBO, BERNABÉ

    1964   *Obras* [*Historia del Nuevo Mundo*] (Francisco Mateos, ed.). Biblioteca de autores
  [1639–53] españoles 91–92. Ediciones Atlas, Madrid.

    1990   *Inca Religion and Customs* (Roland B. Hamilton, trans. and ed.). University of Texas
  [1639–53] Press, Austin.

COE, SOPHIE D.

    1994   *America's First Cuisines.* University of Texas Press, Austin.

CONRAD, GEOFFREY W., AND ARTHUR A. DEMAREST

    1984   *Religion and Empire: The Dynamics of Aztec and Inca Expansionism.* New Studies in
            Archaeology. Cambridge University Press, Cambridge.

D'ALTROY, TERENCE N., AND CHRISTINE A. HASTORF

    1984   The Distribution and Contents of Inka State Storehouses in the Xauxa Region of
            Peru. *American Antiquity* 49(2): 334–349.

DEARBORN, DAVID S. P., KATHARINA J. SCHREIBER, AND RAYMOND E. WHITE

    1987   Intimachay: A December Solstice Observatory at Machu Picchu, Peru. *American*
                Antiquity 52(2): 346–352.

ESTETE, MIGUEL DE

    1968   *Noticia del Perú* . . . In *Biblioteca Peruana*. Primera serie, 1: 345–404. Editores Técnicos
    [1535]   Asociados, Lima.

FARRINGTON, IAN S.

    1995   The Mummy, Estate and Palace of Inka Huayna Capac at Quispeguanca.
                Tawantinsuyu 1: 55–65.

GASPARINI, GRAZIANO, AND LUISE MARGOLIES

    1980   *Inca Architecture* (Patricia J. Lyon, trans.). Indiana University Press, Bloomington.

GEERTZ, CLIFFORD

    1983   Chapter 6: Centers, Kings and Charisma: Reflections on the Symbolics of Power. In
                Local Knowledge: Further Essays in Interpretive Anthropology: 121–146. Basic Books,
                New York.

GONZÁLEZ HOLGUÍN, DIEGO

    1989   *Vocabulario de la lengua general de todo el Perú, llamada lengua qquichua o del Inca.*
    [1590–1600] Facsimile of the Raúl Porras Barrenechea edition of 1952. Universidad Nacional
                Mayor de San Marcos, Lima.

GUAMAN POMA DE AYALA, FELIPE

    1980   *El primer nueva corónica y buen gobierno*, critical ed. (John V. Murra and Rolena Adorno,
    [1615]   eds.; Jorge L. Urioste, trans.). Siglo Veintiuno, Mexico.

HYSLOP, JOHN

    1990   *Inka Settlement Planning*. University of Texas Press, Austin.

MATOS MENDIETA, RAMIRO

    1994   *Pumpu: Centro administrativo Inka de la Puna de Junín*. Arqueología e Historia 10.
                Editorial Horizonte, Lima.

MOLINA, CRISTÓBAL DE ("EL CUSQUEÑO")

    1916   *Relación de las fábulas y ritos de los Incas*. Annotations and concordances by Horacio H.
    [1576]   Urteaga; biographical notes and bibliography by Carlos A. Romero. Colección de
                libros y documentos referentes a la historia del Perú 1. Sanmartí, Lima.

MORRIS, CRAIG

    1992   Huánuco Pampa and Tunsukancha: Major and Minor Nodes in the Inca Storage
                Network. In *Inka Storage Systems* (Terry Y. LeVine, ed.): 151–175. University of
                Oklahoma Press, Norman.

MORRIS, CRAIG, AND DONALD E. THOMPSON

    1985   *Huánuco Pampa: An Inca City and Its Hinterland*. Thames and Hudson, London.

Murúa, Martín de

  1946   *Historia del origen y genealogía real de los reyes Incas del Perú*. Introduction, notes, and
  [1590–1609] arrangement by Constantino Bayle. Consejo Superior de Investigaciones Científicas,
              Instituto Santo Toribio de Mogrovejo, Madrid.

  1985   *Los retratos de los Incas en la Crónica Fray Martín de Murúa*. (Eduardo Jahnsen Friedrich,
  [1611–16]   ed.). Oficina de Asuntos Culturales de la Corporación Financiera de Desarrollo,
              Lima.

Niles, Susan A.

  1987   *Callachaca: Style and Status in an Inca Community*. University of Iowa Press, Iowa City.

  1988   Looking for "Lost" Inca Palaces. *Expedition* 30(3): 56–64.

  1999   *The Shape of Inca History: Narrative and Architecture in an Andean Empire*. University of
              Iowa Press, Iowa City.

Pizarro, Pedro

  1978   *Relación del descubrimiento y conquista del Perú* (Guillermo Lohmann Villena, ed.; notes
  [1571]   by Pierre Duviols). Fondo Editorial, Pontificia Universidad Católica del Perú, Lima.

Posnansky, Arthur

  1957   *Tihuanacu: The Cradle of American Man*, vol. 3. Ministerio de Educación, La Paz.

Protzen, Jean-Pierre, with Stella Nair

  1997   Who Taught the Inca Stonemasons Their Skills? A Comparison of Tiahuanaco and
              Inca Cut-Stone Masonry. *Journal of the Society of Architectural Historians* 56(2): 146–
              167.

Reinhard, Johan

  1991   *Machu Picchu: The Sacred Center*. Nuevas Imágenes S.A., Lima.

Rostworowski de Diez Canseco, María

  1962   Nuevos datos sobre tenencia de tierras reales en el Incario. *Revista del Museo Nacional*
              31: 130–164.

Rowe, John H.

  1947   Inca Culture at the Time of the Spanish Conquest. In *Handbook of South American
              Indians*, vol. 2, *The Andean Civilizations* (Julian H. Steward, ed.): 183–330. Smithsonian
              Institution, Bureau of American Ethnology, Bulletin 143, Washington, D.C.

  1990   Machu Picchu a la luz de documentos del siglo XVI. *Histórica* 14(1): 139–154.

Salazar, Lucy C.

  2001   Religious Ideology and Mortuary Ritual at Machu Picchu. In *Mortuary Practices and
              Ritual Associations: Shamanic Elements in Prehistoric Funerary Contexts in South America*
              (John E. Staller and Elizabeth J. Currie, eds.): 117–127. BAR International Series
              982. Archaeopress, Oxford.

  n.d.   Machu Picchu's Silent Majority: A Consideration of the Inca Cemeteries. Paper
              presented at the Dumbarton Oaks Symposium Variations in the Expression of Inka
              Power, organized by Ramiro Matos Mendieta, Richard Burger, and Craig Morris,
              Washington D.C., October 1997.

SALAZAR, LUCY, AND VUKA ROUSSAKIS

2000   Tejidos y tejedores del Tahuantinsuyo. In *Los Incas: Arte y símbolos*: 269–303. Banco
        de Crédito del Perú, Lima.

SARMIENTO DE GAMBOA, PEDRO

1943   *Historia de los incas* (2d rev. ed.). Colección Hórreo 10. Emecé, Buenos Aires.
[1572]

SCHINDLER, HELMUT

2000   Die Tiwanaku-Sammlung 14-14-1/684 in München. *Münchner Beiträge zur
        Völkerkunde* 6: 355–369. Staatliche Museum für Völkerkunde, Munich.

WRIGHT, KENNETH R., JONATHAN M. KELLY, AND ALFREDO VALENCIA ZEGARRA

1997   Machu Picchu: Ancient Hydraulic Engineering. *Journal of Hydraulic Engineering* 123
[1534] (10): 838–843.

WRIGHT, KENNETH R., GARY D. WITT, AND ALFREDO VALENCIA ZEGARRA

1997   Hydrogeology and Paleohydrology of Ancient Machu Picchu. *Ground Water* 35(4):
        660–666.

XÉREZ, FRANCISCO DE

1968   Verdadera relación de la Conquista del Perú y Provincia del Cuzco llamada la Nueva
        Castilla. In *Biblioteca Peruana: El Perú a través de los siglos*, primera serie, 1: 191–272.
        Editores Técnicos Asociados, Lima.

Body, Presence, and Space in Andean and Mesoamerican Rulership

Stephen D. Houston

BROWN UNIVERSITY

Tom Cummins

HARVARD UNIVERSITY

A palace must be studied in relation to the ruler or noble who occupies it. Such people give meaning to the palace. They are the conscious strategists, transcendent symbols, and sacred beings who, in palatial settings, combine pragmatic self-interest with collective cultural values. However, this chapter does *not* address all architecturally relevant features of kingship, the institutions and strategies of divine rule, the relations between polity and governance, and the many ways of achieving control through invocations, manipulations, and material realizations of the spirit world (Houston and Stuart 1996). Such discussion would require more than one chapter and more than one book. Instead, it explores indigenous ideas about the royal body as a logical coda to a volume on Pre-Columbian palaces. In the chapters that came before, all excellent in their own ways, the royal body loomed as an inescapable yet sometimes unremarked presence. Here we foreground the royal body far more than the stones and structural elements that encased it.

What was the nature of the royal presence in palaces and related spaces of Mesoamerica and the Andes, and how did that presence compare with other bodies? Is such a comparison between diverse regions necessary or even desirable? In our judgment, use of the term *palace*, taken from an Old World tradition that created opulent residences in Rome, makes any such comparison inevitable. At one level, comparison yields useful contrasts that highlight evolving concepts within regional or polity traditions. At another, even the most ardent relativist must acknowledge that Maya and Moche, rulers and ruled, had bodies and that the needs and wishes of those bodies helped to configure monumental space. To the thinking, contemplative human, royal bodies pose precisely the same questions, regardless of time and place, of how humans might establish differences among themselves. This problem is central to rulers who want to stress their social and spiritual prominence. At times, however, the task of considering such topics over two regions has seemed overwhelming to us. For that reason we narrow the debate by featuring broad themes and particularly well-documented traditions, if at the risk of assuming spurious continuities and essential characteristics. Our essay first reviews theoretical frameworks for conceptualizing the body, royal or otherwise. Discussion centers on the symbolic underpinnings of body, space, time, agency, and the properties of what Terence Turner has called the "social skin." The final sections point to conclusions taken from Mesoamerican and Andean evidence, the two categories of cultural information that shape previous chapters in this book. All of the evidence gathered here relates to spaces occupied by the royal presence.

Bodies and Royal Bodies

The human body has three principal properties: (1) it thinks and acts as a phenomenological entity, meaning that it operates as a being that experiences and cognizes the world around it (Scheper-Hughes and Lock 1987: 7); (2) it defines itself through social existence and interaction; and (3) it displays attributes that frame the way we comprehend other matters. The body performs a pivotal role in human existence because of these properties, which merge physicality and concept, image and action. Such properties help us understand *all* bodies, whether royal or nonroyal, and deserve a measure of separate discussion.

Phenomenological and Interactional Bodies

The first two properties are, respectively, phenomenological (having to do with the experience of life) and interactional (concerning the body in society). The body literally makes action and thought possible through physical motion and the firing of synapses. Scholars may refer to disembodied, generalized entities such as "society," "culture," or "state," sometimes imputing intention and agency to them. But it is the body, and the body alone, that hosts intellection and enables humans to act. More deeply still, the body combines sensation, cognition, meaning, and identity. Jacques Lacan would have us believe that this combination occurs when the body and its mind assemble a self-image from countless tactile and kinesthetic experiences. By looking at other beings, by internalizing a "specular image" of other people, the body distills such encounters into a conception of itself as a complete entity, a body with boundaries and a minimal set of features (Lacan 1977: 19; Grosz 1995: 86).[1] In this Lacan accords with George Herbert Mead, who believed "[we] must be others if we are to be ourselves . . . [so that a]ny self is a social self [although] it is restricted to the group whose roles it assumes" (Mead 1964: 292; see also Cooley 1964 and his concept of the "looking glass self"). As a concept and a physical thing, the body can only be understood in relation to other bodies, a point particularly relevant to royalty.

---

[1] Assertions about "complete beings" require some caution, since they presuppose a *gestalt* model of human identity. Recent studies strongly suggest that, within a person, there can cohabit multiple "narrative selves" that "constitute the subject of the person's experience at some point in time" (Lock 1993: 146; see also Young 1990). Leaving to the side the problem of how such selves articulate with one another—can it only be because of a shared body?—there are parallels in Pre-Columbian data. In the formal rhetoric of Maya inscriptions, distinct "narrative selves," usually linked to mythic identities and their tropes, can be attached to the person of Maya lords through dance (inspiriting action) and ritual impersonation (inspiriting ornament; Houston and Stuart 1996: 306).

Along with body images come notions of space and time, either with respect to individuals—the "egocentric" frame of reference that situates the individual as a participant—or with respect to an "absolute" view that involves the mind as a kind of "disengaged theorist" viewing space and time comprehensively, without individual vantage point (Campbell 1994: 5–6). Egocentric space exists in relation to parts of the body—right, left, up, down. The body as an active force resides in the center. In contrast, absolute space corresponds to coordinates that have no central point. So too with time. A body moving through time senses the potential of the future and retains memory of the past. Yet, according to one phenomenological interpretation, it can be said to exist only in its present phase of existence, shuttling from experience to experience (Luckmann 1991: 154). That same body, however, also exists within absolute time, time without end, time that does not depend on individual experience. Patently, space and time are causally connected. A self-conscious human relies on them to act or perform as an agent, since the full use of instruments to achieve desired ends requires spatial sense as well as temporal calculation (Campbell 1994: 38–41). The royal body accentuates egocentric and absolute perspectives. A prime mover of social action and privileged receptor of perception, it also serves conceptually as a central axis of cosmic order (see below).

Shared images of the body permit our very existence as social beings. Through the medium of the body, philosophical subjects (our conscious selves) relate to objects (all that is external to those selves), an existential task of the body emphasized by Lacan and Mead. A result of this interaction is that the body learns that it is not alone, that it coexists, not with projected phantasms of the mind, but with fellow subjects that are equally capable of thought and activity. The result is a capacity to live in human society (Holbrook 1988: 121–122). The body image permits us to confide in "a stable external world and a coherent sense of self-identity" (Giddens 1991: 51) and to synchronize our experiences and actions with those of other bodies (Luckmann 1991: 156).

Symbolic Bodies

The body is central in another way: it possesses attributes that form a natural, forceful, and readily structured model for categorizing other aspects of the world. As such, the body, its symmetries, and asymmetries are, in Robert Hertz's words, "the essential articles of our intellectual equipment" (Hertz 1973: 21)—indeed, the body as an experiential filter unavoidably imprints its properties on the world around it. At once physical entity and cognized image, the body endlessly generates metaphors for ordering thoughts and actions about everything from society to morality, buildings to geography, often linking body space with cosmic and social space (Bourdieu 1990: 77; Eliade 1959: 168, 172–173; Flynn 1998: 46; Lock 1993: 135).[2] Nonetheless, the use of terms like *metaphor* may be misleading.

---

[2] To some, it is doubtful that the body can truly exist in a "natural" or preconceptual state. After all, it is the mind that necessarily organizes perception of the body (Lock 1993: 136). Mark Johnson would put this differently. The meanings of the body arise from the experience of physical acts; abstract concepts (such as institutions or morality) acquire meaning by being likened to recurrent physical actions or entities (Johnson 1987: 98). This metaphorical structuring allows us to comprehend experience.

Conceptually, things presumed to be similar may in fact *share* essences: that is, they do not so much resemble as form part of each other (Scheper-Hughes and Lock 1987: 20–21). Such beliefs closely recall doctrines of monism that acknowledge only one principle or being and that discount Cartesian dualisms between mind and matter.

The body is also a vehicle for meaningful gesture, movement, and ornament. Marcel Mauss noted that "the body is the first and most natural instrument of humanity" (Mauss 1950: 372). What interested Mauss were not so much internal images as the "techniques of the body," how the body was manipulated according to age, sex, prestige, and form of activity. In Mauss's personal experience, these "techniques" varied by society and could change dramatically through time. The body had a "history"; it was not so much "a constant amidst flux but . . . an epitome of that flux" (Csordas 1994: 2; see also Dreyfus and Rabinow 1982: 128–129). Body practices, which Mauss included within his notion of "habitus," were acquired socially as repetitive acts, often learned from childhood, and under the authority of prestigious individuals whose example others tended to follow (Mauss 1950: 368–369). Through habitus, the body became a workable paradox, functioning as "tool, agent, and object" (Csordas 1994: 5). Michel Foucault developed similar ideas, albeit within a history of Western prisons, by showing how bodies undergo "surveillance" from more powerful bodies that, in Foucault's words, "invest it, train it, torture it, force it to carry out tasks, to perform ceremonies, to emit signs" (Foucault 1995: 25; see also Bourdieu 1990: 54–56; Gell 1993: 3–4). We do not have to endorse Foucault's strangely robotic view of human nature to agree that the control of one body by another lies at the heart of social inequality.

Mauss focused on movement and interactions with objects, but one can scarcely avoid another "technique of the body": its ornamentation, whether by dress, paint, tattooing, or physical deformation. Such surface modifications are focal because they involve the "social skin," the "frontier of the social self" that serves as a "symbolic stage upon which the drama of socialization is enacted" (Turner 1980: 112). Some of these modifications or body "disciplines" are more-or-less permanent or accretional, others fleeting and discontinuous, yet all advertise something that a particular body wishes to communicate (Joyce 1998: 157, 159). The social skin inverts Hertz's metaphoric extensions by both projecting and receiving signs from other semantic domains; bodily metaphors help structure the world, and the world semantically structures the body. This complex interplay of meanings results in widespread notions of multiple bodies (Csordas 1994: 5): social and physical bodies (Douglas 1973: 93–112); bodies that experience, that regulate or represent symbols (Scheper-Hughes and Lock 1987: 18–23); medical and consumer bodies (O'Neill 1985: 91–147), each connected to its own realm of thought and behavior but linked physically and compellingly in a visible, fleshy form. As much signboard as mirror, the social skin can equally express inner qualities and conditions (Strathern 1979; Gell 1993: 30–31). Its symbolic density makes it central to understanding meanings that converge on the body.

Royal Bodies

If the body records core concepts of societies, it must also generate social difference and hierarchy, whether of the sexes or of unequals within society (Laqueur 1990: 11). The problem of the royal body assumes primary importance here. What symbolic domains intersect uniquely in the royal body? What is its relation to time, space, and action? How do people establish and mark its singularity? How, in short, are transcendent beings created out of human flesh, and "stranger kings" devised out of kin (Feeley-Harnik 1985: 281)? Along with James Frazer, whose work on divine kings remains topical if controversial, Ernst Kantorowicz showed the way in a study that has influenced historical disciplines as diverse as Egyptology and Classical studies (Bell 1985; Dupont 1989). In late medieval kingship, the royal body conflated the physical presence with corporate symbols. Although it might wither and die, the body attained immortality and ceaseless vitality when conceived as the corporeal representation of high office (Kantorowicz 1957: 23, 506). Such concepts, which in Europe descended principally (but not solely) from Pauline concepts of the body of Christ, came to the fore in rituals and regalia of accession and burial. At accession these rituals merged and then, at burial, disentangled distinct meanings of the body, thus sustaining the seamless dignity of office in the face of physical corruption and the disturbance of office entailed in royal succession; images or immediate inheritance served to ensure that seamless quality (Flynn 1998: 17; but see Brown 1981: 266, who questions the supposed unimportance to kingship of the interred corpse). The royal spouse shared in this ritual processing, but incompletely so: dyads, although necessary in practical terms for royal propagation, symbolically violated the integrity of the monad that should, ideally, encompass the ruler. The Egyptian and Andean cases brought two royal bodies together by the expedient of incest, which concentrated wealth and regal essence (see below). Incest provided another mark of distinction: it differentiated royal practice from that of other people and established parallels with the behavior of gods (see below; Gillespie 1989: 52-55).

Of key importance in medieval mortuary effigies and Roman antecedents was the image (*imago*) that housed—indeed constituted—the body incorruptible, to be fed and paid court as the successor prepared himself for ritual "estrangement" from other mortals (Dupont 1989: 407–409; Flynn 1998: 16–17). Among the Romans the rights to such images (*ius imaginum*) correlated tightly with claims to nobility (Dupont 1989: 410). Such animate images abounded in Classic Maya art as well and accorded with pan-Mesoamerican beliefs in the extension of an individual's essence to other images or objects—the royal "skin," its superficial markers of identity, can also wrap over any number of stelae and altars, multiplying its presences (Houston and Stuart 1998; López Austin 1988, 1: 42). Body and alter-image used clothing and ornament to create a social skin that marked them uniquely. As bodies immortal they neutralized time by appearing forever fresh and regal, in flagrant disregard of decay. And as bodies of centrality they could, as in Southeast Asian models of kingship, exist at a pivotal place from which a gradient descended to other beings. They then gave "way at the periphery to realms of equal but opposite kinds of power" that exhibited disorder and decentered excess (Feeley-Harnik 1985: 25). For this reason, spaces distant from the ruler's body tended to be morally ambiguous and dangerous. The ruler's space was both *egocentric*, focused on his body and its perception, and *absolute*, in that royal space could inherently assign equivalence to other bodies in the regions it occupied. In kingly models, the center of the royal body could be imagined in two ways: as a central, static point around which the world revolved; and as a restless, heroic, and primary force of agency from which other human activities rippled (Tambiah 1976: 112–113, 118–119). Better than anything else, these properties exemplified the body as paradoxical mixture of tool, agent, and subject.

Conceptually, bodily practices of the ruler took place in "monumental time," which was "reductive and generic" and "reduces social experience to collective predictability" (Herzfeld 1991: 10; see also Joyce 1998: 159). Activities were formulaic and repeated from earlier ones—or so traditions alleged. Nonetheless, these practices often originated in common acts, appropriating the form and logic of everyday activities, such as bathing, eating, or planting; these were then modified to the extent that they attained a different order of meaning among rulers (Bloch 1985: 272). From the pull of the familiar and its transformation into actions of striking dissimilarity came the emotional force of these rituals for all who witnessed them. They generalized and exalted the mundane within an idiom shared by the ruler and the ruled, presenting "complements and counterfoils to commoner traditions" (Blier 1995: 346).

Perhaps the most telling example were royal feasts, which historians and anthropologists typically see only in terms of payment and reciprocity or studied ostentation (e.g., Murray 1996: 19). Feasts can certainly be seen in such ways, but the superabundance of food offered to rulers at Hellenistic, Aztec, and Bourbon courts expresses more of the prodigious and singular appetites expected of the royal body, which summoned foodstuffs that no mortal could consume at one sitting. The royal body could also crave, and pretend to satisfy, other pleasures in superhuman quantity, as suggested by the 450 women in the Ottoman harem during the fifteenth century (Necipoğlu 1991: 160). These patterns remind us that royal bodies functioned in a supercharged symbolic realm, culturally and locally idiosyncratic, but essential to understanding the ruler in time and space.

The Ruler's Body in Mesoamerica

A concern with royal bodies was pronounced in Mesoamerica, and in ways that can be understood phenomenologically, interactionally, and symbolically.[3] The so-called "lan-

---

[3] The human body in Mesoamerica cannot be fully explored here, although there are many other elements that deserve study. For example, systems of measurement underscore close connections to the body, especially in the well-known vigesimal notations that abound in Mesoamerica. The interval between extended thumb and forefinger, Classic Mayan *nab* (na-ba or NAB; Kevin Johnston, personal communication, 1985), figures in Classic Maya estimates of what appear to be rubber ball diameters or distances between ball bounces. Personal field observations by Houston suggest that the dimensions of most hieroglyphic texts correspond to multiples of human finger or hand width. Slight discrepancies between texts hint strongly that such measurements were neither codified nor regulated, but reflected the normal variation in the hands of individual artists. Houston, David Stuart, and Karl Taube are now undertaking a study of the Classic Maya body that mirrors Alfredo López-Austin's (1988) investigation of the human body in Nahua thought.

guage of *iya*," employed by early Colonial (and presumably Postclassic) Mixtec of Oaxaca, deployed a variety of special terms used solely in describing the bodies of lords (de los Reyes 1976: 74–81). Other peoples, such as the Nahuatl speakers of the Basin of Mexico, referred to the bodies of kings in terms of unique properties, both internal and external. Rulers and a few others, such as wise, pre-senescent elders, contained and discharged hot "soul force" or *tonalli*, a term linked etymologically to "warmth of sun" (Karttunen 1983: 245–246; López Austin 1988, 1: 290). The faces of lords were "fiery," "laws" came like sparks from their chest, their visages blazed like torches or firebrands (López Austin 1988, 1: 399; Maxwell and Hanson 1992: 179, 176, 179, 182). The sun was not so much a royal metaphor, as in seventeenth-century France, but the primordial ruler himself, whose arrival and subsequent movement triggered diurnal time (King 1994: 131; López Austin 1997: 19; Joyce 1996: 174).[4] The ruler was, in short, active, heated, and warlike (Burkhart 1997: 37). This notion obtained among the Classic Maya as well, for whom *k'inich*, "sunny," was an exalted epithet for lords and high places. To be stripped of that title by enemies indicated the worst kind of ignominy. Similarly, the archetype of the dignified ruler was the Sun God, who in at least one Classic depiction mediated disputes from his seat on a jaguar-pelted throne (Stuart and Stuart 1993: 171). At a somewhat later time, in Colonial Tzotzil, "majesty"— and, revealingly, "tyrant"—equated to the "hot breath, air or wind" (*k'ak'al ik'*) that emanated from the king (Laughlin 1988, 2: 558). The connection of ruler to the sun's presence and its movements help explain the orientation and processional layout of Mesoamerican palaces or causeways. Practically, their relation to the sun would assist in keeping rooms cool and courtly tableaux visible; symbolically, human motion could be tethered explicitly to that of the sun and other celestial bodies.

According to Nahuatl and Classic Maya data, the locus of the blazing royal presence was the forehead, the place wrapped by the royal diadem that also served as the customary platform for display of identity (Houston and Stuart 1998: 83; López Austin 1988, 1: 172). In Aztec and Classic Maya thought, the head was where the *tonalli* or its Maya equivalent lodged and where "name or reputation" shined forth (Furst 1995: 110; León-Portilla 1992: 169–170). It was also part of the social skin that could be modified for display, particularly through body paint and tattooing. Classic Maya figurines and the notoriously deformed foreheads of Classic-era skeletons illustrate this practice. Moreover, if doorways of palaces were "mouths," a pan-Mesoamerican metaphor in Pre-Columbian, Colonial, and ethnographic sources, then the mansard roofs and cornice façades in palaces represented the "foreheads" and "headdresses" that individuated buildings. Cranial modification was, according to several Mexican sources, a positive act that created valiant and morally balanced men (López Austin 1988, 1: 194, 361). Among the Classic Maya, such deformation also likened humans explicitly to the beauty of the high-browed maize god, whose material substance was, according to many accounts, magically transformed into human flesh (Taube 1993: 67).

[4] A theology of celestial light logically attends powerful figures. Consider, in an Old World context, the description of God in Isaiah 60:20: "Thy sun shall no more go down; neither shall thy moon withdraw itself: for the Lord shall be thine everlasting light."

Fig. 1 Jade "flowers" worn as jewelry, Chichén Itzá cenote (Proskouriakoff 1974: pl. 40)

The social skin of royal bodies in Mesoamerica was manipulated in numerous ways. Clothing is relevant here, but its meaning needs further study, especially for the Classic Maya period, when the pictorial data are richest (cf. Anawalt 1981: 173–191; Taylor 1983). In general, for the Maya, these ornaments were not "sets of clothing to be donned in entirety, but assemblages painstakingly arranged and rearranged" (Strathern 1979: 245). Individual decisions doubtless entered into decoration but as channeled by ideal public roles (Gell 1975: 192–193). Recently, David Stuart has made a compelling case that much of the jade ornament worn by Maya lords reproduced the intricate botanical structure of flowers (personal communication, 1994) (Fig. 1). For all Mesoamerican peoples, flowers and their exquisite fragrances associated most closely with aesthetic discernment, eloquence, and merriment—all emblematic of pleasurable, elite life as Mesoamericans understood it (Garibay 1993, 1: 20–42); in the Maya 20-day calendar, not surprisingly, the equivalent of Central Mexican *xochitl,* "flower," was *ajaw,* "lord." But Aztec rhapsodizing about flowers also stressed that, like life, flowers and the joyful senses passed quickly, to be savored despite their brevity. Maya ornament subverted this fatalism by making the impermanent permanent on the body of lords; this was also done by means of tattooing, which an ethnohistoric source described as a way of "converting [the body] into flowers" (Thompson 1946: 22). The Mesoamerican palace, as discussed in this volume by a variety of authors, especially Andrews, Harrison, Inomata, and Webster, represented much the same thinking, since the building or buildings replaced common wood and thatch buildings that lasted only a generation or two with a series of massive, enduring structures. The use of jade flowers also underscored a general observation about Mesoamerican identity, that it derived from the blending of internal attributes with external accouterments: again, the social skin declared internal properties (Burkhart 1997: 45). This held true for the practice of wrapping royalty and their processed bodies in jaguar skin, a predatory creature with whom the lords presumably wished to link themselves symbolically. Similarly, among Nahua-speaking peoples, individuals with special markings, such as double cowlicks, ruddy complexions, or albinism, were thought to possess unusual powers and were more likely to be sacrificed (López Austin 1988, 1: 360).

The flowery metaphor, which led Mesoamericans to garnish the body of the ruler with botanical forms, brings another metaphor to mind. In Mesoamerica, cosmologies often described the forced separation of earth and sky, a rupture maintained by world trees and other mythological supports (López Austin 1997: 10–11). Many scholars have previously commented, perhaps in an overstated manner given the quality of our evidence, on the body of Classic Maya rulers as *axes mundi*, poles that centered the cosmos around their orbit and participated in the maintenance of world order (e.g., Freidel, Schele, and Parker 1993: 137). In Nahuatl poetry, linkages of rulers to precious, flowery trees are plentiful (Garibay 1993, 2: 2, 22). The identity of this vegetation cannot be clearer, in that it corresponded to the fragrant trees of paradise (Tlalolcan and Tamoanchan) that suckled human souls and whose flowers were poets and poetry (López Austin 1997: 118). Around this central tree were four others, each contributing to the quincunx plan that signaled centrality (López Austin 1997: 223); the branches presumably shielded and protected lesser beings, including plebeians. Such trees were symbolically directional yet also structurally stabilizing in that they assisted the central node in separating earth and sky. As such, they represented natural models for ancillary lords at court, an evocation suggested by quadripartite arrangements of royal names in Aztec poetry (e.g., Garibay 1993, 1: 26). The ruler as tree clearly established itself as the body of centrality that ordered space vertically and horizontally. In terms of others' perception, too, he was not only central, but elevated, from which a gradient of humanity flowed: "in public eye, he lives on high . . . He knows there is no one above him, he experiences nothing over him. He alone goes before, he alone is in front" (Maxwell and Hanson 1992: 176). In palaces, then, one would expect such centrality and verticality to be enhanced by architectural means, for palaces would logically and necessarily combine absolute and egocentric space in the person of the ruler.

But the tree-as-ruler had a paradoxical quality. According to Aztec maxims of wisdom, it was something that sprouted, rooted, or germinated itself (Maxwell and Hanson 1992: 183). Elsewhere in these statements are references to the ruler both as a plant that grows and as an agent that furrows, sows, and implants (Maxwell and Hanson 1992: 170, 181). The Aztecs evidently conceived of the use of the digging stick as the primordial masculine activity, which wounded mother earth through slashing, sexual motions, if with fruitful results (López Austin 1988, 1: 347–348). It was thus an ideal example of the pattern described by Maurice Bloch, who emphasized the elite appropriation of common activity as a strategy for buttressing royal authority.[5] In much the same way, Nahuatl poetry contains an expression that openly likened rule to sowing (Maxwell and Hanson 1992: 183). David

---

[5] This pattern applies to another metaphor for rule, the king as "bearer" of burdensome tasks and gods (Maxwell and Hanson 1992: 170; Schroeder 1991: 170–171).

Stuart and Stephen Houston have considered that this may explain the principal means by which Classic Maya lords declared agency or supervision. This glyphic phrase often occurred after initial acts by others and plausibly reads: *u-chab'/kab'-i?-jiiy* (U-CHAB'/KAB'-ji-ya), a locution remarkably similar to one attested in Colonial Tzotzil, *chabi*, "govern," based in turn on a root meaning to "cultivate, plow" (Laughlin 1988, 1: 184; see also the Nahuatl expression *cuitlahui*, meaning both "to care for, raise someone; to fertilize the soil with manure," Karttunen 1983: 73). In the cycle of Mesoamerican agriculture, digging was the act that initiated all such production in conjunction with the "hot, dry, fiery, and solar beings of the dry season" (López Austin 1997: 191, 193)—note again the linkage of rulers and heat. The act of sowing constituted a central act of agency and an appropriate conception of royal action. The ruler "cultivated" not in the field, but in the palace and adjacent architectonic spaces. Palace work was, in a sense, a form of royal horticulture, a concept recalling the Inca practice of tending golden "plants" in the ceremonial gardens of Cuzco.

The social skin of rulers absorbed many changes. Body paint, mentioned in many ethnohistoric accounts, particularly for Postclassic Yucatan, involved the application of bright clays for battle display or, in the case of women, red as a fragrant unguent (Tozzer 1941: 49, 219); the Aztecs connected yellow pigments to beautiful women (Berdan and Anawalt 1997: 146). Not all "inkwells" functioned solely as mixing surfaces for scribes, but may have been used for preparation of body paints (Inomata 1997: 346). According to Diego de Landa, young men adorned themselves with black paint until their marriage, when they were entitled to tattooing: in Yucatan the black accompanied fasting and abnegation, perhaps as part of youthful *rites de passage* (Tozzer 1941: 89). Blue, a common pigment on Classic Maya figurines, had sacred associations, and, to judge from early Colonial documents, the act of smearing it seemed almost as important as its final, lustrous appearance on the body (Tozzer 1941: 159); this alone would suggest that figurines in Classic Maya centers were not so much toys as venerated objects (Schele 1997: 17). The rich images from the Classic Maya show an abundance of body painting, as part of a semiosis of color that has yet to be studied comprehensively, but which may involve subtle keys to standardized emotions, projected qualities, or states of being (MacLaury 1997: 36–37; Sahlins 1976; Strathern 1979: 245).

A brief survey of body paint does not reveal many invariant patterns, although a few tendencies can be seen. Foreheads, lips, and eyes receive the most body paint. The lower body appears with designs on "hot spots," which correspond to the thighs, arms, and torso, in areas where the Maya and earlier Mesoamerican groups attached celt fetishes (Karl Taube, personal communication, 1995; e.g., Kerr 1990: 255, 267). Name glyphs or titular glyphs also occur (Fig. 2) (Kerr 1990: 245; Kerr 1994: 640), especially on women. In some instances, women have the reverse of masculine body paint, on the shoulders and back of the head (Kerr 1994: 650–651). Still, painting schemes do not correlate exclusively with rulers, but may have been contingent on changing ceremonial roles or sheer personal whim.

Painting was fleeting. Less so were the body modifications described by Colonial sources and evident in Pre-Columbian representations. For the Classic Maya the most perplexing consisted of thick, pockmarked "skin" placed over the chin and buccal areas

Fig. 2 Name glyphs painted as body ornament, Late Classic Maya (Kerr # 2573; Kerr 1990: 245)

(Schele 1997: 69–73, 93, 139). It is possible that these represent Maya analogs, found only on men, of the flayed skins worn by Xipe impersonators in Postclassic Mexico; these skin flaps may have been extracted along with the captives' jawbones that occasionally festooned Maya warriors in Classic art (Kerr 1997: 759). The Maya also practiced extensive scarification. The lavish care associated with surface ornament and clothing and the violence commonly linked to tattooing and body scarification would seem, cross-culturally, to protect and define the body in direct proportion to the difficulty and pain of these procedures (Gell 1993: 35). The presence of pricked, bulging brows linked to deities may point to the co-essences or companion spirits of certain lords, which tattooing is known ethnohistorically to indicate (Thompson 1946: 21).

Another form of mutilation, the insertion of labrets and earspools, can be seen not so much as mere ornament, or status markers, as emphatic declarations about the sensory powers of lords. Among the Kayapo of the Amazon, earplugs symbolize "the socialisation of understanding" (as in the noble *orejones* or "big ears" of Inca civilization), and labrets or lip ornaments convey an "ornate and blustering" style of public speaking that comes to mature men (Turner 1980: 120–121). The elaborate gold labrets of Central Mexico depict snakes or raptors and may well have designated the kinds of speech expected of lordly figures (Fig. 3). Certainly in children they bore witness to covenants between children and gods (López Austin 1988, 1, 288); labrets could be easily changed depending on the sociolinguistic context. Dental filings and inlays, of jade or hematite, too, may have referred to some aspect of speech, or they may have transformed and purified inhalations. Earspools potentially betokened kinds of discernment, or anticipated and channeled the statements the royal ear wished to receive.

Fig. 3 Mixtec gold labrets, American Museum of Natural History (Pasztory 1983: color pl. 15)

The emphasis on royal speech reflected a notion of speech as agentive or "actuating force" (Blier 1995: 316). Royal titles, too, stressed the connection between forceful, public speech and governance: Nahuatl *tlahtoani* stemmed from a term "to speak, to issue proclamations and commands" (Karttunen 1983: 266); *ajaw* may have derived from **aj-aw*, "he of the shout, shouter" (Houston and Stuart 1996: 295); and Colonial Tzotzil tells us that *k'opoj*, "speak," means the same as "become a lord" (Laughlin 1988, 2: 569). Among the Mixtec of Mexico, the forceful speech of *caciques* (the title of local lords) was conceived in terms of heat, a notion consistent with the "hot," solar bodies of lords (John Monaghan, personal communication, October 1998). The very notion of the lord as a "speaker" was itself a corporeal reference, the lord serving as the head of the corporate entity he represented. When that lord died the Nahuatl peoples claimed that the lower classes became mute (López Austin 1988, 1: 390).[6] The removal of the jawbone, a customary practice in Mesoamerica with war captives, may have symbolically incapacitated them for further speech. Also present was a refined notion of synesthesia, a mental notion of one sense—speech and sound—being stimulated by another—the sight of labrets and earplugs. The same concept undergirded the speech scrolls that occur throughout Mesoamerican art (Houston and Taube 2000).

Bodily processes were just as important for another sense, that of royal sight. In Classic Maya writing the glyph for "see" was an eyeball that depicts two twirling lines, looping out

---

[6] The idea that the ruler is part of a corporate body makes sense of Nahuatl statements that rulers are "locks of hair of the people, nails of the people" (López Austin 1988, 1: 392), that is, the body parts that grow aggressively despite being cut. It is probably no coincidence that the principal Mesoamerican image of capture involves the grasping of hair, a token of vitality (see Winter 1996: 13, for Mesopotamian beard-cutting as an abridgment of an enemy's vital force).

Fig. 4 Maize god "born from the eye" (Kerr # 2723; Kerr 1990: 275)

to embrace that which was seen. These lines, which sometimes erupt from the pupil, bear a striking similarity to a convention meaning birth, and, indeed, as David Stuart has pointed out (personal communication, 1995), there is one mythological episode in which the maize god, in the reclining position of a newborn, springs forth from the eye of a disembodied head (Kerr 1990: 275); the glyphs state that the figure is "he who is born from the secretion" (a–si–ya–i–chi) (Fig. 4). In Classic Maya practice, the king who "sees" was also the king who validated an event by his presence.

The link to birth is intriguing. It is possible that, for the Maya, sight was essentially a creative or even procreative act, that the existence of an event depended on its apprehension by the lord. For the Nahuatl peoples, too, the eye served as "our total leader, torch, light, clarity, spectator, what we live by . . . it illumines peoples, it lights the way for people, it directs" (López Austin 1988, 1: 177); in the Codex Mendoza, pictorial conventions for sight and for establishing conceptual connections between tableaux were one–and–the–same (Berdan and Anawalt 1997: 147, 180). Moreover, in one Colonial Maya language, to "rise in status" was to "have 'one's eyes open'" (Laughlin 1988, 2: 557). Ethnographic Tzotzil have a keen understanding that "seeing" is a species of "insight," to be collected by cargo holders as they undertake ritual circuits (Vogt 1993: 205). The power of royal sight may also explain why only a few Aztec lords were allowed or able to gaze into the eyes of a Tenochca ruler (López Austin 1988, 1: 399). Such glances could be seen as potentially dangerous emanations.

The great importance of royal sight and perception is underscored by the occurrence in Maya script of a glyphic compound reading *y-ichnal*, cognate with Yucatec Maya *y-iknal* (David Stuart, personal communication, 1987; Hanks 1990: 90–95; Houston and Taube 2000: fig. 22). This term concerns "the body as it engages in movement and action" that is "related to an agent the way one's shadow or perceptual field is" (Hanks 1990: 90, 91). Space within the *y-ichnal* is morally qualified, back and left being "bad," front and right "good" (Hanks 1990: fig. 3.2). William Hanks, who first discussed it ethnographically, was describing all egocentric forms of spatial reference. According to glyphic evidence, however, the body frame for the Classic Maya was unambiguously royal or supernatural, and space was "moral" with respect to the royal body as it moved or remained in one place. To judge from glyphic contexts, the state of being within the royal *y-ichnal* gave great weight to royal agency and supervision. It follows that the places occupied by the royal body—palaces—must be understood in terms of this perceptual field. The emphasis on speech should also prompt more attention to the acoustic study of palaces (see Sennett [1993: 52–61] on the "heat of words" in "spaces to speak" within Periklean Athens).

Much of what we have discussed so far relates the royal body to perception, transformable skin, and self-image. But time has not yet been implicated. Here the royal body achieves a unique prominence, for it can be seen as that of time itself (Stuart 1996: 166–168). In Maya usage, the royal body appears within day cartouches corresponding to *ajaw*, "lord." The day sign *ajaw* corresponds to the seating and wrapping of stone monuments—it presides over points of disjunction in the calendar, and its renewal within a fresh cycle of dates stands metaphorically for the renewal of kingship itself (Stuart 1996: 167). Time afterward is literally regarded as "on its back," as though dates faced earlier time (Stuart 1990: 9). Conversely, this expression could mean that the time elapsed between *ajaw* day signs formed the back or spine of embodied time. A central Mexican representation of much later date (and conceptually Pre-Columbian, according to Alfredo López Austin) shows body parts connected to day signs (López Austin 1988: 1: 348). At work here are notions that, through their bodies, Maya lords defined the very fabric of space and time.

The Royal Body in the Andes

In the Andean region, as elsewhere, the body of the ruling lord performed simultaneously in multiple fields of social, political, and religious domains. Legitimacy came about through the bodily medium of the living ruler, who, in variant ways, according to different systems of knowledge, expressed the essence of dynastic sovereignty (Kantorowicz 1957; Marin 1988). The body of the ruler and its interplay with dynastic relations required a specialized architectural setting in which prescribed rituals could be enacted, specific objects manipulated, and particular representations displayed. Sequential building programs such as at Chan Chan may have marked succession, or the amplification of already standing structures such as at Sipán may have fulfilled the same architectural purpose (Alva and Donnan 1993: 43–55; Kolata 1990: 107–144; Pillsbury and Leonard, this volume). There is also evidence among the Inca in Cuzco that a series of buildings, called palaces by the Spaniards, was sequentially built (Gasparini and Margolies 1980). However, they do not have any special nomenclature, nor do they play a prominent role in foundation myths. Rather, the creation of the plaza, by draining the marsh area, constitutes the primordial royal architectural act. Typologically the palaces were simply termed *hatun wasi* or "big house." This implies the notion of a greater scale as discussed by Salazar and Burger (this volume), but not a differentiation of architectural form. These "palaces" in turn were given the name of the Sapa Inca who may have lived in them.[7]

---

[7] For example, this is the term that Franciso de Avila translates as palace from the Quechua in his sermons: "Chaymantari llapam ymahincacaccapas ppuchucan, manam yntallapas tacyanchu. Maymi cunan ñaupachica manchafcca Yncacuna? Maymi collqquen, ccorin? Toccapuccompincuna, aqquillan, qquerun, chacran, hatunhuacin, huarmincuna? Mana ñam futillantapas yachachicchhtlu" (Avila 1648: 43).

Unlike Aztec, Maya, and perhaps Moche examples, Inca legitimacy was not reiterated on these buildings or on any others in Tawantinsuyu through sculpted or painted images of dynastic ancestors or their mythic/ritual roles. The living ruler did not see himself through the representation of someone or something absent. Rather, among the Inca, the living ruler sat in the plaza between and at the head of the two rows of the actual bodies of his ancestors (Isbell 1997: 38–68). Through his actions the Inca dominated an architectural space designed and still literally occupied by his predecessors. The phenomenological presence of the ruler's ancestors embodied by their adorned and desiccated corpses obviated the need to distinguish between representation and what was being represented in terms of portrait. At one level of understanding, the mummies as the actual bodies of past rulers were therefore pre-iconic in a Piercean sense. The representation of the ancestor was the body of the ancestor, someone who once had been as living as the present ruler. The mummies were not portraits of the ancestors in the sense that they *stood* for the body of the ancestor—they *were* the body of the ancestor.[8] At the same time, the mummies were indexical in that they sat in dynamic relation to the body of the living ruler: the message seemed to be, "what the ruler is now he will become and within the same space of this plaza." The mummy was also indexical to the ancestor: it constituted what remained of the temporal and animate being whose actions were told in the oral histories recounted before the body (Hanks 1996: 39–54; Pierce 1955: 107). As a mummy, it also represented the corporate memory of the Inca as heads of their lineage group, *panaca*, each of which had become a fixed political entity with defined estates. Yet, having experienced death—however death was conceived by the Inca—these bodies were not equivalent to that of the present ruler, just as there was a difference between the estates of the dead and those of living rulers. The property and material goods of the living ruler were in flux, whereas those of the dead were conceived of as static. Nor was the present ruler the same as the ancestors: he occupied the space of the plaza and the palaces as a living corporeal being and therefore functioned as a generative agent; in contrast, the mummies sat in the plaza as inert exemplars of a sociopolitical unit.

The architectural framing of regal space therefore did not necessarily consist in some kind of restricted access to interior rooms of the *hatun wasi* by which the sacred body of the ruler was staged in a process of revelation.[9] Nor was it a tomb that formed the spatial context of the deceased. Rather, as an aggregate, the exterior walls of buildings belonged to the palaces of the living and dead rulers and marked the area of the plaza in which these multileveled relations could be enacted. Within this public space, the ritual disposition of the ancestors and ruler spatially formed a relational expression of hierarchy, kinship, and legitimacy. The mummies were seated in two parallel rows, and the living, active body of the Sapa Inca was seated at the center. His body constituted an axis around which

---

[8] Each Inca dynastic member had a totemic other called *huauques* or "brother." As Maarten van de Guchte has demonstrated, these sculptures were not simply state images of the king's authority. They were his double, composed of parts of him (van de Guchte 1996: 256–268).

[9] This does not mean that the sacred person of the Inca was immediately approachable. Accounts of the first meeting with Atahualpa outside Cajamarca record that he was hidden behind a curtain of fine cloth.

Fig. 5 Illustration from Martín de Murúa's *Historia general del Perú* (1613). J. Paul Getty Museum, Los Angeles, MS Ludwig XIII 16.

sociopolitical space was organized and the various temporalities were represented. Here the embodiment of Inca origins and mythic history came face to face with the present.[10] But since the generative body of the living Inca was the focal point for this spatial and temporal organization, the center of Tawantinsuyu was not, in theory, the fixed geographical site of Cuzco. Instead, the living body of the ruling Inca *was* Cuzco and Cuzco *was* the living Inca. At the very beginning of the Conquest, Spaniards believed the title of the Inca emperor to be Cuzco (Pease 1990: 193). This may have been a simple misunderstanding, but the fact that it existed implies that Cuzco and the body of the living Inca ruler were equally indexical of a concept that intersected place and being. Similar concepts that link body and place occur ethnographically in Bolivia, where distortions in landscapes prompt human illness, and vice versa (Bastien 1985: 596–598).

The ruling Inca's body therefore may have literally embodied the center of whatever conceptually united Tawantinsuyu as a sociopolitical and cultural entity. Wherever he existed or materialized, so too did the center of Tawantinsuyu, and thus there could be a multitude of palaces throughout the empire that became activated through the presence of the Sapa Inca, or perhaps something that had belonged to him. At least this is how one can interpret a watercolor illustration from the 1613 version of Martín de Murúa's manuscript, *Historia general del Perú* (Fig. 5). The Inca is seated aloft in a litter born on the shoulders of

[10] Similar configurations of seated bodies expressing distinctions and hierarchies are still used in the Andes (Urton 1992: 245–252).

Fig. 6 Stirrup spout vessel with "Presentation Theme"/"Sacrifice Ceremony"
of the Moche, Staatliches Museum für Völkerkunde, Munich

four individuals. This is perhaps how most local lords were carried throughout Peru, but
the best descriptions come from the north coast (Ramírez 1996: 20–24; Rostworowski
1961: 15–21). Here the local lords who visited subject communities were carried on litters
and surrounded by a retinue of musicians and servants. The empty litter is also a significant
iconographic element in the "Presentation Theme"/"Sacrifice Ceremony" of the Moche, a
subject to which we shall return (Fig. 6). However, within the colonial narrative of con-

Fig. 7 Inca ruler Atahualpa prior to being seized by Spaniards, from the frontis-
piece of Cristóbal de Mena, *La conquista del Perú llamada la nueva Castilla* (1534)

quest and the violent transfer of power, the litter was the last autonomous royal space from
which the Inca ruler Atahualpa was seized and pulled into the world of European conquest
(Fig. 7). What is important about this act of conquest is the fact that the Inca ruler neither
received the Spaniards in the "capital city" of Cuzco nor in a royal structure in Cajamarca.
Unlike Moctezuma and the unfolding of his dethroning, there is no architectural structure
that frames the events in Tawantinsuyu.

Looking at Murúa's illustration again, we see the Inca seated in a litter and wearing the *mascaipacha* or royal fringe. The four figures carrying the litter are each dressed differently. This is not incidental. By their dress, each figure personifies one of the four parts of Tawantinsuyu. For example, the figure representing Antisuyu carries a bow and sports three long red feathers of some type of jungle bird. The dress of the other figures includes the conical hat of Collasuyu. The point is that we know that the Inca leader was often obliged to travel forth from Cuzco. In doing so, the center of the Tawantinsuyu may have conceptually shifted to wherever his body was transported (Martínez Cereceda 1995). Of course, this is a colonial image, but it exemplifies certain concepts about the nature of the Inca's body and space. And if the Spaniards confused the nature of Cuzco and the Inca sovereign in the early stages of the Conquest, might not this concept have been part of that confusion?

Whether or not Inca rulership was based on a succession of individual rulers similar to European dynastic history, or whether there was some form of dual rulership, originating in the moiety structure of Andean social organization, is not crucial to our description (Zuidema 1964; Wachtel 1973). Even within dual authority in the Andes, there was one body that embodied the pinnacle of the sociopolitical hierarchy (Garcilaso de la Vega 1943 [1609], bk. 1, chap. 24). This was spatially recognized in seating arrangements as well as ritual actions. Clearly, among the Inca, one individual held precedence. It was through this body that the ritual center was configured, in terms of a conceptual center as in Cuzco or in the spatial axis of the seated mummies in the plaza. Among the Inca the title for that corporeal body was the *Sapa Inca*. The term *Sapa* implies uniqueness within the corporate body of the Inca.

Yet how does the living body of an Andean ruler become marked through social institutions and iconographic forms? How does it differ from other bodies or, for that matter, those of the ancestors? To judge from the recent discoveries at Sipán, the Moche leader assumed the persona of a key mythic figure, embodying a critical element of a foundational narrative that not only was orally recounted, and perhaps reenacted, but that was pictorially replicated in various media (Fig. 8). The cosmic relationship between the living individual and rulership was identified through the mythic character, an identification that was achieved by impersonation, a pattern present, if in differing ways, within Mesoamerica (Houston and Stuart 1996: 297–299). The assumption of this role in life was probably performed through rituals of accession: the right to dress in these iconographic signs transformed the body from that of an individual to a sacred being incarnate. The possibility of transformation was already latent in the body of the individual, which inevitably experienced its own life-cycle changes. A similar process of impersonation may account for Wari-Tiahuanaco textile designs that place the wearer within the center of an iconographic program recalling the central figure on the Gateway of the Sun at Tiahuanaco (Fig. 9).

Thus the Inca leader may have embodied the center of Tawantinsuyu. It may also be the case that some *uncus* (tunics), such as the Dumbarton Oaks piece, centered the Inca's body within an abstract representation of the empire. Yet there is no pictorial correlation between Inca iconography as based on mythic narrative and the ritual paraphernalia mark-

Fig. 8 Presentation Theme, Pañamarca

Fig. 9 View of the Gateway of the Sun at
Tiahuanaco, and detail of central figure

ing the specialness of the ruler's body (Cummins n.d.). The body of the Inca ruler did not assume a persona of impersonation that was categorically identical to that in which all other rulers appeared and acted. True, the living being of the Inca was semi-divine, claiming to be the son of the sun. But the Inca ruler did not impersonate the sun in the fashion that a Moche lord might impersonate a mythic being. The Sapa Inca, nonetheless, was marked as both unique in relation to all others and was connected through objects of investiture to the mythic origins of the Inca.

In this context, it is useful to focus on the body of the Sapa Inca as it was transformed by the coronation ritual. We are fortunate in having a number of Spanish eyewitness accounts of the investiture of the last Inca crowned in Cuzco. These descriptions are not in themselves insightful or sensitive to Inca beliefs, but with other colonial texts they permit a more interpretive account to be assembled. The event witnessed by the Spaniards took place in Cuzco's plaza in 1534, or less than two years after Atahualpa had been pulled from his litter. This time the heir to the throne, Manco Capac, was carried into the plaza on a litter along with the mummies of his ancestors. They were seated on their *tianas* (low seats) in two rows; the heir to the throne sat at the center. Feasting and other events continued for a month; however, at some unrecorded point, two related rituals occurred that marked the body of the Sapa Inca as a distinct being.

During the first day of the celebration, the new Sapa Inca, Manco Capac, took a new name, becoming Manco Inca (Betanzos 1996 [1557]: 278). At the same time he was invested with special emblems of sovereignty. His head received the *mascaipacha* or red woolen fringe that hung from a headband and over his forehead (Fig. 10). To either side of the fringe was a white feather. The individual red tassels of the *mascaipacha* are said to represent the heads of *curacas* (lords) of nations brought forcibly under the suzerainty of Tawantinsuyu (Murúa 1613, 1: chap. 9, 35; Zuidema 1983a: 69–70). The two feathers, one taken from the right wing of a male *corequenque* bird, the other from the left wing of a female *corequenque*, symbolized the moiety division of *hanan* and *hurin* (Esquivel y Navía 1980 [1750], 1: 20: Garcilaso de la Vega 1943 [1609–17]: bk. 6: chap. 28: 63–64). As such, the physical head of the Sapa Inca became the metaphysical embodiment of Tawantinsuyu's political and social organization.

The new ruler was also given two other objects called *tupa yauri* and *tupa cusi*. *Tupa* means "anything royal that touches the king" (González Holguín 1989 [1608]: 347). Unlike the *mascaipacha*, these two objects were not, as a class of objects, the unique prerogative of the Sapa Inca; however, as these particular objects belonged only to the sovereign, they were called *tupa*. Moreover, as a royal category of objects, they were not the personal property of the new Inca. Rather, they were "heirlooms" that had come through the hands of all the mummies that sat with the new lord. That is, they were the ultimate manifestation of *tupa* as they had touched the body of every king. The possession of them now situated the body of the new Sapa Inca into the narrative of the Inca's divine origins. The specific names of these objects refer to the items given by Viracocha to the dynastic founder, Manco Capac.

Fig. 10 "Royal Arms of the Inca" with *mascaipacha* in upper left quadrant. Martín de Murúa *Historia general del Perú* (1613). J. Paul Getty Museum, Los Angeles, MS Ludwig XIII 16.

The *tupa yauri* was the scepterlike staff. Shaped like a pickax, the same type of ritual weapon, called simply *yauri*, was given to the Sapa Inca as heir to the throne when he was initiated into manhood during the *huarachicui* ceremony.[11] As the *yauri* was placed in the heir's hands, those who were gathered around him gave the cry *aucacunapac*. *Aucacunapac* meant "for tyrants, traitors, the cruel, the treacherous, and disloyal" (Cieza de León 1967 [1554]: chap. 27, 62). The relation of the heir's *yauri* and the red woolen fringe of his future crown was clarified when the youth was required to run up a mountain slope to show that he was fleet and brave in war. On coming back down, he carried the *yauri* that had tied to it a bit of wool as a sign that he would take the hair and heads of his enemy in battle (Cieza de León 1967 [1554]: chap. 7, 21). The *tupa yauri* given to the new ruler at his coronation was a symbolic weapon representing in general the Inca's military conquest and control that was commanded by the Sapa Inca and symbolized by the unique fringe of his *mascaipacha*.[12]

The second object given to the Sapa Inca represented the benevolent, peaceful, and productive aspects of the state. It was the pair of golden *aquillas*, called *tupa cusi* (Murúa 1613, 1: chap. 22, 54; Santa Cruz Pachacuti 1993 [ca. 1615]: 214; Murúa terms the vessels

[11] According to Titu Cusi Yupanqui, the *tupa yauri* or royal *yauri* was made of gold, whereas those received by the other Inca youths were a mixture of copper and silver ([1570]: 69; see also Larrea 1960a).

[12] Juan Larrea (1960a) demonstrates that the *yauri* was not an actual weapon but was related to the ritual *tumi* knife. He further suggests that the *mascaipacha's* shape derived from the shape of the *tumi* blade (Larrea 1960b: 129–132).

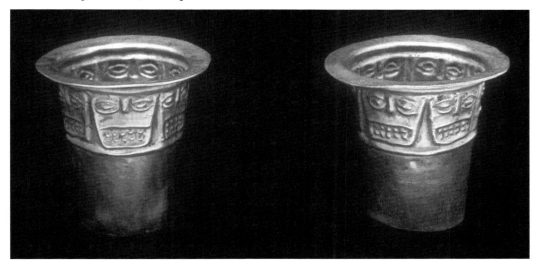

Fig. 11 Pair of golden *aquillas*

tupa cusi napa) (Fig. 11). Like the *tupa yauri*, a similar set of *aquillas* had previously been given to the heir as well as to all other Inca males during their initiation ceremony. At this time the *aquillas* were used by the youths to toast Inca deities and relatives, as well as each other so as to express the social bonds of *hanan* and *hurin* by which they were divided. The *tupa cusi aquillas* given to the new emperor were, however, like the *tupa yauri*, an emblem of royal investiture. Santa Cruz Pachacuti, for example, says that Inca Yupanqui "at last died, and he left his son Ingaruca in command of his state, as his oldest son and heir, giving to him in his hand the *topa yauri*, *topa cusi*, and crown as sign of leaving (him) the kingdom."[13]

At the same time that the new Inca ruler acknowledged his mythic descent by taking possession of these objects, he set himself apart from each of the previous lineages. At the moment of his coronation he left his own descent group and formed his own *panaca*. He began by folding in on himself and becoming fully independent of all alliances. He took his body out of social circulation upon his accession to the throne by marrying the closest living being to himself, his sister. Almost all accounts of Inca history credit the dynastic founder, Manco Capac, with originating royal sister-marriage, but the Inca explained away their inability to follow his example out of their necessity to continue expected patterns of marriage exchange. José de Acosta says that this type of incestuous marriage was relatively new in Tawantinsuyu and that it was Pachacuti's son, Tupac Inca Yupanqui, who was the first Inca to marry his full sister.[14] Other chroniclers record that Inca rulers prior to Tupac Inca Yupanqui

---

[13] "al fin se murió y dexó a su hijo Ingaruca en el señorío de su estado como a hijo mayor y eredero entregándoles en su mano el topa yauri y topa cussi, y a ttopa pichuc llaotta [mascaipacha], en señal de dejación del reino" (Santa Cruz Pachacuti 1993 [ca. 1615]: 214; see also Murúa [1613]).

[14] For references, see Acosta (1940 [1590], 6: chap. 18, 488), Vaca de Castro (1974 [1542–44]: 45), and Cobo (1956 [1653], 14: chap. 7, 250). Cobo copied most of his information from Acosta, but he adds that the rest of the Inca nobility could marry their half-sisters and that the Sapa Inca's marriage to his full sister was "muy moderna."

had married their sisters. However, these early incestuous bonds may have been declared retroactively so that, like the mythological union of Manco Capac to his sister, Mama Qoya, they gave legitimacy both to each royal *panaca* and to the new marital institution itself. Regardless of these historical developments, the relaxation of this fundamental exogamic law is relatively rare, and it seems to have fulfilled for the Inca rulership roughly the same function that it did for the other stratified societies of similar sociopolitical development.

In the African societies of the Swazi, Bantu, Lundu, and Luba, for example, royal incest occurs as part of what is termed "sacred kingship." Inca rule can also be termed a "sacred kingship" for a number of similar reasons, not the least of which was the Sapa Inca's claim to be the "son of the sun." The institution of royal incest in both African and Inca society was used to help elevate the corporeal body of the ruler to this status. The marriage was one of the primary and constitutive signs of power. It joined within a single act permitted only to the sovereign the contradictory states of social belonging and social separation that are inherent aspects of rulership in early state societies (see above).[15]

As a sign of social cohesion or belonging, African royal incest was not necessarily meant to produce a superior stratum of rulers because the heirs to the throne were not the sons of the brother/sister marriage and neither were the Inca heirs. Rather, the marriage referred to the cosmic powers of fertility and fecundity that were attributed to this exceptional union. In Inca mythology, fertility was associated with the paradigmatic incestuous pair of Manco Capac and Mama Qoya. They were credited with leading Andean men and women out of nature into culture by teaching them agriculture and weaving (Garcilaso de la Vega 1943 [1609–17], 1: chap. 16, 42–44). Moreover, all Inca sovereigns presented themselves as the keepers and providers of the people's welfare. Agricultural rituals began with the Inca and his wife as the paradigmatic union whose labor bore fruit throughout Tawantinsuyu. The first plantings were begun by the Sapa Inca and his sister/wife on a field just below Sacsahuaman, the sun temple/fortress above Cuzco (Fig. 12). The incestuous marriage, therefore, benevolently represented the creation of a harmonious world and cosmic order.

At the same time, the marriage denoted separation and difference because the incest prohibition still pertained to everyone else, including all other members of the royal clan. The sole transgression by the sovereign, Sapa Inca, meaning "unique Inca," was a sign of absolute autonomy. He was literally unique, beyond the exogamic rules that structured the rest of society, and, as the embodiment of state power, he was liberated from all dependence on reciprocity. It is therefore not coincidental that the Sapa Inca's coronation and his marriage to his sister occurred together as parts of a single ceremony.[16] The royal investiture

---

[15] Without agreeing with its idealistic conclusions, we base this description of African royal incest and its implications on a study by Marc Abeles (1981: 1–14). The similarity between these African kingdoms and the Inca is not restricted to just the same ideological institution of "sacred kingship." They also share a similar economic structure. This does not mean that other societies with comparable economic structures will also have the same ideological features.

[16] See Cieza de León (1967 [1554]: chap. 7, 22). Santa Cruz Pachacuti describes only two brother/sister marriages, Manco Capac and Mama Coya and Huayna Capac and Coya Mama Cuçi Rimay. Only in the latter case does he say that the coronation and marriage took place on the same day (Santa Cruz Pachacuti 1993 [ca. 1615]: 243).

Fig. 12   Sapa Inca sowing the first field,
Guaman Poma (ca. 1613), *Nueva corónica
y buen gobierno*, folio 260

politically set the Sapa Inca's body above all others, and the marriage placed him outside all
kinship ties that were at the base of *ayllu* community reciprocity. Therefore, upon assuming
the throne, each new Sapa Inca left his father's *panaca*, the lineage into which he had been
born, and began a new one. His body became socially and politically active against the inert
bodies of his ancestors and their wealth. His brothers, sisters, and other close relatives remained within their father's *panaca*; although not inheriting rule, they retained all the wealth
that the dead Sapa Inca had accumulated during his reign. Like the Lere king in Africa, who
incestuously married but without the customary bridewealth, the new Sapa Inca and his
sister/bride had no claim to the wealth of their father's clan.[17] Instead, such riches had to
be accumulated through the means accorded to a living ruler: conquest and agricultural
expansion. At this level the brother/sister marriage signified that the position of the sovereign was absolute and outside the reciprocity of Andean society expressed in the normal
patterns of marriage exchange.[18]

[17] "...tenían por ley ... que el Señor (Sapa Inca) que dellos señoría le embalsamban ... y a estos Señores
les dejaban todo el servicio que habian tenido que vida ... y tenian señaladas sus provincias que les diesen
sustentos. El señor que entraba a governar se habia de servir de nuebos criados; las vajillas habían de ser de palo
y de barro hasta en tanto quel las hiciese de oro y plata y *siempre se aventajaban los que entraban a governor*"
(Pizarro 1917 [1571]: 42; emphasis ours).

[18] María Rostworowski has argued that the Inca's institution of this incestuous marriage was meant to
secure an orderly transfer of power from one generation to the next. Apart from the fact that it did not—
witness the civil war between Atahualpa and Huascar—the incestuous marriage between brother and sister is

Several interrelated points need to be made. First, this marriage marked the very special sanctity and power of the sovereign, a status accompanied by a number of other unique privileges and signs. His divine status represented the aristocratic class that held sway over Tawantinsuyu. The Sapa Inca's unique marriage was a metonymical device that represented the new state order. Or, as Santa Cruz Pachacuti so succinctly puts it in mythological terms, first Manco Capac married his sister "because not finding his equal and he did not want to end his caste and for the rest it was not permitted in any form [incestuous marriage] because before they prohibited it. And thus he began to make the moral laws for the good government of his people."[19]

The physical body of the Sapa Inca therefore came to embody morally the sociopolitical order of Tawantinsuyu, just as it defined its center. The *hatun wasi* or palace was that place built anywhere in the empire's ceremonial centers that provided an architectural framing, as described by Craig Morris (this volume), for the display and exercise of those dimensions. What are important are the architectural elements of the building itself, its walls and doorways. They articulate spaces of interior and exterior action and interaction in which the body of the Sapa Inca is always central, as emphasized in the passage by Murúa as cited by Morris. The unadorned walls become unnoticed in Murúa's description, except for the artistry of the masonry, an observation that is not only textual but also pictorial in Murúa's 1590 manuscript. And therefore, although they are illustrations of the text, that is not what is at issue. The walls of the Inca palaces are rendered stark and unadorned, just as there is a sparseness of architectural description in the text. Only the yellow of the *ichu* grass roof gives color to the otherwise gray color of the stone (Fig. 13). In other words, the descriptive emphasis of Murúa's text finds resonance in the nature of the watercolors' depiction. It is the correspondence between modes of observation and the absence of decorative detail that ensures our understanding of Inca palaces as organizing structures for the actions and representations of the Sapa Inca and that do not represent themselves as anything more or less.

Conclusion

In both Mesoamerica and the Andes, the royal body gives particular meaning to the spaces it occupies. The properties, perceptions, and image of the royal presence establish fields of interaction that globally encompass other bodies. In a point relevant to other contributions to this volume, it follows that the ruler's presence symbolically transforms palatial space while the royal body walks through corridors, over plazas, up stairways, and across platforms. In both Mesoamerica and the Andes, the regal frame had to be made into

---

such a radical disjunction in social conventions that its practice carries much more profound significance, as we have argued, than merely being a means of producing a clearly defined heir to the throne (Rostworowski 1960: 417–427).

[19] "por no aber hallado su ygual, lo uno por no perder la casta y a los demás no los consentieron por ningún modo, que antes lo prohebieron, y assí començó poner leyes morales para el buen gobierno de su gente" (Santa Cruz Pachacuti 1993 [ca. 1615]: 197).

Fig. 13 Inca Palace, Martín de
Murúa, *Historia de la Origen de
los Incas,* 1590, fol 73v, Galvin
collection, Ireland

a body of paradox. Consider: it undertakes at once common yet unique acts. Like other bodies, it wears clothing, but different raiment that encapsulates difference and expresses powerful inner qualities. It senses like mundane bodies, but with elevated discernment. It exists as a body on an earthly plane, but in centered, pivotal, and celestially sustaining fashion. It marries and procreates, yet in ways that violate norms expected of other beings. And, finally, it possesses, not the mere warmth of human bodies, but pure solar fire. The palace that houses the paradoxical body thus becomes a *place* of paradox, the familiar juxtaposed to the unfamiliar, the exotic, the anomalous, and the unsettling. Left for another forum, although partly addressed by Andean information, is the problem of the queen, of making monads out of dyads, and of reconciling unitary and dualistic phenomena (see Joyce 1996). For want of space, this essay also fails to resolve the different royal trajectories of bodily understandings, especially in relation to representation and interlocution with ancestral presences (Houston and Stuart 1996). What unites these disparate data is the evidence of attempts that were palpably successful, from the earliest years of Pre-Columbian kingship to the latest, in achieving singularity in the royal body.

Acknowledgments This chapter has embodied itself through the assistance of Susan Toby Evans and Joanne Pillsbury. John Clark, John Monaghan, David Stuart, and Karl Taube supplied helpful comments that improved the final result.

Bibliography

ABELES, MARC

1981   Sacred Kingship and the Formation of the State. In *The Study of the State* (Henri Claessen and Peter Skalnek, eds.): 1–14. Mouton, The Hague.

ACOSTA, JOSÉ DE

1940   *Historia natural y moral de las Indias.* Fondo de Cultura Económica, México, D.F.
[1590]

ADORNO, ROLENA

1982   On Pictorial Language and the Typology of Culture in a New World Chronicle. *Semiotica* 36 (1/2): 51–106.

ALVA, WALTER, AND CHRISTOPHER DONNAN

1993   *Royal Tombs of Sipán.* Fowler Museum of Cultural History, Los Angeles.

ANAWALT, PATRICIA R.

1981   *Indian Clothing before Cortés: Mesoamerican Costumes from the Codices.* University of Oklahoma Press, Norman.

ARCHAMBAULT, PAUL

1967   The Analogy of the "Body" in Renaissance Political Literature. *Bibliothèque d'Humanisme et Renaissance* 29: 21–63.

ARZE, SILVIA, AND XIMENA MEDINACELI

1991   *Imágenes y presagios: El escudo de los Ayaviri, Mallkus de Charcas.* Hisbol, La Paz.

AVILA, FRANCISCO DE

1648   *Tratado de los Evangelios.* Lima.

BARKAN, LEONARD

1975   *Nature's Work of Art: The Human Body as Image of the World.* Yale University Press, New Haven, Conn.

BASTIEN, JOSEPH

1985   Qollahuaya-Andean Body Concepts: A Topographical-Hydraulic Mode of Physiology. *American Anthropologist* 87: 595–611.

BELL, LANNY

1985   Luxor Temple and the Cult of the Royal Ka. *Journal of Near Eastern Studies* 44(4): 251–294.

BERDAN, FRANCES F., AND PATRICIA R. ANAWALT

1997   *The Essential Codex Mendoza.* University of California Press, Berkeley.

BETANZOS, JUAN DE

1996   *Narrative of the Incas* (Roland B. Hamilton and Dana Buchanan, trans. and eds.).
[1557]   University of Texas Press, Austin.

BLIER, SUZANNE PRESTON

1995   *African Vodun: Art, Psychology, and Power.* University of Chicago Press, Chicago.

BLOCH, MAURICE

1985   The Ritual of the Royal Bath in Madagascar: The Dissolution of Death, Birth, and
Fertility into Authority. In *Rituals of Royalty: Power and Ceremonial in Traditional
Society* (David Cannadine and Simon Price, eds.): 271–297. Cambridge University
Press, Cambridge.

BOURDIEU, PIERRE

1990   *The Logic of Practice.* Stanford University Press, Stanford, Calif.

BROWN, ELIZABETH A. R.

1981   Death and the Human Body in the Later Middle Ages: The Legislation of Boniface
VIII on the Division of the Corpse. *Viator* 12: 221–270.

BURKHART, LOUISE M.

1997   Mexica Women on the Home Front: Housework and Religion in Aztec Mexico. In
Indian Women of Early Mexico (Susan Schroeder, Stephanie Wood, and Robert
Haskett, eds.): 25–54. University of Oklahoma Press, Norman.

CABELLO BALBOA, MIGUEL

1951   *Miscélania Antártica.* Lima: Instituto de Etnología, San Marcos.
[1586]

CAMPBELL, JOHN

1994   *Past, Space, and Self.* MIT Press, Cambridge, Mass.

CIEZA DE LEÓN, PEDRO DE

1967   *El Señorío de los Incas, Segunda parte de la crónica del Perú.* Instituto de Estudios
[1554]   Peruanos, Lima.

CLASSEN, CONSTANCE

1993   *Inca Cosmology and the Human Body.* University of Utah Press, Salt Lake City.

COBO, BERNABÉ

1956   *Historia del Nuevo Mundo.* Biblioteca de autores españoles desde la formación del
[1653]   lenguaje hasta nuestros días 91–92, Madrid.

COOLEY, CHARLES HORTON

1964   *Human Nature and Social Order.* Schocken, New York.

CSORDAS, THOMAS J.

1994   Introduction: The Body as Representation and Being-in-the-World. In *Embodiment
and Experience: The Existential Ground of Culture and Self* (Thomas J. Csordas, ed.): 1–
24. Cambridge University Press, Cambridge.

CUMMINS, TOM

n.d.   Towards a meaning of objects in Tawantinsuyu: *Queros* and *aquillas.* Paper presented at Variations in the Expression of Inka Power, a symposium held at Dumbarton Oaks, Washington, D.C., 1997.

DE LOS REYES, ANTONIO

1976   *Arte en lengua mixteca por Antonio de los Reyes, 1593.* Vanderbilt University Publications in Anthropology 14. Nashville.

DOUGLAS, MARY

1973   *Natural Symbols: Explorations in Cosmology.* Vintage, New York.

DREYFUS, HUBERT L. AND PAUL RABINOW

1982   *Michel Foucault: Beyond Structuralism and Hermeneutics.* University of Chicago Press, Chicago.

DUPONT, FLORENCE

1989   The Emperor-God's Other Body. In *Fragments for a History of the Human Body* (Michel Feher, ed.): 396–419. Zone, New York.

ELIADE, MIRCEA

1959   *The Sacred and the Profane: The Nature of Religion.* Harcourt Brace, New York.

ESQUIVEL Y NAVIA, DIEGO DE

1980   *Noticias cronológicas de la gran ciudad del Cuzco.* 2 vols. Biblioteca Peruana de Cultura,
[1750]   Lima.

FEELEY-HARNIK, GILLIAN

1985   Issues in Divine Kingship. *Annual Review of Anthropology* 14: 273–313.

FLYNN, TOM

1998   *The Body in Three Dimensions.* Abrams, New York.

FOUCAULT, MICHEL

1995   *Discipline and Punish: The Birth of the Prison.* Vintage, New York.

FREIDEL, DAVID, LINDA SCHELE, AND JOY PARKER

1993   *Maya Cosmos: Three Thousand Years on the Shaman's Path.* William Morrow, New York.

FURST, JILL L. M.

1995   *The Natural History of the Soul in Ancient Mexico.* Yale University Press, New Haven, Conn.

GARCILASO DE LA VEGA, EL INCA

1943   *Comentarios Reales de los Incas.* Emece Editores S.A., Buenos Aires.
[1609–17]

GARIBAY, ANGEL M.

    1993   *Poesía Nahuatl.* 2 vols. (2d ed.) Instituto de Investigaciones Históricas, Serie Cultura Nahuátl, Fuente 4. Universidad Nacional Autónoma de México, México, D.F.

GASPARINI, GRAZIANO, AND LOUISE MARGOLIES

    1980   *Inca Architecture.* Indiana University Press, Bloomington.

GELL, ALFRED

    1975   *Metamorphosis of the Cassowaries.* Athlone Press, London.

    1993   *Wrapping in Images: Tatooing in Polynesia.* Oxford Studies in Social and Cultural Anthropology, Cultural Forms. Clarendon Press, Oxford.

GIBSON, CHARLES

    1969   *The Inca Concept of Sovereignty and the Spanish Administration in Peru.* University of Texas Press, Austin.

GIDDENS, ANTHONY

    1991   *Modernity and Self-Identity: Self and Society in the Late Modern Age.* Stanford University Press, Stanford, Calif.

GILLESPIE, SUSAN D.

    1989   *The Aztec Kings: The Construction of Rulership in Mexica History.* University of Arizona Press, Tucson.

GONZÁLEZ HOLGUÍN, DIEGO

    1989   *Vocabulario de la lengua general de Todo Perú llamada Qquichua o del Inca.* Universidad de
    [1608]   San Marcos, Lima.

GRAHAM, IAN

    1996   *Corpus of Maya Hieroglyphic Inscriptions,* vol. 7, pt. 1: *Seibal.* Peabody Museum of Archaeology and Ethnology, Harvard University, Cambridge, Mass.

GRAHAM, IAN, AND ERIC VON EUW

    1975   *Corpus of Maya Hieroglyphic Inscriptions,* vol. 2, pt. 1: *Naranjo.* Peabody Museum of Archaeology and Ethnology, Harvard University, Cambridge, Mass.

GRAHAM, IAN, AND PETER MATHEWS

    1996   *Corpus of Maya Hieroglyphic Inscriptions,* vol. 6, pt. 2: *Tonina.* Peabody Museum of American Archaeology and Ethnology, Cambridge, Mass.

GROSZ, ELIZABETH

    1995   *Space, Time, and Perversion: Essays on the Politics of Bodies.* Routledge, New York.

GUAMAN POMA DE AYALA, FELIPE

    1980   *Nueva corónica y buen gobierno* (John V. Murra and Rolena Adorno, eds.) Siglo
    [ca. 1613] Veintuno, México, D.F.

HANKS, WILLIAM

1990   *Referential Practice: Language and Lived Space among the Maya.* University of Chicago Press, Chicago.

1996   *Language and Communicative Practice.* Westview Press, Boulder.

HERZFELD, MICHAEL

1991   *A Place in History: Social and Monumental Time in a Cretan Town.* Princeton University Press, Princeton, N.J.

HERTZ, ROBERT

1973   The Pre-Eminence of the Right Hand: A Study in Religious Polarity. In *Right and Left: Essays on Dual Symbolic Classification* (Rodney Needham, ed.): 3–31. University of Chicago Press, Chicago.

HOLBROOK, DAVID

1988   *Further Studies in Philosophical Anthropology.* Avebury, Aldershot.

HOUSTON, STEPHEN D., AND DAVID S. STUART

1996   Of Gods, Glyphs, and Kings: Divinity and Rulership among the Classic Maya. *Antiquity* 70: 289–312.

1998   The Ancient Maya Self: Personhood and Portraiture in the Classic Period. *Res: Anthropology and Aesthetics* 33: 73–101.

HOUSTON, STEPHEN D., AND KARL TAUBE

2000   An Archaeology of the Senses: Perception and Cultural Expression in Ancient Mesoamerica. *Cambridge Archaeological Journal* 10(2): 261–294.

INOMATA, TAKESHI

1997   The Last Day of a Fortified Classic Maya Center: Archaeological Investigations at Aguateca, Guatemala. *Ancient Mesoamerica* 8: 337–351.

ISBELL, WILLIAM H.

1997   *Mummies and Mortuary Monuments: A Postprocessual Prehistory of Central Andean Social Organization.* University of Texas Press, Austin.

JOHNSON, MARK

1987   *The Body in the Mind: The Bodily Basis of Meaning, Imagination, and Reason.* University of Chicago Press, Chicago.

JONES, CHRISTOPHER, AND LINTON SATTERTHWAITE

1982   *Tikal Report No. 33, Part A: The Monuments and Inscriptions of Tikal: The Carved Monuments.* University Museum Monograph 44. University Museum, University of Pennsylvania, Philadelphia.

JOYCE, ROSEMARY A.

1996   The Construction of Gender in Classic Maya Monuments. In *Gender and Archaeology* (Rita P. Wright, ed.): 167–195. University of Pennsylvania Press, Philadelphia.

1998   Performing the Body in Pre-Hispanic Central America. *Res: Anthropology and Aesthetics* 33: 147–165.

KANTOROWICZ, ERNST H.

1957   *The King's Two Bodies: A Study in Medieval Political Theology.* Princeton University Press, Princeton, N.J.

KARTTUNEN, FRANCES

1983   *An Analytical Dictionary of Nahuatl.* University of Oklahoma Press, Norman.

KELLOGG, SUSAN

1997   From Parallel to Equivalent to Separate but Unequal: Tenochca Mexica Women, 1500–1700. In *Indian Women of Early Mexico* (Susan Schroeder, Stephanie Wood, and Robert Haskett, eds.): 123–143. University of Oklahoma Press, Norman.

KERR, JUSTIN

1990   *The Maya Vase Book: A Corpus of Rollout Photographs of Maya Vases*, vol. 2. Kerr Associates, New York.

1994   *The Maya Vase Book: A Corpus of Rollout Photographs of Maya Vases*, vol. 4. Kerr Associates, New York.

1997   *The Maya Vase Book: A Corpus of Rollout Photographs of Maya Vases*, vol. 5. Kerr Associates, New York.

KING, MARK B.

1994   Hearing the Echoes of Verbal Art in Mixtec Writing. In *Writing without Words: Alternative Literacies in Mesoamerica and the Andes* (Elizabeth H. Boone and Walter D. Mignolo, eds.): 102–136. Duke University Press, Durham, N.C.

KOLATA, ALAN

1990   The Urban Concept of Chan Chan. In *The Northern Dynasties: Kingship and Statecraft in Chimor* (Michael E. Moseley and Alana Cordy-Collins, eds.): 107–144. Dumbarton Oaks, Washington, D.C.

LACAN, JACQUES

1977   *Écrits: A Selection.* Tavistock, London.

LAQUEUR, THOMAS

1990   *Making Sex: Body and Gender from the Greeks to Freud.* Harvard University Press, Cambridge, Mass.

LARREA, JUAN

1960a   El Yauri, insignia incaíca. In *Corona Incaica*: 59–94. Facultad de Filosofía y Humanidades, Universidad Nacional de Córdoba, Córdoba.

1960b   La Macaipacha, Corona del Imperio. In *Corona Incaica*: 105–152. Facultad de Filosofía y Humanidades, Universidad Nacional de Córdoba, Córdoba.

LAUGHLIN, ROBERT M.

1988   *The Great Tzotzil Dictionary of Santo Domingo Zinacantán.* 3 vols. Smithsonian Contributions to Anthropology 31. Smithsonian Institution Press, Washington, D.C.

LEFEBVRE, HENRI

    1991   *The Production of Space.* Blackwell, Oxford.

LEÓN-PORTILLA, MIGUEL

    1992   *The Aztec Image of Self and Society: An Introduction to Nahua Culture.* University of
            Utah Press, Salt Lake City.

LOCK, MARGARET

    1993   Cultivating the Body: Anthropology and Epistemologies of Bodily Practice and
            Knowledge. *Annual Review of Anthropology* 22: 133–155.

LÓPEZ AUSTIN, ALFREDO

    1988   *The Human Body and Ideology: Concepts of the Ancient Nahuas* (Thelma Ortiz de
            Montellano and Bernard Ortiz de Montellano, trans.). 2 vols. University of Utah
            Press, Salt Lake City.

    1997   *Tamoanchan, Tlalolcan: Places of Mist.* University Press of Colorado, Niwot.

L'ORANGE, HENRI P.

    1947   *Apotheosis in Ancient Portraiture.* H. Aschehoug, Oslo.

LUCKMANN, THOMAS

    1991   The Constitution of Human Life in Time. In *Chronotypes: The Construction of Time*
            (John Bender and David E. Wellbery, eds.): 151–166. Stanford University Press,
            Stanford, Calif.

MacLAURY, ROBERT E.

    1997   *Color and Cognition in Mesoamerica: Constructing Categories as Vantages.* University of
            Texas Press, Austin.

MARIN, LOUIS

    1988   *Portrait of a King.* University of Minnesota Press, Minneapolis.

MARTÍNEZ CERECEDA, JOSÉ LUIS

    1995   *Autoridades en los Andes, los atributos del Señor.* Pontificia Universidad Católica del
            Perú, Fondo Editorial, Lima.

MAUSS, MARCEL

    1950   *Sociologie et anthropologie.* Presses Universitaires de France, Paris.

    1990   *The Gift, Forms and Functions of Exchange in Archaic Societies.* (W. D. Halls, trans.).
            Routledge, London.

MAXWELL, JUDITH M., AND CRAIG A. HANSON

    1992   *Of the Manners of Speaking That the Old Ones Had: The Metaphors of Andrés de Olmos in
            the TULAL Manuscript (Arte para Aprender la Lengua Mexicana 1547).* University of
            Utah Press, Salt Lake City.

MAYER, KARL H.

    1995   *Maya Monuments: Sculptures of Unknown Provenance, Supplement 4.* Academic
            Publishers, Graz, Austria.

MEAD, GEORGE H.

1964   *Selected Writings.* University of Chicago Press, Chicago.

MENA, CRISTÓBAL DE

1534   *La conquista del Perú llamada la nueua Castilla. La qual tierra por diuina voluntad fue marauillosamente conquistada en la felicissima ventura del Emperador y Rey nuestro señor y por la prudencia y esfuerço del muy magnifico y valeroso cauallero el Capitan Francisco piçarro Gouernador y adelantado de la nueua castilla y de su hermano Hernando piçarro y de sus animosos capitanes y fieles y esforçados compañeros que con el se hallaron.* Bartholomé Pérez, Seville.

MORRIS, CRAIG

1982   The Infrastructure of Inka Control in the Peruvian Highlands. In *The Inca and Aztec States 1400–1800* (G. Collier, R. Rosaldo, and J. Wirth, eds.): 153–172. Academic Press, New York.

MOSELEY, MICHAEL, AND ALANA CORDY COLLINS (EDS.)

1990   *The Northern Dynasties: Kingship and Statecraft in Chimor.* Dumbarton Oaks, Washington, D.C.

MURRA, JOHN

1980   *The Economic Organization of the Inca State.* JAI Press, Greenwich, Conn.

MURRAY, OSWIN

1996   Hellenistic Royal Symposia. In *Aspects of Hellenistic Kingship* (Per Bilde, Troels Engberg-Pdersen, Lise Hannestad, and Jan Zahle, eds.): 15–27. Aarhus University Press, Aarhus, Denmark.

MURÚA, MARTÍN DE

1590   *Historia del origen y genaeología real del Incas reyes.* Manuscript, Galvin collection, Ireland.

1613   *Historia general del Perú.* J. Paul Getty Museum, MS Ludwig XIII 16.

NECIPOĞLU, ĞÜLRU

1991   *Architecture, Ceremonial, and Power: The Topkapi Palace in the Fifteenth and Sixteenth Centuries.* MIT Press, Cambridge, Mass.

O'Neill, John

1985   *Five Bodies: The Shape of Modern Society.* Cornell University Press, Ithaca, N.Y.

PASZTORY, ESTHER

1983   *Aztec Art.* H. N. Abrams, New York.

PEASE, FRANKLIN

1990   Los Incas en la colonia. In *El Mundo Andino en la época del descubrimiento.* Comisión Nacional Peruana de V Centenario del Descubrimiento Encuentro de Dos Americas. Taller Impresiones Benito, Lima.

PIERCE, C.S.

1955   *Philosophical Writings of Pierce* (J. Buchler, ed.). Dover, New York.

PIZARRO, PEDRO

1917   *Relación del descubrimiento y conquista de los reinos de Perú.* Colección de libros y
[1571]   documentos referentes a la historia del Perú (Carlos A. Romero and Horacio H.
Urteaga, eds.). 1st series, vol. 6. Sanmartí y Ca, Lima.

POLO DE ONDEGARDO

1916   *Relación de los fundamentos acerca del notable daño que resulta de no guardar a los indios sus*
[1571]   *fueros.* Colección de libros y documentos referentes a la historia del Perú (Carlos A.
Romero and Horacio H. Urteaga, eds.). 1st series, vol. 3: 45–188. Sanmartí y Ca,
Lima.

PROSKOURIAKOFF, TATIANA

1974   *Jades from the Cenotes of Sacrifice, Chichen Itza, Yucatan.* Memoirs of the Peabody
Museum of Archaeology and Ethnology 10(1). Harvard University, Cambridge,
Mass.

PROTZEN, JEAN-PIERRE

1993   *Inca Architecture and Construction at Ollantaytambo.* Oxford University Press, Oxford.

RAMÍREZ, SUSAN

1996   *The World Upside Down: Cross-Cultural Contact and Conflict in Sixteenth-Century Peru.*
Stanford University Press, Stanford, Calif.

REENTS-BUDET, DORIE

1994   *Painting the Maya Universe: Royal Ceramics of the Classic Period.* Duke University Press,
Durham, N.C.

ROSTWOROWSKI DE DIEZ CANSECO, MARÍA

1960   Succession, Cooptation to Kingship, and Royal Incest among the Incas. *Southwestern
Journal of Anthropology* 16(4): 417–427.

1961   *Curacas y sucsesiones, Costa norte.* Imprenta Minerva, Lima.

SAHLINS, MARSHALL

1976   Colors and Cultures. *Semiotica* 16: 1–22.

SALOMON, FRANK

1986   *Native Lords of Quito in the Age of the Incas: The Political Economy of Northern Andean
Chiefdoms.* Cambridge University Press, Cambridge.

SALOMON, FRANK, AND GEORGE L. URIOSTE (TRANS. AND EDS.)

1991   *The Huarochirí Manuscript: A Testament of Ancient and Colonial Andean Religion.*
University of Texas Press, Austin.

SANTA CRUZ PACHACUTI, JOAN DE

1993   *Relación de antigüedades deste reyno del piru.* Cusco: Centro de Estudios Regionales
[ca. 1615]   Andinos Bartolomé de las Casas and Institut Français d'Études Andines.

SARMIENTO DE GAMBOA, PEDRO

    1988   *Historia de los Incas.* Madrid: Miraguano Ediciones.
    [1572]

SCHELE, LINDA

    1997   *Hidden Faces of the Maya.* Alti Publishing, México, D.F.

SCHEPER-HUGHES, NANCY, AND MARGARET LOCK

    1987   The Mindful Body: A Prolegomenon to Future Work in Medical Anthropology. *Medical Anthropology Quarterly* 1: 6–41.

SCHROEDER, SUSAN

    1991   *Chimalpahin and the Kingdoms of Chalco.* University of Arizona Press, Tucson.

SENNETT, RICHARD

    1993   *Flesh and Stone: The Body and the City in Western Civilization.* W. W. Norton, New York.

SHARON, DOUGLAS

    1976   The Inca *Warachikuy* Initiations. In *Enculturation in Latin America: An Anthology* (Johannes Wilbert, ed): 213–236. UCLA Latin American Center Publications, University of California, Los Angeles.

STEWART, T. DALE

    1975   Human Skeletal Remains from Dzibilchaltun, Yucatan, Mexico, with a Review of Cranial Deformity Types in the Maya Region. In *Archaeological Investigations on the Yucatan Peninsula* (E. Wyllys Andrew et al.): 199–225. Middle American Research Institute Publication 31, no. 7. Tulane University, New Orleans.

STONE, ANDREA

    1996   Metaphors of Vitality and Aesthetics in Maya Art. Paper presented at the 95th meeting of the American Anthropological Association, San Francisco, 1996.

STRATHERN, MARILYN

    1979   The Self in Self-Decoration. *Oceania* 49: 241–257.

STUART, DAVID

    1990   A New Carved Panel from the Palenque Area. *Research Reports on Ancient Maya Writing* 32. Center for Maya Research, Washington, D.C.

    1996   Kings of Stone: A Consideration of Stelae in Ancient Maya Ritual and Representation. *Res: Anthropology and Aesthetics* 29/30: 148–171.

STUART, GENE S., AND GEORGE E. STUART

    1993   *Lost Kingdoms of the Maya.* National Geographic Society, Washington, D.C.

TAMBIAH, STANLEY J.

    1976   *World Conqueror and World Renouncer: A Study of Buddhism and Polity in Thailand against a Historical Background.* Cambridge University Press, Cambridge.

TAUBE, KARL

1993   *Aztec and Maya Myths.* British Museum Press, London.

1996   The Olmec Maize God: The Face of Corn in Formative Mesoamerica. *Res: Anthropology and Aesthetics* 29/30: 39–81.

TAYLOR, DICEY

n.d.   Classic Maya Costume: Regional Types of Dress. Ph.D. dissertation, Yale University, New Haven, Conn., 1983.

TAYLOR, GERALD

1983   Camay capac et camasca dans le manuscrit quechua de Huarochirí. *Journal de la Société des Américanistes* 63: 231–244.

THOMPSON, J. ERIC S.

1946   Tattooing and Scarification among the Maya. *Notes on Middle American Archaeology and Ethnology* 63. Division of Historical Research, Carnegie Institution of Washington, D.C.

TITU CUSI YUPANQUI, INGA DIEGO DE CASTRO

1973   *Relación de la conquista del Peru y hechos del Inca Manco II.* Ediciones de la Biblioteca
[1570]   Universitaria, Lima.

TOLEDO, FRANCISCO DE

1874   Información de las idolatrías de las Incas e indios y de como se enterraban . . .
[1571]   *Colección de documentos inéditos relativos al descubrimiento . . . sacadas en su mayor parte de Real Archivo de las Indias,* vol. 21. Madrid.

TOZZER, ALFRED M. (ED.)

1941   *Landa's Relación de las Cosas de Yucatan.* Papers of the Peabody Museum of American Archaeology and Ethnology, Harvard University 18. Cambridge, Mass.

TURNER, TERENCE S.

1980   The Social Skin. In *Not Work Alone: A Cross-Cultural View of Activities Superfluous to Survival* (Jeremy Cherfas and Roger Lewin, eds.): 112–140. Temple Smith, London.

URTON, GARY

1990   *The History of a Myth: Pacariqtambo and the Origin of the Inkas.* University of Texas Press, Austin.

1992   Communialism and Differentiation in an Andean Community. In *Andean Cosmologies through Time: Persistence and Emergence* (R. Dover, K. Seibold, and J. McDowell, eds.): 229–266. Indiana University Press, Bloomington.

VACA DE CASTRO, CRISTÓBAL

1974   *Relación de la descendencía, gobierno y conquista de los Incas.* Ediciones de la Biblioteca
[1542–44] Universitaria, Lima.

VAN DE GUCHTE, MAARTEN

1996   Sculpture and the Concept of the Double among the Inca Kings. *Res: Anthropology and Aesthetics* 29/30: 256–268.

VOGT, EVON Z.

1993   *Tortillas for the Gods: A Symbolic Analysis of Zinacanteco Rituals.* University of Oklahoma Press, Norman.

WACHTEL, NATHAN

1973   Estructuralismo e historia: A propósito de la organización social del Cuzco. In *Sociedad e ideología*: 21–58. Instituto de Investigaciones Peruanos, Lima.

WINTER, IRENE J.

1996   Sex, Rhetoric, and the Public Monument: The Alluring Body of Naram-Sîn. In *Sexuality in Ancient Art: Near East, Egypt, Greece, and Italy* (Natalie B. Kampen, ed.): 11–26. Cambridge University Press, Cambridge.

YOUNG, A.

1990   Moral Conflicts in a Psychiatric Hospital Treating Combat-Related Post-Traumatic Stress Disorder. In *Social Science Perspectives on Medical Ethics* (G. Weisz, ed.): 65–82. Kluwer Academic, Dordrecht.

ZUIDEMA, R. TOM

1964   *The Ceque System of Cuzco: The Social Organization of the Capital of the Inca.* Brill, Leiden.

1983a   The Lion in the City: Royal Symbols of Transition in Cuzco. *Journal of Latin American Lore* 9(1): 39–100.

1983b   Hierarchy and Space in Incaic Social Organization. *Ethnohistory* 30(2): 49–75.

1991   Guaman Poma and the Art of Empire: Toward an Iconography of Inca Royal Dress. In *Transatlantic Encounters: Europeans and Andeans in the Sixteenth Century* (K. Andrien and R. Adorno, eds.): 151–202. University of California Press, Berkeley.

1997   La política matrimonial incaica según Juan de Betanzos: Un ejemplo implicando a los reyes Inca Roca y Yahuar Huácac. In *Arqueología, Antropología, e Historia en Los Andes: Homenaje a María Rostworowski* (R. Varón Gabrai and J. Flores Espinoza, eds.): 288–300. Instituto de Estudios Peruanos, Lima.

Index